The Essential Tversky

The Essential Tversky

Amos Tversky
edited and with an introduction by Eldar Shafir
foreword by Michael Lewis
afterword by Daniel Kahneman

The MIT Press
Cambridge, Massachusetts
London, England

This book was set in ITC Stone Serif Std by Toppan Best-set Premedia Limited. Printed and bound in the United States of America.

Library of Congress Cataloging-in-Publication Data

Names: Tversky, Amos, author. | Shafir, Eldar, editor.
Title: The essential Tversky / Amos Tversky ; edited and with an introduction by Eldar Shafir ; foreword by Michael Lewis ; afterword by Daniel Kahneman.
Description: Cambridge, MA : MIT Press, [2018] | Includes bibliographical references and index.
Identifiers: LCCN 2017047688 | ISBN 9780262535106 (pbk. : alk. paper)
Subjects: LCSH: Cognitive psychology. | Cognition. | Decision making.
Classification: LCC BF201 .T775 2018 | DDC 153--dc23 LC record available at https://lccn.loc.gov/2017047688

10 9 8 7 6 5 4 3 2

Contents

Foreword

Reviving Amos

Michael Lewis

I'm pretty sure that the so-called "Tversky Test" is the briefest intelligence test ever designed. Invented by University of Michigan psychologist Richard Nisbett, it ran as follows: the longer it takes you, upon encountering Amos Tversky, to figure out that Amos Tversky is smarter than you, the stupider you are. I never met Amos Tversky, and so I was never personally subjected to the Tversky test. But I have met all sorts of people who were, and none of them quarreled with its design. The mind of Amos Tversky wasn't simply powerful and interesting. It was a ruler used by others to take a measure of their own. People still do this—even though Amos has been dead for more than twenty years.

Working on a book about Tversky's collaboration with his fellow Israeli psychologist Daniel Kahneman, I encountered many versions of this strange phenomenon. I found a lot of people who had known Amos still asking themselves, twenty years after his death, "What would Amos have thought about this? What would Amos have said?" I met a woman who never married because, she said, in contemplating her suitors, she could not help but ask herself, "What would Amos think of this guy?" (The answer was always "Not much!") I met several big-time intellectuals, all of whom had collaborated with Amos, who said they could still not help but imagine Amos reading whatever paper they were preparing for publication. If the Amos of their imaginations failed to approve of their work, then they returned to the drawing board. I even met former students of Amos's who had preserved, with great care, the most quotidian objects given to them by Amos. An old book, a stapler, and a laser pointer had all become, in effect, holy relics.

Above all, people treasured the shards of wisdom that spilled from Amos with a shocking ease:

The secret to doing good research is always to be a little underemployed. You waste years by not being able to waste hours.

If someone asks you to do something and you don't immediately know you want to do it, wait a day. You'll be amazed how many things that you agreed to do when asked you actually would rather not do.

A part of good science is to see what everyone else can see but think what no one else has ever said.

Some people are just hard to let go of, and Amos Tversky is one of them. But there is some obvious frustration in the many attempts to keep him around. Daniel Kahneman, in his eulogy of Amos, pointed out the difficulty of the problem. At Amos's funeral, Danny explained that Amos had left him to write, under both their names, a preface to a collection of their joint papers, with the instructions, "Trust the model you have of me in your mind." But how could anyone seriously trust his mental model of Amos's mind? The wonder of Amos's mind was the things it did that others could never imagine. Whatever people had rattling around in their heads, when they imagined Amos Tversky, Danny said, was bound to be a cheap imitation of the original.

Amos himself didn't help matters here. It's striking how fiercely Amos resisted commemoration. When they learned that Amos was dying, his students asked if they could videotape his final lectures to Stanford undergraduates: Amos refused. On his deathbed, Amos instructed the president of Stanford University to do nothing to preserve his memory—such as naming some annual lecture after him. (He didn't want his name associated with work whose quality he couldn't control.) To the people closest to him, Amos explained that he felt he had served his purpose in this life, and that he would soon be forgotten, and he was okay with that.

And perhaps he was. But, truly, he isn't.

Introduction

Eldar Shafir

Amos Tversky was a towering figure in the cognitive and decision sciences. His research had enormous influence; he created new areas of study and helped transform neighboring disciplines. His work was exciting, aesthetic, and ingenious, and it changed how the social sciences understand human behavior and society. The influence of Tversky's work was recently made palpable in Michael Lewis's book, *The Undoing Project*, which explores the long-lasting collaboration between Tversky and his colleague and friend, Daniel Kahneman. In the book, Lewis describes his discovery that much of Tversky and Kahneman's thinking, unbeknownst to him, had been the foundation for his earlier and highly influential book, *Moneyball*. The seminal research that Tversky and Kahneman conducted also played a central role in Kahneman's bestseller, *Thinking Fast and Slow*. These and other recent books have introduced Tversky's thinking to audiences much wider than those typically exposed to specialized academic work. The present collection of "classics" is intended to provide readers with a sense of Tversky's thinking through some of his original writings.

This collection brings together fourteen of Tversky's original academic articles, chosen for being highly influential, accessible, and characteristic of Tversky's mind and work. These articles were selected from a larger collection of forty articles chosen in collaboration with Tversky during the last months of his life (Shafir, 2003). Even the original collection represented only a fragment of Tversky's published work and offers a limited sense of his remarkable achievements. (Those who want to read more are invited to explore the original 1,000-page volume or consult the appendix at the end of this book, which includes Tversky's full bibliography.) The present selection covers an array of topics, from medicine and statistics to psychological similarity and economics, while avoiding much of Tversky's more highly technical pieces. It is intended to capture the essence of Tversky's phenomenal mind for those who might have encountered some of his ideas but did not have the fortune to study with him or read his work in greater depth. This collection will hopefully also serve as a cherished memento for those whose lives he personally touched.

Tversky was born on March 16, 1937, in Haifa, Israel. His father was a veterinarian, and his mother was a social worker and later a member of the first Israeli Parliament. He received his Bachelor of Arts degree, majoring in philosophy and psychology, from Hebrew University in Jerusalem in 1961 and his Doctor of Philosophy degree in psychology from the University of Michigan in 1965. Tversky taught at Hebrew University (1966–1978) and Stanford University (1978–1996), where he was the inaugural Davis-Brack Professor of Behavioral Sciences and Principal Investigator at the Stanford Center on Conflict and Negotiation.

Tversky's early work in mathematical psychology focused on the study of individual choice behavior and analysis of psychological measurement. Almost from the beginning, Tversky's work explored the surprising implications of simple and intuitively compelling psychological assumptions for theories that, until then, seemed self-evident. In one heavily cited early work (Tversky, 1969), he relied on the psychology of just noticeable differences to predict violations of transitivity, one of the most basic axioms of the normative theory of choice. This work raised a number of issues that would prove pivotal in Tversky's later work. It hinted at ways in which perfectly reasonable people, making what felt like reasonable decisions, could end up violating the most basic axioms of rational decision making. It also addressed the difficulty of reaching clear conclusions concerning the rational status of such violations in the absence of a compelling analysis of the mechanisms and costs involved. Simplification in the choice process could prove extremely useful, even if occasionally it failed to yield the optimal choice. Of main interest to Tversky was the systematic violation of normative principles and what these violations revealed about the psychological mechanisms governing behavior.

Early in his career as a mathematical psychologist, Tversky developed a deep interest in the formalization and conceptualization of similarity. The notion of similarity is ubiquitous in psychological theorizing, where it plays a fundamental role in theories of learning, memory, knowledge, perception, and judgment, among others. When Tversky began his work in this area, the theoretical analysis of similarity relations had been dominated by geometric models, where each object is represented by a point in some multidimensional coordinate space and the metric distances between points reflect the similarities between the respective objects. Tversky challenged the geometric approach and revolutionized our understanding of similarity assessment. In his now-famous model of similarity (chapter 3, this volume), items are mentally represented as collections of features, with the similarity between them an increasing function of the features that they have in common and a decreasing function of their distinct features. Moreover, similarity judgments lead us to give greater weight to common features (the son and the father look so much alike despite the age difference), whereas dissimilarity judgments give greater importance to distinct features (the son and the father are so different in age despite their similar faces). Among other things, this simple theory was able to explain observed asymmetries in similarity judgments (A may be more similar to B than B is to A), and the fact that item A may be perceived as quite similar to item B and item B quite similar to item C, but items A and C may nevertheless be perceived as highly dissimilar (Tversky & Gati, 1978). These remarkable effects, predicted by Tversky's feature-based model, were incompatible with any of the earlier geometric approaches. In many ways, these early papers foreshadowed the immensely elegant work to come. They were predicated on the technical mastery of relevant normative theories and explored simple and compelling psychological principles until their unexpected theoretical implications became apparent and often striking.

Tversky's long and extraordinarily influential collaboration with Daniel Kahneman began in 1969 and spanned the fields of judgment and decision making. Their first paper, on the belief in the law of small numbers (chapter 10, this volume), suggested that naïve respondents as well as trained scientists have strong but misguided intuitions about random sampling. These expectations were shown to lead to systematic patterns of misperception of chance events, which Tversky and colleagues later applied to the analyses of widely held and apparently misguided beliefs, such as the hot hand in basketball and the belief that arthritis pain is related to the weather (Shafir, 2003, chapters 10, 11, & 15).

Cognitive and perceptual biases that operate regardless of motivational factors formed the core of their remarkably creative and highly influential "heuristics and biases" program. Having recognized that intuitive predictions and judgments of probability do not follow the principles of statistics or the laws of probability, Tversky and Kahneman embarked on the study of biases as a method for investigating judgmental heuristics. In the article in *Science* (chapter 1, this volume), they documented three heuristics—representativeness, availability, and anchoring and adjustment—that people were shown to employ in assessing probabilities and predicting values. In settings where the relevance of simple probabilistic rules is transparent, people often reveal appropriate statistical intuitions. In richer contexts, however, people often rely on heuristics that do not obey simple formal considerations, which can lead to fallacious judgments. When relying on the representativeness heuristic, for example, the likelihood that item A belongs to class B is judged by the degree to which A resembles B. Prior probabilities and sample sizes, both of which are highly relevant to likelihood, have no impact on how representative an item appears and are thus neglected. This can lead to memorable errors such as the "conjunction fallacy," wherein a conjunction, because it appears more representative, is judged more probable than one of its conjuncts (chapter 2, this volume).

The beauty of the work is most apparent in the interplay of psychological intuition with normative theory and is accompanied by memorable demonstrations. The research shows that people exhibit sensitivity to various principles' normative appeal, yet their judgments often violate those basic principles. The coexistence of fallible intuitions and an underlying appreciation for normative judgment yields a subtle picture of probabilistic reasoning. An important theme in Tversky's work is a rejection of the claim that people are not smart or sophisticated enough to grasp the relevant normative considerations. Rather, Tversky attributes people's recurrent and systematic judgmental errors to their reliance on heuristic processes that simply do not abide by the normative criteria. For example, the notion that people focus on the strength of the evidence (e.g., the warmth of a letter of reference) with insufficient regard for its weight (e.g., how well the writer knows the candidate) is used by Dale Griffin and Tversky (chapter 11, this volume) to explain various systematic biases in probabilistic judgment, including the failure to appreciate regression phenomena and people's tendency to be overconfident (when the evidence is remarkable but its weight is low) and occasionally underconfident (when the evidence is unremarkable but its weight is high). This approach runs through much of Tversky's work. The experimental demonstrations are noteworthy not simply because they contradict a popular and highly influential normative theory; rather, they are memorable because people who exhibit these errors typically find the demonstrations highly compelling, yet surprisingly inconsistent with their own assumptions about how they make decisions.

Amos Tversky studied individual choice behavior in his first publication and throughout his career. The work was largely motivated by earlier developments in economics, particularly the publication of von Neumann and Morgenstern's (1947) normative treatment of expected utility, which, with some ensuing modifications, showed that a few compelling axioms, when satisfied, imply that a person's choices can be thought of as favoring the alternative with the highest subjective expected utility. In the 1970s, Tversky and Kahneman worked on a descriptive theory of decision making under risk, known as prospect theory (chapter 4, this volume). Prospect theory incorporates a number of fundamental psychological principles of choice that differ in important ways from those envisioned by the normative account. Among other things, prospect theory posits a value function with three important properties: (1) it is defined on gains and losses rather than total wealth, which captures the fact that people normally treat outcomes as departures from some reference point rather than in terms of final assets; (2) it is steeper for losses than for gains, thus a loss of $X is more aversive than a gain of $X is attractive, yielding what is referred to as "loss aversion"; and (3) it is concave for gains and convex for losses, which yields risk aversion in the domain of gains and risk seeking in the domain of losses (except for low probabilities, where these patterns reverse). These properties are compelling and may seem unobjectionable, yet they lead to normatively problematic consequences. The theory predicts decision patterns that have been empirically confirmed in dozens of studies and contrast directly with the fundamental assumptions of expected utility theory. Loss aversion, for example, also plays an important role in riskless choice, where among other things it accounts for the large disparity often observed between the minimum people are willing to accept to give up a good and the maximum they would be willing to pay to acquire it (chapter 8, this volume). Loss aversion has far-reaching consequences for economic choices and for people's willingness to depart from the status quo. Mathematically elegant and psychologically insightful, prospect theory and its extensions have had a major influence in the social sciences.

Tversky was particularly interested in the relationship between uncertainty and preference. In an investigation of the relation between probability judgments and preferences between bets, Heath and Tversky (chapter 9, this volume) propose the competence hypothesis, according to which people prefer to bet on their beliefs in situations in which they feel competent or knowledgeable but prefer to bet on chance when they feel incompetent or ignorant. Interestingly, this pattern is inconsistent with the familiar "ambiguity aversion," which predicts a general preference for betting on known chances over beliefs whose probability is ambiguous. Along related lines, Fox and Tversky (chapter 12, this volume) present the comparative ignorance hypothesis, according to which aversion to ambiguity, which does not emerge in noncomparative settings, is produced by comparison with less ambiguous events or more knowledgeable individuals.

The foregoing findings call into question the fundamental notion of inferring beliefs from preferences. Most conceptions of decision making under uncertainty—both normative and descriptive—are consequentialist in the sense that decisions are presumed to be determined by an assessment of the potential consequences and their perceived likelihood. However, Shafir and Tversky (chapter 7, this volume) document situations where people reason and make choices in a nonconsequentialist manner. For example, people who will eventually make the same choice no matter how the uncertainty is resolved are observed making a different choice while the situation is still uncertain, contrary to consequentialism.

Foremost in Tversky's research is the realization that preferences are often shaped by psychological processes that are not bound by normative considerations the person might endorse on reflection. Such processes underlie the study of contingent preferences, where purportedly immaterial variations in description, context, or procedure are shown to alter respondents' relative weighting of attributes and, consequently, their preferences. Exploring contingent preferences in medical contexts, Redelmeier and Tversky (chapter 6, this volume) suggest that looking at a problem from different perspectives can change the relative weight assigned to attributes and thus lead to different choices. They find that physicians give more weight to a patient's personal concerns when they consider the patient as an individual and more weight to criteria of effectiveness and cost when they consider the patient as part of a group. As a result, these physicians make different decisions when evaluating an individual patient than when considering a group of comparable patients (a discrepancy also found in the judgments of lay people).

Decision makers often seek and construct reasons to resolve difficult decisions and justify their choice. Alternative frames, contexts, and elicitation procedures highlight different aspects of the options and bring forth different reasons and considerations that influence decision making. Shafir and Tverky (chapter 14, this volume) consider the role of reasons in the making of decisions. An analysis based on reasons can accommodate framing and elicitation effects and can incorporate comparative influences and considerations of perspective, conflict, and context, which typically remain outside the purview of value maximization.

Psychological common sense formed the basis for some of Tversky's most profound and original insights. A fundamental assumption underlying normative theories is the extensionality principle: options that are extensionally equivalent (i.e., are the same in the world no matter how they're described; e.g., "1% fat" vs. "99% fat free") are assigned the same value, and extensionally equivalent events are assigned the same probability. In other words, these theories are about options and events in the world: alternative descriptions of the same thing are still about the same thing and hence similarly evaluated. In contrast, Tversky's analyses focus on the mental representations of the relevant constructs. The extensionality principle is deemed descriptively invalid because alternative descriptions of the same options and events often produce systematically different judgments and preferences. The way a decision problem is described—for example, in terms of gains or losses—can trigger conflicting risk attitudes and thus lead to discrepant preferences with respect to the same final outcomes (chapter 5, this volume). Similarly, alternative descriptions of the same event bring to mind different instances and thus can yield discrepant likelihood judgments (chapter 13, this volume). Preferences as well as judgments appear to be constructed, not merely revealed, in the elicitation process, and their construction depends on the framing of the problem, method of elicitation, and valuations and attitudes that these trigger.

Behavior, Tversky's research made clear, is the outcome of normative ideals that people endorse on reflection, combined with psychological tendencies and processes that intrude on and shape behavior independently of any deliberative intent. Tversky had a unique ability to master the technicalities of the normative treatments and to intuit and then experimentally demonstrate the vagaries and consequences of the psychological processes that impinged on them. He was an intellectual giant whose work has an exceptionally broad appeal; his research is known to economists, philosophers, statisticians, health scholars, political scientists, sociologists, and legal theorists, among others. Many of Tversky's papers are both seminal and definitive. Reading a Tversky paper offers the pleasure of watching a craftsman at work: he provides a clear map of a domain that had previously seemed confusing and then offers a new set of tools and ideas for thinking about the problem. (For a sense of his impact, consider the fact that Tversky has more than 230,000 citations in Google Scholar. The four-teen articles in this collection average more than 8,500 citations each.)

Tversky won many awards and distinctions for his diverse accomplishments. These range from Israel's highest honor for bravery in 1956 for rescuing a soldier, to prestigious academic awards, including a MacArthur Prize in 1984, honorary degrees, and election to several distinguished societies. In October 2002, the Royal Swedish Academy of Sciences awarded the Nobel Memorial Prize in Economic Sciences to Daniel Kahneman, "for hav-ing integrated insights from psychological research into economic science, especially con-cerning human judgment and decision-making under uncertainty." This work, completed together with Amos Tversky, the Nobel citation explained, formulated alternative theories that better account for observed behavior. The Royal Swedish Academy of Sciences does not award prizes posthumously but took the unusual step of acknowledging Tversky in the citation. "Certainly, we would have gotten this together," said Kahneman on the day of the announcement. Two months later, Tversky posthumously won, together with Kahneman, the prestigious 2003 Grawemeyer Award, which recognizes powerful ideas in the arts and sciences. The citation read, "It is difficult to identify a more influential idea than that of Kahneman and Tversky in the human sciences."

Tversky managed to combine discipline and joy in the conduct of his life in a manner that conveyed a great sense of freedom and autonomy. His habit of working through the night helped protect him from interruptions and gave him the time to engage at leisure in his research activities, as well as in other interests, including a lifelong love of Hebrew lit-erature, a fascination with modern physics, and an expert interest in professional basketball. He was tactful but firm in rejecting commitments that would distract him: "For those who like that sort of thing," Amos would say with his characteristic smile as he declined various engagements, "that's the sort of thing they like." To his friends and collaborators, Amos was a delight. He found great joy in sharing ideas and experiences with people close to him, and his joy was contagious. Many friends became research collaborators, and many collaborators became close friends. He would spend countless hours developing, delighting in, and refin-ing an idea. "Let's get this right," he would say—and his ability to do so was unequaled.

1 Judgment under Uncertainty: Heuristics and Biases

Amos Tversky and Daniel Kahneman

Many decisions are based on beliefs concerning the likelihood of uncertain events such as the outcome of an election, the guilt of a defendant, or the future value of the dollar. These beliefs are usually expressed in statements such as "I think that . . . ," "chances are . . . ," "It is unlikely that . . . ," etc. Occasionally, beliefs concerning uncertain events are expressed in numerical form as odds or subjective probabilities. What determines such beliefs? How do people assess the probability of an uncertain event or the value of an uncertain quantity? The theme of the present paper is that people rely on a limited number of heuristic principles which reduce the complex tasks of assessing probabilities and predicting values to simpler judgmental operations. In general, these heuristics are quite useful, but sometimes they lead to severe and systematic errors.

The subjective assessment of probability resembles the subjective assessment of physical quantities such as distance or size. These judgments are all based on data of limited validity, which are processed according to heuristic rules. For example, the apparent distance of an object is determined in part by its clarity. The more sharply the object is seen, the closer it appears to be. This rule has some validity because in any given scene the more distant objects are seen less sharply than nearer objects. However, the reliance on this rule leads to systematic errors in the estimation of distance. Specifically, distances are often overestimated when visibility is poor because the contours of objects are blurred. Distances are often underestimated when visibility is good, however, because the objects are sharply seen. Thus, the reliance on blur as a cue leads to characteristic biases in the judgment of distance. Systematic errors which are associated with heuristic rules are also common in the intuitive judgment of probability. The following sections describe three heuristics that are employed to assess probabilities and to predict values. Biases to which these heuristics lead are enumerated and the applied and theoretical implications of these observations are discussed.

Representativeness

Many of the probabilistic questions with which people are concerned belong to one of the following types: What is the probability that object *A* belongs to class *B*? What is the probability that event *A* originates from process *B*? What is the probability that process *A* will generate event *B*? In answering such questions people typically rely on the representativeness heuristic, in which probabilities are evaluated by the degree to which *A* is representative of *B* (i.e., by the degree of similarity between them). For example, when *A* is highly representative of *B*, the probability that *A* originates from *B* is judged to be high. If *A* is not similar to *B*, however, the probability that *A* originates from *B* is judged to be low.

For an illustration of judgment by representativeness, consider an individual who has been described by a former neighbor as follows: "Steve is very shy and withdrawn, invariably helpful, but with little interest in people, or in the world of reality. A meek and tidy soul, he has a need for order and structure, and a passion for detail." How do people assess the probability that Steve is engaged in each of several occupations (e.g., farmer, salesman, airline pilot, librarian, physician)? How do people order these occupations from most to least likely? In the representativeness heuristic, the probability that Steve is a librarian, for example, is assessed by the degree to which he is representative or similar to the stereotype of a librarian. Indeed, research with problems of this type has shown that people order the occupations by probability and by similarity in exactly the same way.[1] As will be shown below, this approach to the judgment of probability leads to serious errors because similarity, or representativeness, is not influenced by several factors which should affect judgments of probability.

Insensitivity to Prior Probability of Outcomes

One of the factors that have no effect on representativeness but should have a major effect on probability is the prior probability, or base-rate frequency, of the outcomes. In the case of Steve, for example, the fact that there are many more farmers than librarians in the population should enter into any reasonable estimate of the probability that Steve is a librarian rather than a farmer. Considerations of base-rate frequency, however, do not affect the similarity of Steve to the stereotypes of librarians and farmers. If people evaluate probability by representativeness, therefore, prior probabilities will be neglected. This hypothesis was tested in an experiment where prior probabilities were explicitly manipulated.[1] Subjects were shown brief personality descriptions of several individuals, allegedly sampled at random from a group of 100 professionals—engineers and lawyers. The subjects were asked to assess, for each description, the probability that it belonged to an engineer rather than to a lawyer. In one experimental condition, subjects were told that the group from which the descriptions had been drawn consisted of 70 engineers and 30 lawyers. In another condition, subjects were told that the group consisted of 30 engineers and 70 lawyers. The odds that any particular description belongs to an engineer rather than to a lawyer should be higher in the first condition, where there is a majority of engineers, than in the second condition, where there is a majority of lawyers. Specifically, it can be shown by applying Bayes' rule that the ratio of these odds should be $(0.7 / 0.3)^2 = 5.44$ for each description. In a sharp violation of Bayes' rule, the subjects in the two conditions produced essentially the same probability judgments. Apparently, subjects evaluated the likelihood that a particular description belonged to an engineer rather than to a lawyer by the degree to which this description was representative of the two stereotypes, with little or no regard for the prior probabilities of the categories.

The subjects correctly utilized prior probabilities when they had no other information. In the absence of a personality sketch they judged the probability that an unknown individual is an engineer to be 0.7 and 0.3, respectively, in the two base-rate conditions. However, prior probabilities were effectively ignored when a description was introduced, even when this description was totally uninformative. The responses to the following description illustrate this phenomenon:

Dick is a 30-year-old man. He is married with no children. A man of high ability and high motivation, he promises to be quite successful in his field. He is well liked by his colleagues.

This description was intended to convey no information relevant to the question of whether Dick is an engineer or a lawyer. Consequently, the probability that Dick is an engineer should equal the proportion of engineers in the group, as if no description had been given. The subjects, however, judged the probability of Dick being an engineer to be 0.5 regardless of whether the stated proportion of engineers in the group was 0.7 or 0.3. Evidently, people respond differently when given no evidence and when given worthless evidence. When no specific evidence is given—prior probabilities are properly utilized; when worthless evidence is given—prior probabilities are ignored.[1]

Insensitivity to Sample Size

To evaluate the probability of obtaining a particular result in a sample drawn from a specified population, people typically apply the representativeness heuristic. That is, they assess the likelihood of a sample result (e.g., that the average height in a random sample of ten men will be 6′0″) by the similarity of this result to the corresponding parameter (i.e., to the average height in the population of men). The similarity of a sample statistic to a population parameter does not depend on the size of the sample. Consequently, if probabilities are assessed by representativeness, then the judged probability of a sample statistic will be essentially independent of sample size. Indeed, when subjects assessed the distributions of average height for samples of various sizes, they produced identical distributions. For example, the probability of obtaining an average height greater than 6′0″ was assigned the same value for samples of 1000, 100, and 10 men.[2] Moreover, subjects failed to appreciate the role of sample size even when it was emphasized in the formulation of the problem. Consider the following question:

A certain town is served by two hospitals. In the larger hospital about 45 babies are born each day, and in the smaller hospital about 15 babies are born each day. As you know, about 50% of all babies are boys. The exact percentage of baby boys, however, varies from day to day. Sometimes it may be higher than 50%, sometimes lower.

For a period of one year, each hospital recorded the days on which more than 60% of the babies born were boys. Which hospital do you think recorded more such days?

- The larger hospital (21)

- The smaller hospital (21)

- About the same (i.e., within 5% of each other) (53).

The values in parentheses are the number of undergraduate students who chose each answer.

Most subjects judged the probability of obtaining more than 60% boys to be the same in the small and in the large hospital, presumably because these events are described by the same statistic and are therefore equally representative of the general population. In contrast, sampling theory entails that the expected number of days on which more than 60% of the babies are boys is much greater in the small hospital than in the large one because a large sample is less likely to stray from 50%. This fundamental notion of statistics is evidently not part of people's repertoire of intuitions.

A similar insensitivity to sample size has been reported in judgments of posterior probability; that is, of the probability that a sample has been drawn from one population rather than from another. Consider the following example:

Imagine an urn filled with balls, of which 2/3 are of one color and 1/3 of another. One individual has drawn 5 balls from the urn and found that 4 were red and 1 was white. Another individual has drawn 20 balls and found that 12 were red and 8 were white. Which of the two individuals should feel more confident that the urn contains 2/3 red balls and 1/3 white balls, rather than the opposite? What odds should each individual give?

In this problem, the correct posterior odds are 8 to 1 for the 4:1 sample and 16 to 1 for the 12:8 sample, assuming equal prior probabilities. However, most people feel that the first sample provides much stronger evidence for the hypothesis that the urn is predominantly red because the proportion of red balls is larger in the first than in the second sample. Here again, intuitive judgments are dominated by the sample proportion and are essentially unaffected

by the size of the sample, which plays a crucial role in the determination of the actual posterior odds.[2] In addition, intuitive estimates of posterior odds are far less extreme than the
correct values. The underestimation of the impact of evidence has been observed repeatedly
in problems of this type.[3,4] It has been labeled "conservatism."

Misconceptions of Chance

People expect that a sequence of events generated by a random process will represent the
essential characteristics of that process even when the sequence is short. In considering
tosses of a coin, for example, people regard the sequence HTHTTH to be more likely than the
sequence HHHTTT, which does not appear random, and also more likely than the sequence
HHHHTH, which does not represent the fairness of the coin.[2] Thus, people expect that the
essential characteristics of the process will be represented, not only globally in the entire
sequence, but also locally in each of its parts. A locally representative sequence, however,
deviates systematically from chance expectation: it contains too many alternations and too
few runs. Another consequence of the belief in local representativeness is the well-known
gambler's fallacy. After observing a long run of *red* on the roulette wheel, for example, most
people erroneously believe that *black* is now due, presumably because the occurrence of
black will result in a more representative sequence than the occurrence of an additional *red*.
Chance is commonly viewed as a self-correcting process where a deviation in one direction
induces a deviation in the opposite direction to restore the equilibrium. In fact, deviations
are not "corrected" as a chance process unfolds, they are merely diluted.

Misconceptions of chance are not limited to naive subjects. A study of the statistical intuitions of experienced research psychologists[5] revealed a lingering belief in what may be called
the "law of small numbers" according to which even small samples are highly representative
of the populations from which they are drawn. The responses of these investigators reflected
the expectation that a valid hypothesis about a population will be represented by a statistically significant result in a sample—with little regard for its size. As a consequence, the
researchers put too much faith in the results of small samples and grossly overestimated the
replicability of such results. In the actual conduct of research, this bias leads to the selection
of samples of inadequate size and to over-interpretation of findings.

Insensitivity to Predictability

People are sometimes called upon to make numerical predictions about, for example, the
future value of a stock, the demand for a commodity, or the outcome of a football game.
Such predictions are often made by representativeness. For example, suppose one is given

a description of a company and is asked to predict its future profit. If the description of the company is very favorable, a very high profit will appear most representative of that description; if the description is mediocre, a mediocre performance will appear most representative, etc. Now, the degree of favorableness of the description is unaffected by the reliability of that description or by the degree to which it permits accurate prediction. Hence, if people predict solely in terms of the favorableness of the description, their predictions will be insensitive to the reliability of the evidence and to the expected accuracy of the prediction.

This mode of judgment violates the normative statistical theory where the extremeness and the range of predictions are controlled by considerations of predictability. When predictability is nil, the same prediction should be made in all cases. For example, if the descriptions of companies provide no information relevant to profit, then the same value (e.g., average profit) should be predicted for all companies. If predictability is perfect, of course, the values predicted will match the actual values, and hence the range of predictions will equal the range of outcomes. In general, the higher the predictability, the wider the range of predicted values.

Several studies of numerical prediction have demonstrated that intuitive predictions violate this rule, and that subjects show little or no regard for considerations of predictability.[1] In one of these studies, subjects were presented with several paragraphs, each describing the performance of a student-teacher during a particular practice lesson. Some subjects were asked to *evaluate* the quality of the lesson described in the paragraph in percentile scores, relative to a specified population. Other subjects were asked to *predict*, also in percentile scores, the standing of each student-teacher five years after the practice lesson. The judgments made under the two conditions were identical. That is, the prediction of a remote criterion (success of a teacher after five years) was identical to the evaluation of the information on which the prediction was based (the quality of the practice lesson). The students who made these predictions were undoubtedly aware of the limited predictability of teaching competence on the basis of a single trial lesson five years earlier. Nevertheless, their predictions were as extreme as their evaluations.

The Illusion of Validity

As we have seen, people often predict by selecting the outcome (e.g., an occupation) that is most representative of the input (e.g., the description of a person). The confidence they have in their prediction depends primarily on the degree of representativeness (i.e., on the quality of the match between the selected outcome and the input) with little or no regard for the factors that limit predictive accuracy. Thus, people express great confidence in the prediction that a person is a librarian when given a description of his personality which matches the stereotype of librarians, even if the description is scanty, unreliable, or outdated. The unwarranted confidence which is produced by a good fit between the predicted outcome and the input information may be called the illusion of validity. This illusion persists even when the judge is aware of the factors that limit the accuracy of his predictions. It is a common observation that psychologists who conduct selection interviews often experience considerable confidence in their predictions, even when they know of the vast literature that shows selection interviews to be highly fallible. The continued reliance on the clinical interview for selection, despite repeated demonstrations of its inadequacy, amply attests to the strength of this effect.

The internal consistency of a pattern of inputs (e.g., a profile of test scores) is a major determinant of one's confidence in predictions based on these inputs. Thus, people express more confidence in predicting the final grade-point average of a student whose first-year record consists entirely of Bs, than in predicting the grade-point average of a student whose first-year record includes many As and Cs. Highly consistent patterns are most often observed when the input variables are highly redundant or correlated. Hence, people tend to have great confidence in predictions based on redundant input variables. However, an elementary result in the statistics of correlation asserts that, given input variables of stated validity, a prediction based on several such inputs can achieve higher accuracy when they are independent of each other than when they are redundant or correlated. Thus, redundancy among inputs decreases accuracy even as it increases confidence, and people are often confident in predictions that are quite likely to be off the mark.[1]

Misconceptions of Regression

Suppose a large group of children have been examined on two equivalent versions of an aptitude test. If one selects ten children from among those who did best on one of the two versions, one will find their performance on the second version to be somewhat disappointing, on the average. Conversely, if ten children are selected from among those who did the worst on one version, they will be found, on the average, to do somewhat better on the other version. More generally, consider two variables X and Y which have the same distribution. If one selects individuals whose average score deviates from the mean of X by k units, then, by and large, the average deviation from the mean of Y will be less than k. These observations illustrate a general phenomenon known as regression toward the mean, which was first documented by Galton more than one hundred years ago.

In the normal course of life, we encounter many instances of regression toward the mean; for example, in the comparison of the height of fathers and sons, of the intelligence of husbands and wives, or of the performance of individuals on consecutive examinations.

Nevertheless, people do not develop correct intuitions about this phenomenon. First, they do not expect regression in many contexts where it is bound to occur. Second, when they recognize the occurrence of regression, they often invent spurious causal explanations for it.[1] We suggest that the phenomenon of regression remains elusive because it is incompatible with the belief that the predicted outcome should be maximally representative of the input, and hence that the value of the outcome variable should be as extreme as the value of the input variable.

The failure to recognize the import of regression can have pernicious consequences as illustrated by the following observation.[1] In a discussion of flight training, experienced instructors noted that praise for an exceptionally smooth landing is typically followed by a poorer landing on the next try, while harsh criticism after a rough landing is usually followed by an improvement on the next try. The instructors concluded that verbal rewards are detrimental to learning while verbal punishments are beneficial—contrary to accepted psychological doctrine. This conclusion is unwarranted because of the presence of regression toward the mean. As in other cases of repeated examination, an improvement will usually follow a poor performance and a deterioration will usually follow an outstanding performance—even if the instructor does not respond to the trainee's achievement on the first attempt. Because the instructors had praised their trainees after good landings and admonished then after poor ones, they reached the erroneous and potentially harmful conclusion that punishment is more effective than reward.

Thus, the failure to understand the effect of regression leads one to overestimate the effectiveness of punishment and to underestimate the effectiveness of reward. In social interaction as well as in intentional training, rewards are typically administered when performance is good and punishments are typically administered when performance is poor. By regression alone, therefore, behavior is most likely to improve after punishment and most likely to deteriorate after reward. Consequently, the human condition is such that, by chance alone, one is most often rewarded for punishing others and most often punished for rewarding them. People are generally not aware of this contingency. In fact, the elusive role of regression in determining the apparent consequences of reward and punishment seems to have escaped the notice of students of this area.

Availability

There are situations in which people assess the frequency of a class or the probability of an event by the ease with which instances or occurrences can be brought to mind. For example, one may assess the risk of heart attack among middle-aged people by recalling such occurrences among one's acquaintances. Similarly, one may evaluate the probability that a given business venture will fail by imagining various difficulties that it could encounter. This judgmental heuristic is called availability. Availability is a useful clue for assessing frequency or probability because, in general, instances of large classes are recalled better and faster than instances of less frequent classes. However, availability is also affected by other factors besides frequency and probability. Consequently, the reliance on availability leads to predictable biases, some of which are illustrated below.

Biases Due to the Retrievability of Instances

When the frequency of a class is judged by the availability of its instances, a class whose instances are easily retrieved will appear more numerous than a class of equal frequency whose instances are less retrievable. In an elementary demonstration of this effect, subjects heard a list of well-known personalities of both sexes and were subsequently asked to judge whether the list contained more names of men than of women. Different lists were presented to different groups of subjects. In some of the lists the men were relatively more famous than the women, and in others the women were relatively more famous than the men. In each of the lists, the subjects erroneously judged the class consisting of the more famous personalities to be the more numerous.[6]

In addition to familiarity, there are other factors (e.g., salience) which affect the retrievability of instances. For example, the impact of seeing a house burning, on the subjective probability of such accidents, is probably greater than the impact of reading about a fire in the local paper. Furthermore, recent occurrences are likely to be relatively more available than earlier occurrences. It is a common experience that the subjective probability of traffic accidents rises temporarily when one sees a car overturned by the side of the road.

Biases Due to the Effectiveness of a Search Set

Suppose one samples a word (of three letters or more) at random from an English text. Is it more likely that the word starts with r or that r is its third letter? People approach this problem by recalling words that begin with r (e.g., road) and words that have r in the third position (e.g., car) and assess relative frequency by the ease with which words of the two types come to mind. Because it is much easier to search for words by their first than by their third letter, most people judge words that begin with a given consonant to be more numerous than words in which the same consonant appears in the third position. They do so even for consonants (e.g., r or k) that are actually more frequent in the third position than in the first.[6]

Different tasks elicit different search sets. For example, suppose you are asked to rate the frequency with which abstract words (e.g., thought, love) and concrete words (e.g., door, water) appear in written English. A natural way to answer this question is to search for contexts in which the word could appear. It seems easier to think of contexts in which an abstract concept is mentioned (e.g., "love" in love stories) than to think of contexts in which a concrete word (e.g., "door") is mentioned. If the frequency of words is judged by the availability of the contexts in which they appear, abstract words will be judged as relatively more numerous than concrete words. This bias has been observed in a recent study[7] which showed that the judged frequency of occurrence of abstract words was much higher than that of concrete words of the same objective frequency. Abstract words were also judged to appear in a much greater variety of contexts than concrete words.

Biases of Imaginability

Sometimes, one has to assess the frequency of a class whose instances are not stored in memory but can be generated according to a given rule. In such situations, one typically generates several instances and evaluates frequency or probability by the ease with the relevant instances can be constructed. However, the ease of constructing instances does not always reflect their actual frequency, and this mode of evaluation is prone to biases. To illustrate, consider a group of 10 people who form committees of k members, $2 \leq k \leq 8$. How many different committees of k members can be formed? The correct answer to this problem is given by the binomial coefficient $\binom{10}{k}$ which reaches a maximum of 252 for $k = 5$. Clearly, the number of committees of k members equals the number of committees of $(10 - k)$ members because any committee of k members defines a unique group of $(10 - k)$ non-members.

One way to answer this question without computation is to mentally construct committees of k members and to evaluate their number by the ease with which they come to mind. Committees of few members, say 2, are more available than committees of many members, say 8. The simplest scheme for the construction of committees is a partition of the group into disjoint sets. One readily sees that it is easy to construct five disjoint committees of 2 members, while it is impossible to generate even two disjoint committees of 8 members. Consequently, if frequency is assessed by imaginability or by availability for construction, the small committees will appear more numerous than larger committees, in contrast to the correct symmetric bell-shaped function. Indeed, when naive subjects were asked to estimate the number of distinct committees of various sizes, their estimates were a decreasing monotonic function of committee size.[6] For example, the median estimate of the number of committees of 2 members was 70, while the estimate for committees of 8 members was 20 (the correct answer is 45 in both cases).

Imaginability plays an important role in the evaluation of probabilities in real-life situations. The risk involved in an adventurous expedition, for example, is evaluated by imagining contingencies with which the expedition is not equipped to cope. If many such difficulties are vividly portrayed, the expedition can be made to appear exceedingly dangerous, although the ease with which disasters are imagined need not reflect their actual likelihood. Conversely, the risk involved in an undertaking may be grossly underestimated if some possible dangers are either difficult to conceive or simply do not come to mind.

Illusory Correlation

Chapman and Chapman[8] have described an interesting bias in the judgment of the frequency with which two events co-occur. They presented naive judges with information concerning several hypothetical mental patients. The data for each patient consisted of a clinical diagnosis and a drawing of a person made by the patient. Later the judges estimated the frequency with which each diagnosis (e.g., paranoia or suspiciousness) had been accompanied by various features of the drawing (e.g., peculiar eyes). The subjects markedly overestimated the frequency of co-occurrence of natural associates, such as suspiciousness and peculiar eyes. This effect was labeled illusory correlation. In their erroneous judgments of the data to which they had been exposed, naive subjects "rediscovered" much of the common but unfounded clinical lore concerning the interpretation of the draw-a-person test. The illusory correlation effect was extremely resistant to contradictory data. It persisted even when the correlation between symptom and diagnosis was actually negative, and it prevented the judges from detecting relationships that were in fact present.

Availability provides a natural account for the illusory-correlation effect. The judgment of how frequently two events co-occur could be based on the strength of the associative bond between them. When the association is strong, one is likely to conclude that the events have been frequently paired. Consequently, strong associates will be judged to have occurred frequently together. According to this view, the illusory correlation between suspiciousness and peculiar drawing of the eyes, for example, is due to the fact that suspiciousness is more readily associated with the eyes than with any other part of the body.

Life-long experience has taught us that, in general, instances of large classes are recalled better and faster than instances of less frequent classes; that likely occurrences are easier to imagine than unlikely ones; and that the associative connections between events are strengthened when the events frequently co-occur. As a consequence, man has at his disposal a procedure (i.e., the availability heuristic) for estimating the numerosity of a class, the likelihood of an event, or the frequency of co-occurrences, by the ease with which the relevant mental operations of retrieval, construction, or association can be performed. However, as the preceding examples have demonstrated, this valuable estimation procedure is subject to systematic errors.

Adjustment and Anchoring

In many situations, people make estimates by starting from an initial value which is adjusted to yield the final answer. The initial value, or starting point, may be suggested by the formulation of the problem, or else it may be the result of a partial computation. Whatever the source of the initial value, adjustments are typically insufficient.[4] That is, different starting points yield different estimates, which are biased toward the initial values. We call this phenomenon anchoring.

Insufficient Adjustment

In a demonstration of the anchoring effect, subjects were asked to estimate various quantities, stated in percentages (e.g., the percentage of African countries in the U.N.). For each question a starting value between 0 and 100 was determined by spinning a wheel of fortune in the subjects' presence. The subjects were instructed to indicate whether the given (arbitrary) starting value was too high or too low, and then to reach their estimate by moving upward or downward from that value. Different groups were given different starting values for each problem. These arbitrary values had a marked effect on the estimates. For example, the median estimates of the percentage of African countries in the U.N. were 25% and 45%, respectively, for groups which received 10% and 65% as starting points. Payoffs for accuracy did not reduce the anchoring effect.

Anchoring occurs not only when the starting point is given to the subject but also when the subject bases his estimate on the result of some incomplete computation. A study of intuitive numerical estimation illustrates this effect. Two groups of high-school students estimated, within 5 seconds, a numerical expression that was written on the blackboard. One group estimated the product $8 \times 7 \times 6 \times 5 \times 4 \times 3 \times 2 \times 1$, while another group estimated the product $1 \times 2 \times 3 \times 4 \times 5 \times 6 \times 7 \times 8$. To rapidly answer such questions people may perform a few steps of computation and estimate the product by extrapolation or adjustment. Because adjustments are typically insufficient, this procedure should lead to underestimation. Furthermore, because the result of the first few steps of multiplication (performed from left to right) is higher in the descending sequence than in the ascending sequence, the former expression should be judged larger than the latter. Both predictions were confirmed. The median estimate for the ascending sequence was 512, while the median estimate for the descending sequence was 2,250. The correct answer is 40,320.

Biases in the Evaluation of Conjunctive and Disjunctive Events

In a recent study,[9] subjects were given the opportunity to bet on one of two events. Three types of events were used: (i) simple events, such as drawing a red marble from a bag containing 50% red marbles and 50% white marbles; (ii) conjunctive events, such as drawing a red marble 7 times in succession, with replacement, from a bag containing 90% red marbles and 10% white marbles; and (iii) disjunctive events, such as drawing a red marble at least once in 7 successive tries, with replacement, from a bag containing 10% red marbles and 90% white marbles. In this problem, a significant majority of subjects preferred to bet on the conjunctive event (the probability of which is 0.48) rather than on the simple event, the probability of which is 0.50. Subjects also preferred to bet on the simple event rather than on the disjunctive events which has a probability of 0.52. Thus, most subjects bet on the less likely event in both comparisons. This pattern of choices illustrates a general finding. Studies of choice among gambles and of judgments of probability indicate that people tend to overestimate the probability of conjunctive events[10] and to underestimate the probability of disjunctive events. These biases are readily explained as effects of anchoring. The stated probability of the elementary event (e.g., of success at any one stage) provides a natural starting point for the estimation of the probabilities of both conjunctive and disjunctive events. Since adjustment from the starting point is typically insufficient, the final estimates remain too close to the probabilities of the elementary events in both cases. Note that the overall probability of a conjunctive event is lower than the probability of each elementary event, whereas the overall probability of a disjunctive event is higher than the probability of each elementary event. As a consequence of anchoring, the overall probability will be overestimated in conjunctive problems and underestimated in disjunctive problems.

Biases in the evaluation of compound events are particularly significant in the context of planning. The successful completion of an undertaking (e.g., the development of a new product) typically has a conjunctive character: for the undertaking to succeed each of a series of events must occur. Even when each of these events is very likely, the overall probability of success can be quite low if the number of events is large. The general tendency to overestimate the probability of conjunctive events leads to unwarranted optimism in the evaluation of the likelihood that a plan will succeed or that a project will be completed on time. Conversely, disjunctive structures are typically encountered in the evaluation of risks. A complex system (e.g., a nuclear reactor or a human body) will malfunction if any of its essential components fails. Even when the likelihood of failure in each component is slight, the probability of an overall failure can be high if many components are involved. Because of anchoring, people will tend to underestimate the probabilities of failure in complex systems. Thus, the direction of the anchoring bias can sometimes be inferred from the structure of the event. The chain-like structure of conjunctions leads to overestimation, whereas the funnel-like structure of disjunctions leads to underestimation.

Anchoring in the Assessment of Subjective Probability Distributions

For many purposes (e.g., the calculation of posterior probabilities, decision-theoretical analyses) a person is required to express his beliefs about a quantity (e.g., the value of the Dow-Jones on a particular day) in the form of a probability distribution. Such a distribution is usually constructed by asking the person to select values of the quantity that correspond to specified percentiles of his subjective probability distribution. For example, the judge may be asked to select a number X_{90} such that his subjective probability that this number will be higher than the value of the Dow-Jones is 0.90. That is, he should select X_{90} so that he is just willing to accept 9 to 1 odds that the Dow-Jones will not exceed X_{90}. A subjective probability distribution for the value of the Dow-Jones can be constructed from several such judgments corresponding to different percentiles (e.g., X_{10}, X_{25}, X_{75}, X_{99}, etc.).

By collecting subjective probability distributions for many different quantities, it is possible to test the judge for proper calibration. A judge is properly (or externally) calibrated in a set of problems if exactly Π% of the true values of the assessed quantities fall below his stated values of X_{Π}. For example, the true values should fall below X_{01} for 1% of the quantities and above X_{99} for 1% of the quantities. Thus, the true values should fall in the confidence interval between X_{01} and X_{99} on 98% of the problems.

Several investigators (see notes 11, 12, 13) have obtained probability distributions for many quantities from a large number of judges. These distributions indicated large and systematic departures from proper calibration. In most studies, the actual values of the assessed quantities are either smaller than X_{01} or greater than X_{99} for about 30% of the problems. That is, the subjects state overly narrow confidence intervals which reflect more certainty than is justified by their knowledge about the assessed quantities. This bias is common to naive and to sophisticated subjects, and it is not eliminated by introducing proper scoring rules which provide incentives for external calibration. This effect is attributable, in part at least, to anchoring. To select X_{90} for the value of the Dow-Jones, for example, it is natural to begin by thinking about one's best estimate of the Dow-Jones and to adjust this value upward. If this adjustment—like most others—is insufficient, then X_{90} will not be sufficiently extreme. A similar anchoring effect will occur in the selection of X_{10} which is presumably obtained by adjusting one's best estimate downward. Consequently, the confidence interval between X_{10} and X_{90} will be too narrow, and the assessed probability distribution will be too tight. In support of this interpretation it can be shown that subjective probabilities are systematically altered by a procedure in which one's best estimate does not serve as an anchor.

Subjective probability distributions for a given quantity (the Dow-Jones average) can be obtained in two different ways: (i) by asking the subject to select values of the Dow-Jones that correspond to specified percentiles of his probability distribution, and (ii) by asking the subject to assess the probabilities that the true value of the Dow-Jones will exceed some specified values. The two procedures are formally equivalent and should yield identical distributions. However, they suggest different modes of adjustment from different anchors. In procedure (i), the natural starting point is one's best estimate of the quantity. In procedure (ii), on the other hand, the subject may be anchored on the value stated in the question. Alternatively, he may be anchored on even odds, or 50–50 chances, which is a natural starting point in the estimation of likelihood. In either case, procedure (ii) should yield less extreme odds than procedure (i).

To contrast the two procedures, a set of 24 quantities (such as the air distance from New Delhi to Peking) was presented to a group of subjects who assessed either X_{10} or X_{90} for each problem. Another group of subjects received the median judgment of the first group for each of the 24 quantities. They were asked to assess the odds that each of the given values exceeded the true value of the relevant quantity. In the absence of any bias, the second group should retrieve the odds specified to the first group, that is, 9:1. However, if even odds or the stated value serve as anchors, the odds of the second group should be less extreme, that is, closer to 1:1. Indeed, the median odds stated by this group, across all problems, were 3:1. When the judgments of the two groups were tested for external calibration, it was found that subjects in the first group were too extreme, while subjects in the second group were too conservative.

Discussion

This chapter has been concerned with cognitive biases which stem from the reliance on judgmental heuristics. These biases are not attributable to motivational effects such as wishful thinking or the distortion of judgments by payoffs and penalties. Indeed, several of the severe errors of judgment reported earlier were observed despite the fact that subjects were encouraged to be accurate and were rewarded for the correct answers.[2,6]

The reliance on heuristics and the prevalence of biases are not restricted to laymen. Experienced researchers are also prone to the same biases—when they think intuitively. For example, the tendency to predict the outcome that best represents the data, with insufficient regard for prior probability, has been observed in the intuitive judgments of individuals who had extensive training in statistics.[1,5] Although the statistically sophisticated avoid elementary errors (e.g., the gambler's fallacy), their intuitive judgments are liable to similar fallacies in more intricate and less transparent problems.

It is not surprising that useful heuristics such as representativeness and availability are retained, even though they occasionally lead to errors in prediction or estimation. What is perhaps surprising is the failure of people to infer from life-long experience such fundamental statistical rules as regression toward the mean or the effect of sample size on sampling variability. Although everyone is exposed in the normal course of life to numerous examples from which these rules could have been induced, very few people discover the principles of sampling and regression on their own. Statistical principles are not learned from everyday experience because the relevant instances are not coded appropriately. For example, we do not discover that successive lines in a text differ more in average word length than do successive pages because we simply do not attend to the average word length of individual lines or pages. Thus, we do not learn the relation between sample size and sampling variability, although the data for such learning are present in abundance whenever we read.

The lack of an appropriate code also explains why people usually do not detect the biases in their judgments of probability. A person could conceivably learn whether his judgments are externally calibrated by keeping a tally of the proportion of events that actually occur among those to which he assigns the same probability. However, it is not natural to group events by their judged probability. In the absence of such grouping it is impossible for an individual to discover, for example, that only 50% of the predictions to which he has assigned a probability of 0.9 or higher actually came true.

The empirical analysis of cognitive biases has implications for the theoretical and applied role of judged probabilities. Modern decision theory[14,15] regards subjective probability as the quantified opinion of an idealized person. Specifically, the subjective probability of a given event is defined by the set of bets about this event which such a person is willing to accept. An internally consistent, or coherent, subjective probability measure can be derived for an individual if his choices among bets satisfy certain principles (i.e., the axioms of the theory). The derived probability is subjective in the sense that different individuals are allowed to have different probabilities for the same event. The major contribution of this approach is that it provides a rigorous subjective interpretation of probability which is applicable to unique events and is embedded in a general theory of rational decision.

It should perhaps be noted that while subjective probabilities can sometimes be inferred from preferences among bets, they are normally not formed in this fashion. A person bets on Team A rather than on Team B because he believes that Team A is more likely to win; he does not infer this belief from his betting preferences. Thus, in reality, subjective probabilities determine preferences among bets and are not derived from them as in the axiomatic theory of rational decision.[14]

The inherently subjective nature of probability has led many students to the belief that coherence, or internal consistency, is the only valid criterion by which judged probabilities should be evaluated. From the standpoint of the formal theory of subjective probability, any set of internally consistent probability judgments is as good as any other. This criterion is not entirely satisfactory because an internally consistent set of subjective probabilities can be incompatible with other beliefs held by the individual. Consider a person whose subjective probabilities for all possible outcomes of a coin-tossing game reflect the gambler's fallacy. That is, his estimate of the probability of *tails* on any toss increases with the number of consecutive *heads* that preceded that toss. The judgments of such a person could be internally consistent and therefore acceptable as adequate subjective probabilities according to the criterion of the formal theory. These probabilities, however, are incompatible with the generally held belief that a coin has no memory and is therefore incapable of generating sequential dependencies. For judged probabilities to be considered adequate, or rational, internal consistency is not enough. The judgments must be compatible with the entire web of beliefs held by the individual. Unfortunately, there can be no simple formal procedure for assessing the compatibility of a set of probability judgments with the judge's total system of beliefs. The rational judge will nevertheless strive for compatibility, even though internal consistency is more easily achieved and assessed. In particular, he will attempt to make his probability judgments compatible with his knowledge about (i) the subject matter, (ii) the laws of probability, and (iii) his own judgmental heuristics and biases.

Notes

This article was published with minor modifications in *Science* 185 (1974), 1124–1131, 27 September 1974. Copyright 1974 by the American Association for the Advancement of Science whose permission to reproduce it here is gratefully acknowledged.

This research was supported by the Advanced Research Projects Agency of the Department of Defense and was monitored by ONR under Contract No. N00014–73-C-0438 to the Oregon Research Institute. Additional support was provided by the Research and Development Authority of the Hebrew University.

References

1. Kahneman, D., & Tversky, A. (1973). On the psychology of prediction. *Psychological Review, 80,* 237–251.

2. Kahneman, D., & Tversky, A. (1972). Subjective probability: A judgment of representativeness. *Cognitive Psychology, 3,* 430–454.

3. Edwards, W. (1968). Conservatism in human information processing. In B. Kleinmuntz (Ed.), *Formal representation of human judgment* (pp. 17–52). New York, NY: Wiley.

4. Slovic, P., & Lichtenstein, S. (1971). Comparison of Bayesian and regression approaches to the study of information processing in judgment. *Organizational Behavior and Human Performance, 6,* 649–744.

5. Tversky, A., & Kahneman, D. (1971). The belief in the law of small numbers. *Psychological Bulletin, 76,* 105–110.

6. Tversky, A., & Kahneman, D. (1973). Availability: A heuristic for judging frequency and probability. *Cognitive Psychology, 5,* 207–232.

7. Galbraith, R. C., & Underwood, B. J. (1973). Perceived frequency of concrete and abstract words. *Memory & Cognition, 1,* 56–60.

8. Chapman, L. J., & Chapman, J. P. (1967). Genesis of popular but erroneous psychodiagnostic observations. *Journal of Abnormal Psychology, 73,* 193–204; Chapman, L. J., & Chapman, J. P. (1969). Illusory correlation as an obstacle to the use of valid psychodiagnostic signs. *Journal of Abnormal Psychology, 74,* 271–280.

9. Bar-Hillel, M. (1973). Compounding subjective probabilities. *Organizational Behavior and Human Performance, 9,* 396–406.

10. Cohen, J., Chesnick, E. I., & Haran, D. (1972). A confirmation of the inertial-ψ effect in sequential choice and decision. *British Journal of Psychology, 63,* 41–46.

11. Alpert, M., & Raiffa, H. (1969). A report on the training of probability assessors. Unpublished manuscript, Harvard University.

12. Staeël von Holstein, C. (1971). Two techniques for assessment of subjective probability distributions—An experimental study. *Acta Psychologica, 35,* 478–494.

13. Winkler, R. L. (1967). The assessment of prior distributions in Bayesian analysis. *Journal of the American Statistical Association, 62,* 776–800.

14. Savage, L. J. (1954). *The foundations of statistics.* New York, NY: Wiley.

15. de Finetti, B. (1968). Probability: Interpretation. In D. L. Sills (Ed.), *International encyclopedia of the social sciences* (vol. 13) (pp. 496–504). New York, NY: Macmillan.

2   Extensional versus Intuitive Reasoning: The Conjunction Fallacy in Probability Judgment

Amos Tversky and Daniel Kahneman

Uncertainty is an unavoidable aspect of the human condition. Many significant choices must be based on beliefs about the likelihood of such uncertain events as the guilt of a defendant, the result of an election, the future value of the dollar, the outcome of a medical operation, or the response of a friend. Because we normally do not have adequate formal models for computing the probabilities of such events, intuitive judgment is often the only practical method for assessing uncertainty.

The question of how lay people and experts evaluate the probabilities of uncertain events has attracted considerable research interest in the last decade (see, e.g., Einhorn & Hogarth, 1981; Kahneman, Slovic, & Tversky, 1982; Nisbett & Ross, 1980). Much of this research has compared intuitive inferences and probability judgments to the rules of statistics and the laws of probability. The student of judgment uses the probability calculus as a standard of comparison much as a student of perception might compare the perceived sizes of objects to their physical sizes. Unlike the correct size of objects, however, the "correct" probability of events is not easily defined. Because individuals who have different knowledge or who hold different beliefs must be allowed to assign different probabilities to the same event, no single value can be correct for all people. Furthermore, a correct probability cannot always be determined even for a single person. Outside the domain of random sampling, probability theory does not determine the probabilities of uncertain events—it merely imposes constraints on the relations among them. For example, if A is more probable than B, then the complement of A must be less probable than the complement of B.

The laws of probability derive from extensional considerations. A probability measure is defined on a family of events and each event is construed as a set of possibilities, such as the three ways of getting a 10 on a throw of a pair of dice. The probability of an event equals the sum of the probabilities of its disjoint outcomes. Probability theory has traditionally been used to analyze repetitive chance processes, but the theory has also been applied to essentially unique events where probability is not reducible to the relative frequency of "favorable" outcomes. The probability that the man who sits next to you on the plane is unmarried equals the probability that he is a bachelor plus the probability that he is either divorced or widowed. Additivity applies even when probability does not have a frequentistic interpretation and when the elementary events are not equiprobable.

The simplest and most fundamental qualitative law of probability is the extension rule: If the extension of A includes the extension of B (i.e., A ⊃ B) then $P(A) \geq P(B)$. Because the set of possibilities associated with a conjunction A&B is included in the set of possibilities associated with B, the same principle can also be expressed by the conjunction rule $P(A\&B) \leq P(B)$: A conjunction cannot be more probable than one of its constituents. This rule holds regardless of whether A and B are independent and is valid for any probability assignment on the same sample space. Furthermore, it applies not only to the standard probability calculus but also to nonstandard models such as upper and lower probability (Dempster, 1967; Suppes, 1975), belief function (Shafer, 1976), Baconian probability (Cohen, 1977), rational belief (Kyburg, 1983), and possibility theory (Zadeh, 1978).

In contrast to formal theories of belief, intuitive judgments of probability are generally not extensional. People do not normally analyze daily events into exhaustive lists of possibilities or evaluate compound probabilities by aggregating elementary ones. Instead, they commonly use a limited number of heuristics, such as representativeness and availability (Kahneman et al., 1982). Our conception of judgmental heuristics is based on *natural assessments* that are routinely carried out as part of the perception of events and the comprehension of messages. Such natural assessments include computations of similarity and representativeness, attributions of causality, and evaluations of the availability of associations and exemplars. These assessments, we propose, are performed even in the absence of a specific task set, although their results are used to meet task demands as they arise. For example, the mere mention of "horror movies" activates instances of horror movies and evokes an assessment of their availability. Similarly, the statement that Woody Allen's aunt had hoped that he would be a dentist elicits a comparison of the character to the stereotype and an assessment of representativeness. It is presumably the mismatch between Woody Allen's personality and our stereotype of a dentist that makes the thought mildly amusing. Although these assessments are not tied to the estimation of frequency or probability, they are likely to play a dominant role when such judgments are required. The availability of horror movies may be used to answer the question, "What proportion of the movies produced last year were horror movies?", and representativeness may control the judgment that a particular boy is more likely to be an actor than a dentist.

The term *judgmental heuristic* refers to a strategy—whether deliberate or not—that relies on a natural assessment to produce an estimation or a prediction. One of the manifestations of a heuristic is the relative neglect of other considerations. For example, the resemblance of a child to various professional stereotypes may be given too much weight in predicting future vocational choice, at the expense of other pertinent data such as the base-rate frequencies of occupations. Hence, the use of judgmental heuristics gives rise to predictable biases. Natural assessments can affect judgments in other ways, for which the term *heuristic* is less apt. First, people sometimes misinterpret their task and fail to distinguish the required judgment from the natural assessment that the problem evokes. Second, the natural assessment may act as an anchor to which the required judgment is assimilated, even when the judge does not intend to use the one to estimate the other.

Previous discussions of errors of judgment have focused on deliberate strategies and on misinterpretations of tasks. The present treatment calls special attention to the processes of anchoring and assimilation, which are often neither deliberate nor conscious. An example from perception may be instructive: If two objects in a picture of a three-dimensional scene have the same picture size, the one that appears more distant is not only seen as "really" larger but also as larger in the picture. The natural computation of real size evidently influences the (less natural) judgment of picture size, although observers are unlikely to confuse the two values or to use the former to estimate the latter.

The natural assessments of representativeness and availability do not conform to the extensional logic of probability theory. In particular, a conjunction can be more representative than one of its constituents, and instances of a specific category can be easier to retrieve than instances of a more inclusive category. The following demonstration illustrates the point. When they were given 60 seconds to list seven-letter words of a specified form, students at the University of British Columbia (UBC) produced many more words of the form _ _ _ _ing than of the form _ _ _ _ _n_, although the latter class includes the former. The average numbers of words produced in the two conditions were 6.4 and 2.9, respectively ($t(44) = 4.70$, $p < 0.01$). In this test of availability, the increased efficacy of memory search suffices to offset the reduced extension of the target class.

Our treatment of the availability heuristic (Tversky & Kahneman, 1973) suggests that the differential availability of *ing* words and of _n_ words should be reflected in judgments of frequency. The following question tests this prediction.

In four pages of a novel (about 2,000 words), how many words would you expect to find that have the form _ _ _ _ing (seven-letter words that end with "ing")? Indicate your best estimate by circling one of the values below:

0   1–2   3–4   5–7   8–10   11–15   16+.

A second version of the question requested estimates for words of the form _ _ _ _ _n_. The median estimates were 13.4 for *ing* words (N = 52) and 4.7 for _n_ words (N = 53, $p < 0.01$ by median test), contrary to the extension rule. Similar results were obtained for the comparison of words of the form _ _ _ _ _ly with words of the form _ _ _ _ _l_; the median estimates were 8.8 and 4.4, respectively.

This example illustrates the structure of the studies reported in this article. We constructed problems in which a reduction of extension was associated with an increase in availability or representativeness, and we tested the conjunction rule in judgments of frequency or probability. In the next section we discuss the representativeness heuristic and contrast it with the conjunction rule in the context of person perception. The third section describes conjunction fallacies in medical prognoses, sports forecasting, and choice among bets. In the fourth section we investigate probability judgments for conjunctions of causes and effects and describe conjunction errors in scenarios of future events. Manipulations that enable respondents to resist the conjunction fallacy are explored in the fifth section, and the implications of the results are discussed in the last section.

Representative Conjunctions

Modern research on categorization of objects and events (Mervis & Rosch, 1981; Rosch, 1978; Smith & Medin, 1981) has shown that information is commonly stored and processed in relation to mental models, such as prototypes and schemata. It is therefore natural and economical for the probability of an event to be evaluated by the degree to which that event is representative of an appropriate mental model (Kahneman & Tversky, 1972, 1973; Tversky & Kahneman, 1971, 1982). Because many of the results reported here are attributed to this heuristic, we first briefly analyze the concept of representativeness and illustrate its role in probability judgment.

Representativeness is an assessment of the degree of correspondence between a sample and a population, an instance and a category, an act and an actor, or, more generally, between an outcome and a model. The model may refer to a person, a coin, or the world economy, and the respective outcomes could be marital status, a sequence of heads and tails, or the current price of gold. Representativeness can be investigated empirically by asking people, for example, which of two sequences of heads and tails is more representative of a fair coin or which of two professions is more representative of a given personality. This relation differs from other notions of proximity in that it is distinctly directional. It is natural to describe a sample as more or less representative of its parent population or a species (e.g., robin, penguin) as more or less representative of a superordinate category (e.g., bird). It is awkward to describe a population as representative of a sample or a category as representative of an instance.

When the model and the outcomes are described in the same terms, representativeness is reducible to similarity. Because a sample and a population, for example, can be described by the same attributes (e.g., central tendency and variability), the sample appears representative if its salient statistics match the corresponding parameters of the population. In the same manner, a person seems representative of a social group if his or her personality resembles the stereotypical member of that group. Representativeness, however, is not always reducible to similarity; it can also reflect causal and correlational beliefs (see, e.g., Chapman & Chapman, 1967; Jennings, Amabile, & Ross, 1982; Nisbett & Ross, 1980). A particular act (e.g., suicide) is representative of a person because we attribute to the actor a disposition to commit the act, not because the act resembles the person. Thus, an outcome is representative of a model if the salient features match or if the model has a propensity to produce the outcome.

Representativeness tends to covary with frequency: Common instances and frequent events are generally more representative than unusual instances and rare events. The representative summer day is warm and sunny, the representative American family has two children, and the representative height of an adult male is about 5 feet 10 inches. However, there are notable circumstances where representativeness is at variance with both actual and perceived frequency. First, a highly specific outcome can be representative but infrequent. Consider a numerical variable, such as weight, that has a unimodal frequency distribution in a given population. A narrow interval near the mode of the distribution is generally more representative of the population than a wider interval near the tail. For example, 68% of a group of Stanford University undergraduates ($N = 105$) stated that it is more representative for a female Stanford student "to weigh between 124 and 125 pounds" than "to weigh more than 135 pounds." On the other hand, 78% of a different group ($N = 102$) stated that among female Stanford students there are more "women who weigh more than 135 pounds" than "women who weigh between 124 and 125 pounds." Thus, the narrow modal interval (124–125 pounds) was judged to be more representative but less frequent than the broad tail interval (above 135 pounds).

Second, an attribute is representative of a class if it is very diagnostic, that is, if the relative frequency of this attribute is much higher in that class than in a relevant reference class. For example, 65% of the subjects ($N = 105$) stated that it is more representative for a Hollywood actress "to be divorced more than 4 times" than "to vote Democratic." Having multiple divorces is diagnostic of Hollywood actresses because it is part of the stereotype that the incidence of divorce is higher among Hollywood actresses than among other women. However, 83% of a different group ($N = 102$) stated that, among Hollywood actresses, there are more "women who vote Democratic" than "women who are divorced more than 4 times." Thus, the more diagnostic attribute was judged to be more representative but less frequent than an attribute (voting Democratic) of lower diagnosticity. Third, an unrepresentative instance of a category can be fairly representative of a superordinate category. For example, chicken is a worse exemplar of a bird than of an animal, and rice is an unrepresentative vegetable, although it is a representative food.

The preceding observations indicate that representativeness is nonextensional: It is not determined by frequency, and it is not bound by class inclusion. Consequently, the test of the conjunction rule in probability judgments offers the sharpest contrast between the extensional logic of probability theory and the psychological principles of representativeness. Our first set of studies of the conjunction rule were conducted in 1974, using occupation and political affiliation as target attributes to be predicted singly or in conjunction from brief personality sketches (see Tversky & Kahneman, 1982, for a brief summary). The studies described in the present section replicate and extend our earlier work. We used the following personality sketches of two fictitious individuals, Bill and Linda, followed by a set of occupations and avocations associated with each of them.

Bill is 34 years old. He is intelligent, but unimaginative, compulsive, and generally lifeless. In school, he was strong in mathematics but weak in social studies and humanities.

Bill is a physician who plays poker for a hobby.

Bill is an architect.

Bill is an accountant. (A)

Bill plays jazz for a hobby. (J)

Bill surfs for a hobby.

Bill is a reporter.

Bill is an accountant who plays jazz for a hobby. (A&J)

Bill climbs mountains for a hobby.

Linda is 31 years old, single, outspoken, and very bright. She majored in philosophy. As a student, she was deeply concerned with issues of discrimination and social justice, and she also participated in antinuclear demonstrations.

Linda is a teacher in elementary school.

Linda works in a bookstore and takes yoga classes.

Linda is active in the feminist movement. (F)

Linda is a psychiatric social worker.

Linda is a member of the League of Women Voters.

Linda is a bank teller. (T)

Linda is an insurance salesperson.

Linda is a bank teller and is active in the feminist movement. (T&F)

As the reader has probably guessed, the description of Bill was constructed to be representative of an accountant (A) and unrepresentative of a person who plays jazz for a hobby (J). The description of Linda was constructed to be representative of an active feminist (F) and unrepresentative of a bank teller (T). We also expected the ratings of representativeness to be higher for the classes defined by a conjunction of attributes (A&J for Bill, T&F for Linda) than for the less representative constituent of each conjunction (J and T, respectively).

A group of 88 undergraduates at UBC ranked the eight statements associated with each description by "the degree to which Bill (Linda) resembles the typical member of that class." The results confirmed our expectations. The percentages of respondents who displayed the predicted order (A > A&J > J for Bill; F > T&F > T for Linda) were 87% and 85%, respectively. This finding is neither surprising nor objectionable. If, like similarity and prototypicality, representativeness depends on both common and distinctive features (Tversky, 1977), it should be enhanced by the addition of shared features. Adding eyebrows to a schematic face makes it more similar to another schematic face with eyebrows (Gati & Tversky, 1982). Analogously, the addition of feminism to the profession of bank teller improves the match of Linda's current activities to her personality. More surprising and less acceptable is the finding that the great majority of subjects also rank the conjunctions (A&J and T&F) as more *probable* than their less representative constituents (J and T). The following sections describe and analyze this phenomenon.

Indirect and Subtle Tests

Experimental tests of the conjunction rule can be divided into three types: *indirect* tests, *direct-subtle* tests, and *direct-transparent* tests. In the indirect tests, one group of subjects evaluates the probability of the conjunction, and another group of subjects evaluates the probability of its constituents. No subject is required to compare a conjunction (e.g., "Linda is a bank teller and a feminist") to its constituents. In the direct-subtle tests, subjects compare the conjunction to its less representative constituent, but the inclusion relation between the events is not emphasized. In the direct-transparent tests, the subjects evaluate or compare the probabilities of the conjunction and its constituent in a format that highlights the relation between them.

The three experimental procedures investigate different hypotheses. The indirect procedure tests whether probability judgments conform to the conjunction rule, the direct-subtle procedure tests whether people will take advantage of an opportunity to compare the critical events, and the direct-transparent procedure tests whether people will obey the conjunction rule when they are compelled to compare the critical events. This sequence of tests also describes the course of our investigation, which began with the observation of violations of the conjunction rule in indirect tests and proceeded—to our increasing surprise—to the finding of stubborn failures of that rule in several direct-transparent tests.

Three groups of respondents took part in the main study. The statistically *naive* group consisted of undergraduate students at Stanford University and UBC who had no background in probability or statistics. The *informed* group consisted of first-year graduate students in psychology and in education and of medical students at Stanford who were all familiar with the basic concepts of probability after one or more courses in statistics. The *sophisticated* group consisted of doctoral students in the decision science program of the Stanford Business School who had taken several advanced courses in probability, statistics, and decision theory.

Subjects in the main study received one problem (either Bill or Linda) first in the format of a direct test. They were asked to rank all eight statements associated with that problem (including the conjunction, its separate constituents, and five filler items) according to their probability, using 1 for the most probable and 8 for the least probable. The subjects then received the remaining problem in the format of an indirect test in which the list of alternatives included either the conjunction or its separate constituents. The same five filler items were used in both the direct and the indirect versions of each problem.

Table 2.1 presents the average ranks (R) of the conjunction R(A&B) and of its less representative constituents R(B), relative to the set of five filler items. The percentage of violations of the conjunction rule in the direct test is denoted by V. The results can be summarized as follows: (a) the conjunction is ranked higher than its less likely constituents in all 12 comparisons, (b) there is no consistent difference between the ranks of the alternatives in the direct and indirect tests, (c) the overall incidence of violations of the conjunction rule in direct tests is 88%, which virtually coincides with the incidence of the corresponding pattern in judgments of representativeness, and (d) there is no effect of statistical sophistication in either indirect or direct tests.

The violation of the conjunction rule in a direct comparison of B to A&B is called the *conjunction fallacy*. Violations inferred from between-subjects comparisons are called *conjunction*

Table 2.1

Tests of the Conjunction Rule in Likelihood Rankings

Subjects	Problem	Direct test				Indirect test		
		V	R(A&B)	R(B)	N	R(A&B)	R(B)	Total N
Naive	Bill	92	2.5	4.5	94	2.3	4.5	88
	Linda	89	3.3	4.4	88	3.3	4.4	86
Informed	Bill	86	2.6	4.5	56	2.4	4.2	56
	Linda	90	3.0	4.3	53	2.9	3.9	55
Sophisticated	Bill	83	2.6	4.7	32	2.5	4.6	32
	Linda	85	3.2	4.3	32	3.1	4.3	32

Note: V = percentage of violations of the conjunction rule; R(A&B) and R(B) = mean rank assigned to A&B and to B, respectively; N = number of subjects in the direct test; Total N = total number of subjects in the indirect test, who were about equally divided between the two groups.

errors. Perhaps the most surprising aspect of table 2.1 is the lack of any difference between indirect and direct tests. We had expected the conjunction to be judged more probable than the less likely of its constituents in an indirect test, in accord with the pattern observed in judgments of representativeness. However, we also expected that even naive respondents would notice the repetition of some attributes, alone and in conjunction with others, and that they would then apply the conjunction rule and rank the conjunction below its constituents. This expectation was violated, not only by statistically naive undergraduates but even by highly sophisticated respondents. In both direct and indirect tests, the subjects apparently ranked the outcomes by the degree to which Bill (or Linda) matched the respective stereotypes. The correlation between the mean ranks of probability and representativeness was 0.96 for Bill and 0.98 for Linda. Does the conjunction rule hold when the relation of inclusion is made highly transparent? The studies described in the next section abandon all subtlety in an effort to compel the subjects to detect and appreciate the inclusion relation between the target events.

Transparent Tests

This section describes a series of increasingly desperate manipulations designed to induce subjects to obey the conjunction rule. We first presented the description of Linda to a group of 142 undergraduates at UBC and asked them to check which of two alternatives was more probable:

Linda is a bank teller. (T)

Linda is a bank teller and is active in the feminist movement. (T&F)

The order of alternatives was inverted for one half of the subjects, but this manipulation had no effect. Overall, 85% of respondents indicated that T&F was more probable than T, in a flagrant violation of the conjunction rule.

Surprised by the finding, we searched for alternative interpretations of the subjects' responses. Perhaps the subjects found the question too trivial to be taken literally and consequently interpreted the inclusive statement T as T&not-F; that is, "Linda is a bank teller and is *not* a feminist." In such a reading, of course, the observed judgments would not violate the conjunction rule. To test this interpretation, we asked a new group of subjects ($N = 119$) to assess the probability of T and of T&F on a 9-point scale ranging from 1 (extremely unlikely) to 9 (extremely likely). Because it is sensible to rate probabilities even when one of the events includes the other, there was no reason for respondents to interpret T as T&not-F. The pattern of responses obtained with the new version was the same as before. The mean ratings of probability were 3.5 for T and 5.6 for T&F, and 82% of subjects assigned a higher rating to T&F than they did to T.

Although subjects do not spontaneously apply the conjunction rule, perhaps they can recognize its validity. We presented another group of UBC undergraduates with the description of Linda followed by the two statements, T and T&F, and asked them to indicate which of the following two arguments they found more convincing.

Argument 1. Linda is more likely to be a bank teller than she is to be a feminist bank teller because every feminist bank teller is a bank teller, but some women bank tellers are not feminists, and Linda could be one of them.

Argument 2. Linda is more likely to be a feminist bank teller than she is likely to be a bank teller because she resembles an active feminist more than she resembles a bank teller.

The majority of subjects (65%, $n = 58$) chose the invalid resemblance argument (argument 2) over the valid extensional argument (argument 1). Thus, a deliberate attempt to induce a reflective attitude did not eliminate the appeal of the representativeness heuristic.

We made a further effort to clarify the inclusive nature of the event T by representing it as a disjunction. (Note that the conjunction rule can also be expressed as a disjunction rule $P(A$ or $B) \geq P(B)$.) The description of Linda was used again, with a 9-point rating scale for judgments of probability, but the statement T was replaced by

Linda is a bank teller whether or not she is active in the feminist movement. (T*)

This formulation emphasizes the inclusion of T&F in T. Despite the transparent relation between the statements, the mean ratings of likelihood were 5.1 for T&F and 3.8 for T* ($p <$ 0.01, by t test). Furthermore, 57% of the subjects ($n = 75$) committed the conjunction fallacy by rating T&F higher than T*, and only 16% gave a lower rating to T&F than to T*.

The violations of the conjunction rule in direct comparisons of T&F to T* are remarkable because the extension of "Linda is a bank teller whether or not she is active in the feminist movement" clearly includes the extension of "Linda is a bank teller and is active in the feminist movement." Many subjects evidently failed to draw extensional inferences from the phrase "whether or not," which may have been taken to indicate a weak disposition. This interpretation was supported by a between-subjects comparison, in which different subjects evaluated T, T*, and T&F on a 9-point scale after evaluating the common filler statement, "Linda is a psychiatric social worker." The average ratings were 3.3 for T, 3.9 for T*, and 4.5 for T&F, with each mean significantly different from both others. The statements T and T* are of course extensionally equivalent, but they are assigned different probabilities. Because feminism fits Linda, the mere mention of this attribute makes T* more likely than T, and a definite commitment to it makes the probability of T&F even higher!

Modest success in loosening the grip of the conjunction fallacy was achieved by asking subjects to choose whether to bet on T or on T&F. The subjects were given Linda's description, with the following instruction:

If you could win $10 by betting on an event, which of the following would you choose to bet on? (Check one)

The percentage of violations of the conjunction rule in this task was "only" 56% ($n = 60$), much too high for comfort but substantially lower than the typical value for comparisons of the two events in terms of probability. We conjecture that the betting context draws attention to the conditions in which one bet pays off whereas the other does not, allowing some subjects to discover that a bet on T dominates a bet on T&F.

The respondents in the studies described in this section were statistically naive undergraduates at UBC. Does statistical education eradicate the fallacy? To answer this question, 64 graduate students of social sciences at the University of California, Berkeley and at Stanford University, all with credit for several statistics courses, were given the rating-scale version of the direct test of the conjunction rule for the Linda problem. For the first time in this series of studies, the mean rating for T&F (3.5) was lower than the rating assigned to T (3.8), and only 36% of respondents committed the fallacy. Thus, statistical sophistication produced a majority who conformed to the conjunction rule in a transparent test, although the incidence of violations was fairly high even in this group of intelligent and sophisticated respondents.

Elsewhere (Kahneman & Tversky, 1982a), we distinguished between positive and negative accounts of judgments and preferences that violate normative rules. A positive account focuses on the factors that produce a particular response; a negative account seeks to explain why the correct response was not made. The positive analysis of the Bill and Linda problems invokes the representativeness heuristic. The stubborn persistence of the conjunction fallacy in highly transparent problems, however, lends special interest to the characteristic question of a negative analysis: Why do intelligent and reasonably well-educated people fail to recognize the applicability of the conjunction rule in transparent problems? Postexperimental interviews and class discussions with many subjects shed some light on this question. Naive as well as sophisticated subjects generally noticed the nesting of the target events in the direct-transparent test, but the naive, unlike the sophisticated, did not appreciate its significance for probability assessment. On the other hand, most naive subjects did not attempt to defend their responses. As one subject said after acknowledging the validity of the conjunction rule, "I thought you only asked for my opinion."

The interviews and the results of the direct-transparent tests indicate that naive subjects do not spontaneously treat the conjunction rule as decisive. Their attitude is reminiscent of children's responses in a Piagetian experiment. The child in the preconservation stage is not altogether blind to arguments based on conservation of volume and typically expects quantity to be conserved (Bruner, 1966). What the child fails to see is that the conservation argument is decisive and should overrule the perceptual impression that the tall container holds more water than the short one. Similarly, naive subjects generally endorse the conjunction rule in the abstract, but their application of this rule to the Linda problem is blocked by the compelling impression that T&F is more representative of her than T is. In this context, the adult subjects reason as if they had not reached the stage of formal operations. A full understanding of a principle of physics, logic, or statistics requires knowledge of the conditions under which it prevails over conflicting arguments, such as the height of the liquid in a container or the representativeness of an outcome. The recognition of the decisive nature of rules distinguishes different developmental stages in studies of conservation; it also distinguishes different levels of statistical sophistication in the present series of studies.

More Representative Conjunctions

The preceding studies revealed massive violations of the conjunction rule in the domain of person perception and social stereotypes. Does the conjunction rule fare better in other areas of judgment? Does it hold when the uncertainty regarding the target events is attributed to chance rather than to partial ignorance? Does expertise in the relevant subject matter protect against the conjunction fallacy? Do financial incentives help respondents see the light? The following studies were designed to answer these questions.

Medical Judgment

In this study we asked practicing physicians to make intuitive predictions on the basis of clinical evidence.[1] We chose to study medical judgment because physicians possess expert knowledge and because intuitive judgments often play an important role in medical decision making. Two groups of physicians took part in the study. The first group consisted of 37 internists from the greater Boston area who were taking a postgraduate course at Harvard University. The second group consisted of 66 internists with admitting privileges in the New England Medical Center. They were given problems of the following type:

A 55-year-old woman had pulmonary embolism documented angiographically 10 days after a cholecystectomy.

Please rank order the following in terms of the probability that they will be among the conditions experienced by the patient (use 1 for the most likely and 6 for the least likely). Naturally, the patient could experience more than one of these conditions.

dyspnea and hemiparesis (A&B)	syncope and tachycardia
calf pain	hemiparesis (B)
pleuritic chest pain	hemoptysis

1. We are grateful to Barbara J. McNeil, Harvard Medical School, Stephen G. Pauker, Tufts University School of Medicine, and Edward Baer, Stanford Medical School, for their help in the construction of the clinical problems and in the collection of the data.

The symptoms listed for each problem included one, denoted B, which was judged by our consulting physicians to be nonrepresentative of the patient's condition, and the conjunction of B with another highly representative symptom denoted A. In the above example of pulmonary embolism (blood clots in the lung), dyspnea (shortness of breath) is a typical symptom, whereas hemiparesis (partial paralysis) is very atypical. Each participant first received three (or two) problems in the indirect format, where the list included either B or the conjunction A&B, but not both, followed by two (or three) problems in the direct format illustrated above. The design was balanced so that each problem appeared about an equal number of times in each format. An independent group of 32 physicians from Stanford University were asked to rank each list of symptoms "by the degree to which they are representative of the clinical condition of the patient."

The design was essentially the same as in the Bill and Linda study. The results of the two experiments were also very similar. The correlation between mean ratings by probability and by representativeness exceeded 0.95 in all five problems. For every one of the five problems, the conjunction of an unlikely symptom with a likely one was judged more probable than the less likely constituent. The ranking of symptoms was the same in direct and indirect tests: The overall mean ranks of A&B and of B, respectively, were 2.7 and 4.6 in the direct tests and 2.8 and 4.3 in the indirect tests. The incidence of violations of the conjunction rule in direct tests ranged from 73% to 100%, with an average of 91%. Evidently, substantive expertise does not displace representativeness and does not prevent conjunction errors.

Can the results be interpreted without imputing to these experts a consistent violation of the conjunction rule? The instructions used in the present study were especially designed to eliminate the interpretation of symptom B as an exhaustive description of the relevant facts, which would imply the absence of symptom A. Participants were instructed to rank symptoms in terms of the probability "that they will be among the conditions experienced by the patient." They were also reminded that "the patient could experience more than one of these conditions." To test the effect of these instructions, the following question was included at the end of the questionnaire:

In assessing the probability that the patient described has a particular symptom X, did you assume that (check one)

X is the *only* symptom experienced by the patient?

X is *among* the symptoms experienced by the patient?

Sixty of the 62 physicians who were asked this question checked the second answer, rejecting an interpretation of events that could have justified an apparent violation of the conjunction rule.

An additional group of 24 physicians, mostly residents at Stanford Hospital, participated in a group discussion in which they were confronted with their conjunction fallacies in the same questionnaire. The respondents did not defend their answers, although some references were made to "the nature of clinical experience." Most participants appeared surprised and dismayed to have made an elementary error of reasoning. Because the conjunction fallacy is easy to expose, people who committed it are left with the feeling that they should have known better.

Predicting Wimbledon

The uncertainty encountered in the previous studies regarding the prognosis of a patient or the occupation of a person is normally attributed to incomplete knowledge rather than to the operation of a chance process. Recent studies of inductive reasoning about daily events, conducted by Nisbett, Krantz, Jepson, and Kunda (1983), indicated that statistical principles (e.g., the law of large numbers) are commonly applied in domains such as sports and gambling, which include a random element. The next two studies test the conjunction rule in predictions of the outcomes of a sports event and of a game of chance, where the random aspect of the process is particularly salient.

A group of 93 subjects, recruited through an advertisement in the University of Oregon newspaper, were presented with the following problem in October 1980:

Suppose Bjorn Borg reaches the Wimbledon finals in 1981. Please rank order the following outcomes from most to least likely.

A. Borg will win the match (1.7)

B. Borg will lose the first set (2.7)

C. Borg will lose the first set but win the match (2.2)

D. Borg will win the first set but lose the match (3.5)

The average rank of each outcome (1 = most probable, 2 = second most probable, etc.) is given in parentheses. The outcomes were chosen to represent different levels of strength for the player, Borg, with A indicating the highest strength; C, a rather lower level because it indicates a weakness in the first set; B, lower still because it only mentions this weakness; and D, lowest of all.

After winning his fifth Wimbledon title in 1980, Borg seemed extremely strong. Consequently, we hypothesized that Outcome C would be judged more probable than Outcome B, contrary to the conjunction rule, because C represents a better performance for Borg than does B. The mean rankings indicate that this hypothesis was confirmed; 72% of the respondents assigned a higher rank to C than to B, violating the conjunction rule in a direct test.

Is it possible that the subjects interpreted the target events in a nonextensional manner that could justify or explain the observed ranking? It is well known that connectives (e.g., *and, or, if)* are often used in ordinary language in ways that depart from their logical definitions. Perhaps the respondents interpreted the conjunction (A and B) as a disjunction (A or B), an implication (A implies B), or a conditional statement (A if B). Alternatively, the event B could be interpreted in the presence of the conjunction as B and not-A. To investigate these possibilities, we presented to another group of 56 naive subjects at Stanford University the hypothetical results of the relevant tennis match, coded as sequences of wins and losses. For example, the sequence LWWLW denotes a five-set match in which Borg lost (L) the first and the third sets but won (W) the other sets and the match. For each sequence the subjects were asked to examine the four target events of the original Borg problem and to indicate, by marking + or –, whether the given sequence was consistent or inconsistent with each of the events.

With very few exceptions, all of the subjects marked the sequences according to the standard (extensional) interpretation of the target events. A sequence was judged consistent with the conjunction "Borg will lose the first set but win the match" when both constituents were satisfied (e.g., LWWLW) but not when either one or both constituents failed. Evidently, these subjects did not interpret the conjunction as an implication, a conditional statement, or a disjunction. Furthermore, both LWWLW and LWLWL were judged consistent with the inclusive event "Borg will lose the first set," contrary to the hypothesis that the inclusive event B is understood in the context of the other events as "Borg will lose the first set and the match." The classification of sequences therefore indicated little or no ambiguity regarding the extension of the target events. In particular, all sequences that were classified as instances of B&A were also classified as instances of B, but some sequences that were classified as instances of B were judged inconsistent with B&A, in accord with the standard interpretation in which the conjunction rule should be satisfied.

Another possible interpretation of the conjunction error maintains that instead of assessing the probability $P(B/E)$ of hypothesis B (e.g., that Linda is a bank teller) in light of evidence E (Linda's personality), subjects assess the inverse probability $P(E/B)$ of the evidence given to the hypothesis in question. Because $P(E/A\&B)$ may well exceed $P(E/B)$, the subjects' responses could be justified under this interpretation. Whatever plausibility this account may have in the case of Linda, it is surely inapplicable to the present study where it makes no sense to assess the conditional probability that Borg will reach the finals given the outcome of the final match.

Risky Choice

If the conjunction fallacy cannot be justified by a reinterpretation of the target events, can it be rationalized by a nonstandard conception of probability? On this hypothesis, representativeness is treated as a legitimate nonextensional interpretation of probability rather than as a fallible heuristic. The conjunction fallacy, then, may be viewed as a misunderstanding regarding the meaning of the word *probability*. To investigate this hypothesis we tested the conjunction rule in the following decision problem, which provides an incentive to choose the most probable event, although the word *probability* is not mentioned.

Consider a regular six-sided die with four green faces and two red faces. The die will be rolled 20 times and the sequence of greens (G) and reds (R) will be recorded. You are asked to select one sequence, from a set of three, and you will win $25 if the sequence you chose appears on successive rolls of the die. Please check the sequence of greens and reds on which you prefer to bet.

1. RGRRR

2. GRGRRR

3. GRRRRR

Note that sequence 1 can be obtained from sequence 2 by deleting the first G. By the conjunction rule, therefore, sequence 1 must be more probable than sequence 2. Note also that all three sequences are rather unrepresentative of the die because they contain more Rs than Gs. However, sequence 2 appears to be an improvement over sequence 1 because it contains a higher proportion of the more likely color. A group of 50 respondents were asked to rank the events by the degree to which they are representative of the die; 88% ranked sequence 2 highest and sequence 3 lowest. Thus, sequence 2 is favored by representativeness, although it is dominated by sequence 1.

A total of 260 students at UBC and Stanford University were given the choice version of the problem. There were no significant differences between the populations, and their results were pooled. The subjects were run in groups of 30 to 50 in a classroom setting. About one half of the subjects ($N = 125$) actually played the gamble with real payoffs. The choice was hypothetical for the other subjects. The percentages of subjects who chose the dominated option of sequence 2 were 65% with real payoffs and 62% in the hypothetical format. Only 2% of the subjects in both groups chose sequence 3.

To facilitate the discovery of the relation between the two critical sequences, we presented a new group of 59 subjects with a (hypothetical) choice problem in which sequence 2 was replaced by RGRRRG. This new sequence was preferred over sequence 1, RGRRR, by 63% of the respondents, although the first five elements of the two sequences were identical. These results suggest that subjects coded each sequence in terms of the proportion of Gs and Rs and ranked the sequences by the discrepancy between the proportions in the two sequences (1/5 and 1/3) and the expected value of 2/3.

It is apparent from these results that conjunction errors are not restricted to misunderstandings of the word *probability*. Our subjects followed the representativeness heuristic even when the word was not mentioned and even in choices involving substantial payoffs. The results further show that the conjunction fallacy is not restricted to esoteric interpretations of the connective *and* because that connective was also absent from the problem. The present test of the conjunction rule was direct, in the sense defined earlier, because the subjects were required to compare two events, one of which included the other. However, informal interviews with some of the respondents suggest that the test was subtle: The relation of inclusion between sequences 1 and 2 was apparently noted by only a few of the subjects. Evidently, people are not attuned to the detection of nesting among events, even when these relations are clearly displayed.

Suppose that the relation of dominance between sequences 1 and 2 is called to the subjects' attention. Do they immediately appreciate its force and treat it as a decisive argument for sequence 1? The original choice problem (without sequence 3) was presented to a new group of 88 subjects at Stanford University. These subjects, however, were not asked to select the sequence on which they preferred to bet but only to indicate which of the following two arguments, if any, they found correct.

Argument 1: The first sequence (RGRRR) is more probable than the second (GRGRRR) because the second sequence is the same as the first with an additional G at the beginning. Hence, every time the second sequence occurs, the first sequence must also occur. Consequently, you can win on the first and lose on the second, but you can never win on the second and lose on the first.
Argument 2: The second sequence (GRGRRR) is more probable than the first (RGRRR) because the proportions of R and G in the second sequence are closer than those of the first sequence to the expected proportions of R and G for a die with four green and two red faces.

Most of the subjects (76%) chose the valid extensional argument over an argument that formulates the intuition of representativeness. Recall that a similar argument in the case of Linda was much less effective in combating the conjunction fallacy. The success of the present manipulation can be attributed to the combination of a chance setup and a gambling task, which promotes extensional reasoning by emphasizing the conditions under which the bets will pay off.

Fallacies and Misunderstandings

We have described violations of the conjunction rule in direct tests as a fallacy. The term *fallacy* is used here as a psychological hypothesis, not as an evaluative epithet. A judgment is appropriately labeled a fallacy when most of the people who make it are disposed, after suitable explanation, to accept the following propositions: (a) They made a nontrivial error, which they probably would have repeated in similar problems; (b) the error was conceptual, not merely verbal or technical; and (c) they *should* have known the correct answer or a procedure to find it. Alternatively, the same judgment could be described as a failure of communication if the subject misunderstands the question or if the experimenter misinterprets the answer. Subjects who have erred because of a misunderstanding are likely to reject the propositions listed above and to claim (as students often do after an examination) that they knew the correct answer all along, and that their error, if any, was verbal or technical rather than conceptual.

A psychological analysis should apply interpretive charity and should avoid treating genuine misunderstandings as if they were fallacies. It should also avoid the temptation to rationalize any error of judgment by ad hoc interpretations that the respondents themselves would not endorse. The dividing line between fallacies and misunderstandings, however, is not always clear. In one of our earlier studies, for example, most respondents stated that a particular description is more likely to belong to a physical education teacher than to a teacher. Strictly speaking, the latter category includes the former, but it could be argued that *teacher* was understood in this problem in a sense that excludes physical education teacher, much as *animal* is often used in a sense that excludes insects. Hence, it was unclear whether the apparent violation of the extension rule in this problem should be described as a fallacy or as a misunderstanding. A special effort was made in the present studies to avoid ambiguity by defining the critical event as an intersection of well-defined classes, such as bank tellers and feminists. The comments of the respondents in postexperimental discussions supported the conclusion that the observed violations of the conjunction rule in direct tests are genuine fallacies, not just misunderstandings.

Causal Conjunctions

The problems discussed in previous sections included three elements: a causal model M (Linda's personality); a basic target event B, which is unrepresentative of M (she is a bank teller); and an added event A, which is highly representative of the model M (she is a feminist). In these problems, the model M is positively associated with A and is negatively associated with B. This structure, called the M → A paradigm, is depicted on the left-hand side of figure 2.1. We found that when the sketch of Linda's personality was omitted and she was identified merely as a "31-year-old woman," almost all respondents obeyed the conjunction rule and ranked the conjunction (bank teller and active feminist) as less probable than its constituents. The conjunction error in the original problem is therefore attributable to the relation between M and A, not to the relation between A and B.

The conjunction fallacy was common in the Linda problem despite the fact that the stereotypes of bank teller and feminist are mildly incompatible. When the constituents of a conjunction are highly incompatible, the incidence of conjunction errors is greatly reduced. For example, the conjunction "Bill is bored by music and plays jazz for a hobby" was judged as less probable (and less representative) than its constituents, although "bored by music" was

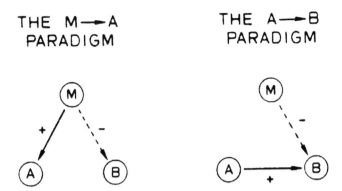

Figure 2.1
Schematic representation of two experimental paradigms used to test the conjunction rule. (Solid and broken arrows denote strong positive and negative association, respectively, among the model M, the basic target B, and the added target A.)

perceived as a probable (and representative) attribute of Bill. Quite reasonably, the incompatibility of the two attributes reduced the judged probability of their conjunction.

The effect of compatibility on the evaluation of conjunctions is not limited to near contradictions. For instance, it is more representative (as well as more probable) for a student to be in the upper half of the class in both mathematics and physics or to be in the lower half of the class in both fields than to be in the upper half in one field and in the lower half in the other. Such observations imply that the judged probability (or representativeness) of a conjunction cannot be computed as a function (e.g., product, sum, minimum, weighted average) of the scale values of its constituents. This conclusion excludes a large class of formal models that ignore the relation between the constituents of a conjunction. The viability of such models of conjunctive concepts has generated a spirited debate (Jones, 1982; Osherson & Smith, 1981, 1982; Zadeh, 1982; Lakoff, reference note 1).

The preceding discussion suggests a new formal structure, called the A → B paradigm, which is depicted on the right-hand side of figure 2.1. Conjunction errors occur in the A → B paradigm because of the direct connection between A and B, although the added event, A, is not particularly representative of the model, M. In this section of the article we investigate problems in which the added event, A, provides a plausible cause or motive for the occurrence of B. Our hypothesis is that the strength of the causal link, which has been shown in previous work to bias judgments of conditional probability (Tversky & Kahneman, 1980), will also bias judgments of the probability of conjunctions (see Beyth-Marom, reference note 2). Just as the thought of a personality and a social stereotype naturally evokes an assessment of their similarity, the thought of an effect and a possible cause evokes an assessment of causal impact (Ajzen, 1977). The natural assessment of propensity is expected to bias the evaluation of probability.

To illustrate this bias in the A → B paradigm, consider the following problem, which was presented to 115 undergraduates at Stanford University and UBC:

A health survey was conducted in a representative sample of adult males in British Columbia of all ages and occupations. Mr. F. was included in the sample. He was selected by chance from the list of participants.

Which of the following statements is more probable? (check one)

Mr. F. has had one or more heart attacks.

Mr. F. has had one or more heart attacks and he is over 55 years old.

This seemingly transparent problem elicited a substantial proportion (58%) of conjunction errors among statistically naive respondents. To test the hypothesis that these errors are produced by the causal (or correlational) link between advanced age and heart attacks, rather than by a weighted average of the component probabilities, we removed this link by uncoupling the target events without changing their marginal probabilities.

A health survey was conducted in a representative sample of adult males in British Columbia of all ages and occupations. Mr. F. and Mr. G. were both included in the sample. They were unrelated and were selected by chance from the list of participants.

Which of the following statements is more probable? (check one)

Mr. F. has had one or more heart attacks.

Mr. F. has had one or more heart attacks and Mr. G. is over 55 years old.

Assigning the critical attributes to two independent individuals eliminates in effect the A → B connection by making the events (conditionally) independent. Accordingly, the incidence of conjunction errors dropped to 29% (N = 90).

The A → B paradigm can give rise to dual conjunction errors where A&B is perceived as more probable than each of its constituents, as illustrated in the next problem.

Peter is a junior in college who is training to run the mile in a regional meet. In his best race, earlier this season, Peter ran the mile in 4:06 min. Please rank the following outcomes from most to least probable.

Peter will run the mile under 4:06 min.

Peter will run the mile under 4 min.

Peter will run the second half-mile under 1:55 min.

Peter will run the second half-mile under 1:55 min. and will complete the mile under 4 min.

Peter will run the first half-mile under 2:05 min.

The critical event (a sub–1:55-minute second half *and* a sub–4-minute mile) is clearly defined as a conjunction and not as a conditional. Nevertheless, 76% of a group of undergraduate students from Stanford University ($N = 96$) ranked it above one of its constituents, and 48% of the subjects ranked it above both constituents. The natural assessment of the relation between the constituents apparently contaminated the evaluation of their conjunction. In contrast, no one violated the extension rule by ranking the second outcome (a sub–4-minute mile) above the first (a sub–4:06-minute mile). The preceding results indicate that the judged probability of a conjunction cannot be explained by an averaging model because in such a model P(A&B) lies between P(A) and P(B). An averaging process, however, may be responsible for some conjunction errors, particularly when the constituent probabilities are given in a numerical form.

Motives and Crimes

A conjunction error in a motive–action schema is illustrated by the following problem—one of several of the same general type administered to a group of 171 students at UBC:

John P. is a meek man, 42 years old, married with two children. His neighbors describe him as mild-mannered, but somewhat secretive. He owns an import–export company based in New York City, and he travels frequently to Europe and the Far East. Mr. P. was convicted once for smuggling precious stones and metals (including uranium) and received a suspended sentence of 6 months in jail and a large fine. Mr. P. is currently under police investigation.

Please rank the following statements by the probability that they will be among the conclusions of the investigation. Remember that other possibilities exist and that more than one statement may be true. Use 1 for the most probable statement, 2 for the second, etc.

Mr. P. is a child molester.

Mr. P. is involved in espionage and the sale of secret documents.

Mr. P. is a drug addict.

Mr. P. killed one of his employees.

One half of the subjects ($n = 86$) ranked the events above. Other subjects ($n = 85$) ranked a modified list of possibilities in which the last event was replaced by

Mr. P. killed one of his employees to prevent him from talking to the police.

Although the addition of a possible motive clearly reduces the extension of the event (Mr. P. might have killed his employee for other reasons, such as revenge or self-defense), we hypothesized that the mention of a plausible but nonobvious motive would increase the perceived likelihood of the event. The data confirmed this expectation. The mean rank of the conjunction was 2.90, whereas the mean rank of the inclusive statement was 3.17 ($p < 0.05$, by t test). Furthermore, 50% of the respondents ranked the conjunction as more likely than the event that Mr. P. was a drug addict, but only 23% ranked the more inclusive target event as more likely than drug addiction. We have found in other problems of the same type that the mention of a cause or motive tends to increase the judged probability of an action when the suggested motive (a) offers a reasonable explanation of the target event, (b) appears fairly likely on its own, and (c) is nonobvious, in the sense that it does not immediately come to mind when the outcome is mentioned.

We have observed conjunction errors in other judgments involving criminal acts in both the A → B and the M → A paradigms. For example, the hypothesis that a policeman described as violence prone was involved in the heroin trade was ranked less likely (relative to a standard comparison set) than a conjunction of allegations—that he is involved in the heroin trade and that he recently assaulted a suspect. In that example, the assault was not causally linked to the involvement in drugs, but it made the combined allegation more representative of the suspect's disposition. The implications of the psychology of judgment to the evaluation of legal evidence deserve careful study because the outcomes of many trials depend on the ability of a judge or a jury to make intuitive judgments on the basis of partial and fallible data (see Rubinstein, 1979; Saks & Kidd, 1981).

Forecasts and Scenarios

The construction and evaluation of scenarios of future events are not only a favorite pastime of reporters, analysts, and news watchers. Scenarios are often used in the context of planning, and their plausibility influences significant decisions. Scenarios for the past are also important in many contexts, including criminal law and the writing of history. It is of interest, then, to evaluate whether the forecasting or reconstruction of real-life events is subject to conjunction errors. Our analysis suggests that a scenario that includes a possible cause and an outcome could appear more probable than the outcome on its own. We tested this hypothesis in two populations: statistically naive students and professional forecasters.

A sample of 245 UBC undergraduates was requested in April 1982 to evaluate the probability of occurrence of several events in 1983. A 9-point scale was used, defined by the following categories: less than 0.01%, 0.1%, 0.5%, 1%, 2%, 5%, 10%, 25%, and 50% or more. Each problem was presented to different subjects in two versions: one that included only the basic outcome and another that included a more detailed scenario leading to the same outcome. For example, one half of the subjects evaluated the probability of a massive flood somewhere in North America in 1983, in which more than 1000 people drown. The other half of the subjects evaluated the probability of an earthquake in California sometime in 1983, causing a flood in which more than 1000 people drown.

The estimates of the conjunction (earthquake and flood) were significantly higher than the estimates of the flood ($p < 0.01$, by a Mann–Whitney test). The respective geometric means were 3.1% and 2.2%. Thus, a reminder that a devastating flood could be caused by the anticipated California earthquake made the conjunction of an earthquake and a flood appear more probable than a flood. The same pattern was observed in other problems.

The subjects in the second part of the study were 115 participants in the Second International Congress on Forecasting held in Istanbul, Turkey, in July 1982. Most of the subjects were professional analysts, employed by industry, universities, or research institutes. They were professionally involved in forecasting and planning, and many had used scenarios in their work. The research design and the response scales were the same as before. One group of forecasters evaluated the probability of a complete suspension of diplomatic relations between the USA and the Soviet Union, sometime in 1983.

The other respondents evaluated the probability of the same outcome embedded in the following scenario: a Russian invasion of Poland, and a complete suspension of diplomatic relations between the USA and the Soviet Union, sometime in 1983.

Although *suspension* is necessarily more probable than *invasion and suspension*, a Russian invasion of Poland offered a plausible scenario leading to the breakdown of diplomatic relations between the superpowers. As expected, the estimates of probability were low for both problems but significantly higher for the conjunction *invasion and suspension* than for *suspension* ($p < 0.01$, by a Mann–Whitney test). The geometric means of estimates were 0.47% and 0.14%, respectively. A similar effect was observed in the comparison of the following outcomes:

a 30% drop in the consumption of oil in the US in 1983.

a dramatic increase in oil prices and a 30% drop in the consumption of oil in the US in 1983.

The geometric means of the estimated probability of the first and second outcomes, respectively, were 0.22% and 0.36%. We speculate that the effect is smaller in this problem (although still statistically significant) because the basic target event (a large drop in oil consumption) makes the added event (a dramatic increase in oil prices) highly available, even when the latter is not mentioned.

Conjunctions involving hypothetical causes are particularly prone to error because it is more natural to assess the probability of the effect given the cause than the joint probability of the effect and the cause. We do not suggest that subjects deliberately adopt this interpretation; rather we propose that the higher conditional estimate serves as an anchor that makes the conjunction appear more probable.

Attempts to forecast events such as a major nuclear accident in the United States or an Islamic revolution in Saudi Arabia typically involve the construction and evaluation of scenarios. Similarly, a plausible story of how the victim might have been killed by someone other than the defendant may convince a jury of the existence of reasonable doubt. Scenarios can usefully serve to stimulate the imagination, to establish the feasibility of outcomes, or to set bounds on judged probabilities (Kirkwood & Pollock, 1982; Zentner, 1982). However, the use of scenarios as a prime instrument for the assessment of probabilities can be highly misleading. First, this procedure favors a conjunctive outcome produced by a sequence of likely steps (e.g., the successful execution of a plan) over an equally probable disjunctive outcome (e.g., the failure of a careful plan), which can occur in many unlikely ways (Bar-Hillel, 1973; Tversky & Kahneman, 1973). Second, the use of scenarios to assess probability is especially vulnerable to conjunction errors. A detailed scenario consisting of causally linked and representative events may appear more probable than a subset of these events (Slovic, Fischhoff, & Lichtenstein, 1976). This effect contributes to the appeal of scenarios and to the illusory insight that they often provide. The attorney who fills in guesses regarding unknown facts, such as motive or mode of operation, may strengthen a case by improving its coherence, although such additions can only lower probability. Similarly, a political analyst can improve scenarios by adding plausible causes and representative consequences. As Pooh-Bah in the *Mikado* explains, such additions provide "corroborative details intended to give artistic verisimilitude to an otherwise bald and unconvincing narrative."

Extensional Cues

The numerous conjunction errors reported in this article illustrate people's affinity for non-extensional reasoning. It is nonetheless obvious that people can understand and apply the extension rule. What cues elicit extensional considerations and what factors promote conformity to the conjunction rule? In this section we focus on a single estimation problem and report several manipulations that induce extensional reasoning and reduce the incidence of the conjunction fallacy. The participants in the studies described in this section were statistically naive students at UBC. Mean estimates are given in parentheses.

A health survey was conducted in a sample of adult males in British Columbia, of all ages and occupations.

Please give your best estimate of the following values:

What percentage of the men surveyed have had one or more heart attacks? (18%)

What percentage of the men surveyed both are over 55 years old and have had one or more heart attacks? (30%)

This version of the health-survey problem produced a substantial number of conjunction errors among statistically naive respondents: 65% of the respondents ($N = 147$) assigned a strictly higher estimate to the second question than to the first.[2] Reversing the order of the constituents did not significantly affect the results.

The observed violations of the conjunction rule in estimates of relative frequency are attributed to the A → B paradigm. We propose that the probability of the conjunction is biased toward the natural assessment of the strength of the causal or statistical link between age and heart attacks. Although the statement of the question appears unambiguous, we considered the hypothesis that the respondents who committed the fallacy had actually interpreted the second question as a request to assess a conditional probability. A new group of UBC undergraduates received the same problem, with the second question amended as follows:

Among the men surveyed who are over 55 years old, what percentage have had one or more heart attacks?

The mean estimate was 59% ($N = 55$). This value is significantly higher than the mean of the estimates of the conjunction (45%) given by those subjects who had committed the fallacy in the original problem. Subjects who violate the conjunction rule therefore do not simply substitute the conditional $P(B/A)$ for the conjunction $P(A\&B)$.

A seemingly inconsequential change in the problem helps many respondents avoid the conjunction fallacy. A new group of subjects ($N = 159$) were given the original questions but were also asked to assess the "percentage of the men surveyed who are over 55 years old" prior to assessing the conjunction. This manipulation reduced the incidence of conjunction error from 65% to 31%. It appears that many subjects were appropriately cued by the requirement to assess the relative frequency of both classes before assessing the relative frequency of their intersection.

The following formulation also facilitates extensional reasoning:

A health survey was conducted in a sample of 100 adult males in British Columbia, of all ages and occupations.

Please give your best estimate of the following values:

How many of the 100 participants have had one or more heart attacks?

How many of the 100 participants both are over 55 years old and have had one or more heart attacks?

The incidence of the conjunction fallacy was only 25% in this version ($N = 117$). Evidently, an explicit reference to the number of individual cases encourages subjects to set up a representation of the problems in which class inclusion is readily perceived and appreciated. We have replicated this effect in several other problems of the same general type. The

2. The incidence of the conjunction fallacy was considerably lower (28%) for a group of advanced undergraduates at Stanford University ($N = 62$) who had completed one or more courses in statistics.

rate of errors was further reduced to a record 11% for a group ($N = 360$) who also estimated the number of participants over 55 years of age prior to the estimation of the conjunctive category. The present findings agree with the results of Beyth-Marom (reference note 2), who observed higher estimates for conjunctions in judgments of probability than in assessments of frequency.

The results of this section show that nonextensional reasoning sometimes prevails even in simple estimates of relative frequency in which the extension of the target event and the meaning of the scale are completely unambiguous. On the other hand, we found that the replacement of percentages by frequencies and the request to assess both constituent categories markedly reduced the incidence of the conjunction fallacy. It appears that extensional considerations are readily brought to mind by seemingly inconsequential cues. A contrast worthy of note exists between the effectiveness of extensional cues in the health-survey problem and the relative inefficacy of the methods used to combat the conjunction fallacy in the Linda problem (argument, betting, "whether or not"). The force of the conjunction rule is more readily appreciated when the conjunctions are defined by the intersection of concrete classes than by a combination of properties. Although classes and properties are equivalent from a logical standpoint, they give rise to different mental representations in which different relations and rules are transparent. The formal equivalence of properties to classes is apparently not programmed into the lay mind.

Discussion

In the course of this project we studied the extension rule in a variety of domains; we tested more than 3,000 subjects on dozens of problems, and we examined numerous variations of these problems. The results reported in this article constitute a representative though not exhaustive summary of this work.

The data revealed widespread violations of the extension rule by naive and sophisticated subjects in both indirect and direct tests. These results were interpreted within the framework of judgmental heuristics. We proposed that a judgment of probability or frequency is commonly biased toward the natural assessment that the problem evokes. Thus, the request to estimate the frequency of a class elicits a search for exemplars, the task of predicting vocational choice from a personality sketch evokes a comparison of features, and a question about the co-occurrence of events induces an assessment of their causal connection. These assessments are not constrained by the extension rule. Although an arbitrary reduction in the extension of an event typically reduces its availability, representativeness, or causal coherence, there are numerous occasions in which these assessments are higher for the restricted than for the inclusive event. Natural assessments can bias probability judgment in three ways: The respondents may (a) use a natural assessment deliberately as a strategy of estimation, (b) be primed or anchored by it, or (c) fail to appreciate the difference between the natural and the required assessments.

Logic versus Intuition

The conjunction error demonstrates with exceptional clarity the contrast between the extensional logic that underlies most formal conceptions of probability and the natural assessments that govern many judgments and beliefs. However, probability judgments are not always dominated by nonextensional heuristics. Rudiments of probability theory have become part of the culture, and even statistically naive adults can enumerate possibilities and calculate odds in simple games of chance (Edwards, 1975). Furthermore, some real-life contexts encourage the decomposition of events. The chances of a team to reach the playoffs, for example, may be evaluated as follows: "Our team will make it if we beat team B, which we should be able to do since we have a better defense, or if team B loses to both C and D, which is unlikely since neither one has a strong offense." In this example, the target event (reaching the playoffs) is decomposed into more elementary possibilities that are evaluated in an intuitive manner.

Judgments of probability vary in the degree to which they follow a decompositional or a holistic approach and in the degree to which the assessment and the aggregation of probabilities are analytic or intuitive (see, e.g., Hammond & Brehmer, 1973). At one extreme there are questions (e.g., What are the chances of beating a given hand in poker?) that can be answered by calculating the relative frequency of "favorable" outcomes. Such an analysis possesses all the features associated with an extensional approach: It is decompositional, frequentistic, and algorithmic. At the other extreme, there are questions (e.g., What is the probability that the witness is telling the truth?) that are normally evaluated in a holistic, singular, and intuitive manner (Kahneman & Tversky, 1982b). Decomposition and calculation provide some protection against conjunction errors and other biases, but the intuitive element cannot be entirely eliminated from probability judgments outside the domain of random sampling.

A direct test of the conjunction rule pits an intuitive impression against a basic law of probability. The outcome of the conflict is determined by the nature of the evidence, the formulation of the question, the transparency of the event structure, the appeal of the heuristic, and the sophistication of the respondents. Whether people obey the conjunction rule in any particular direct test depends on the balance of these factors. For example, we found it difficult to induce naive subjects to apply the conjunction rule in the Linda problem, but minor variations in the health-survey question had a marked effect on conjunction errors. This conclusion is consistent with the results of Nisbett et al. (1983), who showed that lay people can apply certain statistical principles (e.g., the law of large numbers) to everyday problems and that the accessibility of these principles varied with the content of the problem and increased significantly with the sophistication of the respondents. We found, however, that sophisticated and naive respondents answered the Linda problem similarly in indirect tests and only parted company in the most transparent versions of the problem. These observations suggest that statistical sophistication did not alter intuitions of representativeness, although it enabled the respondents to recognize in direct tests the decisive force of the extension rule.

Judgment problems in real life do not usually present themselves in the format of a within-subjects design or of a direct test of the laws of probability. Consequently, subjects' performance in a between-subjects test may offer a more realistic view of everyday reasoning. In the indirect test it is very difficult even for a sophisticated judge to ensure that an event has no subset that would appear more probable than it does and no superset that would appear less probable. The satisfaction of the extension rule could be ensured, without direct comparisons of A&B to B, if all events in the relevant ensemble were expressed as disjoint unions of elementary possibilities. In many practical contexts, however, such analysis is not feasible. The physician, judge, political analyst, or entrepreneur typically focuses on a critical target event and is rarely prompted to discover potential violations of the extension rule.

Studies of reasoning and problem solving have shown that people often fail to understand or apply an abstract logical principle even when they can use it properly in concrete familiar contexts. Johnson-Laird and Wason (1977), for example, showed that people who err in the verification of *if then* statements in an abstract format often succeed when the problem evokes a familiar schema. The present results exhibit the opposite pattern: People generally accept the conjunction rule in its abstract form (B is more probable than A&B) but defy it in concrete examples, such as the Linda and Bill problems, where the rule conflicts with an intuitive impression.

The violations of the conjunction rule were not only prevalent in our research, they were also sizable. For example, subjects' estimates of the frequency of seven-letter words ending with *ing* were three times as high as their estimates of the frequency of seven-letter words ending with _n_. A correction by a factor of three is the smallest change that would eliminate the inconsistency between the two estimates. However, the subjects surely know that there are many _n_ words that are not *ing* words (e.g., *present, content*). If they believe, for example, that only one half of the *n* words end with *ing*, then a 6:1 adjustment would be required to make the entire system coherent. The ordinal nature of most of our experiments did not permit an estimate of the adjustment factor required for coherence. Nevertheless, the size of the effect was often considerable. In the rating-scale version of the Linda problem, for example, there was little overlap between the distributions of ratings for T&F and for T. Our problems, of course, were constructed to elicit conjunction errors, and they do not provide an unbiased estimate of the prevalence of these errors. Note, however, that the conjunction error is only a symptom of a more general phenomenon: People tend to overestimate the probabilities of representative (or available) events and/or underestimate the probabilities of less representative events. The violation of the conjunction rule demonstrates this tendency even when the "true" probabilities are unknown or unknowable. The basic phenomenon may be considerably more common than the extreme symptom by which it was illustrated.

Previous studies of the subjective probability of conjunctions (e.g., Bar-Hillel, 1973; Cohen & Hansel, 1957; Goldsmith, 1978; Wyer, 1976; Beyth-Marom, reference note 2) focused primarily on testing the multiplicative rule $P(A\&B) = P(B)P(A/B)$. This rule is strictly stronger than the conjunction rule; it also requires cardinal rather than ordinal assessments of probability. The results showed that people generally overestimate the probability of conjunctions in the sense that $P(A\&B) > P(B)P(A/B)$. Some investigators, notably Wyer and Beyth-Marom, also reported data that are inconsistent with the conjunction rule.

Conversing under Uncertainty

The representativeness heuristic generally favors outcomes that make good stories or good hypotheses. The conjunction *feminist bank teller* is a better hypothesis about Linda than *bank teller*, and the scenario of a Russian invasion of Poland followed by a diplomatic crisis makes a better story than simply *diplomatic crisis*. The notion of a good story can be illuminated by extending the Gricean concept of cooperativeness (Grice, 1975) to conversations under uncertainty. The standard analysis of conversation rules assumes that the speaker knows the truth. The maxim of quality enjoins him or her to say only the truth. The maxim of quantity enjoins the speaker to say all of it, subject to the maxim of relevance, which restricts the message to what the listener needs to know. What rules of cooperativeness apply to an uncertain speaker, that is, one who is uncertain of the truth? Such a speaker can guarantee absolute quality only for tautological statements (e.g., "Inflation will continue so long as prices rise"), which are unlikely to earn high marks as contributions to the conversation. A useful contribution must convey the speaker's relevant beliefs even if they are not certain. The rules of cooperativeness for an uncertain speaker must therefore allow for a trade-off of quality and quantity in the evaluation of messages. The expected value of a message can be defined by its information value if it is true, weighted by the probability that it is true. An uncertain speaker may wish to follow the maxim of value: Select the message that has the highest expected value.

The expected value of a message can sometimes be improved by increasing its content, although its probability is thereby reduced. The statement "Inflation will be in the range of 6% to 9% by the end of the year" may be a more valuable forecast than "Inflation will be in the range of 3% to 12%," although the latter is more likely to be confirmed. A good forecast is a compromise between a point estimate, which is sure to be wrong, and a 99.9% credible interval, which is often too broad. The selection of hypotheses in science is subject to the same trade-off: A hypothesis must risk refutation to be valuable, but its value declines if refutation is nearly certain. Good hypotheses balance informativeness against probable truth (Good, 1971). A similar compromise obtains in the structure of natural categories. The basic-level category *dog* is much more informative than the more inclusive category *animal* and only slightly less informative than the narrower category *beagle*. Basic-level categories have a privileged position in language and thought, presumably because they offer an optimal combination of scope and content (Rosch, 1978). Categorization under uncertainty is a case in point. A moving object dimly seen in the dark may be appropriately labeled *dog*, where the subordinate *beagle* would be rash and the super-ordinate *animal* far too conservative.

Consider the task of ranking possible answers to the question, "What do you think Linda is up to these days?" The maxim of value could justify a preference for T&F over T in this task because the added attribute *feminist* considerably enriches the description of Linda's current activities, at an acceptable cost in probable truth. Thus, the analysis of conversation under uncertainty identifies a pertinent question that is legitimately answered by ranking the conjunction above its constituent. We do not believe, however, that the maxim of value provides a fully satisfactory account of the conjunction fallacy. First, it is unlikely that our respondents interpret the request to rank statements by their probability as a request to rank them by their expected (informational) value. Second, conjunction fallacies have been observed in numerical estimates and in choices of bets, to which the conversational analysis simply does not apply. Nevertheless, the preference for statements of high expected (informational) value could hinder the appreciation of the extension rule. As we suggested in the discussion of the interaction of picture size and real size, the answer to a question can be biased by the availability of an answer to a cognate question—even when the respondent is well aware of the distinction between them.

The same analysis applies to other conceptual neighbors of probability. The concept of surprise is a case in point. Although surprise is closely tied to expectations, it does not follow the laws of probability (Kahneman & Tversky, 1982b). For example, the message that a tennis champion lost the first set of a match is more surprising than the message that she lost the first set but won the match, and a sequence of four consecutive heads in a coin toss is more surprising than four heads followed by two tails. It would be patently absurd, however, to bet on the less surprising event in each of these pairs. Our discussions with subjects provided no indication that they interpreted the instruction to judge probability as an instruction to evaluate surprise. Furthermore, the surprise interpretation does not apply to the conjunction fallacy observed in judgments of frequency. We conclude that surprise and informational value do not properly explain the conjunction fallacy, although they may well contribute to the ease with which it is induced and to the difficulty of eliminating it.

Cognitive Illusions

Our studies of inductive reasoning have focused on systematic errors because they are diagnostic of the heuristics that generally govern judgment and inference. In the words of Helmholtz (1881/1903), "It is just those cases that are not in accordance with reality which are particularly instructive for discovering the laws of the processes by which normal perception originates." The focus on bias and illusion is a research strategy that exploits human error, although it neither assumes nor entails that people are perceptually or cognitively inept. Helmholtz's position implies that perception is not usefully analyzed into a normal process that produces accurate percepts and a distorting process that produces errors and illusions. In cognition, as in perception, the same mechanisms produce both valid and invalid judgments. Indeed, the evidence does not seem to support a "truth plus error" model, which assumes a coherent system of beliefs that is perturbed by various sources of distortion and error. Hence, we do not share Dennis Lindley's optimistic opinion that "inside every incoherent person there is a coherent one trying to get out" (Lindley, reference note 3), and we suspect that incoherence is more than skin deep (Tversky & Kahneman, 1981).

It is instructive to compare a structure of beliefs about a domain (e.g., the political future of Central America) to the perception of a scene (e.g., the view of Yosemite Valley from Glacier Point). We have argued that intuitive judgments of all relevant marginal, conjunctive, and conditional probabilities are not likely to be coherent, that is, to satisfy the constraints of probability theory. Similarly, estimates of distances and angles in the scene are unlikely to satisfy the laws of geometry. For example, there may be pairs of political events for which $P(A)$ is judged greater than $P(B)$ but $P(A/B)$ is judged less than $P(B/A)$—see Tversky and Kahneman (1980). Analogously, the scene may contain a triangle ABC for which the A angle appears greater than the B angle, although the BC distance appears to be smaller than the AC distance.

The violations of the qualitative laws of geometry and probability in judgments of distance and likelihood have significant implications for the interpretation and use of these judgments. Incoherence sharply restricts the inferences that can be drawn from subjective estimates. The judged ordering of the sides of a triangle cannot be inferred from the judged ordering of its angles, and the ordering of marginal probabilities cannot be deduced from the ordering of the respective conditionals. The results of the present study show that it is even unsafe to assume that $P(B)$ is bounded by $P(A\&B)$. Furthermore, a system of judgments that does not obey the conjunction rule cannot be expected to obey more complicated principles that presuppose this rule, such as Bayesian updating, external calibration, and the maximization of expected utility. The presence of bias and incoherence does not diminish the normative force of these principles, but it reduces their usefulness as descriptions of behavior and hinders their prescriptive applications. Indeed, the elicitation of unbiased judgments and the reconciliation of incoherent assessments pose serious problems that presently have no satisfactory solution (Lindley, Tversky, & Brown, 1979; Shafer & Tversky, reference note 4).

The issue of coherence has loomed larger in the study of preference and belief than in the study of perception. Judgments of distance and angle can readily be compared to objective reality and can be replaced by objective measurements when accuracy matters. In contrast, objective measurements of probability are often unavailable, and most significant choices under risk require an intuitive evaluation of probability. In the absence of an objective criterion of validity, the normative theory of judgment under uncertainty has treated the coherence of belief as the touchstone of human rationality. Coherence has also been assumed in many descriptive analyses in psychology, economics, and other social sciences. This assumption is attractive because the strong normative appeal of the laws of probability makes violations appear implausible. Our studies of the conjunction rule show that normatively inspired theories that assume coherence are descriptively inadequate, whereas psychological analyses that ignore the appeal of normative rules are, at best, incomplete. A comprehensive account of human judgment must reflect the tension between compelling logical rules and seductive nonextensional intuitions.

Note

This research was supported by Grant NR 179–058 from the U.S. Office of Naval Research. We are grateful to friends and colleagues, too numerous to list by name, for their useful comments and suggestions on an earlier draft of this article.

Reference Notes

1. Lakoff, G. (1982). *Categories and cognitive models* (Cognitive Science Report No. 2). Berkeley: University of California.

2. Beyth-Marom, R. (1981). *The subjective probability of conjunctions* (Decision Research Report No. 81–12). Eugene, OR: Decision Research.

3. Lindley, D., Personal communication, 1980.

4. Shafer, G., & Tversky, A. (1983). *Weighing evidence: The design and comparisons of probability thought experiments*. Unpublished manuscript, Stanford University, Stanford, CA.

References

Ajzen, I. (1977). Intuitive theories of events and the effects of base-rate information on prediction. *Journal of Personality and Social Psychology, 35*, 303–314.

Bar-Hillel, M. (1973). On the subjective probability of compound events. *Organizational Behavior and Human Performance, 9*, 396–406.

Bruner, J. S. (1966). On the conservation of liquids. In J. S. Bruner, R. R. Olver, P. M. Greenfield, et al. (Eds.), *Studies in cognitive growth* (pp. 183–207). New York, NY: Wiley.

Chapman, L. J., & Chapman, J. P. (1967). Genesis of popular but erroneous psychodiagnostic observations. *Journal of Abnormal Psychology, 73*, 193–204.

Cohen, J., & Hansel, C. M. (1957). The nature of decision in gambling: Equivalence of single and compound subjective probabilities. *Acta Psychologica, 13*, 357–370.

Cohen, L. J. (1977). *The probable and the provable*. Oxford, England: Clarendon Press.

Dempster, A. P. (1967). Upper and lower probabilities induced by a multivalued mapping. *Annals of Mathematical Statistics, 38*, 325–339.

Edwards, W. (1975). Comment. *Journal of the American Statistical Association, 70*, 291–293.

Einhorn, H. J., & Hogarth, R. M. (1981). Behavioral decision theory: Processes of judgment and choice. *Annual Review of Psychology, 32*, 53–88.

Gati, I., & Tversky, A. (1982). Representations of qualitative and quantitative dimensions. *Journal of Experimental Psychology: Human Perception and Performance, 8*, 325–340.

Goldsmith, R. W. (1978). Assessing probabilities of compound events in a judicial context. *Scandinavian Journal of Psychology, 19*, 103–110.

Good, I. J. (1971). The probabilistic explication of information, evidence, surprise, causality, explanation, and utility. In V. P. Godambe & D. A. Sprott (Eds.), *Foundations of statistical inference: Proceedings on the foundations of statistical inference* (pp. 108–127). Toronto, ON: Holt, Rinehart & Winston.

Grice, H. P. (1975). Logic and conversation. In G. Harman & D. Davidson (Eds.), *The logic of grammar* (pp. 64–75). Encino, CA: Dickinson.

Hammond, K. R., & Brehmer, B. (1973). Quasi-rationality and distrust: Implications for international conflict. In L. Rappoport & D. A. Summers (Eds.), *Human judgment and social interaction* (pp. 338–391). New York, NY: Holt, Rinehart & Winston.

von Helmholtz, H. (1903). *Popular lectures on scientific subjects* (E. Atkinson, Trans.). New York, NY: Green. (Original work published 1881).

Jennings, D., Amabile, T., & Ross, L. (1982). Informal covariation assessment. In D. Kahneman, P. Slovic, & A. Tversky (Eds.), *Judgment under uncertainty: Heuristics and biases* (pp. 211–230). New York, NY: Cambridge University Press.

Johnson-Laird, P. N., & Wason, P. C. (1977). A theoretical analysis of insight into a reasoning task. In P. N. Johnson-Laird & P. C. Wason (Eds.), *Thinking: Readings in cognitive science* (pp. 143–157). Cambridge, England: Cambridge University Press.

Jones, G. V. (1982). Stacks not fuzzy sets: An ordinal basis for prototype theory of concepts. *Cognition, 12*, 281–290.

Kahneman, D., Slovic, P., & Tversky, A. (Eds.). (1982). *Judgment under uncertainty: Heuristics and biases.* New York, NY: Cambridge University Press.

Kahneman, D., & Tversky, A. (1972). Subjective probability: A judgment of representativeness. *Cognitive Psychology, 3*, 430–454.

Kahneman, D., & Tversky, A. (1973). On the psychology of prediction. *Psychological Review, 80*, 237–251.

Kahneman, D., & Tversky, A. (1982a). On the study of statistical intuitions. *Cognition, 11*, 123–141.

Kahneman, D., & Tversky, A. (1982b). Variants of uncertainty. *Cognition, 11*, 143–157.

Kirkwood, C. W., & Pollock, S. M. (1982). Multiple attribute scenarios, bounded probabilities, and threats of nuclear theft. *Futures, 14*, 545–553.

Kyburg, H. E. (1983). Rational belief. *Behavioral and Brain Sciences, 6*, 231–245.

Lindley, D. V., Tversky, A., & Brown, R. V. (1979). On the reconciliation of probability assessments. *Journal of the Royal Statistical Society. Series A (General), 142*, 146–180.

Mervis, C. B., & Rosch, E. (1981). Categorization of natural objects. *Annual Review of Psychology, 32*, 89–115.

Nisbett, R. E., Krantz, D. H., Jepson, C., & Kunda, Z. (1983). The use of statistical heuristics in everyday inductive reasoning. *Psychological Review, 90*, 339–363.

Nisbett, R., & Ross, L. (1980). *Human inference: Strategies and shortcomings of social judgment.* Englewood Cliffs, NJ: Prentice-Hall.

Osherson, D. N., & Smith, E. E. (1981). On the adequacy of prototype theory as a theory of concepts. *Cognition, 9*, 35–38.

Osherson, D. N., & Smith, E. E. (1982). Gradedness and conceptual combination. *Cognition, 12*, 299–318.

Rosch, E. (1978). Principles of categorization. In E. Rosch & B. B. Lloyd (Eds.), *Cognition and categorization* (pp. 27–48). Hillsdale, NJ: Erlbaum.

Rubinstein, A. (1979). False probabilistic arguments vs. faulty intuition. *Israel Law Review, 14*, 247–254.

Saks, M. J., & Kidd, R. F. (1981). Human information processing and adjudication: Trials by heuristics. *Law & Society Review, 15*, 123–160.

Shafer, G. (1976). *A mathematical theory of evidence.* Princeton, NJ: Princeton University Press.

Slovic, P., Fischhoff, B., & Lichtenstein, S. (1976). Cognitive processes and societal risk taking. In J. S. Carroll & J. W. Payne (Eds.), *Cognition and social behavior* (pp. 165–184). Potomac, MD: Erlbaum.

Smith, E. E., & Medin, D. L. (1981). *Categories and concepts*. Cambridge, MA: Harvard University Press.

Suppes, P. (1975). Approximate probability and expectation of gambles. *Erkenntnis, 9*, 153–161.

Tversky, A. (1977). Features of similarity. *Psychological Review, 84*, 327–352.

Tversky, A., & Kahneman, D. (1971). Belief in the law of small numbers. *Psychological Bulletin, 76*, 105–110.

Tversky, A., & Kahneman, D. (1973). Availability: A heuristic for judging frequency and probability. *Cognitive Psychology, 5*, 207–232.

Tversky, A., & Kahneman, D. (1980). Causal schemas in judgments under uncertainty. In M. Fishbein (Ed.), *Progress in social psychology* (pp. 49–72). Hillsdale, NJ: Erlbaum.

Tversky, A., & Kahneman, D. (1981). The framing of decisions and the psychology of choice. *Science, 211*, 453–458.

Tversky, A., & Kahneman, D. (1982). Judgments of and by representativeness. In D. Kahneman, P. Slovic, & A. Tversky (Eds.), *Judgment under uncertainty: Heuristics and biases* (pp. 84–98). New York, NY: Cambridge University Press.

Wyer, R. S., Jr. (1976). An investigation of the relations among probability estimates. *Organizational Behavior and Human Performance, 15*, 1–18.

Zadeh, L. A. (1978). Fuzzy sets as a basis for a theory of possibility. *Fuzzy Sets and Systems, 1*, 3–28.

Zadeh, L. A. (1982). A note on prototype theory and fuzzy sets. *Cognition, 12*, 291–297.

Zentner, R. D. (1982). Scenarios, past, present and future. *Long Range Planning, 15*, 12–20.

3 Features of Similarity

Amos Tversky

Similarity plays a fundamental role in theories of knowledge and behavior. It serves as an organizing principle by which individuals classify objects, form concepts, and make generalizations. Indeed, the concept of similarity is ubiquitous in psychological theory. It underlies the accounts of stimulus and response generalization in learning, it is employed to explain errors in memory and pattern recognition, and it is central to the analysis of connotative meaning.

Similarity or dissimilarity data appear in different forms: ratings of pairs, sorting of objects, communality between associations, errors of substitution, and correlation between occurrences. Analyses of these data attempt to explain the observed similarity relations and to capture the underlying structure of the objects under study.

The theoretical analysis of similarity relations has been dominated by geometric models. These models represent objects as points in some coordinate space such that the observed dissimilarities between objects correspond to the metric distances between the respective points. Practically all analyses of proximity data have been metric in nature, although some (e.g., hierarchical clustering) yield tree-like structures rather than dimensionally organized spaces. However, most theoretical and empirical analyses of similarity assume that objects can be adequately represented as points in some coordinate space and that dissimilarity behaves like a metric distance function. Both dimensional and metric assumptions are open to question.

It has been argued by many authors that dimensional representations are appropriate for certain stimuli (e.g., colors, tones) but not for others. It seems more appropriate to represent faces, countries, or personalities in terms of many qualitative features than in terms of a few quantitative dimensions. The assessment of similarity between such stimuli, therefore, may be better described as a comparison of features rather than as the computation of metric distance between points.

A metric distance function, δ, is a scale that assigns to every pair of points a nonnegative number, called their distance, in accord with the following three axioms:

Minimality:

$\delta(a, b) \geq \delta(a, a) = 0.$

Symmetry:

$\delta(a, b) = \delta(b, a).$

The triangle inequality:

$\delta(a, b) + \delta(b, c) \geq \delta(a, c).$

To evaluate the adequacy of the geometric approach, let us examine the validity of the metric axioms when δ is regarded as a measure of dissimilarity. The minimality axiom implies that the similarity between an object and itself is the same for all objects. This assumption, however, does not hold for some similarity measures. For example, the probability of judging two identical stimuli as "same" rather than "different" is not constant for all stimuli. Moreover, in recognition experiments the off-diagonal entries often exceed the diagonal entries; that is, an object is identified as another object more frequently than it is identified as itself. If identification probability is interpreted as a measure of similarity, then these observations violate minimality and are, therefore, incompatible with the distance model.

Similarity has been viewed by both philosophers and psychologists as a prime example of a symmetric relation. Indeed, the assumption of symmetry underlies essentially all theoretical treatments of similarity. Contrary to this tradition, the present paper provides empirical evidence for asymmetric similarities and argues that similarity should not be treated as a symmetric relation.

Similarity judgments can be regarded as extensions of similarity statements, that is, statements of the form "a is like b." Such a statement is directional; it has a subject, a, and a referent, b, and it is not equivalent in general to the converse similarity statement "b is like a." In fact, the choice of subject and referent depends, at least in part, on the relative salience of the objects. We tend to select the more salient stimulus, or the prototype, as a referent, and the less salient stimulus, or the variant, as a subject. We say "the portrait resembles the person" rather than "the person resembles the portrait." We say "the son resembles the father" rather than "the father resembles the son." We say "an ellipse is like a circle," not "a circle is like an ellipse," and we say "North Korea is like Red China" rather than "Red China is like North Korea."

As will be demonstrated later, this asymmetry in the *choice* of similarity statements is associated with asymmetry in *judgments* of similarity. Thus, the judged similarity of North Korea to Red China exceeds the judged similarity of Red China to North Korea. Likewise, an ellipse is more similar to a circle than a circle is to an ellipse. Apparently, the direction of asymmetry is determined by the relative salience of the stimuli; the variant is more similar to the prototype than vice versa.

The directionality and asymmetry of similarity relations are particularly noticeable in similes and metaphors. We say "Turks fight like tigers" and not "tigers fight like Turks." Since the tiger is renowned for its fighting spirit, it is used as the referent rather than the subject of the simile. The poet writes "my love is as deep as the ocean," not "the ocean is as deep as my love," because the ocean epitomizes depth. Sometimes both directions are used but they carry different meanings. "A man is like a tree" implies that man has roots; "a tree is like a man" implies that the tree has a life history. "Life is like a play" says that people play roles. "A play is like life" says that a play can capture the essential elements of human life. The relations between the interpretation of metaphors and the assessment of similarity are briefly discussed in the final section.

The triangle inequality differs from minimality and symmetry in that it cannot be formulated in ordinal terms. It asserts that one distance must be smaller than the sum of two others, and hence it cannot be readily refuted with ordinal or even interval data. However, the triangle inequality implies that if a is quite similar to b, and b is quite similar to c, then a and c cannot be very dissimilar from each other. Thus, it sets a lower limit to the similarity between a and c in terms of the similarities between a and b and between b and c. The following example (based on William James) casts some doubts on the psychological validity of this assumption. Consider the similarity between countries: Jamaica is similar to Cuba (because of geographical proximity) and Cuba is similar to Russia (because of their political affinity), but Jamaica and Russia are not similar at all.

This example shows that similarity, as one might expect, is not transitive. In addition, it suggests that the perceived distance of Jamaica to Russia exceeds the perceived distance of Jamaica to Cuba, plus that of Cuba to Russia—contrary to the triangle inequality. Although such examples do not necessarily refute the triangle inequality, they indicate that it should not be accepted as a cornerstone of similarity models.

It should be noted that the metric axioms, by themselves, are very weak. They are satisfied, for example, by letting $\delta(a, b) = 0$ if $a = b$, and $\delta(a, b) = 1$ if $a \neq b$. To specify the distance function, additional assumptions are made (e.g., intradimensional subtractivity and interdimensional additivity) relating the dimensional structure of the objects to their metric distances. For an axiomatic analysis and a critical discussion of these assumptions, see Beals, Krantz, and Tversky (1968), Krantz and Tversky (1975), and Tversky and Krantz (1970).

In conclusion, it appears that despite many fruitful applications (see e.g., Carroll & Wish, 1974; Shepard, 1974), the geometric approach to the analysis of similarity faces several difficulties. The applicability of the dimensional assumption is limited, and the metric axioms are questionable. Specifically, minimality is somewhat problematic, symmetry is apparently false, and the triangle inequality is hardly compelling.

The next section develops an alternative theoretical approach to similarity, based on feature matching, which is neither dimensional nor metric in nature. In subsequent sections this approach is used to uncover, analyze, and explain several empirical phenomena, such as the role of common and distinctive features, the relations between judgments of similarity and difference, the presence of asymmetric similarities, and the effects of context on similarity. Extensions and implications of the present development are discussed in the final section.

Feature Matching

Let $\Delta = \{a, b, c, \dots\}$ be the domain of objects (or stimuli) under study. Assume that each object in Δ is represented by a set of features or attributes, and let A, B, C denote the sets of features associated with the objects a, b, c, respectively. The features may correspond to components such as eyes or mouth, they may represent concrete properties such as size or color, and they may reflect abstract attributes such as quality or complexity. The characterization of stimuli as feature sets has been employed in the analysis of many cognitive processes such as speech perception (Jakobson, Fant, & Halle, 1961), pattern recognition (Neisser, 1967), perceptual learning (Gibson, 1969), preferential choice (Tversky, 1972), and semantic judgment (Smith, Shoben, & Rips, 1974).

Two preliminary comments regarding feature representations are in order. First, it is important to note that our total database concerning a particular object (e.g., a person, a country, or a piece of furniture) is generally rich in content and complex in form. It includes appearance, function, relation to other objects, and any other property of the object that can be deduced from our general knowledge of the world. When faced with a particular task (e.g., identification or similarity assessment) we extract and compile from our database a limited list of relevant features on the basis of which we perform the required task. Thus, the representation of an object as a collection of features is viewed as a product of a prior process of extraction and compilation.

Second, the term *feature* usually denotes the value of a binary variable (e.g., voiced vs. voiceless consonants) or the value of a nominal variable (e.g., eye color). Feature representations, however, are not restricted to binary or nominal variables; they are also applicable to ordinal or cardinal variables (i.e., dimensions). A series of tones that differ only in loudness, for example, could be represented as a sequence of nested sets where the feature set associated with each tone is included in the feature sets associated with louder tones. Such a representation is isomorphic to a directional unidimensional structure. A nondirectional unidimensional structure (e.g., a series of tones that differ only in pitch) could be represented by a chain of overlapping sets. The set-theoretical representation of qualitative and quantitative dimensions has been investigated by Restle (1959).

Let s(a, b) be a measure of the similarity of a to b defined for all distinct a, b in Δ. The scale s is treated as an ordinal measure of similarity. That is, s(a, b) > s(c, d) means that a is more similar to b than c is to d. The present theory is based on the following assumptions.

1. Matching:

$s(a, b) = F(A \cap B, A - B, B - A)$.

The similarity of a to b is expressed as a function F of three arguments: $A \cap B$, the features that are common to both a and b; $A - B$, the features that belong to a but not to b; $B - A$, the features that belong to b but not to a. A schematic illustration of these components is presented in figure 3.1.

2. Monotonicity:

$s(a, b) \geq s(a, c)$

whenever

$A \cap B \supset A \cap C, \quad A - B \subset A - C,$

and

$B - A \subset C - A$.

Moreover, the inequality is strict whenever either inclusion is proper.

That is, similarity increases with addition of common features and/or deletion of distinctive features (i.e., features that belong to one object but not to the other). The monotonicity

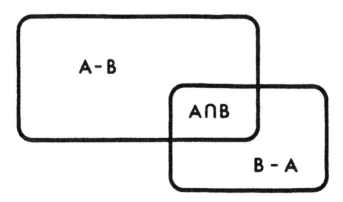

Figure 3.1
A graphical illustration of the relation between two feature sets.

axiom can be readily illustrated with block letters if we identify their features with the component (straight) lines. Under this assumption, E should be more similar to F than to I because E and F have more common features than E and I. Furthermore, I should be more similar to F than to E because I and F have fewer distinctive features than I and E.

Any function F satisfying assumptions 1 and 2 is called a *matching function*. It measures the degree to which two objects—viewed as sets of features—match each other. In the present theory, the assessment of similarity is described as a feature-matching process. It is formulated, therefore, in terms of the set-theoretical notion of a matching function rather than in terms of the geometric concept of distance.

In order to determine the functional form of the matching function, additional assumptions about the similarity ordering are introduced. The major assumption of the theory (independence) is presented next; the remaining assumptions and the proof of the representation theorem are presented in the appendix. Readers who are less interested in formal theory can skim or skip the following paragraphs up to the discussion of the representation theorem.

Let Φ denote the set of all features associated with the objects of Δ, and let X, Y, Z, . . . , etc. denote collections of features (i.e., subsets of Φ). The expression F(X, Y, Z) is defined whenever there exists a, b in Δ such that $A \cap B = X$, $A - B = Y$, and $B - A = Z$, whence $s(a, b) = F(A \cap B, A - B, B - A) = F(X, Y, Z)$. Next, define $V \simeq W$ if one or more of the following hold for some X, Y, Z: F(V, Y, Z) = F(W, Y, Z), F(X, V, Z) = F(X, W, Z), F(X, Y, V) = F(X, Y, W).

The pairs (a, b) and (c, d) are said to *agree* on one, two, or three components, respectively, whenever one, two, or three of the following hold: $(A \cap B) \simeq (C \cap D)$, $(A - B) \simeq (C - D)$, $(B - A) \simeq (D - C)$.

3. Independence

Suppose the pairs (a, b) and (c, d), as well as the pairs (a′, b′) and (c′, d′), agree on the same two components, while the pairs (a, b) and (a′, b′), as well as the pairs (c, d) and (c′, d′), agree on the remaining (third) component. Then

$$s(a, b) \geq s(a', b') \quad \text{iff} \quad s(c, d) \geq s(c', d').$$

To illustrate the force of the independence axiom consider the stimuli presented in figure 3.2, where

$A \cap B = C \cap D = $ round profile $= X,$

$A' \cap B' = C' \cap D' = $ sharp profile $= X',$

$A - B = C - D = $ smiling mouth $= Y,$

$A' - B' = C' - D' = $ frowning mouth $= Y',$

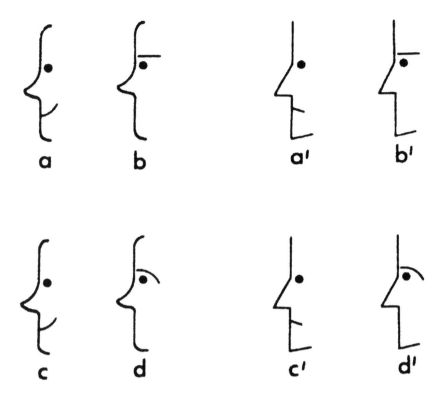

Figure 3.2
An illustration of independence.

B – A = B′ – A′ = straight eyebrow = Z,

D – C = D′ – C′ = curved eyebrow = Z′.

By independence, therefore,

$$s(a, b) = F(A \cap B, A - B, B - A)$$
$$= F(X, Y, Z) \geq F(X', Y', Z)$$
$$= F(A' \cap B', A' - B', B' - A')$$
$$= s(a', b')$$

if and only if

$$s(c, d) = F(C \cap D, C - D, D - C)$$
$$= F(X, Y, Z') \geq F(X', Y', Z')$$
$$= F(C' \cap D', C' - D', D' - C')$$
$$= s(c', d').$$

Thus, the ordering of the joint effect of any two components (e.g., X, Y vs. X', Y') is independent of the fixed level of the third factor (e.g., Z or Z').

It should be emphasized that any test of the axioms presupposes an interpretation of the features. The independence axiom, for example, may hold in one interpretation and fail in another. Experimental tests of the axioms, therefore, test jointly the adequacy of the interpretation of the features and the empirical validity of the assumptions. Furthermore, the above examples should not be taken to mean that stimuli (e.g., block letters, schematic faces) can be properly characterized in terms of their components. To achieve an adequate feature representation of visual forms, more global properties (e.g., symmetry, connectedness) should also be introduced. For an interesting discussion of this problem, in the best tradition of Gestalt psychology, see Goldmeier (1972; originally published in 1936).

In addition to matching (1), monotonicity (2), and independence (3), we also assume solvability (4), and invariance (5). Solvability requires that the feature space under study be sufficiently rich that certain (similarity) equations can be solved. Invariance ensures that the equivalence of intervals is preserved across factors. A rigorous formulation of these assumptions is given in the Appendix, along with a proof of the following result.

Representation Theorem Suppose assumptions 1, 2, 3, 4, and 5 hold. Then there exist a similarity scale S and a nonnegative scale f such that for all a, b, c, d in D,

(i) $S(a, b) \geq S(c, d)$ iff $s(a, b) \geq s(c, d)$;

(ii) $S(a, b) = \theta f(A \cap B) - \alpha f(A - B) - \beta f(B - A)$, for some $\theta, \alpha, \beta \geq 0$;

(iii) f and S are interval scales.

The theorem shows that under assumptions 1–5, there exists an interval similarity scale S that preserves the observed similarity order and expresses similarity as a linear combination, or a contrast, of the measures of the common and the distinctive features. Hence, the representation is called the *contrast model*. In parts of the following development we also assume that f satisfies feature additivity. That is, $f(X \cup Y) = f(X) + f(Y)$ whenever X and Y are disjoint, and all three terms are defined.[1]

Note that the contrast model does not define a single similarity scale, but rather a family of scales characterized by different values of the parameters θ, α, and β. For example, if $\theta = 1$ and α and β vanish, then $S(a, b) = f(A \cap B)$; that is, the similarity between objects is the measure of their common features. If, however, $\alpha = \beta = 1$ and θ vanishes, then $-S(a, b) = f(A - B) + f(B - A)$; that is, the dissimilarity between objects is the measure of the symmetric difference between the respective feature sets. Restle (1961) has proposed these forms as models of similarity and psychological distance, respectively. Note that in the former model ($\theta = 1$, $\alpha = \beta = 0$), similarity between objects is determined only by their common features, whereas in the latter model ($\theta = 0$, $\alpha = \beta = 1$), it is determined by their distinctive features only. The contrast model expresses similarity between objects as a weighted difference of the measures of their common and distinctive features, thereby allowing for a variety of similarity relations over the same domain.

The major constructs of the present theory are the contrast rule for the assessment of similarity, and the scale f, which reflects the salience or prominence of the various features. Thus, f measures the contribution of any particular (common or distinctive) feature to the similarity between objects. The scale value f(A) associated with stimulus a is regarded, therefore, as a measure of the overall salience of that stimulus. The factors that contribute to the salience of a stimulus include intensity, frequency, familiarity, good form, and informational content. The manner in which the scale f and the parameters (θ, α, β) depend on the context and the task are discussed in the following sections.

Let us recapitulate what is assumed and what is proven in the representation theorem. We begin with a set of objects, described as collections of features, and a similarity ordering, which is assumed to satisfy the axioms of the present theory. From these assumptions, we derive a measure f on the feature space and prove that the similarity ordering of object pairs coincides with the ordering of their contrasts, defined as linear combinations of the respective common and distinctive features. Thus, the measure f and the contrast model are derived from qualitative axioms regarding the similarity of objects.

The nature of this result may be illuminated by an analogy to the classical theory of decision under risk (von Neumann & Morgenstern, 1947). In that theory, one starts with a set of prospects, characterized as probability distributions over some consequence space, and a preference order that is assumed to satisfy the axioms of the theory. From these assumptions one derives a utility scale on the consequence space and proves that the preference order between prospects coincides with the order of their expected utilities. Thus, the utility scale and the expectation principle are derived from qualitative assumptions about preferences. The present theory of similarity differs from the expected-utility model in that the characterization of objects as feature sets is perhaps more problematic than the characterization of uncertain options as probability distributions. Furthermore, the axioms of utility theory are proposed as (normative) principles of rational behavior, whereas the axioms of the present theory are intended to be descriptive rather than prescriptive.

The contrast model is perhaps the simplest form of a matching function, yet it is not the only form worthy of investigation. Another matching function of interest is the *ratio model*,

$$S(a, b) = \frac{f(A \cap B)}{f(A \cap B) + \alpha f(A - B) + \beta f(B - A)}, \quad \alpha, \beta \geq 0,$$

where similarity is normalized so that S lies between 0 and 1. The ratio model generalizes several set-theoretical models of similarity proposed in the literature. If $\alpha = \beta = 1$, S(a, b) reduces to $f(A \cap B)/f(A \cup B)$ (see Gregson, 1975; Sjöberg, 1972). If $\alpha = \beta = \frac{1}{2}$, $S(a, b)$ equals $2f(A \cap B)/(f(A) + f(B))$ (see Eisler & Ekman, 1959). If $\alpha = 1$ and $\beta = 0$, $S(a, b)$ reduces to $f(A \cap B)/f(A)$ (see Bush & Mosteller, 1951). The present framework, therefore, encompasses a wide variety of similarity models that differ in the form of the matching function F and in the weights assigned to its arguments.

In order to apply and test the present theory in any particular domain, some assumptions about the respective feature structure must be made. If the features associated with each object are explicitly specified, we can test the axioms of the theory directly and scale the features according to the contrast model. This approach, however, is generally limited to stimuli (e.g., schematic faces, letters, strings of symbols) that are constructed from a fixed feature set. If the features associated with the objects under study cannot be readily specified, as is often the case with natural stimuli, we can still test several predictions of the contrast model that involve only general qualitative assumptions about the feature structure of the objects. Both approaches were employed in a series of experiments conducted by Itamar Gati and the present author. The following three sections review and discuss our main findings, focusing primarily on the test of qualitative predictions. A more detailed description of the stimuli and the data are presented in Tversky and Gati (1978).

Asymmetry and Focus

According to the present analysis, similarity is not necessarily a symmetric relation. Indeed, it follows readily (from either the contrast or the ratio model) that

$$s(a, b) = s(b, a) \quad \text{iff} \quad \alpha f(A - B) + \beta f(B - A) = \alpha f(B - A) + \beta f(A - B)$$
$$\text{iff} \quad (\alpha - \beta)f(A - B) = (\alpha - \beta)f(B - A).$$

Hence, $s(a, b) = s(b, a)$ if either $\alpha = \beta$, or $f(A - B) = f(B - A)$, which implies $f(A) = f(B)$, provided feature additivity holds. Thus, symmetry holds whenever the objects are equal in measure ($f(A) = f(B)$) or the task is nondirectional ($\alpha = \beta$). To interpret the latter condition, compare the following two forms:

(i) Assess the degree to which a and b are similar to each other.

(ii) Assess the degree to which a is similar to b.

In (i), the task is formulated in a nondirectional fashion; hence, it is expected that $\alpha = \beta$ and $s(a, b) = s(b, a)$. In (ii), however, the task is directional, and hence α and β may differ and symmetry need not hold.

If $s(a, b)$ is interpreted as the degree to which a is similar to b, then a is the subject of the comparison and b is the referent. In such a task, one naturally focuses on the subject of the comparison. Hence, the features of the subject are weighted more heavily than the features of the referent (i.e., $\alpha > \beta$). Consequently, similarity is reduced more by the distinctive features of the subject than by the distinctive features of the referent. It follows readily that whenever $\alpha > \beta$,

$$s(a, b) > s(b, a) \quad \text{iff} \quad f(B) > f(A).$$

Thus, the focusing hypothesis (i.e., $\alpha > \beta$) implies that the direction of asymmetry is determined by the relative salience of the stimuli so that the less salient stimulus is more similar to the salient stimulus than vice versa. In particular, the variant is more similar to the prototype than the prototype is to the variant because the prototype is generally more salient than the variant.

Similarity of Countries

Twenty-one pairs of countries served as stimuli. The pairs were constructed so that one element was more prominent than the other (e.g., Red China—North Vietnam, USA—Mexico, Belgium—Luxemburg). To verify this relation, we asked a group of 69 subjects[2] to select in each pair the country they regarded as more prominent. The proportion of subjects that agreed with the a priori ordering exceeded $\frac{2}{3}$ for all pairs except one. A second group of 69 subjects was asked to choose which of two phrases they preferred to use: "country a is similar to country b" or "country b is similar to country a." In all 21 cases, most of the subjects chose the phrase in which the less prominent country served as the subject and the more prominent country as the referent. For example, 66 subjects selected the phrase "North Korea is similar to Red China" and only 3 selected the phrase "Red China is similar to North Korea." These results demonstrate the presence of marked asymmetries in the choice of similarity statements, whose direction coincides with the relative prominence of the stimuli.

To test for asymmetry in direct judgments of similarity, we presented two groups of 77 subjects each with the same list of 21 pairs of countries and asked subjects to rate their similarity on a 20-point scale. The only difference between the two groups was the order of the countries within each pair. For example, one group was asked to assess "the degree to which the USSR is similar to Poland," whereas the second group was asked to assess "the degree to which Poland is similar to the USSR." The lists were constructed so that the more prominent country appeared about an equal number of times in the first and second positions.

For any pair (p, q) of stimuli, let p denote the more prominent element, and let q denote the less prominent element. The average $s(q, p)$ was significantly higher than the average $s(p, q)$ across all subjects and pairs: t test for correlated samples yielded $t(20) = 2.92$, $p < 0.01$. To obtain a statistical test based on individual data, we computed for each subject a directional asymmetry score defined as the average similarity for comparisons with a prominent referent; that is, s(q, p), minus the average similarity for comparisons with a prominent subject, s(p, q). The average difference was significantly positive: $t(153) = 2.99$, $p < 0.01$.

The above study was repeated using judgments of difference instead of judgments of similarity. Two groups of 23 subjects each participated in this study. They received the same list of 21 pairs except that one group was asked to judge the degree to which country a differed from country b, denoted d(a, b), whereas the second group was asked to judge the degree to which country b was different from country a, denoted d(b, a). If judgments of difference follow the contrast model, and $\alpha > \beta$, then we expect the prominent stimulus p to differ from the less prominent stimulus q more than q differs from p; that is, d(p, q) > d(q, p). This hypothesis was tested using the same set of 21 pairs of countries and the prominence ordering established earlier. The average d(p, q), across all subjects and pairs, was significantly higher than the average d(q, p): t test for correlated samples yielded $t(20) = 2.72$, $p < 0.01$. Furthermore, the average asymmetry score, computed as above for each subject, was significantly positive ($t(45) = 2.24$, $p < 0.05$).

Similarity of Figures

A major determinant of the salience of geometric figures is goodness of form. Thus, a "good figure" is likely to be more salient than a "bad figure," although the latter is generally more complex. However, when two figures are roughly equivalent with respect to goodness of form, the more complex figure is likely to be more salient. To investigate these hypotheses and to test the asymmetry prediction, two sets of eight pairs of geometric figures were constructed. In the first set, one figure in each pair (denoted p) had better form than the other (denoted q). In the second set, the two figures in each pair were roughly matched in goodness of form, but one figure (denoted p) was richer or more complex than the other (denoted q). Examples of pairs of figures from each set are presented in figure 3.3.

A group of 69 subjects was presented with the entire list of 16 pairs of figures, where the two elements of each pair were displayed side by side. For each pair, the subjects were asked to indicate which of the following two statements they preferred to use: "The left figure is similar to the right figure" or "The right figure is similar to the left figure." The positions of the stimuli were randomized so that p and q appeared an equal number of times on the left and on the right. The results showed that in each one of the pairs, most of the subjects selected the form "q is similar to p." Thus, the more salient stimulus was generally chosen as the referent rather than the subject of similarity statements.

To test for asymmetry in judgments of similarity, we presented two groups of 67 subjects each with the same 16 pairs of figures and asked the subjects to rate (on a 20-point scale) the degree to which the figure on the left was similar to the figure on the right. The two groups received identical booklets, except that the left and right positions of the figures in each pair

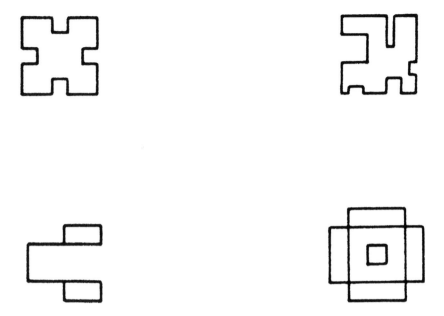

Figure 3.3
Examples of pairs of figures used to test the prediction of asymmetry. The top two figures are examples of a pair (from the first set) that differs in goodness of form. The bottom two are examples of a pair (from the second set) that differs in complexity.

were reversed. The results showed that the average s(q, p) across all subjects and pairs was significantly higher than the average s(p, q). A *t* test for correlated samples yielded $t(15) = 2.94$, $p < 0.01$. Furthermore, in both sets the average asymmetry scores, computed as above for each subject, were significantly positive: In the first set $t(131) = 2.96$, $p < 0.01$; and in the second set $t(131) = 2.79$, $p < 0.01$.

Similarity of Letters

A common measure of similarity between stimuli is the probability of confusing them in a recognition or an identification task: The more similar the stimuli, the more likely they are to be confused. While confusion probabilities are often asymmetric (i.e., the probability of confusing a with b is different from the probability of confusing b with a), this effect is typically attributed to a response bias. To eliminate this interpretation of asymmetry, one could employ an experimental task where the subject merely indicates whether the two stimuli presented to him (sequentially or simultaneously) are identical or not. This procedure was employed by Yoav Cohen and the present author in a study of confusion among block letters.

The following eight block letters served as stimuli: г, c, п, ▫, F, ᴇ, ᴚ, ʙ. All pairs of letters were displayed on a cathode-ray tube, side by side, on a noisy background. The letters were presented sequentially, each for approximately 1 msec. The right letter always followed the left letter with an interval of 630 msec in between. After each presentation the subject pressed one of two keys to indicate whether the two letters were identical or not.

A total of 32 subjects participated in the experiment. Each subject was tested individually. On each trial, one letter (known in advance) served as the standard. For one half of the subjects the standard stimulus always appeared on the left, and for the other half of the subjects the standard always appeared on the right. Each one of the eight letters served as a standard. The trials were blocked into groups of 10 pairs in which the standard was paired once with each of the other letters and three times with itself. Since each letter served as a standard in one block, the entire design consisted of eight blocks of 10 trials each. Every subject was presented with three replications of the entire design (i.e., 240 trials). The order of the blocks in each design and the order of the letters within each block were randomized.

According to the present analysis, people compare the variable stimulus, which serves the role of the subject, to the standard (i.e., the referent). The choice of standard, therefore, determines the directionality of the comparison. A natural partial ordering of the letters with respect to prominence is induced by the relation of inclusion among letters. Thus, one letter is assumed to have a larger measure than another if the former includes the latter. For example, ᴇ includes F and г but not ▫. For all 19 pairs in which one letter includes the other, let p denote the more prominent letter and q denote the less prominent letter. Furthermore, let s(a, b) denote the percentage of times that the subject judged the variable stimulus a to be the same as the standard b.

It follows from the contrast model, with $\alpha > \beta$, that the proportion of "same" responses should be larger when the variable is included in the standard than when the standard is included in the variable, that is, s(q, p) > s(p, q). This prediction was borne out by the data. The average s(q, p) across all subjects and trials was 17.1%, whereas the average s(p, q) across all subjects and trials was 12.4%. To obtain a statistical test, we computed for each subject the difference between s(q, p) and s(p, q) across all trials. The difference was significantly positive ($t(31) = 4.41$, $p < 0.001$). These results demonstrate that the prediction of directional asymmetry derived from the contrast model applies to confusion data and not merely to rated similarity.

Similarity of Signals

Rothkopf (1957) presented 598 subjects with all ordered pairs of the 36 Morse Code signals and asked them to indicate whether the two signals in each pair were the same or not. The pairs were presented in a randomized order without a fixed standard. Each subject judged about one fourth of all pairs.

Let s(a, b) denote the percentage of "same" responses to the ordered pair (a, b); that is, the percentage of subjects who judged the first signal a to be the same as the second signal b. Note that a and b refer here to the first and second signals and not to the variable and the standard as in the previous section. Obviously, Morse Code signals are partially ordered according to temporal length. For any pair of signals that differ in temporal length, let p and q denote, respectively, the longer and shorter elements of the pair.

From the total of 555 comparisons between signals of different length, reported in Rothkopf (1957), s(q, p) exceeds s(p, q) in 336 cases, s(p, q) exceeds s(q, p) in 181 cases, and s(q, p) equals s(p, q) in 38 cases ($p < 0.001$ by sign test). The average difference between s(q, p) and s(p, q) across all pairs is 3.3%, which is also highly significant. A t test for correlated samples yields $t(554) = 9.17$, $p < 0.001$.

The asymmetry effect is enhanced when we consider only those comparisons in which one signal is a proper subsequence of the other. (e.g., $\cdot\cdot$ is a subsequence of $\cdot\cdot\cdot$ as well as of $\cdot\cdot\cdot$). From a total of 195 comparisons of this type, s(q, p) exceeds s(p, q) in 128 cases, s(p, q) exceeds s(q, p) in 55 cases, and s(q, p) equals s(p, q) in 12 cases ($p < 0.001$ by sign test). The average difference between s(q, p) and s(p, q) in this case is 4.7% ($t(194) = 7.58$, $p < 0.001$).

A later study following the same experimental paradigm with somewhat different signals was conducted by Wish (1967). His signals consisted of three tones separated by two silent intervals, where each component (i.e., a tone or a silence) was either short or long. Subjects were presented with all pairs of 32 signals generated in this fashion and judged whether the two members of each pair were the same or not.

The above analysis is readily applicable to Wish's (1967) data. From a total of 386 comparisons between signals of different length, s(q, p) exceeds s(p, q) in 241 cases, s(p, q) exceeds s(q, p) in 117 cases, and s(q, p) equals s(p, q) in 28 cases. These data are clearly asymmetric ($p < 0.001$ by sign test). The average difference between s(q, p) and s(p, q) is 5.9%, which is also highly significant ($t(385) = 9.23$, $p < 0.001$).

In the studies of Rothkopf and Wish there is no a priori way to determine the directionality of the comparison or, equivalently, to identify the subject and the referent. However, if we accept the focusing hypothesis ($\alpha > \beta$) and the assumption that longer signals are more prominent than shorter ones, then the direction of the observed asymmetry indicates that the first signal serves as the subject that is compared with the second signal that serves the role of the referent. Hence, the directionality of the comparison is determined, according to the present analysis, from the prominence ordering of the stimuli and the observed direction of asymmetry.

Rosch's Data

Rosch (1973, 1975) has articulated and supported the view that perceptual and semantic categories are naturally formed and defined in terms of focal points, or prototypes. Because of the special role of prototypes in the formation of categories, she hypothesized that (i) in sentence frames involving hedges such as "a is essentially b," focal stimuli (i.e., prototypes) appear in the second position; and (ii) the perceived distance from the prototype to the variant is greater than the perceived distance from the variant to the prototype. To test these hypotheses, Rosch (1975) used three stimulus domains: color, line orientation, and number. Prototypical colors were focal (e.g., pure red), while the variants were either non-focal (e.g., off-red) or less saturated. Vertical, horizontal, and diagonal lines served as prototypes for line orientation, and lines of other angles served as variants. Multiples of 10 (e.g., 10, 50, 100) were taken as prototypical numbers, and other numbers (e.g., 11, 52, 103) were treated as variants.

Hypothesis (i) was strongly confirmed in all three domains. When presented with sentence frames such as "_____ is virtually _____," subjects generally placed the prototype in the second blank and the variant in the first. For instance, subjects preferred the sentence "103 is virtually 100" to the sentence "100 is virtually 103." To test hypothesis (ii), one stimulus (the standard) was placed at the origin of a semicircular board, and the subject was instructed to place the second (variable) stimulus on the board so as "to represent his feeling of the distance between that stimulus and the one fixed at the origin." As hypothesized, the measured distance between stimuli was significantly smaller when the prototype, rather than the variant, was fixed at the origin, in each of the three domains.

If focal stimuli are more salient than non-focal stimuli, then Rosch's findings support the present analysis. The hedging sentences (e.g., "a is roughly b") can be regarded as a particular type of similarity statements. Indeed, the hedges data are in perfect agreement with the choice of similarity statements. Furthermore, the observed asymmetry in distance placement follows from the present analysis of asymmetry and the natural assumptions that the standard and the variable serve, respectively, as referent and subject in the distance-placement task. Thus, the placement of b at distance t from a is interpreted as saying that the (perceived) distance from b to a equals t.

Rosch (1975) attributed the observed asymmetry to the special role of distinct prototypes (e.g., a perfect square or a pure red) in the processing of information. In the present theory, however, asymmetry is explained by the relative salience of the stimuli. Consequently, it implies asymmetry for pairs that do not include the prototype (e.g., two levels of distortion of the same form). If the concept of prototypicality, however, is interpreted in a relative sense (i.e., a is more prototypical than b) rather than in an absolute sense, then the two interpretations of asymmetry practically coincide.

Discussion

The conjunction of the contrast model and the focusing hypothesis implies the presence of asymmetric similarities. This prediction was confirmed in several experiments of perceptual and conceptual similarity using both judgmental methods (e.g., rating) and behavioral methods (e.g., choice).

The asymmetries discussed in the previous section were observed in *comparative* tasks in which the subject compares two given stimuli to determine their similarity. Asymmetries were also observed in *production* tasks in which the subject is given a single stimulus and asked to produce the most similar response. Studies of pattern recognition, stimulus identification, and word association are all examples of production tasks. A common pattern observed in such studies is that the more salient object occurs more often as a response to the less salient object than vice versa. For example, "tiger" is a more likely associate to "leopard" than "leopard" is to "tiger." Similarly, Garner (1974) instructed subjects to select from a given set of dot patterns one that is similar—but not identical—to a given pattern. His results show that "good" patterns are usually chosen as responses to "bad" patterns and not conversely.

This asymmetry in production tasks has commonly been attributed to the differential availability of responses. Thus, "tiger" is a more likely associate to "leopard" than vice versa, because "tiger" is more common and hence a more available response than "leopard." This account is probably more applicable to situations where the subject must actually produce the response (as in word association or pattern recognition) than to situations where the subject merely selects a response from some specified set (as in Garner's task).

Without questioning the importance of response availability, the present theory suggests another reason for the asymmetry observed in production tasks. Consider the following translation of a production task to a question-and-answer scheme. Question: What is a like? Answer: a is like b. If this interpretation is valid and the given object a serves as a subject rather than as a referent, then the observed asymmetry of production follows from the present theoretical analysis, since $s(a, b) > s(b, a)$ whenever $f(B) > f(A)$.

In summary, it appears that proximity data from both comparative and production tasks reveal significant and systematic asymmetries whose direction is determined by the relative salience of the stimuli. Nevertheless, the symmetry assumption should not be rejected altogether. It seems to hold in many contexts, and it serves as a useful approximation in many others. It cannot be accepted, however, as a universal principle of psychological similarity.

Common and Distinctive Features

In the present theory, the similarity of objects is expressed as a linear combination, or a contrast, of the measures of their common and distinctive features. This section investigates the relative impact of these components and their effect on the relation between the assessments of similarity and difference. The discussion concerns only symmetric tasks, where $\alpha = \beta$, and hence $s(a, b) = s(b, a)$.

Elicitation of Features

The first study employs the contrast model to predict the similarity between objects from features that were produced by the subjects. The following 12 vehicles served as stimuli: bus, car, truck, motorcycle, train, airplane, bicycle, boat, elevator, cart, raft, sled. One group of 48 subjects rated the similarity between all 66 pairs of vehicles on a scale from 1 (no similarity) to 20 (maximal similarity). Following Rosch and Mervis (1975), we instructed a second group of 40 subjects to list the characteristic features of each one of the vehicles. Subjects were given 70 sec to list the features that characterized each vehicle. Different orders of presentation were used for different subjects.

The number of features per vehicle ranged from 71 for airplane to 21 for sled. Altogether, 324 features were listed by the subjects, of which 224 were unique and 100 were shared by two or more vehicles. For every pair of vehicles, we counted the number of features that were attributed to both (by at least one subject) and the number of features that were attributed to one vehicle but not to the other. The frequency of subjects that listed each common or distinctive feature was computed.

In order to predict the similarity between vehicles from the listed features, the measures of their common and distinctive features must be defined. The simplest measure is obtained by counting the number of common and distinctive features produced by the subjects. The product-moment correlation between the (average) similarity of objects and the number of their common features was 0.68. The correlation between the similarity of objects and the number of their distinctive features was –0.36. The multiple correlation between similarity and the numbers of common and distinctive features (i.e., the correlation between similarity and the contrast model) was 0.72.

The counting measure assigns equal weight to all features regardless of their frequency of mention. To take this factor into account, let X_a denote the proportion of subjects who attributed feature X to object a, and let N_X denote the number of objects that share feature X. For any a, b, define the measure of their common features by $f(A \cap B) = \sum X_a X_b / N_X$, where the summation is over all X in $A \cap B$, and the measure of their distinctive features by

$$f(A - B) + f(B - A) = \sum Y_a + \sum Z_b$$

where the summations range over all $Y \in A - B$ and $Z \in B - A$, that is, the distinctive features of a and b, respectively. The correlation between similarity and the above measure of the common features was 0.84, and the correlation between similarity and the above measure of the distinctive features was −0.64. The multiple correlation between similarity and the measures of the common and the distinctive features was 0.87.

Note that the above methods for defining the measure f were based solely on the elicited features and did not utilize the similarity data at all. Under these conditions, a perfect correlation between the two should not be expected because the weights associated with the features are not optimal for the prediction of similarity. A given feature may be frequently mentioned because it is easily labeled or recalled, although it does not have a great impact on similarity, and vice versa. Indeed, when the features were scaled using the additive tree procedure (Sattath & Tversky, 1977) in which the measure of the features is derived from the similarities between the objects, the correlation between the data and the model reached 0.94.

The results of this study indicate that (i) it is possible to elicit from subjects detailed features of semantic stimuli such as vehicles (see Rosch & Mervis, 1975), (ii) the listed features can be used to predict similarity according to the contrast model with a reasonable degree of success, and (iii) the prediction of similarity is improved when frequency of mention and not merely the number of features is taken into account.

Similarity versus Difference

It has been generally assumed that judgments of similarity and difference are complementary; that is, judged difference is a linear function of judged similarity with a slope of −1. This hypothesis has been confirmed in several studies. For example, Hosman and Kuennapas (1972) obtained independent judgments of similarity and difference for all pairs of lowercase letters on a scale from 0 to 100. The product–moment correlation between the judgments was −0.98, and the slope of the regression line was −0.91. We also collected judgments of similarity and difference for 21 pairs of countries using a 20-point rating scale. The sum of the two judgments for each pair was quite close to 20 in all cases. The product–moment correlation between the ratings was again −0.98. This inverse relation between similarity and difference, however, does not always hold.

Naturally, an increase in the measure of the common features increases similarity and decreases difference, whereas an increase in the measure of the distinctive features decreases similarity and increases difference. However, the relative weight assigned to the common and the distinctive features may differ in the two tasks. In the assessment of similarity between objects the subject may attend more to their common features, whereas in the assessment of difference between objects the subject may attend more to their distinctive features. Thus, the relative weight of the common features will be greater in the former task than in the latter task.

Let d(a, b) denote the perceived difference between a and b. Suppose d satisfies the axioms of the present theory with the reverse inequality in the monotonicity axiom, that is, d(a, b)

$\leq d(a, c)$ whenever $A \cap B \supset A \cap C$, $A - B \subset A - C$, and $B - A \subset C - A$. Furthermore, suppose s also satisfies the present theory and assume (for simplicity) that both d and s are symmetric. According to the representation theorem, therefore, there exist a nonnegative scale f and nonnegative constants θ and λ such that for all a, b, c, e,

$$s(a, b) > s(c, e) \quad \text{iff} \quad \theta f(A \cap B) - f(A - B) - f(B - A)$$
$$> \theta f(C \cap E) - f(C - E) - f(E - C),$$

and

$$d(a, b) > d(c, e) \quad \text{iff} \quad f(A - B) + f(B - A) - \lambda f(A \cap B)$$
$$> f(C - E) + f(E - C) - \lambda f(C \cap E).$$

The weights associated with the distinctive features can be set equal to 1 in the symmetric case with no loss of generality. Hence, θ and λ reflect the *relative* weight of the common features in the assessment of similarity and difference, respectively.

Note that if θ is very large, then the similarity ordering is essentially determined by the common features. By contrast, if λ is very small, then the difference ordering is determined primarily by the distinctive features. Consequently, both $s(a, b) > s(c, e)$ and $d(a, b) > d(c, e)$ may be obtained whenever

$$f(A \cap B) > f(C \cap E)$$

and

$$f(A - B) + f(B - A) > f(C - E) + f(E - C).$$

That is, if the common features are weighed more heavily in judgments of similarity than in judgments of difference, then a pair of objects with many common and many distinctive features may be perceived as both more similar and more different than another pair of objects with fewer common and fewer distinctive features.

To test this hypothesis, 20 sets of four countries were constructed on the basis of a pilot test. Each set included two pairs of countries: a prominent pair and a nonprominent pair. The prominent pairs consisted of countries that were well known to our subjects (e.g., USA—USSR, Red China—Japan). The nonprominent pairs consisted of countries that were known to the subjects, but not as well as the prominent ones (e.g., Tunis—Morocco, Paraguay—Ecuador). All subjects were presented with the same 20 sets. One group of 30 subjects selected between the two pairs in each set the pair of countries that were more *similar*. Another group of 30 subjects selected between the two pairs in each set the pair of countries that were more *different*.

Let Π_s and Π_d denote, respectively, the percentage of choices where the prominent pair of countries was selected as more similar or as more different. If similarity and difference are complementary (i.e., $\theta = \lambda$), then $\Pi_s + \Pi_d$ should equal 100 for all pairs. If $\theta > \lambda$, however, then $\Pi_s + \Pi_d$ should exceed 100. The average value of $\Pi_s + \Pi_d$, across all sets, was 113.5, which is significantly greater than 100 ($t(59) = 3.27$, $p < 0.01$).

Moreover, on the average, the prominent pairs were selected more frequently than the nonprominent pairs in both the similarity and the difference tasks. For example, 67% of the subjects in the similarity group selected West Germany and East Germany as more similar to each other than Ceylon and Nepal, whereas 70% of the subjects in the difference group selected West Germany and East Germany as more different from each other than Ceylon and Nepal. These data demonstrate how the relative weight of the common and the distinctive features varies with the task and support the hypothesis that people attend more to the common features in judgments of similarity than in judgments of difference.

Similarity in Context

Like other judgments, similarity depends on context and frame of reference. Sometimes the relevant frame of reference is specified explicitly, as in the questions, "How similar are English and French with respect to sound?" and "What is the similarity of a pear and an apple with respect to taste?" In general, however, the relevant feature space is not specified explicitly but rather inferred from the general context.

When subjects are asked to assess the similarity between the USA and the USSR, for instance, they usually assume that the relevant context is the set of countries and that the relevant frame of reference includes all political, geographical, and cultural features. The relative weights assigned to these features, of course, may differ for different people. With natural, integral stimuli such as countries, people, colors, and sounds, there is relatively little ambiguity regarding the relevant feature space. However, with artificial, separable stimuli, such as figures varying in color and shape, or lines varying in length and orientation, subjects sometimes experience difficulty in evaluating overall similarity and occasionally tend to evaluate similarity with respect to one factor or the other (Shepard, 1964) or change the relative weights of attributes with a change in context (Torgerson, 1965).

In the present theory, changes in context or frame of reference correspond to changes in the measure of the feature space. When asked to assess the political similarity between countries, for example, the subject presumably attends to the political aspects of the countries and ignores, or assigns a weight of zero to, all other features. In addition to such restrictions of the feature space induced by explicit or implicit instructions, the salience of features and hence the similarity of objects are also influenced by the effective context (i.e., the set of objects under consideration). To understand this process, let us examine the factors that determine the salience of a feature and its contribution to the similarity of objects.

The Diagnosticity Principle

The salience (or the measure) of a feature is determined by two types of factors: intensive and diagnostic. The former refers to factors that increase intensity or signal-to-noise ratio, such as the brightness of a light, the loudness of a tone, the saturation of a color, the size of a letter, the frequency of an item, the clarity of a picture, or the vividness of an image. The diagnostic factors refer to the classificatory significance of features, that is, the importance or prevalence of the classifications that are based on these features. Unlike the intensive factors, the diagnostic factors are highly sensitive to the particular object set under study. For example, the feature "real" has no diagnostic value in the set of actual animals since it is shared by all actual animals and hence cannot be used to classify them. This feature, however, acquires considerable diagnostic value if the object set is extended to include legendary animals, such as a centaur, a mermaid, or a phoenix.

When faced with a set of objects, people often sort them into clusters to reduce information load and facilitate further processing. Clusters are typically selected so as to maximize the similarity of objects within a cluster and the dissimilarity of objects from different clusters. Hence, the addition and/or deletion of objects can alter the clustering of the remaining objects. A change of clusters, in turn, is expected to increase the diagnostic value of features on which the new clusters are based and, therefore, the similarity of objects that share these features. This relation between similarity and grouping—called the diagnosticity hypothesis—is best explained in terms of a concrete example. Consider the two sets of four schematic faces (displayed in figure 3.4), which differ in only one of their elements (p and q).

The four faces of each set were displayed in a row and presented to a different group of 25 subjects who were instructed to partition them into two pairs. The most frequent partition of set 1 was c and p (smiling faces) versus a and b (nonsmiling faces). The most common partition of set 2 was b and q (frowning faces) versus a and c (nonfrowning faces). Thus, the replacement of p by q changed the grouping of a: In set 1 a was paired with b, whereas in set 2 a was paired with c.

According to the above analysis, smiling has a greater diagnostic value in set 1 than in set 2, whereas frowning has a greater diagnostic value in set 2 than in set 1. By the diagnosticity hypothesis, therefore, similarity should follow the grouping. That is, the similarity of a (which has a neutral expression) to b (which is frowning) should be greater in set 1, where they are grouped together, than in set 2, where they are grouped separately. Likewise, the similarity of a to c (which is smiling) should be greater in set 2, where they are grouped together, than in set 1, where they are not.

To test this prediction, two different groups of 50 subjects were presented with sets 1 and 2 (in the form displayed in figure 3.4) and asked to select one of the three faces below (called the choice set) that was most similar to the face on the top (called the target). The percentage

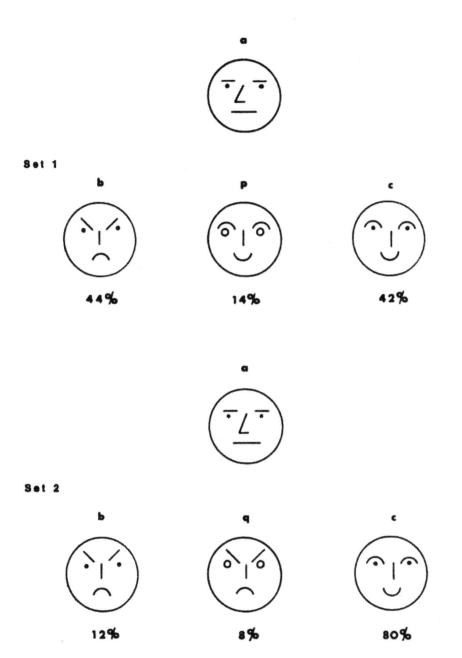

Figure 3.4
Two sets of schematic faces used to test the diagnosticity hypothesis. The percentage of subjects who selected each face (as most similar to the target) is presented below the face.

of subjects who selected each of the three elements of the choice set is presented below the face. The results confirmed the diagnosticity hypothesis: b was chosen more frequently in set 1 than in set 2, whereas c was chosen more frequently in set 2 than in set 1. Both differences are statistically significant ($p < 0.01$). Moreover, the replacement of p by q actually reversed the similarity ordering: In set 1, b is more similar to a than c, whereas in set 2, c is more similar to a than b.

A more extensive test of the diagnosticity hypothesis was conducted using semantic rather than visual stimuli. The experimental design was essentially the same, except that countries served as stimuli instead of faces. Twenty pairs of matched sets of four countries of the form {a, b, c, p} and {a, b, c, q} were constructed. An example of two matched sets is presented in figure 3.5.

Note that the two matched sets (1 and 2) differ only by one element (p and q). The sets were constructed so that a (in this case Austria) is likely to be grouped with b (e.g., Sweden) in set 1 and with c (e.g., Hungary) in set 2. To validate this assumption, we presented two groups of 25 subjects with all sets of four countries and asked them to partition each quadruple into two pairs. Each group received one of the two matched quadruples, which were displayed in a row in random order. The results confirmed our prior hypothesis regarding the grouping of countries. In every case but one, the replacement of p by q changed the pairing

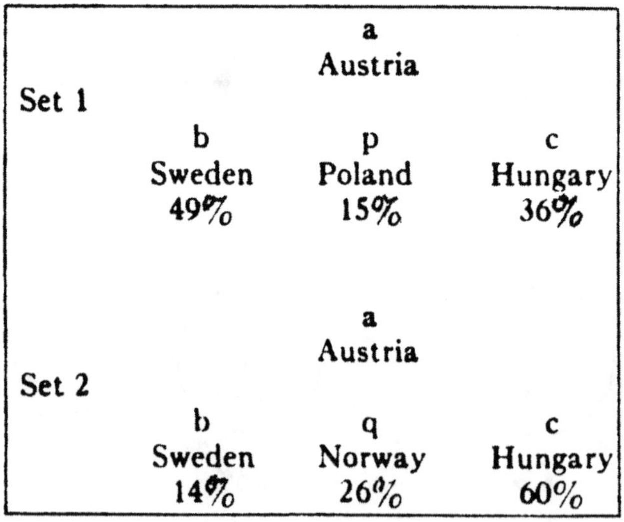

Set 1

	a Austria	
b Sweden 49%	**p** Poland 15%	**c** Hungary 36%

Set 2

	a Austria	
b Sweden 14%	**q** Norway 26%	**c** Hungary 60%

Figure 3.5
Two sets of countries used to test the diagnosticity hypothesis. The percentage of subjects who selected each country (as most similar to Austria) is presented below the country.

of the target country in the predicted direction ($p < 0.01$ by sign test). For example, Austria was paired with Sweden by 60% of the subjects in set 1, and it was paired with Hungary by 96% of the subjects in set 2.

To test the diagnosticity hypothesis, we presented two groups of 35 subjects with 20 sets of four countries in the format displayed in figure 3.5. These subjects were asked to select, for each quadruple, the country in the choice set that was most similar to the target country. Each group received exactly one quadruple from each pair. If the similarity of b to a, say, is independent of the choice set, then the proportion of subjects who chose b rather than c as most similar to a should be the same regardless of whether the third element in the choice set is p or q. For example, the proportion of subjects who select Sweden rather than Hungary as most similar to Austria should be independent of whether the odd element in the choice set is Norway or Poland.

In contrast, the diagnosticity hypothesis implies that the change in grouping, induced by the substitution of the odd element, will change the similarities in a predictable manner. Recall that in set 1 Poland was paired with Hungary, and Austria with Sweden, whereas in set 2 Norway was paired with Sweden, and Austria with Hungary. Hence, the proportion of subjects who select Sweden rather than Hungary (as most similar to Austria) should be higher in set 1 than in set 2. This prediction is strongly supported by the data in figure 3.5, which show that Sweden was selected more frequently than Hungary in set 1, whereas Hungary was selected more frequently than Sweden in set 2.

Let b(p) denote the percentage of subjects who chose country b as most similar to a when the odd element in the choice set is p, and so on. As in the above examples, the notation is chosen so that b is generally grouped with q, and c is generally grouped with p. The differences b(p) – b(q) and c(q) – c(p), therefore, reflect the effects of the odd elements, p and q, on the similarity of b and c to the target a. In the absence of context effects, both differences should equal 0, whereas under the diagnosticity hypothesis both differences should be positive. In figure 3.5, for example, b(p) – b(q) = 49 – 14 = 35, and c(q) – c(p) = 60 – 36 = 24. The average difference, across all pairs of quadruples, equals 9%, which is significantly positive ($t(19) = 3.65$, $p < 0.01$).

Several variations of the experiment did not alter the nature of the results. The diagnosticity hypothesis was also confirmed when (i) each choice set contained four elements rather than three, (ii) the subjects were instructed to rank the elements of each choice set according to their similarity to the target rather than to select the most similar element, and (iii) the target consisted of two elements, and the subjects were instructed to select one element of the choice set that was most similar to the two target elements. For further details, see Tversky and Gati (1978).

The Extension Effect

Recall that the diagnosticity of features is determined by the classifications that are based on them. Features that are shared by all the objects under consideration cannot be used to classify these objects and are, therefore, devoid of diagnostic value. When the context is extended by the enlargement of the object set, some features that had been shared by all objects in the original context may not be shared by all objects in the broader context. These features then acquire diagnostic value and increase the similarity of the objects that share them. Thus, the similarity of a pair of objects in the original context will usually be smaller than their similarity in the extended context.

Essentially the same account was proposed and supported by Sjöberg[3] in studies of similarity between animals and between musical instruments. For example, Sjöberg showed that the similarities between string instruments (banjo, violin, harp, electric guitar) were increased when a wind instrument (clarinet) was added to this set. Since the string instruments are more similar to each other than to the clarinet, however, the above result may be attributed, in part at least, to subjects' tendency to standardize the response scale, that is, to produce the same average similarity for any set of comparisons.

This effect can be eliminated by the use of a somewhat different design, employed in the following study. Subjects were presented with pairs of countries having a common border and assessed their similarity on a 20-point scale. Four sets of eight pairs were constructed. Set 1 contained eight pairs of European countries (e.g., Italy—Switzerland). Set 2 contained eight pairs of American countries (e.g., Brazil—Uruguay). Set 3 contained four pairs from set 1 and four pairs from set 2, whereas set 4 contained the remaining pairs from sets 1 and 2. Each one of the four sets was presented to a different group of 30–36 subjects.

According to the diagnosticity hypothesis, the features "European" and "American" have no diagnostic value in sets 1 and 2, although they both have a diagnostic value in sets 3 and 4. Consequently, the overall average similarity in the heterogeneous sets (3 and 4) is expected to be higher than the overall average similarity in the homogeneous sets (1 and 2). This prediction was confirmed by the data ($t(15) = 2.11$, $p < 0.05$).

In the present study all similarity assessments involve only homogeneous pairs (i.e., pairs of countries from the same continent sharing a common border). Unlike Sjöberg's[3] study, which extended the context by introducing nonhomogeneous pairs, our experiment extended the context by constructing heterogeneous sets composed of homogeneous pairs. Hence, the increase of similarity with the enlargement of context, observed in the present study, cannot be explained by subjects' tendency to equate the average similarity for any set of assessments.

The Two Faces of Similarity

According to the present analysis, the salience of features has two components: intensity and diagnosticity. The intensity of a feature is determined by perceptual and cognitive factors that are relatively stable across contexts. The diagnostic value of a feature is determined by the prevalence of the classifications that are based on it, which change with the context. The effects of context on similarity, therefore, are treated as changes in the diagnostic value of features induced by the respective changes in the grouping of the objects.

This account was supported by the experimental finding that changes in grouping (produced by the replacement or addition of objects) lead to corresponding changes in the similarity of the objects. These results shed light on the dynamic interplay between similarity and classification. It is generally assumed that classifications are determined by similarities among the objects. The preceding discussion supports the converse hypothesis: that the similarity of objects is modified by the manner in which they are classified. Thus, similarity has two faces: causal and derivative. It serves as a basis for the classification of objects, but it is also influenced by the adopted classification. The diagnosticity principle that underlies this process may provide a key to the analysis of the effects of context on similarity.

Discussion

In this section we relate the present development to the representation of objects in terms of clusters and trees, discuss the concepts of prototypicality and family resemblance, and comment on the relation between similarity and metaphor.

Features, Clusters, and Trees

There is a well-known correspondence between features or properties of objects and the classes to which the objects belong. A red flower, for example, can be characterized as having the feature "red," or as being a member of the class of red objects. In this manner, we associate with every feature in Φ the class of objects in Δ that possesses that feature. This correspondence between features and classes provides a direct link between the present theory and the clustering approach to the representation of proximity data.

In the contrast model, the similarity between objects is expressed as a function of their common and distinctive features. Relations among overlapping sets are often represented in a Venn diagram (see figure 3.1). However, this representation becomes cumbersome when the number of objects exceeds four or five. To obtain useful graphic representations of the contrast model, two alternative simplifications are entertained.

First, suppose the objects under study are all equal in prominence, that is, f(A) = f(B) for all a, b in Δ. Although this assumption is not strictly valid in general, it may serve as a reasonable approximation in certain contexts. Assuming feature additivity and symmetry, we obtain

$$S(a, b) = \theta f(A \cap B) - f(A - B) - f(B - A)$$
$$= \theta f(A \cap B) + 2f(A \cap B) - f(A - B) - f(B - A) - 2f(A \cap B)$$
$$= (\theta + 2)f(A \cap B) - f(A) - f(B)$$
$$= \lambda f(A \cap B) + \mu,$$

since f(A) = f(B) for all a, b in Δ. Under the present assumptions, therefore, similarity between objects is a linear function of the measure of their common features.

Since f is an additive measure, f(A ∩ B) is expressible as the sum of the measures of all the features that belong to both a and b. For each subset Λ of Δ, let Φ(Λ) denote the set of features that are shared by all objects in Λ and are not shared by any object that does not belong to Λ. Hence,

$$S(a, b) = \lambda f(A \cap B) + \mu$$
$$= \lambda \left(\sum f(X) \right) + \mu \quad X \in A \cap B$$
$$= \lambda \left(\sum f(\Phi(\Lambda)) \right) + \mu \quad \Lambda \supset \{a, b\}.$$

Since the summation ranges over all subsets of Δ that include both a and b, the similarity between objects can be expressed as the sum of the weights associated with all the sets that include both objects.

This form is essentially identical to the additive clustering model proposed by Shepard and Arabie.[4] These investigators have developed a computer program, ADCLUS, which selects a relatively small collection of subsets and assigns weight to each subset so as to maximize the proportion of (similarity) variance accounted for by the model. Shepard and Arabie[4] applied ADCLUS to several studies, including Shepard, Kilpatric, and Cunningham's (1975) on judgments of similarity between the integers 0 through 9 with respect to their abstract numerical character. A solution with 19 subsets accounted for 95% of the variance. The nine major subsets (with the largest weights) are displayed in table 3.1 along with a suggested interpretation. Note that all the major subsets are readily interpretable, and they are overlapping rather than hierarchical.

The above model expresses similarity in terms of common features only. Alternatively, similarity may be expressed exclusively in terms of distinctive features. It has been shown by Sattath[5] that for any symmetric contrast model with an additive measure f, there exists a measure g defined on the same feature space such that

$$S(a, b) = \theta f(A \cap B) - f(A - B) - f(B - A)$$
$$= \lambda - g(A - B) - g(B - A) \quad \text{for some } \lambda > 0.$$

Table 3.1
ADCLUS Analysis of the Similarities among the Integers 0 through 9 (from Shepard & Arabie[4])

Rank	Weight	Elements of subset	Interpretation of subset
1st	.305	2 4 8	powers of two
2nd	.288	6 7 8 9	large numbers
3rd	.279	3 6 9	multiples of three
4th	.202	0 1 2	very small numbers
5th	.202	1 3 5 7 9	odd numbers
6th	.175	1 2 3	small nonzero numbers
7th	.163	5 6 7	middle numbers (largish)
8th	.160	0 1	additive and multiplicative identities
9th	.146	0 1 2 3 4	smallish numbers

This result allows a simple representation of dissimilarity whenever the feature space Φ is a tree (i.e., whenever any three objects in Δ can be labeled so that $A \cap B = A \cap C \subset B \cap C$). Figure 3.6 presents an example of a feature tree, constructed by Sattath and Tversky (1977) from judged similarities between lowercase letters, obtained by Kuennapas and Janson (1969). The major branches are labeled to facilitate the interpretation of the tree.

Each (horizontal) arc in the graph represents the set of features shared by all the objects (i.e., letters) that follow from that arc, and the arc length corresponds to the measure of that set. The features of an object are the features of all the arcs which lead to that object, and its measure is its (horizontal) distance to the root. The tree distance between objects a and b is the (horizontal) length of the path joining them, that is, $f(A - B) + f(B - A)$. Hence, if the contrast model holds, $\alpha = \beta$, and Φ is a tree, then dissimilarity (i.e., $-S$) is expressible as tree distance.

A feature tree can also be interpreted as a hierarchical clustering scheme where each arc length represents the weight of the cluster consisting of all the objects that follow from that arc. Note that the tree in figure 3.6 differs from the common hierarchical clustering tree in that the branches differ in length. Sattath and Tversky (1977) describe a computer program, ADDTREE, for the construction of additive feature trees from similarity data and discuss its relation to other scaling methods.

It follows readily from the above discussion that if we assume both that the feature set Φ is a tree and that $f(A) = f(B)$ for all a, b in Δ, then the contrast model reduces to the well-known hierarchical clustering scheme. Hence, the additive clustering model (Shepard & Arabie[4]), the additive similarity tree (Sattath & Tversky, 1977), and the hierarchical clustering scheme (Johnson, 1967) are all special cases of the contrast model. These scaling models can thus be used to discover the common and distinctive features of the objects under study. The present

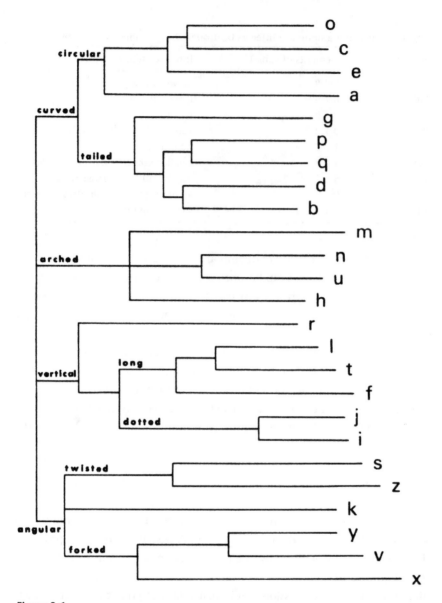

Figure 3.6
The representation of letter similarity as an additive (feature) tree. From Sattath and Tversky (1977).

development, in turn, provides theoretical foundations for the analysis of set-theoretical methods for the representation of proximities.

Similarity, Prototypicality, and Family Resemblance

Similarity is a relation of proximity that holds between two objects. There exist other proximity relations such as prototypicality and representativeness that hold between an object and a class. Intuitively, an object is prototypical if it exemplifies the category to which it belongs. Note that the prototype is not necessarily the most typical or frequent member of its class. Recent research has demonstrated the importance of prototypicality or representativeness in perceptual learning (Posner & Keele, 1968; Reed, 1972), inductive inference (Kahneman & Tversky, 1973), semantic memory (Smith, Rips, & Shoben, 1974), and the formation of categories (Rosch & Mervis, 1975). The following discussion analyzes the relations of prototypicality and family resemblance in terms of the present theory of similarity.

Let $P(a, \Lambda)$ denote the (degree of) prototypicality of object a with respect to class Λ, with cardinality n, defined by

$$P(a, \Lambda) = p_n \left(\lambda \sum f(A \cap B) - \sum (f(A - B) + f(B - A)) \right),$$

where the summations are over all b in Λ. Thus, $P(a, \Lambda)$ is defined as a linear combination (i.e., a contrast) of the measures of the features of a that are shared with the elements of Λ and the features of a that are not shared with the elements of Λ. An element a of Λ is a *prototype* if it maximizes $P(a, \Lambda)$. Note that a class may have more than one prototype.

The factor p_n reflects the effect of category size on prototypicality, and the constant λ determines the relative weights of the common and the distinctive features. If $p_n = 1/n$, $\lambda = \theta$, and $\alpha = \beta = 1$, then $P(a, \Lambda) = 1/n \sum S(a, b)$ (i.e., the prototypicality of a with respect to Λ equals the average similarity of a to all members of Λ). However, in line with the focusing hypotheses discussed earlier, it appears likely that the common features are weighted more heavily in judgments of prototypicality than in judgments of similarity.

Some evidence concerning the validity of the proposed measure was reported by Rosch and Mervis (1975). They selected 20 objects from each one of six categories (furniture, vehicle, fruit, weapon, vegetable, clothing) and instructed subjects to list the attributes associated with each one of the objects. The prototypicality of an object was defined by the number of attributes or features it shared with each member of the category. Hence, the prototypicality of a with respect to Λ was defined by $\sum N(a, b)$, where $N(a, b)$ denotes the number of attributes shared by a and b, and the summation ranges over all b in Λ. Clearly, the measure of prototypicality employed by Rosch and Mervis (1975) is a special case of the proposed measure, where λ is large and $f(A \cap B) = N(a, b)$.

These investigators also obtained direct measures of prototypicality by instructing subjects to rate each object on a 7-point scale according to the extent to which it fits the "idea or image of the meaning of the category." The rank correlations between these ratings and the above measure were quite high in all categories: furniture, 0.88; vehicle, 0.92; weapon, 0.94; fruit, 0.85; vegetable, 0.84; clothing, 0.91. The rated prototypicality of an object in a category, therefore, is predictable by the number of features it shares with other members of that category.

In contrast to the view that natural categories are definable by a conjunction of critical features, Wittgenstein (1953) argued that several natural categories (e.g., a game) do not have any attribute that is shared by all their members, and by them alone. Wittgenstein proposed that natural categories and concepts are commonly characterized and understood in terms of family resemblance, that is, a network of similarity relations that link the various members of the class. The importance of family resemblance in the formation and processing of categories has been effectively underscored by the work of Rosch and her collaborators (Rosch, 1973; Rosch & Mervis, 1975; Rosch, Mervis, Gray, Johnson, & Boyes-Braem, 1976). This research demonstrated that both natural and artificial categories are commonly perceived and organized in terms of prototypes, or focal elements, and some measure of proximity from the prototypes. Furthermore, it lent substantial support to the claim that people structure their world in terms of basic semantic categories that represent an optimal level of abstraction. Chair, for example, is a basic category; furniture is too general and kitchen chair is too specific. Similarly, car is a basic category; vehicle is too general and sedan is too specific. Rosch argued that the basic categories are selected so as to maximize family resemblance—defined in terms of cue validity.

The present development suggests the following measure for family resemblance, or category resemblance. Let Λ be some subset of Δ with cardinality n. The category resemblance of Λ denoted $R(\Lambda)$ is defined by

$$R(\Lambda) = r_n \left(\lambda \sum f(A \cap B) - \sum (f(A - B) + f(B - A)) \right),$$

the summations being over all a, b in Λ. Hence, category resemblance is a linear combination of the measures of the common and the distinctive features of all pairs of objects in that category. The factor r_n reflects the effect of category size on category resemblance, and the constant λ determines the *relative* weight of the common and distinctive features. If $\lambda = \theta$, $\alpha = \beta = 1$, and $r_n = 2/n(n-1)$, then

$$R(\Lambda) = \frac{\sum S(a, b)}{\binom{n}{2}},$$

the summation being over all a, b in Λ; that is, category resemblance equals average similarity between all members of Λ. Although the proposed measure of family resemblance differs from Rosch's, it nevertheless captures her basic notion that family resemblance is highest for those categories that "have the most attributes common to members of the category and the least attributes shared with members of other categories" (Rosch et al., 1976, p. 435).

The maximization of category resemblance could be used to explain the formation of categories. Thus, the set Λ rather than Γ is selected as a natural category whenever $R(\Lambda) > R(\Gamma)$. Equivalently, an object a is added to a category Λ whenever $R(\{\Lambda \cup a\}) > R(\Lambda)$. The fact that the preferred (basic) categories are neither the most inclusive nor the most specific imposes certain constraints on r_n.

If $r_n = 2/n(n - 1)$, then $R(\Lambda)$ equals the average similarity between all members of Λ. This index leads to the selection of minimal categories because average similarity can generally be increased by deleting elements. The average similarity between sedans, for example, is surely greater than the average similarity between cars; nevertheless, car rather than sedan serves as a basic category. If $r_n = 1$, then $R(\Lambda)$ equals the sum of the similarities between all members of Λ. This index leads to the selection of maximal categories because the addition of objects increases total similarity, provided S is nonnegative.

In order to explain the formation of intermediate-level categories, therefore, category resemblance must be a compromise between an average and a sum. That is, r_n must be a decreasing function of n that exceeds $2/n(n - 1)$. In this case, $R(\Lambda)$ increases with category size whenever average similarity is held constant, and vice versa. Thus, a considerable increase in the extension of a category could outweigh a small reduction in average similarity.

Although the concepts of similarity, prototypicality, and family resemblance are intimately connected, they have not been previously related in a formal explicit manner. The present development offers explications of similarity, prototypicality, and family resemblance within a unified framework, in which they are viewed as contrasts, or linear combinations, of the measures of the appropriate sets of common and distinctive features.

Similes and Metaphors

Similes and metaphors are essential ingredients of creative verbal expression. Perhaps the most interesting property of metaphoric expressions is that despite their novelty and nonliteral nature, they are usually understandable and often informative. For example, the statement that Mr. X resembles a bulldozer is readily understood as saying that Mr. X is a gross, powerful person who overcomes all obstacles in getting a job done. An adequate analysis of connotative meaning should account for man's ability to interpret metaphors without specific prior learning. Because the message conveyed by such expressions is often pointed and specific, they cannot be explained in terms of a few generalized dimensions of connotative meaning, such as evaluation or potency (Osgood, 1962). It appears that people interpret similes by scanning the feature space and selecting the features of the referent that are applicable to the subject (e.g., by selecting features of the bulldozer that are applicable to the person). The nature of this process is left to be explained.

There is a close tie between the assessment of similarity and the interpretation of metaphors. In judgments of similarity one assumes a particular feature space, or a frame of reference, and assesses the quality of the match between the subject and the referent. In the interpretation of similes, one assumes a resemblance between the subject and the referent and searches for an interpretation of the space that would maximize the quality of the match. The same pair of objects, therefore, can be viewed as similar or different depending on the choice of a frame of reference.

One characteristic of good metaphors is the contrast between the prior, literal interpretation, and the posterior, metaphoric interpretation. Metaphors that are too transparent are uninteresting; obscure metaphors are uninterpretable. A good metaphor is like a good detective story. The solution should not be apparent in advance to maintain the reader's interest, yet it should seem plausible after the fact to maintain coherence of the story. Consider the simile "An essay is like a fish." At first, the statement is puzzling. An essay is not expected to be fishy, slippery, or wet. The puzzle is resolved when we recall that (like a fish) an essay has a head and a body, and it occasionally ends with a flip of the tail.

This paper benefited from fruitful discussions with Y. Cohen, I. Gati, D. Kahneman, L. Sjöberg, and S. Sattath.

Notes

1. To derive feature additivity from qualitative assumptions, we must assume the axioms of an extensive structure and the compatibility of the extensive and the conjoint scales; see Krantz et al. (1971, Section 10.7).

2. The subjects in all our experiments were Israeli college students, ages 18–28. The material was presented in booklets and administered in a group setting.

3. Sjöberg, L. A cognitive theory of similarity. *Göteborg Psychological Reports* (No. 10), 1972.

4. Shepard, R. N., & Arabie, P. Additive cluster analysis of similarity data. *Proceedings of the U.S.–Japan Seminar on Theory, Methods, and Applications of Multidimensional Scaling and Related Techniques.* San Diego, August 1975.

5. Sattath, S. *An equivalence theorem.* Unpublished note, Hebrew University, 1976.

References

Beals, R., Krantz, D. H., & Tversky, A. (1968). Foundations of multidimensional scaling. *Psychological Review, 75*, 127–142.

Bush, R. R., & Mosteller, F. (1951). A model for stimulus generalization and discrimination. *Psychological Review, 58*, 413–423.

Carroll, J. D., & Wish, M. (1974). Multidimensional perceptual models and measurement methods. In E. C. Carterette & M. P. Friedman (Eds.), *Handbook of perception: Psychophysical judgment and measurement* (Vol. 2, pp. 391–447). New York, NY: Academic Press.

Eisler, H., & Ekman, G. (1959). A mechanism of subjective similarity. *Acta Psychologica, 16*, 1–10.

Garner, W. R. (1974). *The processing of information and structure.* New York, NY: Halsted Press.

Gibson, E. (1969). *Principles of perceptual learning and development.* New York, NY: Appleton-Century-Crofts.

Goldmeier, E. (1972). Similarity in visually perceived forms. *Psychological Issues, 8*, 1–136.

Gregson, R. A. M. (1975). *Psychometrics of similarity.* New York, NY: Academic Press.

Hosman, J., & Kuennapas, T. (1972). *On the relation between similarity and dissimilarity estimates* (Report No. 354). University of Stockholm, Psychological Laboratories.

Jakobson, R., Fant, G. G. M., & Halle, M. (1961). *Preliminaries to speech analysis: The distinctive features and their correlates.* Cambridge, MA: MIT Press.

Johnson, S. C. (1967). Hierarchical clustering schemes. *Psychometrika, 32*, 241–254.

Kahneman, D., & Tversky, A. (1973). On the psychology of prediction. *Psychological Review, 80*, 237–251.

Krantz, D. H., Luce, R. D., Suppes, P., & Tversky, A. (1971). *Foundations of measurement* (Vol. 1). New York, NY: Academic Press.

Krantz, D. H., & Tversky, A. (1975). Similarity of rectangles: An analysis of subjective dimensions. *Journal of Mathematical Psychology, 12*, 4–34.

Kuennapas, T., & Janson, A. J. (1969). Multidimensional similarity of letters. *Perceptual and Motor Skills, 28*, 3–12.

Neisser, U. (1967). *Cognitive psychology.* New York, NY: Appleton-Century-Crofts.

Osgood, C. E. (1962). Studies on the generality of affective meaning systems. *American Psychologist, 17*, 10–28.

Posner, M. I., & Keele, S. W. (1968). On the genesis of abstract ideas. *Journal of Experimental Psychology, 77*, 353–363.

Reed, S. K. (1972). Pattern recognition and categorization. *Cognitive Psychology, 3*, 382–407.

Restle, F. (1959). A metric and an ordering on sets. *Psychometrika, 24*, 207–220.

Restle, F. (1961). *Psychology of judgment and choice*. New York, NY: Wiley.

Rosch, E. (1973). On the internal structure of perceptual and semantic categories. In T. E. Moore (Ed.), *Cognitive development and the acquisition of language* (pp. 111–144). New York, NY: Academic Press.

Rosch, E. (1975). Cognitive reference points. *Cognitive Psychology, 7*, 532–547.

Rosch, E., & Mervis, C. B. (1975). Family resemblances: Studies in the internal structure of categories. *Cognitive Psychology, 7*, 573–603.

Rosch, E., Mervis, C. B., Gray, W., Johnson, D., & Boyes-Braem, P. (1976). Basic objects in natural categories. *Cognitive Psychology, 8*, 382–439.

Rothkopf, E. Z. (1957). A measure of stimulus similarity and errors in some paired-associate learning tasks. *Journal of Experimental Psychology, 53*, 94–101.

Sattath, S., & Tversky, A. (1977). Additive similarity trees. *Psychometrika, 42*, 319–345.

Shepard, R. N. (1964). Attention and the metric structure of the stimulus space. *Journal of Mathematical Psychology, 1*, 54–87.

Shepard, R. N. (1974). Representation of structure in similarity data: Problems and prospects. *Psychometrika, 39*, 373–421.

Shepard, R. N., Kilpatric, D. W., & Cunningham, J. P. (1975). The internal representation of numbers. *Cognitive Psychology, 7*, 82–138.

Smith, E. E., Rips, L. J., & Shoben, E. J. (1974). Semantic memory and psychological semantics. In G. H. Bower (Ed.), *The psychology of learning and motivation* (Vol. 8, pp. 1–45). New York, NY: Academic Press.

Smith, E. E., Shoben, E. J., & Rips, L. J. (1974). Structure and process in semantic memory: A featural model for semantic decisions. *Psychological Review, 81*, 214–241.

Torgerson, W. S. (1965). Multidimensional scaling of similarity. *Psychometrika, 30*, 379–393.

Tversky, A. (1972). Elimination by aspects: A theory of choice. *Psychological Review, 79*, 281–299.

Tversky, A., & Gati, I. (1978). Studies of similarity. In E. Rosch & B. Lloyd (Eds.), *On the nature and principle of formation of categories* (pp. 79–98). Hillsdale, NJ: Erlbaum.

Tversky, A., & Krantz, D. H. (1970). The dimensional representation and the metric structure of similarity data. *Journal of Mathematical Psychology, 7*, 572–597.

von Neumann, J., & Morgenstern, O. (1947). *Theory of games and economic behavior*. Princeton, NJ: Princeton University Press.

Wish, M. (1967). A model for the perception of Morse Code-like signals. *Human Factors, 9*, 529–540.

Wittgenstein, L. (1953). *Philosophical investigations*. New York, NY: Macmillan.

Appendix: An Axiomatic Theory of Similarity

Let $\Delta = \{a, b, c, \ldots\}$ be a collection of objects characterized as sets of features, and let A, B, C, denote the sets of features associated with a, b, c, respectively. Let s(a, b) be an ordinal measure of the similarity of a to b, defined for all distinct a, b in Δ. The present theory is based on the following five axioms. Because the first three axioms are discussed in the paper, they are merely restated here; the remaining axioms are briefly discussed.

1. MATCHING: $s(a, b) = F(A \cap B, A - B, B - A)$ where F is some real-valued function in three arguments.

2. MONOTONICITY: $s(a, b) \geq s(a, c)$ whenever $A \cap B \supset A \cap C$, $A - B \subset A - C$, and $B - A \subset C - A$. Moreover, if either inclusion is proper, then the inequality is strict.

Let Φ be the set of all features associated with the objects of Δ, and let X, Y, Z, etc. denote subsets of Φ. The expression F(X, Y, Z) is defined whenever there exist a, b in Δ such that $A \cap B = X$, $A - B = Y$, and $B - A = Z$, whence s(a, b) = F(X, Y, Z). Define $V \simeq W$ if one or more of the following hold for some X, Y, Z: F(V, Y, Z) = F(W, Y, Z), F(X, V, Z) = F(X, W, Z), F(X, Y, V) = F(X, Y, W). The pairs (a, b) and (c, d) *agree* on one, two, or three components, respectively, whenever one, two, or three of the following hold: $(A \cap B) \simeq (C \cap D)$, $(A - B) \simeq (C - D)$, $(B - A) \simeq (D - C)$.

3. INDEPENDENCE: Suppose the pairs (a, b) and (c, d), as well as the pairs (a', b') and (c', d'), agree on the same two components, while the pairs (a, b) and (a', b'), as well as the pairs (c, d) and (c', d'), agree on the remaining (third) component. Then

$$s(a, b) \geq s(a', b') \quad \text{iff} \quad s(c, d) \geq s(c', d').$$

4. SOLVABILITY:

(i) For all pairs (a, b), (c, d), (e, f), of objects in Δ there exists a pair (p, q) that agrees with them, respectively, on the first, second, and third components; that is, $P \cap Q \simeq A \cap B$, $P - Q \simeq C - D$, and $Q - P \simeq F - E$.

(ii) Suppose s(a, b) > t > s(c, d). Then there exist e, f with s(e, f) = t, such that if (a, b) and (c, d) agree on one or two components, then (e, f) agrees with them on these components.

(iii) There exist pairs (a, b) and (c, d) of objects in Δ that do not agree on any component.

Unlike the other axioms, solvability does not impose constraints on the similarity order; it merely asserts that the structure under study is sufficiently rich so that certain equations can be solved. The first part of axiom 4 is analogous to the existence of a factorial structure. The second part of the axiom implies that the range of s is a real interval: There exist objects in Δ

whose similarity matches any real value that is bounded by two similarities. The third part of axiom 4 ensures that all arguments of F are essential.

Let Φ_1, Φ_2, and Φ_3 be the sets of features that appear, respectively, as first, second, or third arguments of F. (Note that $\Phi_2 = \Phi_3$.) Suppose X and X′ belong to Φ_1, while Y and Y′ belong to Φ_2. Define $(X, X')_1 \simeq (Y, Y')_2$ whenever the two intervals are matched, that is, whenever there exist pairs (a, b) and (a′, b′) of equally similar objects in Δ that agree on the third factor. Thus, $(X, X')_1 \simeq (Y, Y')_2$ whenever

$$s(a, b) = F(X, Y, Z) = F(X', Y', Z) = s(a', b').$$

This definition is readily extended to any other pair of factors. Next, define $(V, V')_i \simeq (W, W')_i$, i = 1, 2, 3 whenever $(V, V')_i \simeq (X, X')_j \simeq (W, W')_i$, for some $(X, X')_j$, $j \neq i$. Thus, two intervals on the same factor are equivalent if both match the same interval on another factor. The following invariance axiom asserts that if two intervals are equivalent on one factor, then they are also equivalent on another factor.

5. INVARIANCE: Suppose V, V′, W, W′ belong to both Φ_i and Φ_j, i, j = 1, 2, 3. Then

$$(V, V')_i \simeq (W, W')_i \quad \text{iff} \quad (V, V')_j \simeq (W, W')_j.$$

Representation Theorem

Suppose axioms 1–5 hold. Then there exist a similarity scale S and a nonnegative scale f such that for all a, b, c, d in Δ

(i) $S(a, b) \geq S(c, d)$ iff $s(a, b) \geq s(c, d)$;

(ii) $S(a, b) = \theta f(A \cap B) - \alpha f(A - B) - \beta f(B - A)$, for some θ, α, $\beta \geq 0$;

(iii) f and S are interval scales.

While a self-contained proof of the representation theorem is quite long, the theorem can be readily reduced to previous results.

Recall that Φ_i is the set of features that appear as the ith argument of F, and let $\Psi_i = \Phi_i/\simeq$, i = 1, 2, 3. Thus, Ψ_i is the set of equivalence classes of Φ_i with respect to $\simeq$. It follows from axioms 1 and 3 that each Ψ_i is well defined, and it follows from axiom 4 that $\Psi = \Psi_1 \times \Psi_2 \times \Psi_3$ is equivalent to the domain of F. We wish to show that Ψ, ordered by F, is a three-component, additive conjoint structure, in the sense of Krantz, Luce, Suppes, and Tversky (1971, Section 6.11.1).

This result, however, follows from the analysis of decomposable similarity structures, developed by Tversky and Krantz (1970). In particular, the proof of part (c) of theorem 1 in that paper implies that, under axioms 1, 3, and 4, there exist nonnegative functions f_i defined on Ψ_i, i = 1, 2, 3, so that for all a, b, c, d in Δ

$s(a, b) \geq s(c, d)$ iff $S(a, b) \geq S(c, d)$

where

$S(a, b) = f_1(A \cap B) + f_2(A - B) + f_3(B - A),$

and f_1, f_2, f_3 are interval scales with a common unit.

According to axiom 5, the equivalence of intervals is preserved across factors. That is, for all V, V', W, W' in $\Phi_i \cap \Phi_j$, i, j = 1, 2, 3,

$f_i(V) - f_i(V') = f_i(W) - f_i(W')$ iff $f_j(V) - f_j(V') = f_j(W) - f_j(W').$

Hence, by part (i) of theorem 6.15 of Krantz et al. (1971), there exist a scale f and constants θ_i such that $f_i(X) = \theta_i f(X)$, i = 1, 2, 3. Finally, by axiom 2, S increases in f_1 and decreases in f_2 and f_3. Hence, it is expressible as

$S(a, b) = \theta f(A \cap B) - \alpha f(A - B) - \beta f(B - A),$

for some nonnegative constants θ, α, β.

4 Prospect Theory: An Analysis of Decision under Risk

Daniel Kahneman and Amos Tversky

Introduction

Expected utility theory has dominated the analysis of decision making under risk. It has been generally accepted as a normative model of rational choice [24] and is widely applied as a descriptive model of economic behavior (e.g., [15, 4]). Thus, it is assumed that all reasonable people would wish to obey the axioms of the theory [47, 36], and that most people actually do, most of the time.

The present chapter describes several classes of choice problems in which preferences systematically violate the axioms of expected utility theory. In light of these observations, we argue that utility theory, as it is commonly interpreted and applied, is not an adequate descriptive model of choice under risk.

Critique

Decision making under risk can be viewed as a choice between prospects or gambles. A prospect $(x_1, p_1; \ldots; x_n, p_n)$ is a contract that yields outcome x_i with probability p_i, where $p_1 + p_2 + \cdots + p_n = 1$. To simplify notation, we omit null outcomes and use (x, p) to denote the prospect $(x, p; 0, 1 - p)$ that yields x with probability p and 0 with probability $1 - p$. The (riskless) prospect that yields x with certainty is denoted by (x). The present discussion is restricted to prospects with so-called objective or standard probabilities.

The application of expected utility theory to choices between prospects is based on the following three tenets.

(i) Expectation: $U (x_1, p_1; \ldots; x_n, p_n) = p_1 u(x_1) + \cdots + p_n u(x_n)$.

That is, the overall utility of a prospect, denoted by U, is the expected utility of its outcomes.

(ii) Asset Integration: $(x_1, p_1; \ldots; x_n, p_n)$ is acceptable at asset position w iff $U (w + x_1, p_1; \ldots; w + x_n, p_n) > u(w)$.

That is, a prospect is acceptable if the utility resulting from integrating the prospect with one's assets exceeds the utility of those assets alone. Thus, the domain of the utility function is final states (which include one's asset position) rather than gains or losses.

Although the domain of the utility function is not limited to any particular class of consequences, most applications of the theory have been concerned with monetary outcomes. Furthermore, most economic applications introduce the following additional assumption.

(iii) Risk Aversion: u is concave ($u'' < 0$).

A person is risk averse if he prefers the certain prospect (x) to any risky prospect with expected value x. In expected utility theory, risk aversion is equivalent to the concavity of the utility function. The prevalence of risk aversion is perhaps the best known generalization regarding risky choices. It led the early decision theorists of the eighteenth century to propose that utility is a concave function of money, and this idea has been retained in modern treatments (Pratt [33], Arrow [4]).

In the following sections we demonstrate several phenomena that violate these tenets of expected utility theory. The demonstrations are based on the responses of students and university faculty to hypothetical choice problems. The respondents were presented with problems of the type illustrated below.

Which of the following would you prefer?

A: 50% chance to win 1,000, 50% chance to win nothing;

B: 450 for sure.

The outcomes refer to Israeli currency. To appreciate the significance of the amounts involved, note that the median net monthly income for a family is about 3,000 Israeli pounds. The respondents were asked to imagine that they were actually faced with the choice described in the problem and to indicate the decision they would have made in such a case. The responses were anonymous, and the instructions specified that there was no "correct" answer to such problems, and that the aim of the study was to find out how people choose among risky prospects. The problems were presented in questionnaire form, with at most a dozen problems per booklet. Several forms of each questionnaire were constructed so that subjects were exposed to the problems in different orders. In addition, two versions of each problem were used in which the left-right position of the prospects was reversed.

The problems described in this paper are selected illustrations of a series of effects. Every effect has been observed in several problems with different outcomes and probabilities. Some of the problems have also been presented to groups of students and faculty at the University of Stockholm and at the University of Michigan. The pattern of results was essentially identical to the results obtained from Israeli subjects.

The reliance on hypothetical choices raises obvious questions regarding the validity of the method and the generalizability of the results. We are keenly aware of these problems. However, all other methods that have been used to test utility theory also suffer from severe drawbacks. Real choices can be investigated either in the field, by naturalistic or statistical observations of economic behavior, or in the laboratory. Field studies can only provide for rather crude tests of qualitative predictions because probabilities and utilities cannot be adequately measured in such contexts. Laboratory experiments have been designed to obtain precise measures of utility and probability from actual choices, but these experimental studies typically involve contrived gambles for small stakes and a large number of repetitions of very similar problems. These features of laboratory gambling complicate the interpretation of the results and restrict their generality.

By default, the method of hypothetical choices emerges as the simplest procedure by which a large number of theoretical questions can be investigated. The use of the method relies on the assumption that people often know how they would behave in actual situations of choice, and on the further assumption that the subjects have no special reason to disguise their true preferences. If people are reasonably accurate in predicting their choices, the presence of common and systematic violations of expected utility theory in hypothetical problems provides presumptive evidence against that theory.

Certainty, Probability, and Possibility

In expected utility theory, the utilities of outcomes are weighted by their probabilities. The present section describes a series of choice problems in which people's preferences systematically violate this principle. We first show that people overweight outcomes that are considered certain, relative to outcomes that are merely probable—a phenomenon that we label the *certainty effect*.

The best known counterexample to expected utility theory, which exploits the certainty effect, was introduced by the French economist Maurice Allais in 1953 [2]. Allais's example has been discussed from both normative and descriptive standpoints by many authors [28, 38]. The following pair of choice problems is a variation of Allais's example, which differs from the original in that it refers to moderate rather than to extremely large gains. The number of respondents who answered each problem is denoted by N, and the percentage who chose each option is given in brackets.

Problem 1: Choose between

A:	2,500 with probability	0.33,	B:	2,400 with certainty.	
	2,400 with probability	0.66,			
	0 with probability	0.01;			
N = 72	[18]			[82]*	

Problem 2: Choose between

C:	2,500 with probability	0.33,	D:	2,400 with probability	0.34,
	0 with probability	0.67;		0 with probability	0.66.
$N = 72$	[83]*			[17]	

The data show that 82% of the subjects chose B in problem 1, and 83% of the subjects chose C in problem 2. Each of these preferences is significant at the 0.01 level, as denoted by the asterisk. Moreover, the analysis of individual patterns of choice indicates that a majority of respondents (61%) made the modal choice in both problems. This pattern of preferences violates expected utility theory in the manner originally described by Allais. According to that theory, with $u(0) = 0$, the first preference implies

$$u(2,400) > .33u(2,500) + .66u(2,400) \quad \text{or} \quad .34u(2,400) > .33u(2,500)$$

while the second preference implies the reverse inequality. Note that problem 2 is obtained from problem 1 by eliminating a 0.66 chance of winning 2,400 from both prospects under consideration. Evidently, this change produces a greater reduction in desirability when it alters the character of the prospect from a sure gain to a probable one than when both the original and the reduced prospects are uncertain.

A simpler demonstration of the same phenomenon, involving only two-outcome gambles, is given below. This example is also based on Allais [2].

Problem 3:

A:	(4,000, 0.80),	or B:	(3,000).
$N = 95$	[20]		[80]*

Problem 4:

C:	(4,000, 0.20),	or D:	(3,000, 0.25).
$N = 95$	[65]*		[35]

In this pair of problems as well as in all other problem-pairs in this section, over half the respondents violated expected utility theory. To show that the modal pattern of preferences in problems 3 and 4 is not compatible with the theory, set $u(0) = 0$, and recall that the choice of B implies $u(3,000)/u(4,000) > 4/5$, whereas the choice of C implies the reverse inequality. Note that the prospect $C = (4,000, 0.20)$ can be expressed as $(A, 0.25)$, while the prospect $D = (3,000, 0.25)$ can be rewritten as $(B, 0.25)$. The substitution axiom of utility theory asserts that if B is preferred to A, then any (probability) mixture (B, p) must be preferred to the mixture (A, p). Our subjects did not obey this axiom. Apparently, reducing the probability of winning from 1.0 to 0.25 has a greater effect than the reduction from 0.8 to 0.2. The following pair of choice problems illustrates the certainty effect with non-monetary outcomes.

Problem 5:

A: 50% chance to win a three-week   B: A one-week tour of
        tour of England, France, and Italy;   England with certainty.
N = 72   [22]   [78]*

Problem 6:

C: 5% chance to win a three-week   D: 10% chance to win a one-
        tour of England, France, and Italy;   week tour of England.
N = 72   [67]*   [33]

The certainty effect is not the only type of violation of the substitution axiom. Another situation in which this axiom fails is illustrated by the following problems.

Problem 7:

A: (6,000, 0.45),   B: (3,000, 0.90).
N = 66   [14]   [86]*

Problem 8:

C: (6,000, 0.001),   D: (3,000, 0.002).
N = 66   [73]*   [27]

Note that in problem 7 the probabilities of winning are substantial (0.90 and 0.45), and most people choose the prospect where winning is more probable. In problem 8, there is a *possibility* of winning, although the probabilities of winning are minuscule (0.002 and 0.001) in both prospects. In this situation where winning is possible but not probable, most people choose the prospect that offers the larger gain. Similar results have been reported by Mac-Crimmon and Larsson [28].

The above problems illustrate common attitudes toward risk or chance that cannot be captured by the expected utility model. The results suggest the following empirical generalization concerning the manner in which the substitution axiom is violated. If (y, pq) is equivalent to (x, p), then (y, pqr) is preferred to (x, pr), $0 < p, q, r < 1$. This property is incorporated into an alternative theory, developed in the second part of the chapter.

The Reflection Effect

The previous section discussed preferences between positive prospects (i.e., prospects that involve no losses). What happens when the signs of the outcomes are reversed so that gains are replaced by losses? The left-hand column of table 4.1 displays four of the choice problems that were discussed in the previous section, and the right-hand column displays choice problems in which the signs of the outcomes are reversed. We use $-x$ to denote the loss of x and > to denote the prevalent preference, i,e., the choice made by the majority of subjects.

Table 4.1
Preferences between Positive and Negative Prospects

Positive prospects				Negative prospects			
Problem 3:	(4,000, .80)	<	(3,000).	Problem 3′:	(−4,000, .80)	>	(−3,000).
N = 95	[20]		[80]*	N = 95	[92]*		[8]
Problem 4:	(4,000, .20)	>	(3,000, .25).	Problem 4′:	(4,000, .20)	<	(−3,000, .25).
N = 95	[65]*		[35]	N = 95	[42]		[58]
Problem 7:	(3,000, .90)	>	(6,000, .45).	Problem 7′:	(−3,000, .90)	<	(−6,000, .45).
N = 66	[86]*		[14]	N = 66	[8]		[92]*
Problem 8:	(3,000, .002)	<	(6,000, .001).	Problem 8′:	(−3,000, .002)	>	(−6,000, .001).
N = 66	[27]		[73]*	N = 66	[70]*		[30]

In each of the four problems in table 4.1, the preference between negative prospects is the mirror image of the preference between positive prospects. Thus, the reflection of prospects around 0 reverses the preference order. We label this pattern the *reflection effect.*

Let us turn now to the implications of these data. First, note that the reflection effect implies that risk aversion in the positive domain is accompanied by risk seeking in the negative domain. In problem 3′, for example, the majority of subjects were willing to accept a risk of 0.80 to lose 4,000, in preference to a sure loss of 3,000, although the gamble has a lower expected value. The occurrence of risk seeking in choices between negative prospects was noted early by Markowitz [29]. Williams [48] reported data where a translation of outcomes produces a dramatic shift from risk aversion to risk seeking. For example, his subjects were indifferent between (100, 0.65; −100, 0.35) and (0), indicating risk aversion. They were also indifferent between (−200, 0.80) and (−100), indicating risk seeking. A recent review by Fishburn and Kochenberger [14] documents the prevalence of risk seeking in choices between negative prospects.

Second, recall that the preferences between the positive prospects in table 4.1 are inconsistent with expected utility theory. The preferences between the corresponding negative prospects also violate the expectation principle in the same manner. For example, problems 3′ and 4′, like problems 3 and 4, demonstrate that outcomes which are obtained with certainty are overweighted relative to uncertain outcomes. In the positive domain, the certainty effect contributes to a risk-averse preference for a sure gain over a larger gain that is merely probable. In the negative domain, the same effect leads to a risk seeking preference for a loss that is merely probable over a smaller loss that is certain. The same psychological principle—the overweighting of certainty—favors risk aversion in the domain of gains and risk seeking in the domain of losses.

Third, the reflection effect eliminates aversion for uncertainty or variability as an explanation of the certainty effect. Consider, for example, the prevalent preferences for (3,000) over (4,000, 0.80) and for (4,000, 0.20) over (3,000, 0.25). To resolve this apparent inconsistency one could invoke the assumption that people prefer prospects that have high expected value and small variance (see, e.g., Allais [2]; Markowitz [30]; Tobin [41]). Because (3,000) has no variance whereas (4,000, 0.80) has large variance, the former prospect could be chosen despite its lower expected value. When the prospects are reduced, however, the difference in variance between (3,000, 0.25) and (4,000, 0.20) may be insufficient to overcome the difference in expected value. Because (−3,000) has both higher expected value and lower variance than (−4,000, 0.80), this account entails that the sure loss should be preferred, contrary to the data. Thus, our data are incompatible with the notion that certainty is generally desirable. Rather, it appears that certainty increases the aversiveness of losses as well as the desirability of gains.

Probabilistic Insurance

The prevalence of the purchase of insurance against both large and small losses has been regarded by many as strong evidence for the concavity of the utility function for money. Why otherwise would people spend so much money to purchase insurance policies at a price that exceeds the expected actuarial cost? However, an examination of the relative attractiveness of various forms of insurance does not support the notion that the utility function for money is concave everywhere. For example, people often prefer insurance programs that offer limited coverage with low or zero deductible over comparable policies that offer higher maximal coverage with higher deductibles—contrary to risk aversion (see, e.g., Fuchs [16]). Another type of insurance problem in which people's responses are inconsistent with the concavity hypothesis may be called probabilistic insurance. To illustrate this concept, consider the following problem, which was presented to 95 Stanford University students.

Problem 9: Suppose you consider the possibility of insuring some property against damage (e.g., fire or theft). After examining the risks and the premium, you find that you have no clear preference between the options of purchasing insurance or leaving the property uninsured.

It is then called to your attention that the insurance company offers a new program called *probabilistic insurance*. In this program you pay half of the regular premium. In case of damage, there is a 50% chance that you pay the other half of the premium and the insurance company covers all the losses; and there is a 50% chance that you get back your insurance payment and suffer all the losses. For example, if an accident occurs on an odd day of the month, you pay the other half of the regular premium and your losses are covered; but if the accident occurs on an even day of the month, your insurance payment is refunded and your losses are not covered.

Recall that the premium for full coverage is such that you find this insurance barely worth its cost.

Under these circumstances, would you purchase probabilistic insurance?

	Yes,	No.
$N = 95$	[20]	[80]*

Although problem 9 may appear contrived, it is worth noting that probabilistic insurance represents many forms of protective action where one pays a certain cost to reduce the probability of an undesirable event—without eliminating it altogether. The installation of a burglar alarm, the replacement of old tires, and the decision to stop smoking can all be viewed as probabilistic insurance.

The responses to problem 9 and to several other variants of the same question indicate that probabilistic insurance is generally unattractive. Apparently, reducing the probability of a loss from p to $p/2$ is less valuable than reducing the probability of that loss from $p/2$ to 0.

In contrast to these data, expected utility theory (with a concave u) implies that probabilistic insurance is superior to regular insurance. That is, if at asset position w one is just willing to pay a premium y to insure against a probability p of losing x, then one should definitely be willing to pay a smaller premium ry to reduce the probability of losing x from p to $(1 - r)p$, $0 < r < 1$. Formally, if one is indifferent between $(w - x, p; w, 1 - p)$ and $(w - y)$, then one should prefer probabilistic insurance $(w - x, (1 - r)p; w - y, rp; w - ry, 1 - p)$ over regular insurance $(w - y)$:

To prove this proposition, we show that

$$pu(w - x) + (1 - p)u(w) = u(w - y)$$

implies

$$(1 - r)pu(w - x) + rpu(w - y) + (1 - p)u(w - ry) > u(w - y).$$

Without loss of generality, we can set $u(w - x) = 0$ and $u(w) = 1$. Hence, $u(w - y) = 1 - p$, and we wish to show that

$$rp(1 - p) + (1 - p)u(w - ry) > 1 - p \quad \text{or} \quad u(w - ry) > 1 - rp$$

which holds if and only if u is concave.

This is a rather puzzling consequence of the risk-aversion hypothesis of utility theory because probabilistic insurance appears intuitively riskier than regular insurance, which entirely eliminates the element of risk. Evidently, the intuitive notion of risk is not adequately captured by the assumed concavity of the utility function for wealth.

The aversion for probabilistic insurance is particularly intriguing because all insurance is, in a sense, probabilistic. The most avid buyer of insurance remains vulnerable to many financial and other risks that his policies do not cover. There appears to be a significant difference between probabilistic insurance and what may be called contingent insurance, which provides the certainty of coverage for a specified type of risk. Compare, for example, probabilistic insurance against all forms of loss or damage to the contents of your home and contingent insurance that eliminates all risk of loss from theft, say, but does not cover other risks (e.g., fire). We conjecture that contingent insurance will be generally more attractive than probabilistic insurance when the probabilities of unprotected loss are equated. Thus, two prospects that are equivalent in probabilities and outcomes could have different values depending on their formulation. Several demonstrations of this general phenomenon are described in the next section.

The Isolation Effect

In order to simplify the choice between alternatives, people often disregard components that the alternatives share and focus on the components that distinguish them (Tversky [44]). This approach to choice problems may produce inconsistent preferences because a pair of prospects can be decomposed into common and distinctive components in more than one way, and different decompositions sometimes lead to different preferences. We refer to this phenomenon as the *isolation effect*.

Problem 10: Consider the following two-stage game. In the first stage, there is a probability of .75 to end the game without winning anything and a probability of .25 to move into the second stage. If you reach the second stage you have a choice between (4,000, .80) and (3,000).

Your choice must be made before the game starts; that is, before the outcome of the first stage is known.

Note that in this game, one has a choice between $0.25 \times 0.80 = 0.20$ chance to win 4,000, and a $0.25 \times 1.0 = 0.25$ chance to win 3,000. Thus, in terms of final outcomes and probabilities one faces a choice between (4,000, 0.20) and (3,000, 0.25), as in problem 4 above. However, the dominant preferences are different in the two problems. Of 141 subjects who answered problem 10, 78% chose the latter prospect, contrary to the modal preference in problem 4. Evidently, people ignored the first stage of the game, whose outcomes are shared by both prospects, and considered problem 10 as a choice between (3,000) and (4,000, 0.80), as in problem 3 above.

The standard and the sequential formulations of problem 4 are represented as decision trees in figures 4.1 and 4.2, respectively. Following the usual convention, squares denote decision nodes and circles denote chance nodes. The essential difference between the two representations is in the location of the decision node. In the standard form (figure 4.1), the decision maker faces a choice between two risky prospects, whereas in the sequential form

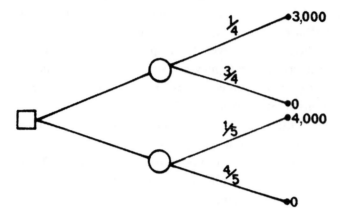

Figure 4.1
The representation of problem 4 as a decision tree (standard formulation).

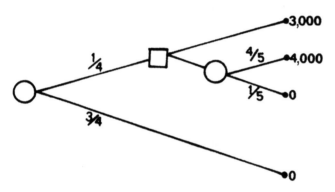

Figure 4.2
The representation of problem 10 as a decision tree (sequential formulation).

(figure 4.2) he faces a choice between a risky and a riskless prospect. This is accomplished by introducing a dependency between the prospects without changing either probabilities or outcomes. Specifically, the event "not winning 3,000" is included in the event "not winning 4,000" in the sequential formulation, whereas the two events are independent in the standard formulation. Thus, the outcome of winning 3,000 has a certainty advantage in the sequential formulation, which it does not have in the standard formulation.

The reversal of preferences due to the dependency among events is particularly significant because it violates the basic supposition of a decision-theoretical analysis: that choices between prospects are determined solely by the probabilities of final states.

It is easy to think of decision problems that are most naturally represented in one of the forms above rather than in the other. For example, the choice between two different risky ventures is likely to be viewed in the standard form. On the other hand, the following problem is most likely to be represented in the sequential form. One may invest money in a venture with some probability of losing one's capital if the venture fails, and with a choice between a fixed agreed return and a percentage of earnings if it succeeds. The isolation effect implies that the contingent certainty of the fixed return enhances the attractiveness of this option, relative to a risky venture with the same probabilities and outcomes.

The preceding problem illustrated how preferences may be altered by different representations of probabilities. We now show how choices may be altered by varying the representation of outcomes.

Consider the following problems, which were presented to two different groups of subjects.

Problem 11: In addition to whatever you own, you have been given 1,000. You are now asked to choose between

A: (1,000, 0.50),   and B: (500).
N = 70   [16]   [84]*

Problem 12: In addition to whatever you own, you have been given 2,000. You are now asked to choose between

C: (−1,000, 0.50),   and D: (−500).
N = 68   [69]*   [31]

The majority of subjects chose B in the first problem and C in the second. These preferences conform to the reflection effect observed in table 4.1, which exhibits risk aversion for positive prospects and risk seeking for negative ones. Note, however, that when viewed in terms of final states, the two choice problems are identical. Specifically,

A = (2,000, 0.50; 1,000, 0.50) = C,   and   B = (1,500) = D.

In fact, problem 12 is obtained from problem 11 by adding 1,000 to the initial bonus and subtracting 1,000 from all outcomes. Evidently, the subjects did not integrate the bonus with the prospects. The bonus did not enter into the comparison of prospects because it was common to both options in each problem.

The pattern of results observed in problems 11 and 12 is clearly inconsistent with utility theory. In that theory, for example, the same utility is assigned to a wealth of $100,000, regardless of whether it was reached from a prior wealth of $95,000 or $105,000. Consequently, the choice between a total wealth of $100,000 and even chances to own $95,000 or $105,000 should be independent of whether one currently owns the smaller or the larger of these two amounts. With the added assumption of risk aversion, the theory entails that the certainty of owning $100,000 should always be preferred to the gamble. However, the responses to problem 12 and to several of the previous questions suggest that this pattern will be obtained if the individual owns the smaller amount but not if he owns the larger amount.

The apparent neglect of a bonus that was common to both options in problems 11 and 12 implies that the carriers of value or utility are changes of wealth, rather than final asset positions that include current wealth. This conclusion is the cornerstone of an alternative theory of risky choice, which is described in the following sections.

Theory

The preceding discussion reviewed several empirical effects that appear to invalidate expected utility theory as a descriptive model. The remainder of the chapter presents an alternative account of individual decision making under risk, called prospect theory. The theory is developed for simple prospects with monetary outcomes and stated probabilities, but it can be extended to more involved choices. Prospect theory distinguishes two phases in the choice process: an early phase of editing and a subsequent phase of evaluation. The editing phase consists of a preliminary analysis of the offered prospects, which often yields a simpler representation of these prospects. In the second phase, the edited prospects are evaluated and the prospect of highest value is chosen. We next outline the editing phase and develop a formal model of the evaluation phase.

The function of the editing phase is to organize and reformulate the options so as to simplify subsequent evaluation and choice. Editing consists of the application of several operations that transform the outcomes and probabilities associated with the offered prospects. The major operations of the editing phase are described below.

Coding.   The evidence discussed in the previous section shows that people normally perceive outcomes as gains and losses, rather than as final states of wealth or welfare. Gains and losses, of course, are defined relative to some neutral reference point. The reference point usually corresponds to the current asset position, in which case gains and losses coincide with the actual amounts that are received or paid. However, the location of the reference point, and the consequent coding of outcomes as gains or losses, can be affected by the formulation of the offered prospects and the expectations of the decision maker.

Combination.   Prospects can sometimes be simplified by combining the probabilities associated with identical outcomes. For example, the prospect (200, 0.25; 200, 0.25) will be reduced to (200, 0.50) and evaluated in this form.

Segregation.   Some prospects contain a riskless component that is segregated from the risky component in the editing phase. For example, the prospect (300, 0.80; 200, 0.20) is naturally decomposed into a sure gain of 200 and the risky prospect (100, 0.80). Similarly, the prospect (−400, 0.40; −100, 0.60) is readily seen to consist of a sure loss of 100 and of the prospect (−300, 0.40).

The preceding operations are applied to each prospect separately. The following operation is applied to a set of two or more prospects.

Cancellation. The essence of the isolation effects described earlier is the discarding of components that are shared by the offered prospects. Thus, our respondents apparently ignored the first stage of the sequential game presented in problem 10 because this stage was common to both options, and they evaluated the prospects with respect to the results of the second stage (see figure 4.2). Similarly, they neglected the common bonus that was added to the prospects in problems 11 and 12. Another type of cancellation involves the discarding of common constituents (i.e., outcome–probability pairs). For example, the choice between (200, 0.20; 100, 0.50; −50, 0.30) and (200, 0.20; 150, 0.50; −100, 0.30) can be reduced by cancellation to a choice between (100, 0.50; −50, 0.30) and (150, 0.50; −100, 0.30).

Two additional operations that should be mentioned are simplification and the detection of dominance. The first refers to the simplification of prospects by rounding probabilities or outcomes. For example, the prospect (101, 0.49) is likely to be recoded as an even chance to win 100. A particularly important form of simplification involves the discarding of extremely unlikely outcomes. The second operation involves the scanning of offered prospects to detect dominated alternatives, which are rejected without further evaluation.

Because the editing operations facilitate the task of decision, it is assumed that they are performed whenever possible. However, some editing operations either permit or prevent the application of others. For example, (500, 0.20; 101, 0.49) will appear to dominate (500, 0.15; 99, 0.51) if the second constituents of both prospects are simplified to (100, 0.50). The final edited prospects could, therefore, depend on the sequence of editing operations, which is likely to vary with the structure of the offered set and the format of the display. A detailed study of this problem is beyond the scope of the present treatment. In this paper we discuss choice problems where it is reasonable to assume either that the original formulation of the prospects leaves no room for further editing or that the edited prospects can be specified without ambiguity.

Many anomalies of preference result from the editing of prospects. For example, the inconsistencies associated with the isolation effect result from the cancellation of common components. Some intransitivities of choice are explained by a simplification that eliminates small differences between prospects (see Tversky [43]). More generally, the preference order between prospects need not be invariant across contexts because the same offered prospect could be edited in different ways depending on the context in which it appears.

Following the editing phase, the decision maker is assumed to evaluate each of the edited prospects and to choose the prospect of highest value. The overall value of an edited prospect, denoted V, is expressed in terms of two scales, π and υ.

The first scale, π, associates with each probability p a decision weight $\pi(p)$, which reflects the impact of p on the overall value of the prospect. However, π is not a probability measure, and it will be shown later that $\pi(p) + \pi(1 - p)$ is typically less than unity. The second scale, υ, assigns to each outcome x a number $\upsilon(x)$, which reflects the subjective value of that outcome. Recall that outcomes are defined relative to a reference point, which serves as the zero point of the value scale. Hence, υ measures the value of deviations from that reference point (i.e., gains and losses).

The present formulation is concerned with simple prospects of the form $(x, p; y, q)$, which have at most two non-zero outcomes. In such a prospect, one receives x with probability p, y with probability q, and nothing with probability $1 - p - q$, where $p + q \leq 1$. An offered prospect is strictly positive if its outcomes are all positive (i.e., if $x, y > 0$ and $p + q = 1$); it is strictly negative if its outcomes are all negative. A prospect is regular if it is neither strictly positive nor strictly negative.

The basic equation of the theory describes the manner in which π and υ are combined to determine the overall value of regular prospects.

If $(x, p; y, q)$ is a regular prospect (i.e., either $p + q < 1$, $x \geq 0 \geq y$, or $x \leq 0 \leq y$), then

$$V(x, p; y, q) = \pi(p)\upsilon(x) + \pi(q)\upsilon(y) \tag{1}$$

where $\upsilon(0) = 0$, $\pi(0) = 0$, and $\pi(1) = 1$. As in utility theory, V is defined on prospects, whereas υ is defined on outcomes. The two scales coincide for sure prospects, where $V(x, 1.0) = V(x) = \upsilon(x)$.

Equation (1) generalizes expected utility theory by relaxing the expectation principle. An axiomatic analysis of this representation is sketched in the appendix, which describes conditions that ensure the existence of a unique π and a ratio-scale υ satisfying equation (1).

The evaluation of strictly positive and strictly negative prospects follows a different rule. In the editing phase such prospects are segregated into two components: (i) the riskless component (i.e., the minimum gain or loss that is certain to be obtained or paid); and (ii) the risky component (i.e., the additional gain or loss that is actually at stake). The evaluation of such prospects is described in the next equation.

If $p + q = 1$ and either $x > y > 0$ or $x < y < 0$, then

$$V(x, p; y, q) = \upsilon(y) + \pi(p)[\upsilon(x) - \upsilon(y)]. \tag{2}$$

That is, the value of a strictly positive or strictly negative prospect equals the value of the riskless component plus the value difference between the outcomes, multiplied by the weight associated with the more extreme outcome. For example, $V(400, 0.25; 100, 0.75)$

= $v(100) + \pi(0.25)[v(400) - v(100)]$. The essential feature of equation (2) is that a decision weight is applied to the value difference $v(x) - v(y)$, which represents the risky component of the prospect, but not to $v(y)$, which represents the riskless component. Note that the right-hand side of equation (2) equals $\pi(p)v(x) + [1 - \pi(p)]v(y)$. Hence, equation (2) reduces to equation (1) if $\pi(p) + \pi(1 - p) = 1$. As will be shown later, this condition is not generally satisfied.

Many elements of the evaluation model have appeared in previous attempts to modify expected utility theory. Markowitz [29] was the first to propose that utility be defined on gains and losses rather than on final asset positions, an assumption that has been implicitly accepted in most experimental measurements of utility (see, e.g., [7, 32]). Markowitz also noted the presence of risk seeking in preferences among positive as well as among negative prospects, and he proposed a utility function that has convex and concave regions in both the positive and negative domains. His treatment, however, retains the expectation principle; hence, it cannot account for the many violations of this principle; see, e.g., table 4.1.

The replacement of probabilities by more general weights was proposed by Edwards [9], and this model was investigated in several empirical studies (e.g., [3, 42]). Similar models were developed by Fellner [12], who introduced the concept of decision weight to explain aversion for ambiguity, and by van Dam [46], who attempted to scale decision weights. For other critical analyses of expected utility theory and alternative choice models, see Allais [2], Coombs [6], Fishburn [13], and Hansson [22].

The equations of prospect theory retain the general bilinear form that underlies expected utility theory. However, in order to accommodate the effects described in the first part of the paper, we are compelled to assume that values are attached to changes rather than to final states, and that decision weights do not coincide with stated probabilities. These departures from expected utility theory must lead to normatively unacceptable consequences, such as inconsistencies, intransitivities, and violations of dominance. Such anomalies of preference are normally corrected by the decision maker when he realizes that his preferences are inconsistent, intransitive, or inadmissible. In many situations, however, the decision maker does not have the opportunity to discover that his preferences could violate decision rules that he wishes to obey. In these circumstances the anomalies implied by prospect theory are expected to occur.

The Value Function

An essential feature of the present theory is that the carriers of value are changes in wealth or welfare, rather than final states. This assumption is compatible with basic principles of perception and judgment. Our perceptual apparatus is attuned to the evaluation of changes or differences rather than to the evaluation of absolute magnitudes. When we respond to attributes such as brightness, loudness, or temperature, the past and present contexts of experience define an adaptation level, or reference point, and stimuli are perceived in relation to this reference point [23]. Thus, an object at a given temperature may be experienced as hot or cold to the touch depending on the temperature to which one has adapted. The same principle applies to non-sensory attributes such as health, prestige, and wealth. The same level of wealth, for example, may imply abject poverty for one person and great riches for another—depending on their current assets.

The emphasis on changes as the carriers of value should not be taken to imply that the value of a particular change is independent of initial position. Strictly speaking, value should be treated as a function in two arguments: the asset position that serves as a reference point, and the magnitude of the change (positive or negative) from that reference point. An individual's attitude to money, say, could be described by a book, where each page presents the value function for changes at a particular asset position. Clearly, the value functions described on different pages are not identical: they are likely to become more linear with increases in assets. However, the preference order of prospects is not greatly altered by small or even moderate variations in asset position. The certainty equivalent of the prospect (1,000, 0.50), for example, lies between 300 and 400 for most people, in a wide range of asset positions. Consequently, the representation of value as a function in one argument generally provides a satisfactory approximation.

Many sensory and perceptual dimensions share the property that the psychological response is a concave function of the magnitude of physical change. For example, it is easier to discriminate between a change of 3° and a change of 6° in room temperature than it is to discriminate between a change of 13° and a change of 16°. We propose that this principle applies in particular to the evaluation of monetary changes. Thus, the difference in value between a gain of 100 and a gain of 200 appears to be greater than the difference between a gain of 1,100 and a gain of 1,200. Similarly, the difference between a loss of 100 and a loss of 200 appears greater than the difference between a loss of 1,100 and a loss of 1,200, unless the larger loss is intolerable. Thus, we hypothesize that the value function for changes of wealth is normally concave above the reference point ($v''(x) < 0$, for $x > 0$) and often convex below it ($v''(x) > 0$, for $x < 0$). That is, the marginal value of both gains and losses generally decreases with their magnitude. Some support for this hypothesis has been reported by Galanter and Pliner [17], who scaled the perceived magnitude of monetary and non-monetary gains and losses.

The above hypothesis regarding the shape of the value function was based on responses to gains and losses in a riskless context. We propose that the value function which is derived from risky choices shares the same characteristics, as illustrated in the following problems.

Problem 13:

(6,000, 0.25),   or   (4,000, 0.25; 2,000, 0.25).

$N = 68$ [18]   [82]*

Problem 13':

(−6,000, 0.25),   or   (−4,000, 0.25; −2,000, 0.25).

$N = 64$ [70]*   [30]

Applying equation (1) to the modal preference in these problems yields

$$\pi(.25)v(6,000) < \pi(.25)[v(4,000) + v(2,000)]$$

and

$$\pi(.25)v(-6,000) > \pi(.25)[v(-4,000) + v(-2,000)].$$

Hence, $v(6,000) < v(4,000) + v(2,000)$ and $v(-6,000) > v(-4,000) + v(-2,000)$. These preferences are in accord with the hypothesis that the value function is concave for gains and convex for losses.

Any discussion of the utility function for money must leave room for the effect of special circumstances on preferences. For example, the utility function of an individual who needs $60,000 to purchase a house may reveal an exceptionally steep rise near the critical value. Similarly, an individual's aversion to losses may increase sharply near the loss that would compel him to sell his house and move to a less desirable neighborhood. Hence, the derived value (utility) function of an individual does not always reflect "pure" attitudes to money because it could be affected by additional consequences associated with specific amounts. Such perturbations can readily produce convex regions in the value function for gains and concave regions in the value function for losses. The latter case may be more common because large losses often necessitate changes in life style.

A salient characteristic of attitudes to changes in welfare is that losses loom larger than gains. The aggravation that one experiences in losing a sum of money appears to be greater than the pleasure associated with gaining the same amount [17]. Indeed, most people find symmetric bets of the form $(x, 0.50; -x, 0.50)$ distinctly unattractive. Moreover, the aversiveness of symmetric fair bets generally increases with the size of the stake. That is, if $x > y \geq 0$, then $(y, 0.50; -y, 0.50)$ is preferred to $(x, 0.50; -x, 0.50)$. According to equation (1), therefore,

$$v(y) + v(-y) > v(x) + v(-x) \quad \text{and} \quad v(-y) - v(-x) > v(x) - v(y).$$

Setting $y = 0$ yields $v(x) < -v(-x)$, and letting y approach x yields $v'(x) < v'(-x)$, provided v', the derivative of v, exists. Thus, the value function for losses is steeper than the value function for gains.

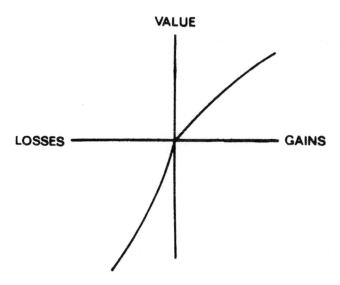

Figure 4.3
A hypothetical value function.

In summary, we have proposed that the value function is (i) defined on deviations from the reference point, (ii) generally concave for gains and commonly convex for losses, and (iii) steeper for losses than for gains. A value function that satisfies these properties is displayed in figure 4.3. Note that the proposed S-shaped value function is steepest at the reference point, in marked contrast to the utility function postulated by Markowitz [29], which is relatively shallow in that region.

Although the present theory can be applied to derive the value function from preferences between prospects, the actual scaling is considerably more complicated than in utility theory because of the introduction of decision weights. For example, decision weights could produce risk aversion and risk seeking even with a linear value function. Nevertheless, it is of interest that the main properties ascribed to the value function have been observed in a detailed analysis of von Neumann–Morgenstern utility functions for changes of wealth (Fishburn and Kochenberger [14]). The functions had been obtained from thirty decision makers in various fields of business in five independent studies [5, 18, 19, 21, 40]. Most utility functions for gains were concave, most functions for losses were convex, and only three individuals exhibited risk aversion for both gains and losses. With a single exception, utility functions were considerably steeper for losses than for gains.

The Weighting Function

In prospect theory, the value of each outcome is multiplied by a decision weight. Decision weights are inferred from choices between prospects much as subjective probabilities are inferred from preferences in the Ramsey–Savage approach. However, decision weights are not probabilities: they do not obey the probability axioms and they should not be interpreted as measures of degree or belief.

Consider a gamble in which one can win 1,000 or nothing, depending on the toss of a fair coin. For any reasonable person, the probability of winning is 0.50 in this situation. This can be verified in a variety of ways; for example, by showing that the subject is indifferent between betting on heads or tails, or by his verbal report that he considers the two events equiprobable. As will be shown below, however, the decision weight $\pi(0.50)$, which is derived from choices, is likely to be smaller than 0.50. Decision weights measure the impact of events on the desirability of prospects and not merely the perceived likelihood of these events. The two scales coincide (i.e., $\pi(p) = p$) if the expectation principle holds, but not otherwise.

The choice problems discussed in the present paper were formulated in terms of explicit numerical probabilities, and our analysis assumes that the respondents adopted the stated values of p. Furthermore, because the events were identified only by their stated probabilities, it is possible in this context to express decision weights as a function of stated probability. In general, however, the decision weight attached to an event could be influenced by other factors (e.g., ambiguity [10, 11]).

We turn now to discuss the salient properties of the weighting function π, which relates decision weights to stated probabilities. Naturally, π is an increasing function of p, with $\pi(0) = 0$ and $\pi(1) = 1$. That is, outcomes contingent on an impossible event are ignored, and the scale is normalized so that $\pi(p)$ is the ratio of the weight associated with the probability p to the weight associated with the certain event.

We first discuss some properties of the weighting function for small probabilities. The preferences in problems 8 and 8' suggest that for small values of p, π is a subadditive function of p (i.e., $\pi(rp) > r\pi(p)$ for $0 < r < 1$). Recall that in problem 8, (6,000, 0.001) is preferred to (3,000, 0.002). Hence,

$$\frac{\pi(.001)}{\pi(.002)} > \frac{v(3,000)}{v(6,000)} > \frac{1}{2} \quad \text{by the concavity of } v.$$

The reflected preferences in problem 8' yield the same conclusion. The pattern of preferences in problems 7 and 7', however, suggests that subadditivity need not hold for large values of p.

Furthermore, we propose that very low probabilities are generally overweighted, that is, $\pi(p) > p$ for small p. Consider the following choice problems.

Problem 14:

    (5,000, 0.001),   or   (5).
N = 72   [72]*   [28]

Problem 14′:

    (−5,000, 0.001),   or   (−5).
N = 72   [17]   [83]*

Note that in problem 14, people prefer what is in effect a lottery ticket over the expected value of that ticket. In problem 14′, by contrast, they prefer a small loss, which can be viewed as the payment of an insurance premium over a small probability of a large loss. Similar observations have been reported by Markowitz [29]. In the present theory, the preference for the lottery in problem 14 implies $\pi(0.001)v(5,000) > v(5)$, hence, $\pi(0.001) > v(5)/v(5,000) > 0.001$, assuming the value function for gains is concave. The readiness to pay for insurance in problem 14′ implies the same conclusion, assuming the value function for losses is convex.

It is important to distinguish overweighting, which refers to a property of decision weights, from the overestimation that is commonly found in the assessment of the probability of rare events. Note that the issue of overestimation does not arise in the present context, where the subject is assumed to adopt the stated value of p. In many real-life situations, overestimation and overweighting may both operate to increase the impact of rare events.

Although $\pi(p) > p$ for low probabilities, evidence suggests that, for all $0 < p < 1$, $\pi(p) + \pi(1 -p) < 1$. We label this property subcertainty. It is readily seen that the typical preferences in any version of Allais's example (see, e.g., problems 1 and 2) imply subcertainty for the relevant value of p. Applying equation (1) to the prevalent preferences in problems 1 and 2 yields, respectively,

$$v(2,400) > \pi(.66)v(2,400) + \pi(.33)v(2,500),$$

that is,

$$[1 - \pi(.66]v(2,400) > \pi(.33)v(2,500);$$

and

$$\pi(.33)v(2,500) > \pi(.34)v(2,400).$$

Hence,

$$1 - \pi(.66) > \pi(.34), \quad \text{or} \quad \pi(.66) + \pi(.34) < 1.$$

Applying the same analysis to Allais's original example yields $\pi(0.89) + \pi(0.11) < 1$, and some data reported by MacCrimmon and Larsson [28] imply subcertainty for additional values of p.

The slope of π in the interval (0, 1) can be viewed as a measure of the sensitivity of preferences to changes in probability. Subcertainty entails that π is regressive with respect to p; that is, that preferences are generally less sensitive to variations of probability than the expectation principle would dictate. Thus, subcertainty captures an essential element of people's attitudes to uncertain events; namely, that the sum of the weights associated with complementary events is typically less than the weight associated with the certain event.

Recall that the violations of the substitution axiom discussed earlier in this paper conform to the following rule: If (x, p) is equivalent to (y, pq), then (x, pr) is not preferred to (y, pqr), $0 < p, q, r \le 1$. By equation (1),

$$\pi(p)v(x) = \pi(pq)v(y) \quad \text{implies} \quad \pi(pr)v(x) \le \pi(pqr)v(y);$$

hence,

$$\frac{\pi(pq)}{\pi(p)} \le \frac{\pi(pqr)}{\pi(pr)}.$$

Thus, for a fixed ratio of probabilities, the ratio of the corresponding decision weights is closer to unity when the probabilities are low than when they are high. This property of π, called subproportionality, imposes considerable constraints on the shape of π: it holds if and only if log π is a convex function of log p.

It is of interest to note that subproportionality together with the overweighting of small probabilities imply that π is subadditive over that range. Formally, it can be shown that if $\pi(p) > p$ and subproportionality holds, then $\pi(rp) > r\pi(p)$, $0 < r < 1$, provided p is monotone and continuous over (0, 1).

Figure 4.4 presents a hypothetical weighting function that satisfies overweighting and subadditivity for small values of p, as well as subcertainty and subproportionality. These properties entail that π is relatively shallow in the open interval and changes abruptly near the end points where $\pi(0) = 0$ and $\pi(1) = 1$. The sharp drops or apparent discontinuities of π at the end points are consistent with the notion that there is a limit to how small a decision weight can be attached to an event, if it is given any weight at all. A similar quantum of doubt could impose an upper limit on any decision weight that is less than unity. This quantal effect may reflect the categorical distinction between certainty and uncertainty. However, the simplification of prospects in the editing phase can lead the individual to discard events of extremely low probability and to treat events of extremely high probability as if they were certain. Because people are limited in their ability to comprehend and evaluate extreme probabilities, highly unlikely events are either ignored or overweighted, and the difference between high probability and certainty is either neglected or exaggerated. Consequently, π is not well behaved near the end points.

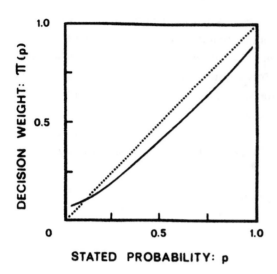

Figure 4.4
A hypothetical weighting function.

The following example, due to Zeckhauser, illustrates the hypothesized nonlinearity of π. Suppose you are compelled to play Russian roulette but are given the opportunity to purchase the removal of one bullet from the loaded gun. Would you pay as much to reduce the number of bullets from four to three as you would to reduce the number of bullets from one to zero? Most people feel that they would be willing to pay much more for a reduction of the probability of death from 1/6 to zero than for a reduction from 4/6 to 3/6. Economic considerations would lead one to pay more in the latter case, where the value of money is presumably reduced by the considerable probability that one will not live to enjoy it.

An obvious objection to the assumption that $\pi(p) \neq p$ involves comparisons between prospects of the form $(x, p; x, q)$ and $(x, p'; x, q')$, where $p + q = p' + q' < 1$. Because any individual will surely be indifferent between the two prospects, it could be argued that this observation entails $\pi(p) + \pi(q) = \pi(p') + \pi(q')$, which in turn implies that π is the identity function. This argument is invalid in the present theory, which assumes that the probabilities of identical outcomes are combined in the editing of prospects. A more serious objection to the nonlinearity of π involves potential violations of dominance. Suppose $x > y > 0$, $p > p'$, and $p + q = p' + q' < 1$; hence, $(x, p; y, q)$ dominates $(x, p'; y, q')$. If preference obeys dominance, then

$$\pi(p)v(x) + \pi(q)v(y) > \pi(p')v(x) + \pi(q')v(y),$$

or

$$\frac{\pi(p) - \pi(p')}{\pi(q') - \pi(q)} > \frac{\upsilon(y)}{\upsilon(x)}.$$

Hence, as y approaches x, $\pi(p) - \pi(p')$ approaches $\pi(q') - \pi(q)$. Because $p - p' = q' - q$, π must be essentially linear, or else dominance must be violated.

Direct violations of dominance are prevented, in the present theory, by the assumption that dominated alternatives are detected and eliminated prior to the evaluation of prospects. However, the theory permits indirect violations of dominance, such as triples of prospects so that A is preferred to B, B is preferred to C, and C dominates A. For an example, see Raiffa [34, p. 75].

Finally, it should be noted that the present treatment concerns the simplest decision task in which a person chooses between two available prospects. We have not treated in detail the more complicated production task (e.g., bidding) where the decision maker generates an alternative that is equal in value to a given prospect. The asymmetry between the two options in this situation could introduce systematic biases. Indeed, Lichtenstein and Slovic [27] have constructed pairs of prospects A and B, such that people generally prefer A over B but bid more for B than for A. This phenomenon has been confirmed in several studies, with both hypothetical and real gambles (see, e.g., Grether and Plott [20]). Thus, it cannot be generally assumed that the preference order of prospects can be recovered by a bidding procedure.

Because prospect theory has been proposed as a model of choice, the inconsistency of bids and choices implies that the measurement of values and decision weights should be based on choices between specified prospects rather than on bids or other production tasks. This restriction makes the assessment of υ and π more difficult because production tasks are more convenient for scaling than pair comparisons.

Discussion

In the final section we show how prospect theory accounts for observed attitudes toward risk, discuss alternative representations of choice problems induced by shifts of reference point, and sketch several extensions of the present treatment.

Risk Attitudes

The dominant pattern of preferences observed in Allais's example (problems 1 and 2) follows from the present theory iff

$$\frac{\pi(.33)}{\pi(.34)} > \frac{\upsilon(2,400)}{\upsilon(2,500)} > \frac{\pi(.33)}{1 - \pi(.66)}.$$

Hence, the violation of the independence axiom is attributed in this case to subcertainty, and more specifically to the inequality $\pi(0.34) < 1 - \pi(0.66)$. This analysis shows that an Allais-type violation will occur whenever the v-ratio of the two non-zero outcomes is bounded by the corresponding π-ratios.

Problems 3 through 8 share the same structure; hence, it suffices to consider one pair, say problems 7 and 8. The observed choices in these problems are implied by the theory iff

$$\frac{\pi(.001)}{\pi(.002)} > \frac{v(3,000)}{v(6,000)} > \frac{\pi(.45)}{\pi(.90)}.$$

The violation of the substitution axiom is attributed in this case to the subproportionality of π. Expected utility theory is violated in the above manner, therefore, whenever the v-ratio of the two outcomes is bounded by the respective π-ratios. The same analysis applies to other violations of the substitution axiom, in both the positive and the negative domain.

We next prove that the preference for regular insurance over probabilistic insurance, observed in Problem 9, follows from prospect theory—provided the probability of loss is overweighted. That is, if $(-x, p)$ is indifferent to $(-y)$, then $(-y)$ is preferred to $(-x, p/2; -y, p/2; -y/2, 1 -p)$. For simplicity, we define for $x \geq 0$, $f(x) = -v(-x)$. Because the value function for losses is convex, f is a concave function of x. Applying prospect theory, with the natural extension of equation 2, we wish to show that

$$\pi(p)f(x) = f(y)$$

implies

$$f(y) \leq f(y/2) + \pi(p/2)[f(y) - f(y/2)] + \pi(p/2)[f(x) - f(y/2)]$$
$$= \pi(p/2)f(x) + \pi(p/2)f(y) + [1 - 2\pi(p/2)]f(y/2).$$

Substituting for $f(x)$ and using the concavity of f, it suffices to show that

$$f(y) \leq \frac{\pi(p/2)}{\pi(p)}f(y) + \pi(p/2)f(y) + f(y)/2 - \pi(p/2)f(y)$$

or

$$\pi(p)/2 \leq \pi(p/2),$$

which follows from the subadditivity of π.

According to the present theory, attitudes toward risk are determined jointly by v and π, and not solely by the utility function. It is therefore instructive to examine the conditions under which risk aversion or risk seeking are expected to occur. Consider the choice between the gamble (x, p) and its expected value (px). If $x > 0$, risk seeking is implied whenever $\pi(p) > v(px)/v(x)$, which is greater than p if the value function for gains is concave. Hence, overweighting ($\pi(p) > p$) is necessary but not sufficient for risk seeking in the domain of gains. Precisely the same condition is necessary but not sufficient for risk aversion when $x < 0$. This analysis restricts risk seeking in the domain of gains and risk aversion in the domain of losses to small probabilities, where overweighting is expected to hold. Indeed these are the typical conditions under which lottery tickets and insurance policies are sold. In prospect theory, the overweighting of small probabilities favors both gambling and insurance, whereas the S-shaped value function tends to inhibit both behaviors.

Although prospect theory predicts both insurance and gambling for small probabilities, we feel that the present analysis falls far short of a fully adequate account of these complex phenomena. Indeed, there is evidence from both experimental studies [37], survey research [26], and observations of economic behavior such as service and medical insurance, that the purchase of insurance often extends to the medium range of probabilities, and that small probabilities of disaster are sometimes entirely ignored. Furthermore, the evidence suggests that minor changes in the formulation of the decision problem can have marked effects on the attractiveness of insurance [37]. A comprehensive theory of insurance behavior should consider, in addition to pure attitudes toward uncertainty and money, such factors as the value of security, social norms of prudence, the aversiveness of a large number of small payments spread over time, information and misinformation regarding probabilities and outcomes, and many others. Some effects of these variables could be described within the present framework; for example, as changes of reference point, transformations of the value function, or manipulations of probabilities or decision weights. Other effects may require the introduction of variables or concepts that have not been considered in this treatment.

Shifts of Reference

So far in this paper, gains and losses were defined by the amounts of money that are obtained or paid when a prospect is played, and the reference point was taken to be the status quo, or one's current assets. Although this is probably true for most choice problems, there are situations in which gains and losses are coded relative to an expectation or aspiration level that differs from the status quo. For example, an unexpected tax withdrawal from a monthly pay check is experienced as a loss, not as a reduced gain. Similarly, an entrepreneur who is weathering a slump with greater success than his competitors may interpret a small loss as a gain, relative to the larger loss he had reason to expect.

The reference point in the preceding examples corresponded to an asset position that one had expected to attain. A discrepancy between the reference point and the current asset position may also arise because of recent changes in wealth to which one has not yet adapted [29]. Imagine a person who is involved in a business venture, has already lost 2,000, and is now facing a choice between a sure gain of 1,000 and an even chance to win 2,000 or nothing.

If he has not yet adapted to his losses, he is likely to code the problem as a choice between (−2,000, 0.50) and (−1,000) rather than as a choice between (2,000, 0.50) and (1,000). As we have seen, the former representation induces more adventurous choices than the latter.

A change of reference point alters the preference order for prospects. In particular, the present theory implies that a negative translation of a choice problem, such as arises from incomplete adaptation to recent losses, increases risk seeking in some situations. Specifically, if a risky prospect $(x, p; -y, 1 - p)$ is just acceptable, then $(x - z, p; y - z, 1 - p)$ is preferred over $(-z)$ for $x, y, z > 0$, with $x > z$.

To prove this proposition, note that

$$V(x, p; y, 1 - p) = 0 \quad \text{iff} \quad \pi(p)v(x) = -\pi(1 - p)v(-y).$$

Furthermore,

$$
\begin{aligned}
V(x &- z, p; -y - z, 1 - p) \\
&= \pi(p)v(x - z) + \pi(1 - p)v(-y - z) \\
&> \pi(p)v(x) - \pi(p)v(z) + \pi(1 - p)v(-y) \\
&\quad + \pi(1 - p)v(-z) \quad \text{by the properties of } v, \\
&= -\pi(1 - p)v(-y) - \pi(p)v(z) + \pi(1 - p)v(-y) \\
&\quad + \pi(1 - p)v(-z) \quad \text{by substitution,} \\
&= -\pi(p)v(z) + \pi(1 - p)v(-z) \\
&> v(-z)[\pi(p) + \pi(1 - p)] \quad \text{since } v(-z) < -v(z), \\
&> v(-z) \quad \text{by subcertainty.}
\end{aligned}
$$

This analysis suggests that a person who has not made peace with his losses is likely to accept gambles that would be unacceptable to him otherwise. The well-known observation [31] that the tendency to bet on long shots increases in the course of the betting day provides some support for the hypothesis that a failure to adapt to losses or to attain an expected gain induces risk seeking. For another example, consider an individual who expects to purchase insurance, perhaps because he has owned it in the past or because his friends do. This individual may code the decision to pay a premium y to protect against a loss x as a choice between $(-x + y, p; y, 1 - p)$ and (0) rather than as a choice between $(-x, p)$ and $(-y)$. The preceding argument entails that insurance is likely to be more attractive in the former representation than in the latter.

Another important case of a shift of reference point arises when a person formulates his decision problem in terms of final assets, as advocated in decision analysis, rather than in terms of gains and losses, as people usually do. In this case, the reference point is set to zero on the scale of wealth and the value function is likely to be concave everywhere [39]. According to the present analysis, this formulation essentially eliminates risk seeking, except for gambling with low probabilities. The explicit formulation of decision problems in terms of final assets is perhaps the most effective procedure for eliminating risk seeking in the domain of losses.

Many economic decisions involve transactions in which one pays money in exchange for a desirable prospect. Current decision theories analyze such problems as comparisons between the status quo and an alternative state that includes the acquired prospect minus its cost. For example, the decision whether to pay 10 for the gamble (1,000, 0.01) is treated as a choice between (990, 0.01; −10, 0.99) and (0). In this analysis, readiness to purchase the positive prospect is equated to willingness to accept the corresponding mixed prospect.

The prevalent failure to integrate riskless and risky prospects, dramatized in the isolation effect, suggests that people are unlikely to perform the operation of subtracting the cost from the outcomes in deciding whether to buy a gamble. Instead, we suggest that people usually evaluate the gamble and its cost separately and decide to purchase the gamble if the combined value is positive. Thus, the gamble (1,000, 0.01) will be purchased for a price of 10 if $\pi(0.01)v(1,000) + v(-10) > 0$.

If this hypothesis is correct, the decision to pay 10 for (1,000, 0.01), for example, is no longer equivalent to the decision to accept the gamble (990, 0.01; −10, 0.99). Furthermore, prospect theory implies that if one is indifferent between $(x(1 - p), p; -px, 1 - p)$ and (0), then one will not pay px to purchase the prospect (x, p). Thus, people are expected to exhibit more risk seeking in deciding whether to accept a fair gamble than in deciding whether to purchase a gamble for a fair price. The location of the reference point and the manner in which choice problems are coded and edited emerge as critical factors in the analysis of decisions.

Extensions

In order to encompass a wider range of decision problems, prospect theory should be extended in several directions. Some generalizations are immediate; others require further development. The extension of equations (1) and (2) to prospects with any number of outcomes is straightforward. When the number of outcomes is large, however, additional editing operations may be invoked to simplify evaluation. The manner in which complex options such as compound prospects are reduced to simpler ones is yet to be investigated.

Although the present chapter has been concerned mainly with monetary outcomes, the theory is readily applicable to choices involving other attributes; for example, quality of life or the number of lives that could be lost or saved as a consequence of a policy decision. The main properties of the proposed value function for money should apply to other attributes as well. In particular, we expect outcomes to be coded as gains or losses relative to a neutral reference point and losses to loom larger than gains.

The theory can also be extended to the typical situation of choice, where the probabilities of outcomes are not explicitly given. In such situations, decision weights must be attached to particular events rather than to stated probabilities, but they are expected to exhibit the essential properties that were ascribed to the weighting function. For example, if A and B are complementary events and neither is certain, $\pi(A) + \pi(B)$ should be less than unity—a natural analogue to subcertainty.

The decision weight associated with an event will depend primarily on the perceived likelihood of that event, which could be subject to major biases [45]. In addition, decision weights may be affected by other considerations, such as ambiguity or vagueness. Indeed, the work of Ellsberg [10] and Fellner [12] implies that vagueness reduces decision weights. Consequently, subcertainty should be more pronounced for vague than for clear probabilities.

The present analysis of preference between risky options has developed two themes. The first theme concerns editing operations that determine how prospects are perceived. The second theme involves the judgmental principles that govern the evaluation of gains and losses and the weighting of uncertain outcomes. Although both themes should be developed further, they appear to provide a useful framework for the descriptive analysis of choice under risk.

Appendix

In this appendix we sketch an axiomatic analysis of prospect theory. Because a complete self-contained treatment is long and tedious, we merely outline the essential steps and exhibit the key ordinal properties needed to establish the bilinear representation of equation (1). Similar methods could be extended to axiomatize equation (2).

Consider the set of all regular prospects of the form $(x, p; y, q)$ with $p + q < 1$. The extension to regular prospects with $p + q = 1$ is straightforward. Let $\gtrsim$ denote the relation of preference between prospects that is assumed to be connected, symmetric, and transitive, and let $\simeq$ denote the associated relation of indifference. Naturally, $(x, p; y, q) \simeq (y, q; x, p)$. We also assume, as is implicit in our notation, that $(x, p; 0, q) \simeq (x, p; 0, r)$ and $(x, p; y, 0) \simeq (x, p; z, 0)$. That is, the null outcome and the impossible event have the property of a multiplicative zero.

Note that the desired representation (equation (1)) is additive in the probability–outcome pairs. Hence, the theory of additive conjoint measurement can be applied to obtain a scale V, which preserves the preference order, and interval scales f and g in two arguments such that

$$V(x, p; y, q) = f(x, p) + g(y, q).$$

The key axioms used to derive this representation are:

Independence: $(x, p; y, q) \succsim (x, p; y' \, q')$ iff $(x', p'; y, q) \succsim (x', p'; y', q')$.

Cancellation: If $(x, p; y' \, q') \succsim (x', p'; y, q)$ and $(x', p'; y'', q'') \succsim (x'', p''; y', q')$, then $(x, p; y'', q'') \succsim (x'', p''; y, q)$.

Solvability: If $(x, p; y, q) \succsim (z, r) \succsim (x, p; y' \, q')$ for some outcome z and probability r, then there exist y'', q'' such that $(x, p; y'' \, q'') \simeq (z, r)$.

It has been shown that these conditions are sufficient to construct the desired additive representation, provided the preference order is Archimedean [8, 25]. Furthermore, because $(x, p; y, q) \simeq (y, q; x, p)$, $f(x, p) + g(y, q) = f(y, q) + g(x, p)$, and letting $q = 0$ yields $f = g$.

Next, consider the set of all prospects of the form (x, p) with a single non-zero outcome. In this case, the bilinear model reduces to $V(x, p) = \pi(p)v(x)$. This is the multiplicative model, investigated in [35] and [25]. To construct the multiplicative representation we assume that the ordering of the probability–outcome pairs satisfies independence, cancellation, solvability, and the Archimedean axiom. In addition, we assume sign dependence [25] to ensure the proper multiplication of signs. It should be noted that the solvability axiom used in [35] and [25] must be weakened because the probability factor permits only bounded solvability.

Combining the additive and the multiplicative representations yields

$$V(x, p; y, q) = f[\pi(p)v(x)] + f[\pi(q)v(y)].$$

Finally, we impose a new distributivity axiom:

$$(x, p; y, p) \simeq (z, p) \quad \text{iff} \quad (x, q; y, q) \simeq (z, q).$$

Applying this axiom to the above representation, we obtain

$$f[\pi(p)v(x)] + f[\pi(p)v(y)] = f[\pi(p)v(z)]$$

implies

$$f[\pi(q)v(x)] + f[\pi(q)v(y)] = f[\pi(q)v(z)].$$

Assuming, with no loss of generality, that $\pi(q) < \pi(p)$, and letting $\alpha = \pi(p)v(x)$, $\beta = \pi(p)v(y)$, $\gamma = \pi(p)v(z)$, and $\theta = \pi(q)/\pi(p)$, yields $f(\alpha) + f(\beta) = f(\gamma)$ implies $f(\theta\alpha) + f(\theta\beta) = f(\theta\gamma)$ for all $0 < \theta < 1$.

Because f is strictly monotonic we can set $\gamma = f^{-1}[f(\alpha) + f(\beta)]$. Hence, $\theta\gamma = \theta f^{-1}[f(\alpha) + f(\beta)] = f^{-1}[f(\theta\alpha) + f(\theta\beta)]$.

The solution to this functional equation is $f(\alpha) = k\alpha^c$ [1]. Hence, $V(x, p; y, q) = k[\pi(p)v(x)]^c + k[\pi(q)v(y)]^c$, for some $k, c > 0$. The desired bilinear form is obtained by redefining the scales π, v, and V so as to absorb the constants k and c.

Notes

This work was supported in part by grants from the Harry F. Guggenheim Foundation and from the Advanced Research Projects Agency of the Department of Defense and was monitored by the Office of Naval Research under Contract N00014–78-C-0100 (ARPA Order No. 3469) under Subcontract 78–072–0722 from Decisions and Designs, Inc. to Perceptronics, Inc. We also thank the Center for Advanced Study in the Behavioral Sciences at Stanford for its support.
    We are indebted to David H. Krantz for his help in the formulation of the appendix.

References

1. Aczél, J. (1966). *Lectures on functional equations and their applications.* New York, NY: Academic Press.

2. Allais, M. (1953). Le comportement de l'homme rationnel devant le risque: Critique des postulats et axiomes de l'école americaine. *Econometrica, 21,* 503–546.

3. Anderson, N. H., & Shanteau, J. C. (1970). Information integration in risky decision making. *Journal of Experimental Psychology, 84,* 441–451.

4. Arrow, K. J. (1971). *Essays in the theory of risk-bearing.* Chicago, IL: Markham.

5. Barnes, J. D., & Reinmuth, J. E. (1976). Comparing imputed and actual utility functions in a competitive bidding setting. *Decision Sciences, 7,* 801–812.

6. Coombs, C. H. (1975). Portfolio theory and the measurement of risk. In M. F. Kaplan & S. Schwartz (Eds.), *Human judgment and decision processes* (pp. 63–85). New York, NY: Academic Press.

7. Davidson, D., Suppes, P., & Siegel, S. (1957). *Decision-making: An experimental approach.* Stanford, CA: Stanford University Press.

8. Debreu, G. (1960). Topological methods in cardinal utility theory. In K. J. Arrow, S. Karlin, & P. Suppes (Eds.), *Mathematical methods in the social sciences* (pp. 16–26). Stanford, CA: Stanford University Press.

9. Edwards, W. (1962). Subjective probabilities inferred from decisions. *Psychological Review, 69,* 109–135.

10. Ellsberg, D. (1961). Risk, ambiguity and the savage axioms. *Quarterly Journal of Economics, 75,* 643–669.

11. Fellner, W. (1961). Distortion of subjective probabilities as a reaction to uncertainty. *Quarterly Journal of Economics, 75,* 670–690.

12. Fellner, W. (1965). *Probability and profit—A study of economic behavior along Bayesian lines.* Homewood, IL: Richard D. Irwin.

13. Fishburn, P. C. (1977). Mean-risk analysis with risk associated with below-target returns. *American Economic Review, 67*, 116–126.

14. Fishburn, P. C., & Kochenberger, G. A. (1979). Two-piece von Neumann–Morgenstern utility functions. *Decision Sciences, 10*, 503–518.

15. Friedman, M., & Savage, L. J. (1948). The utility analysis of choices involving risks. *Journal of Political Economy, 56*, 279–304.

16. Fuchs, V. R. (1976). From Bismark to Woodcock: The "irrational" pursuit of national health insurance. *Journal of Law & Economics, 19*, 347–359.

17. Galanter, E., & Pliner, P. (1974). Cross-modality matching of money against other continua. In H. R. Moskowitz, et al. (Eds.), *Sensation and measurement* (pp. 65–76). Dordrecht, the Netherlands: Reidel.

18. Grayson, C. J. (1960). *Decisions under uncertainty: Drilling decisions by oil and gas operators.* Cambridge, MA: Harvard University Graduate School of Business.

19. Green, P. E. (1963). Risk attitudes and chemical investment decisions. *Chemical Engineering Progress, 59*, 35–40.

20. Grether, D. M., & Plott, C. R. (1979). Economic theory of choice and the preference reversal phenomenon. *American Economic Review, 69*, 623–638.

21. Halter, A. N., & Dean, G. W. (1971). *Decisions under uncertainty.* Cincinnati, OH: South Western Publishing Co.

22. Hansson, B. (1975). The appropriateness of the expected utility model. *Erkenntnis, 9*, 175–194.

23. Helson, H. (1964). *Adaptation-level theory.* New York, NY: Harper.

24. Keeney, R. L., & Raiffa, H. (1976). *Decisions with multiple objectives: preferences and value tradeoffs.* New York, NY: Wiley.

25. Krantz, D. H., Luce, D. R., Suppes, P., & Tversky, A. (1971). *Foundations of measurement.* New York, NY: Academic Press.

26. Kunreuther, H., Ginsberg, R., Miller, L., Sagi, P., Slovic, P., Borkan, B., et al. (1978). *Disaster insurance protection: Public policy lessons.* New York, NY: Wiley.

27. Lichtenstein, S., & Slovic, P. (1971). Reversal of preference between bids and choices in gambling decisions. *Journal of Experimental Psychology, 89*, 46–55.

28. MacCrimmon, K. R., & Larsson, S. (1979). Utility theory: Axioms versus paradoxes. In M. Allais & O. Hagen (Eds.), *Expected utility hypothesis and the Allais paradox* (pp. 333–409). Dordrecht, the Netherlands: Springer.

29. Markowitz, H. (1952). The utility of wealth. *Journal of Political Economy, 60*, 151–158.

30. Markowitz, H. (1959). *Portfolio selection: Efficient diversification of investments.* New York, NY: Wiley.

31. McGlothlin, W. H. (1956). Stability of choices among uncertain alternatives. *American Journal of Psychology, 69*, 604–615.

32. Mosteller, F., & Nogee, P. (1951). An experimental measurement of utility. *Journal of Political Economy, 59*, 371–404.

33. Pratt, J. W. (1964). Risk aversion in the small and in the large. *Econometrica, 32*, 122–136.

34. Raiffa, H. (1968). *Decision analysis: Introductory lectures on choices under uncertainty.* Reading, MA: Addison-Wesley.

35. Roskies, R. (1965). A measurement axiomatization for an essentially multiplicative representation of two factors. *Journal of Mathematical Psychology, 2*, 266–276.

36. Savage, L. J. (1954). *The foundations of statistics.* New York, NY: Wiley.

37. Slovic, P., Fischhoff, B., Lichtenstein, S., Corrigan, B., & Coombs, B. (1977). Preference for insuring against probable small losses: insurance implications. *Journal of Risk and Insurance, 44*, 237–258.

38. Slovic, P., & Tversky, A. (1974). Who accepts savage's axiom? *Behavioral Science, 19*, 368–373.

39. Spetzler, C. S. (1968). The development of corporate risk policy for capital investment decisions. *IEEE Transactions on Systems Science and Cybernetics, SSC-4*, 279–300.

40. Swalm, R. O. (1966). Utility theory—Insights into risk taking. *Harvard Business Review, 44*, 123–136.

41. Tobin, J. (1958). Liquidity preferences as behavior towards risk. *Review of Economic Studies, 26*, 65–86.

42. Tversky, A. (1967). Additivity, utility, and subjective probability. *Journal of Mathematical Psychology, 4*, 175–201.

43. Tversky, A. (1969). Intransitivity of preferences. *Psychological Review, 76*, 31–48.

44. Tversky, A. (1972). Elimination by aspects: A theory of choice. *Psychological Review, 79*, 281–299.

45. Tversky, A., & Kahneman, D. (1974). Judgment under uncertainty: Heuristics and biases. *Science, 185*, 1124–1131.

46. van Dam, C. Another Look at Inconsistency in Financial Decision-Making, presented at the Seminar on Recent Research in Finance and Monetary Economics, Cergy-Pontoise, March, 1975.

47. von Neumann, J., & Morgenstern, O. (1944). *Theory of Games and Economic Behavior.* Princeton, NJ: Princeton University Press.

48. Williams, A. C. (1966). Attitudes toward speculative risks as an indicator of attitudes toward pure risks. *Journal of Risk and Insurance, 33*, 577–586.

5 Rational Choice and the Framing of Decisions

Amos Tversky and Daniel Kahneman

The modern theory of decision making under risk emerged from a logical analysis of games of chance rather than from a psychological analysis of risk and value. The theory was conceived as a normative model of an idealized decision maker, not as a description of the behavior of real people. In Schumpeter's words, it "has a much better claim to being called a logic of choice than a psychology of value" (1954, p. 1058).

The use of a normative analysis to predict and explain actual behavior is defended by several arguments. First, people are generally thought to be effective in pursuing their goals, particularly when they have incentives and opportunities to learn from experience. It seems reasonable, then, to describe choice as a maximization process. Second, competition favors rational individuals and organizations. Optimal decisions increase the chances of survival in a competitive environment, and a minority of rational individuals can sometimes impose rationality on the whole market. Third, the intuitive appeal of the axioms of rational choice makes it plausible that the theory derived from these axioms should provide an acceptable account of choice behavior.

The thesis of the present chapter is that, in spite of these a priori arguments, the logic of choice does not provide an adequate foundation for a descriptive theory of decision making. We argue that the deviations of actual behavior from the normative model are too widespread to be ignored, too systematic to be dismissed as random error, and too fundamental to be accommodated by relaxing the normative system. We first sketch an analysis of the foundations of the theory of rational choice and then show that the most basic rules of the theory are commonly violated by decision makers. We conclude from these findings that the normative and the descriptive analyses cannot be reconciled. A descriptive model of choice is presented, which accounts for preferences that are anomalous in the normative theory.

A Hierarchy of Normative Rules

The major achievement of the modern theory of decision under risk is the derivation of the expected utility rule from simple principles of rational choice that make no reference to long-run considerations (von Neumann & Morgenstern, 1944). The axiomatic analysis of the foundations of expected utility theory reveals four substantive assumptions—cancellation, transitivity, dominance, and invariance—besides the more technical assumptions of comparability and continuity. The substantive assumptions can be ordered by their normative appeal, from the cancellation condition, which has been challenged by many theorists, to invariance, which has been accepted by all. We briefly discuss these assumptions.

Cancellation. The key qualitative property that gives rise to expected utility theory is the "cancellation" or elimination of any state of the world that yields the same outcome regardless of one's choice. This notion has been captured by different formal properties, such as the substitution axiom of von Neumann and Morgenstern (1944), the extended sure-thing principle of Savage (1954), and the independence condition of Luce and Krantz (1971). Thus, if A is preferred to B, then the prospect of winning A if it rains tomorrow (and nothing otherwise) should be preferred to the prospect of winning B if it rains tomorrow because the two prospects yield the same outcome (nothing) if there is no rain tomorrow. Cancellation is necessary to represent preference between prospects as the maximization of expected utility. The main argument for cancellation is that only one state will actually be realized, which makes it reasonable to evaluate the outcomes of options separately for each state. The choice between options should therefore depend only on states in which they yield different outcomes.

Transitivity. A basic assumption in models of both risky and riskless choice is the transitivity of preference. This assumption is necessary and essentially sufficient for the representation of preference by an ordinal utility scale u such that A is preferred to B whenever $u(A) > u(B)$. Thus transitivity is satisfied if it is possible to assign to each option a value that does not depend on the other available options. Transitivity is likely to hold when the options are evaluated separately but not when the consequences of an option depend on the alternative to which it is compared, as implied, for example, by considerations of regret. A common argument for transitivity is that cyclic preferences can support a "money pump," in which the intransitive person is induced to pay for a series of exchanges that returns to the initial option.

Dominance. This is perhaps the most obvious principle of rational choice: if one option is better than another in one state and at least as good in all other states, the dominant option should be chosen. A slightly stronger condition—called stochastic dominance—asserts that, for unidimensional risky prospects, A is preferred to B if the cumulative distribution of A is to the right of the cumulative distribution of B. Dominance is both simpler and more compelling than cancellation and transitivity, and it serves as the cornerstone of the normative theory of choice.

Invariance. An essential condition for a theory of choice that claims normative status is the principle of invariance: different representations of the same choice problem should yield the same preference. That is, the preference between options should be independent of their description. Two characterizations that the decision maker, on reflection, would view as alternative descriptions of the same problem should lead to the same choice—even without the benefit of such reflection. This principle of invariance (or extensionality [Arrow 1982]) is so basic that it is tacitly assumed in the characterization of options rather than explicitly stated as a testable axiom. For example, decision models that describe the objects of choice as random variables all assume that alternative representations of the same random variables should be treated alike. Invariance captures the normative intuition that variations of form that do not affect the actual outcomes should not affect the choice. A related concept, called consequentialism, has been discussed by Hammond (1985).

The four principles underlying expected utility theory can be ordered by their normative appeal. Invariance and dominance seem essential, transitivity could be questioned, and cancellation has been rejected by many authors. Indeed, the ingenious counterexamples of Allais (1953) and Ellsberg (1961) led several theorists to abandon cancellation and the expectation principle in favor of more general representations. Most of these models assume transitivity, dominance, and invariance (e.g., Hansson, 1975; Allais, 1979; Hagen, 1979; Machina, 1982; Quiggin, 1982; Weber, 1982; Chew, 1983; Fishburn, 1983; Schmeidler, 1984; Segal, 1984; Yaari, 1984; Luce & Narens, 1985). Other developments abandon transitivity but maintain invariance and dominance (e.g., Bell, 1982; Fishburn, 1982, 1984; Loomes & Sugden, 1982). These theorists responded to observed violations of cancellation and transitivity by weakening the normative theory in order to retain its status as a descriptive model. However, this strategy cannot be extended to the failures of dominance and invariance that we shall document. Because invariance and dominance are normatively essential and descriptively invalid, a theory of rational decision cannot provide an adequate description of choice behavior.

We next illustrate failures of invariance and dominance and then review a descriptive analysis that traces these failures to the joint effects of the rules that govern the framing of prospects, the evaluation of outcomes, and the weighting of probabilities. Several phenomena of choice that support the present account are described.

Failures of Invariance

In this section we consider two illustrative examples in which the condition of invariance is violated and discuss some of the factors that produce these violations.

The first example comes from a study of preferences between medical treatments (McNeil et al., 1982). Respondents were given statistical information about the outcomes of two treatments of lung cancer. The same statistics were presented to some respondents in terms of mortality rates and to others in terms of survival rates. The respondents then indicated their preferred treatment. The information was presented as follows.[1]

Problem 1 (Survival frame)

Surgery: Of 100 people having surgery, 90 live through the post-operative period, 68 are alive at the end of the first year, and 34 are alive at the end of five years.

Radiation Therapy: Of 100 people having radiation therapy, all live through the treatment, 77 are alive at the end of one year, and 22 are alive at the end of five years.

Problem 1 (Mortality frame)

Surgery: Of 100 people having surgery, 10 die during surgery or the post-operative period, 32 die by the end of the first year, and 66 die by the end of five years.

Radiation Therapy: Of 100 people having radiation therapy, none die during treatment, 23 die by the end of one year, and 78 die by the end of five years.

The inconsequential difference in formulation produced a marked effect. The overall percentage of respondents who favored radiation therapy rose from 18% in the survival frame ($N = 247$) to 44% in the mortality frame ($N = 336$). The advantage of radiation therapy over surgery evidently looms larger when stated as a reduction of the risk of immediate death from 10% to 0% rather than as an increase from 90% to 100% in the rate of survival. The framing effect was not smaller for experienced physicians or for statistically sophisticated business students than for a group of clinic patients.

Our next example concerns decisions between conjunctions of risky prospects with monetary outcomes. Each respondent made two choices, one between favorable prospects and one between unfavorable prospects (Tversky & Kahneman, 1981, p. 454). It was assumed that the two selected prospects would be played independently.

Problem 2 ($N = 150$). Imagine that you face the following pair of concurrent decisions. First examine both decisions, then indicate the options you prefer.

Decision (i) Choose between:

A. a sure gain of $240 [84%]

B. 25% chance to gain $1000 and 75% chance to gain nothing [16%]

Decision (ii) Choose between:

C. a sure loss of $750 [13%]

D. 75% chance to lose $1000 and 25% chance to lose nothing [87%]

The total number of respondents is denoted by *N*, and the percentage who chose each option is indicated in brackets. (Unless otherwise specified, the data were obtained from undergraduate students at Stanford University and at the University of British Columbia.) The majority choice in decision i is risk averse, whereas the majority choice in decision ii is risk seeking. This is a common pattern: choices involving gains are usually risk averse, and choices involving losses are often risk seeking—except when the probability of winning or losing is small (Fishburn & Kochenberger, 1979; Kahneman & Tversky, 1979; Hershey & Schoemaker, 1980).

Because the subjects considered the two decisions simultaneously, they expressed, in effect, a preference for the portfolio A and D over the portfolio B and C. However, the preferred portfolio is actually dominated by the rejected one! The combined options are as follows.

A & D: 25% chance to win $240 and 75% chance to lose $760.

B & C: 25% chance to win $250 and 75% chance to lose $750.

When the options are presented in this aggregated form, the dominant option is invariably chosen. In the format of problem 2, however, 73% of respondents chose the dominated combination A and D, and only 3% chose B and C. The contrast between the two formats illustrates a violation of invariance. The findings also support the general point that failures of invariance are likely to produce violations of stochastic dominance and vice versa.

The respondents evidently evaluated decisions i and ii separately in problem 2, where they exhibited the standard pattern of risk aversion in gains and risk seeking in losses. People who are given these problems are very surprised to learn that the combination of two preferences that they considered quite reasonable led them to select a dominated option. The same pattern of results was also observed in a scaled-down version of problem 2, with real monetary payoff (see Tversky & Kahneman, 1981, p. 458).

As illustrated by the preceding examples, variations in the framing of decision problems produce systematic violations of invariance and dominance that cannot be defended on normative grounds. It is instructive to examine two mechanisms that could ensure the invariance of preferences: canonical representations and the use of expected actuarial value.

Invariance would hold if all formulations of the same prospect were transformed to a standard canonical representation (e.g., a cumulative probability distribution of the same random variable) because the various versions would then all be evaluated in the same manner. In problem 2, for example, invariance and dominance would both be preserved if the outcomes of the two decisions were aggregated prior to evaluation. Similarly, the same choice would be made in both versions of the medical problem if the outcomes were coded in terms of one dominant frame (e.g., rate of survival). The observed failures of invariance indicate that people do not spontaneously aggregate concurrent prospects or transform all outcomes into a common frame.

The failure to construct a canonical representation in decision problems contrasts with other cognitive tasks in which such representations are generated automatically and effortlessly. In particular, our visual experience consists largely of canonical representations: objects do not appear to change in size, shape, brightness, or color when we move around them or when illumination varies. A white circle seen from a sharp angle in dim light appears circular and white, not ellipsoid and grey. Canonical representations are also generated in the process of language comprehension, where listeners quickly recode much of what they hear into an abstract propositional form that no longer discriminates, for example, between the active and the passive voice and often does not distinguish what was actually said from what was implied or presupposed (Clark & Clark, 1977). Unfortunately, the mental machinery that transforms percepts and sentences into standard forms does not automatically apply to the process of choice.

Invariance could be satisfied even in the absence of a canonical representation if the evaluation of prospects were separately linear, or nearly linear, in probability and monetary value. If people ordered risky prospects by their actuarial values, invariance and dominance would always hold. In particular, there would be no difference between the mortality and the survival versions of the medical problem. Because the evaluation of outcomes and probabilities is generally non-linear, and because people do not spontaneously construct canonical representations of decisions, invariance commonly fails. Normative models of choice, which assume invariance, therefore cannot provide an adequate descriptive account of choice behavior. In the next section we present a descriptive account of risky choice, called prospect theory, and explore its consequences. Failures of invariance are explained by framing effects that control the representation of options, in conjunction with the nonlinearities of value and belief.

Framing and Evaluation of Outcomes

Prospect theory distinguishes two phases in the choice process: a phase of framing and editing, followed by a phase of evaluation (Kahneman & Tversky, 1979). The first phase consists of a preliminary analysis of the decision problem, which frames the effective acts, contingencies, and outcomes. Framing is controlled by the manner in which the choice problem is presented as well as by norms, habits, and expectancies of the decision maker. Additional operations that are performed prior to evaluation include cancellation of common components and the elimination of options that are seen to be dominated by others. In the second phase, the framed prospects are evaluated, and the prospect of highest value is selected. The theory distinguishes two ways of choosing between prospects: by detecting that one dominates another or by comparing their values.

For simplicity, we confine the discussion to simple gambles with numerical probabilities and monetary outcomes. Let $(x; p; y; q)$ denote a prospect that yields x with probability p and y with probability q and that preserves the status quo with probability $(1 - p - q)$. According to prospect theory, there are values $v(\cdot)$, defined on gains and losses, and decision weights $\pi(\cdot)$, defined on stated probabilities, such that the overall value of the prospect equals $\pi(p)v(x) + \pi(q)v(y)$. A slight modification is required if all outcomes of a prospect have the same sign.[2]

The Value Function

Following Markowitz (1952), outcomes are expressed in prospect theory as positive or negative deviations (gains or losses) from a neutral reference outcome, which is assigned a value of zero. Unlike Markowitz, however, we propose that the value function is commonly S shaped, concave above the reference point, and convex below it, as illustrated in figure 5.1. Thus the difference in subjective value between a gain of $100 and a gain of $200 is greater than the subjective difference between a gain of $1,100 and a gain of $1,200. The same

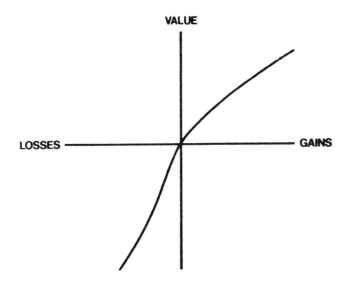

Figure 5.1
A typical value function.

relation between value differences holds for the corresponding losses. The proposed function expresses the property that the effect of a marginal change decreases with the distance from the reference point in either direction. These hypotheses regarding the typical shape of the value function may not apply to ruinous losses or to circumstances in which particular amounts assume special significance.

A significant property of the value function, called *loss aversion*, is that the response to losses is more extreme than the response to gains. The common reluctance to accept a fair bet on the toss of a coin suggests that the displeasure of losing a sum of money exceeds the pleasure of winning the same amount. Thus the proposed value function is (i) defined on gains and losses, (ii) generally concave for gains and convex for losses, and (iii) steeper for losses than for gains. These properties of the value function have been supported in many studies of risky choice involving monetary outcomes (Fishburn & Kochenberger, 1979; Kahneman & Tversky, 1979; Hershey & Schoemaker, 1980; Payne, Laughhunn, & Crum, 1980) and human lives (Tversky, 1977; Eraker & Sox, 1981; Tversky & Kahneman, 1981; Fischhoff, 1983). Loss aversion may also contribute to the observed discrepancies between the amount of money people are willing to pay for a good and the compensation they demand to give it up (Bishop & Heberlein, 1979; Knetsch & Sinden, 1984). This effect is implied by the value function if the good is valued as a gain in the former context and as a loss in the latter.

Framing Outcomes

The framing of outcomes and the contrast between traditional theory and the present analysis are illustrated in the following problems.

Problem 3 (N = 126): Assume yourself richer by $300 than you are today. You have to choose between

a sure gain of $100 [72%]

50% chance to gain $200 and 50% chance to gain nothing [28%]

Problem 4 (N = 128): Assume yourself richer by $500 than you are today. You have to choose between

a sure loss of $100 [36%]

50% chance to lose nothing and 50% chance to lose $200 [64%]

As implied by the value function, the majority choice is risk averse in problem 3 and risk seeking in problem 4, although the two problems are essentially identical. In both cases one faces a choice between $400 for sure and an even chance of $500 or $300. Problem 4 is obtained from problem 3 by increasing the initial endowment by $200 and subtracting this amount from both options. This variation has a substantial effect on preferences. Additional questions showed that variations of $200 in initial wealth have little or no effect on choices. Evidently, preferences are quite insensitive to small changes of wealth but highly sensitive to corresponding changes in reference point. These observations show that the effective carriers of values are gains and losses, or changes in wealth, rather than states of wealth as implied by the rational model.

The common pattern of preferences observed in problems 3 and 4 is of special interest because it violates not only expected utility theory but practically all other normatively based models of choice. In particular, these data are inconsistent with the model of regret advanced by Bell (1982) and by Loomes and Sugden (1982) and axiomatized by Fishburn (1982). This follows from the fact that problems 3 and 4 yield identical outcomes and an identical regret structure. Furthermore, regret theory cannot accommodate the combination of risk aversion in problem 3 and risk seeking in problem 4—even without the corresponding changes in endowment that make the problems extensionally equivalent.

Shifts of reference can be induced by different decompositions of outcomes into risky and riskless components, as in the above problems. The reference point can also be shifted by a mere labeling of outcomes, as illustrated in the following problems (Tversky & Kahneman, 1981, p. 453).

Problem 5 (N = 152): Imagine that the United States is preparing for the outbreak of an unusual Asian disease, which is expected to kill 600 people. Two alternative programs to combat the disease have been proposed. Assume that the exact scientific estimates of the consequences of the programs are as follows:

If Program A is adopted, 200 people will be saved. [72%]

If Program B is adopted, there is 1/3 probability that 600 people will be saved and 2/3 probability that no people will be saved. [28%]

In problem 5 the outcomes are stated in positive terms (lives saved), and the majority choice is accordingly risk averse. The prospect of certainly saving 200 lives is more attractive than a risky prospect of equal expected value. A second group of respondents was given the same cover story with the following descriptions of the alternative programs.

Problem 6 (N = 155):

If Program C is adopted, 400 people will die. [22%]

If Program D is adopted, there is 1/3 probability that nobody will die and 2/3 probability that 600 people will die. [78%]

In problem 6 the outcomes are stated in negative terms (lives lost), and the majority choice is accordingly risk seeking. The certain death of 400 people is less acceptable than a two-thirds chance that 600 people will die. Problems 5 and 6, however, are essentially identical. They differ only in that the former is framed in terms of the number of lives saved (relative to an expected loss of 600 lives if no action is taken), whereas the latter is framed in terms of the number of lives lost.

On several occasions we presented both versions to the same respondents and discussed with them the inconsistent preferences evoked by the two frames. Many respondents expressed a wish to remain risk averse in the "lives saved" version and risk seeking in the "lives lost" version, although they also expressed a wish for their answers to be consistent. In the persistence of their appeal, framing effects resemble visual illusions more than computational errors.

Discounts and Surcharges

Perhaps the most distinctive intellectual contribution of economic analysis is the systematic consideration of alternative opportunities. A basic principle of economic thinking is that opportunity costs and out-of-pocket costs should be treated alike. Preferences should depend only on relevant differences between options, not on how these differences are labeled. This principle runs counter to the psychological tendencies that make preferences susceptible to superficial variations in form. In particular, a difference that favors outcome A over outcome B can sometimes be framed either as an advantage of A or as a disadvantage of B by suggesting either B or A as the neutral reference point. Because of loss aversion, the difference will loom larger when A is neutral and B-A is evaluated as a loss than when B is neutral and A-B is evaluated as a gain. The significance of such variations of framing has been noted in several contexts.

Thaler (1980) drew attention to the effect of labeling a difference between two prices as a surcharge or a discount. It is easier to forgo a discount than to accept a surcharge because the same price difference is valued as a gain in the former case and as a loss in the latter. Indeed, the credit card lobby is said to insist that any price difference between cash and card purchases should be labeled a cash discount rather than a credit surcharge. A similar idea could be invoked to explain why the price response to slack demand often takes the form of discounts or special concessions (Stigler & Kindahl, 1970). Customers may be expected to show less resistance to the eventual cancellation of such temporary arrangements than to outright price increases. Judgments of fairness exhibit the same pattern (Kahneman, Knetsch, & Thaler, 1986a).

Schelling (1981) has described a striking framing effect in a context of tax policy. He points out that the tax table can be constructed by using as a default case either the childless family (as is in fact done) or, say, the modal two-child family. The tax difference between a childless family and a two-child family is naturally framed as an exemption (for the two-child family) in the first frame and as a tax premium (on the childless family) in the second frame. This seemingly innocuous difference has a large effect on judgments of the desired relation between income, family size, and tax. Schelling reported that his students rejected the idea of granting the rich a larger exemption than the poor in the first frame but favored a larger tax premium on the childless rich than on the childless poor in the second frame.

Because the exemption and the premium are alternative labels for the same tax differences in the two cases, the judgments violate invariance. Framing the consequences of a public policy in positive or in negative terms can greatly alter its appeal.

The notion of a money illusion is sometimes applied to workers' willingness to accept, in periods of high inflation, increases in nominal wages that do not protect their real income— although they would strenuously resist equivalent wage cuts in the absence of inflation. The essence of the illusion is that, whereas a cut in the nominal wage is always recognized as a loss, a nominal increase that does not preserve real income may be treated as a gain. Another manifestation of the money illusion was observed in a study of the perceived fairness of economic actions (Kahneman, Knetsch, & Thaler, 1986b). Respondents in a telephone interview evaluated the fairness of the action described in the following vignette, which was presented in two versions that differed only in the bracketed clauses.

A company is making a small profit. It is located in a community experiencing a recession with substantial unemployment [but no inflation/and inflation of 12%]. The company decides to [decrease wages and salaries 7%/increase salaries only 5%] this year.

Although the loss of real income is very similar in the two versions, the proportion of respondents who judged the action of the company "unfair" or "very unfair" was 62% for a nominal reduction but only 22% for a nominal increase.

Bazerman (1983) has documented framing effects in experimental studies of bargaining. He compared the performance of experimental subjects when the outcomes of bargaining were formulated as gains or as losses. Subjects who bargained over the allocation of losses more often failed to reach agreement and more often failed to discover a Pareto-optimal solution. Bazerman attributed these observations to the general propensity toward risk seeking in the domain of losses, which may increase the willingness of both participants to risk the negative consequences of a deadlock.

Loss aversion presents an obstacle to bargaining whenever the participants evaluate their own concessions as losses and the concessions obtained from the other party as gains. In negotiating over missiles, for example, the subjective loss of security associated with dismantling a missile may loom larger than the increment of security produced by a similar action on the adversary's part. If the two parties both assign a two-to-one ratio to the values of the concessions they make and of those they obtain, the resulting four-to-one gap may be difficult to bridge. Agreement will be much easier to achieve by negotiators who trade in "bargaining chips" that are valued equally, regardless of whose hand they are in. In this mode of trading, which may be common in routine purchases, loss aversion tends to disappear (Kahneman & Tversky, 1984).

The Framing and Weighting of Chance Events

In expected utility theory, the utility of each possible outcome is weighted by its probability. In prospect theory, the value of an uncertain outcome is multiplied by a decision weight $\pi(p)$, which is a monotonic function of p but is not a probability. The weighting function p has the following properties. First, impossible events are discarded, that is, $\pi(0) = 0$, and the scale is normalized so that $\pi(1) = 1$, but the function is not well behaved near the end points (Kahneman & Tversky, 1979). Second, for low probabilities, $\pi(p) > p$, but $\pi(p) + \pi(1 - p) \leq 1$ (subcertainty). Thus low probabilities are overweighted, moderate and high probabilities are underweighted, and the latter effect is more pronounced than the former. Third, $\pi(pr)/\pi(p) < \pi(pqr)/\pi(pq)$ for all $0 < p, q, r \leq 1$ (subproportionality). That is, for any fixed probability ratio r, the ratio of decision weights is closer to unity when the probabilities are low than when they are high, for example, $\pi(0.1)/\pi(0.2) > \pi(0.4)/\pi(0.8)$. A hypothetical weighting function that satisfies these properties is shown in figure 5.2. Its consequences are discussed in the next section.[3]

Nontransparent Dominance

The major characteristic of the weighting function is the overweighting of probability differences involving certainty and impossibility, for example, $\pi(1.0) - \pi(0.9)$ or $\pi(0.1) - \pi(0)$,

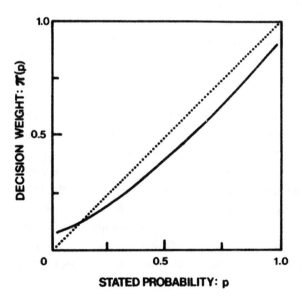

Figure 5.2
A typical weighting function.

relative to comparable differences in the middle of the scale, for example, $\pi(0.3) - \pi(0.2)$. In particular, for small p, π is generally subadditive, for example, $\pi(0.01) + \pi(0.06) > \pi(0.07)$. This property can lead to violations of dominance, as illustrated in the following pair of problems.

Problem 7 ($N = 88$). Consider the following two lotteries, described by the percentage of marbles of different colors in each box and the amount of money you win or lose depending on the color of a randomly drawn marble. Which lottery do you prefer?

Option A

90% white	6% red	1% green	1% blue	2% yellow
$0	win $45	win $30	lose $15	lose $15

Option B

90% white	6% red	1% green	1% blue	2% yellow
$0	win $45	win $45	lose $10	lose $15

It is easy to see that option B dominates option A: for every color the outcome of B is at least as desirable as the outcome of A. Indeed, all respondents chose B over A. This observation is hardly surprising because the relation of dominance is highly transparent, so the dominated prospect is rejected without further processing. The next problem is effectively identical to problem 7, except that colors yielding identical outcomes (red and green in B and yellow and blue in A) are combined. We have proposed that this operation is commonly performed by the decision maker if no dominated prospect is detected.

Problem 8 ($N = 124$). Which lottery do you prefer?

Option C

90% white	6% red	1% green	3% yellow
$0	win $45	win $30	lose $15

Option D

90% white	7% red	1% green	2% yellow
$0	win $45	lose $10	lose $15

The formulation of problem 8 simplifies the options but masks the relation of dominance. Furthermore, it enhances the attractiveness of C, which has two positive outcomes and one negative, relative to D, which has two negative outcomes and one positive. As an inducement to consider the options carefully, participants were informed that one-tenth of them, selected at random, would actually play the gambles they chose. Although this announcement aroused much excitement, 58% of the participants chose the dominated alternative C. In answer to another question the majority of respondents also assigned a higher cash equivalent to C than to D. These results support the following propositions. (i) Two formulations of the same problem elicit different preferences, in violation of invariance. (ii) The dominance rule is obeyed when its application is transparent. (iii) Dominance is masked by a frame in which the inferior option yields a more favorable outcome in an identified state

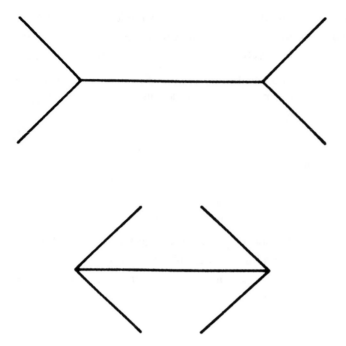

Figure 5.3
The Müller-Lyer illusion.

of the world (e.g., drawing a green marble). (iv) The discrepant preferences are consistent with the subadditivity of decision weights. The role of transparency may be illuminated by a perceptual example. Figure 5.3 presents the well-known Müller-Lyer illusion: the top line appears longer than the bottom line, although it is in fact shorter. In figure 5.4, the same patterns are embedded in a rectangular frame, which makes it apparent that the protruding bottom line is longer than the top one. This judgment has the nature of an inference, in contrast to the perceptual impression that mediates judgment in figure 5.3. Similarly, the finer partition introduced in problem 7 makes it possible to conclude that option D is superior to C, without assessing their values. Whether the relation of dominance is detected depends on framing as well as on the sophistication and experience of the decision maker. The dominance relation in problems 8 and 1 could be transparent to a sophisticated decision maker, although it was not transparent to most of our respondents.

Certainty and Pseudocertainty

The overweighting of outcomes that are obtained with certainty relative to outcomes that are merely probable gives rise to violations of the expectation rule, as first noted by Allais

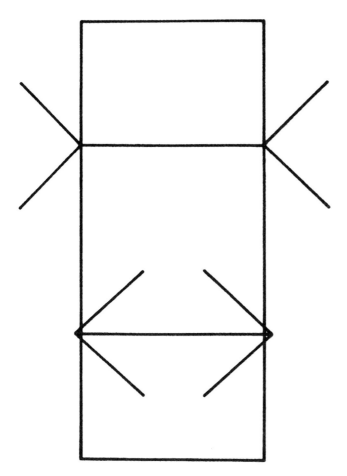

Figure 5.4
A transparent version of the Müller-Lyer illusion.

(1953). The next series of problems (Tversky & Kahneman, 1981, p. 455) illustrates the phenomenon discovered by Allais and its relation to the weighting of probabilities and to the framing of chance events. Chance events were realized by drawing a single marble from a bag containing a specified number of favorable and unfavorable marbles. To encourage thoughtful answers, one-tenth of the participants, selected at random, were given an opportunity to play the gambles they chose. The same respondents answered problems 9–11, in that order.

Problem 9 ($N = 77$). Which of the following options do you prefer?

A. a sure gain of $30 [78%]

B. 80% chance to win $45 and 20% chance to win nothing [22%]

Problem 10 (N = 81). Which of the following options do you prefer?

C.   25% chance to win \$30 and 75% chance to win nothing [42%]

D.   20% chance to win \$45 and 80% chance to win nothing [58%]

Note that problem 10 is obtained from problem 9 by reducing the probabilities of winning by a factor of four. In expected utility theory a preference for A over B in problem 9 implies a preference for C over D in problem 10. Contrary to this prediction, the majority preference switched from the lower prize (\$30) to the higher one (\$45) when the probabilities of winning were substantially reduced. We called this phenomenon the *certainty effect* because the reduction of the probability of winning from certainty to 0.25 has a greater effect than the corresponding reduction from 0.8 to 0.2. In prospect theory, the modal choice in problem 9 implies $v(45)\pi(0.80) < v(30)\pi(1.0)$, whereas the modal choice in problem 10 implies $v(45)\pi(0.20) > v(30)\pi(0.25)$. The observed violation of expected utility theory, then, is implied by the curvature of p (see figure 5.2) if

$$\frac{\pi(.20)}{\pi(.25)} > \frac{v(30)}{v(45)} > \frac{\pi(.80)}{\pi(1.0)}.$$

Allais's problem has attracted the attention of numerous theorists, who attempted to provide a normative rationale for the certainty effect by relaxing the cancellation rule (see, e.g., Allais, 1979; Fishburn, 1982, 1983; Machina, 1982; Quiggin, 1982; Chew, 1983). The following problem illustrates a related phenomenon, called the *pseudocertainty effect*, which cannot be accommodated by relaxing cancellation because it also involves a violation of invariance.

Problem 11 (N = 85): Consider the following two-stage game. In the first stage, there is a 75% chance to end the game without winning anything and a 25% chance to move into the second stage. If you reach the second stage you have a choice between:

E.   a sure win of \$30 [74%]

F.   80% chance to win \$45 and 20% chance to win nothing [26%]

Your choice must be made before the outcome of the first stage is known.

Because there is one chance in four to move into the second stage, prospect E offers a 0.25 probability of winning \$30, and prospect F offers a $0.25 \times 0.80 = 0.20$ probability of winning \$45. Problem 11 is therefore identical to problem 10 in terms of probabilities and outcomes. However, the preferences in the two problems differ: most subjects made a risk-averse choice in problem 11 but not in problem 10. We call this phenomenon the pseudocertainty effect because an outcome that is actually uncertain is weighted as if it were certain. The framing of problem 11 as a two-stage game encourages respondents to apply cancellation: the event of failing to reach the second stage is discarded prior to evaluation because it yields the same outcomes in both options. In this framing problems 11 and 9 are evaluated alike.

Although problems 10 and 11 are identical in terms of final outcomes and their probabilities, problem 11 has a greater potential for inducing regret. Consider a decision maker who chooses F in problem 11, reaches the second stage, but fails to win the prize. This individual knows that the choice of E would have yielded a gain of $30. In problem 10, by contrast, an individual who chooses D and fails to win cannot know with certainty what the outcome of the other choice would have been. This difference could suggest an alternative interpretation of the pseudocertainty effect in terms of regret (e.g., Loomes & Sugden, 1982). However, the certainty and the pseudocertainty effects were found to be equally strong in a modified version of problems 9–11 in which opportunities for regret were equated across problems. This finding does not imply that considerations of regret play no role in decisions. (For examples, see Kahneman & Tversky, 1982, p. 710.) It merely indicates that Allais's example and the pseudocertainty effect are primarily controlled by the nonlinearity of decision weights and the framing of contingencies rather than by the anticipation of regret.[4]

The certainty and pseudocertainty effects are not restricted to monetary outcomes. The following problem illustrates these phenomena in a medical context. The respondents were 72 physicians attending a meeting of the California Medical Association. Essentially the same pattern of responses was obtained from a larger group ($N = 180$) of college students.

Problem 12 ($N = 72$). In the treatment of tumors there is sometimes a choice between two types of therapies: (i) a radical treatment such as extensive surgery, which involves some risk of imminent death; and (ii) a moderate treatment, such as limited surgery or radiation therapy. Each of the following problems describes the possible outcome of two alternative treatments, for three different cases. In considering each case, suppose the patient is a 40-year-old male. Assume that without treatment death is imminent (within a month) and that only one of the treatments can be applied. Please indicate the treatment you would prefer in each case.

Case 1

Treatment A: 20% chance of imminent death and 80% chance of normal life, with an expected longevity of 30 years. [35%]

Treatment B: certainty of a normal life, with an expected longevity of 18 years. [65%]

Case 2

Treatment C: 80% chance of imminent death and 20% chance of normal life, with an expected longevity of 30 years. [68%]

Treatment D: 75% chance of imminent death and 25% chance of normal life, with an expected longevity of 18 years. [32%]

Case 3

Consider a new case where there is a 25% chance that the tumor is treatable and a 75% chance that it is not. If the tumor is not treatable, death is imminent. If the tumor is treatable, the outcomes of the treatment are as follows:

Treatment E: 20% chance of imminent death and 80% chance of normal life, with an expected longevity of 30 years. [32%]

Treatment F: certainty of normal life, with an expected longevity of 18 years. [68%]

The three cases of this problem correspond, respectively, to problems 9–11, and the same pattern of preferences is observed. In case 1, most respondents make a risk-averse choice in favor of certain survival with reduced longevity. In case 2, the moderate treatment no longer ensures survival, and most respondents choose the treatment that offers the higher expected longevity. In particular, 64% of the physicians who chose B in case 1 selected C in case 2. This is another example of Allais's certainty effect.

The comparison of cases 2 and 3 provides another illustration of pseudocertainty. The cases are identical in terms of the relevant outcomes and their probabilities, but the preferences differ. In particular, 56% of the physicians who chose C in case 2 selected F in case 3. The conditional framing induces people to disregard the event of the tumor not being treatable because the two treatments are equally ineffective in this case. In this frame, treatment F enjoys the advantage of pseudocertainty. It appears to ensure survival, but the assurance is conditional on the treatability of the tumor. In fact, there is only a 0.25 chance of surviving a month if this option is chosen.

The conjunction of certainty and pseudocertainty effects has significant implications for the relation between normative and descriptive theories of choice. Our results indicate that cancellation is actually obeyed in choices—in those problems that make its application transparent. Specifically, we find that people make the same choices in problems 11 and 9 and in cases 3 and 1 of problem 12. Evidently, people "cancel" an event that yields the same outcomes for all options, in two-stage or nested structures. Note that in these examples cancellation is satisfied in problems that are formally equivalent to those in which it is violated. The empirical validity of cancellation therefore depends on the framing of the problems.

The present concept of framing originated from the analysis of Allais's problems by Savage (1954, pp. 101–104) and Raiffa (1968, pp. 80–86), who reframed these examples in an attempt to make the application of cancellation more compelling. Savage and Raiffa were right: naive respondents indeed obey the cancellation axiom when its application is sufficiently transparent.[5] However, the contrasting preferences in different versions of the same choice (problems 10 and 11 and cases 2 and 3 of problem 12) indicate that people do not follow the same axiom when its application is not transparent. Instead, they apply (nonlinear) decision weights to the probabilities as stated. The status of cancellation is therefore similar to that of dominance: both rules are intuitively compelling as abstract principles of choice, consistently obeyed in transparent problems and frequently violated in nontransparent ones. Attempts to rationalize the preferences in Allais's example by discarding the cancellation axiom face a major difficulty: they do not distinguish transparent formulations in which cancellation is obeyed from nontransparent ones in which it is violated.

Discussion

In the preceding sections we challenged the descriptive validity of the major tenets of expected utility theory and outlined an alternative account of risky choice. In this section we discuss alternative theories and argue against the reconciliation of normative and descriptive analyses. Some objections of economists to our analysis and conclusions are addressed.

Descriptive and Normative Considerations

Many alternative models of risky choice, designed to explain the observed violations of expected utility theory, have been developed in the last decade. These models divide into the following four classes. (i) Nonlinear functionals (e.g., Allais, 1953, 1979; Machina, 1982) are obtained by eliminating the cancellation condition altogether. These models do not have axiomatizations leading to a (cardinal) measurement of utility, but they impose various restrictions (i.e., differentiability) on the utility functional. (ii) The expectations quotient model (axiomatized by Chew & MacCrimmon, 1979; Weber, 1982; Chew, 1983; Fishburn, 1983) replaces cancellation by a weaker substitution axiom and represents the value of a prospect by the ratio of two linear functionals. (iii) Bilinear models with nonadditive probabilities (e.g., Kahneman & Tversky, 1979; Quiggin, 1982; Schmeidler, 1984; Segal, 1984; Yaari, 1984; Luce & Narens, 1985) assume various restricted versions of cancellation (or substitution) and construct a bilinear representation in which the utilities of outcomes are weighted by a nonadditive probability measure or by some nonlinear transform of the probability scale. (iv) Nontransitive models represent preferences by a bivariate utility function. Fishburn (1982, 1984) axiomatized such models, while Bell (1982) and Loomes and Sugden (1982) interpreted them in terms of expected regret. For further theoretical developments, see Fishburn (1985).

The relation between models and data is summarized in table 5.1. The stub column lists the four major tenets of expected utility theory. Column 1 lists the major empirical violations of these tenets and cites a few representative references. Column 2 lists the subset of models discussed above that are consistent with the observed violations.

The conclusions of table 5.1 may be summarized as follows. First, all the above models (as well as some others) are consistent with the violations of cancellation produced by the certainty effect.[6] Therefore, Allais's "paradox" cannot be used to compare or evaluate competing nonexpectation models. Second, bivariate (nontransitive) models are needed to explain observed intransitivities. Third, only prospect theory can accommodate the observed

Table 5.1
Summary of Empirical Violations and Explanatory Models

Tenet	Empirical violation	Explanatory model
Cancellation	Certainty effect (Allais, 1953, 1979; Kahneman & Tversky, 1979) (problems 9–10, and 12 [cases 1 and 2])	All models
Transitivity	Lexicographic semiorder (Tversky, 1969) Preference reversals (Slovic & Lichtenstein, 1983)	Bivariate models
Dominance	Contrasting risk attitudes (problem 2) Subadditive decision weights (problem 8)	Prospect theory
Invariance	Framing effects (problems 1, 3–4, 5–6, 7–8, 10–11, and 12)	Prospect theory

violations of (stochastic) dominance and invariance. Although some models (e.g., Loomes & Sugden, 1982; Luce & Narens, 1985) permit some limited failures of invariance, they do not account for the range of framing effects described in this article.

Because framing effects and the associated failures of invariance are ubiquitous, no adequate descriptive theory can ignore these phenomena. However, because invariance (or extensionality) is normatively indispensable, no adequate prescriptive theory should permit its violation. Consequently, the dream of constructing a theory that is acceptable both descriptively and normatively appears unrealizable (see also Tversky & Kahneman, 1983).

Prospect theory differs from the other models mentioned above in being unabashedly descriptive and in making no normative claims. It is designed to explain preferences, whether or not they can be rationalized. Machina (1982, p. 292) claimed that prospect theory is "unacceptable as a descriptive model of behavior toward risk" because it implies violations of stochastic dominance. But since the violations of dominance predicted by the theory have actually been observed (see problems 2 and 8), Machina's objection appears invalid.

Perhaps the major finding of the present article is that the axioms of rational choice are generally satisfied in transparent situations and often violated in nontransparent ones. For example, when the relation of stochastic dominance is transparent (as in the aggregated version of problem 2 and in problem 7), practically everyone selects the dominant prospect. However, when these problems are framed so that the relation of dominance is no longer transparent (as in the segregated version of problem 2 and in problem 8), most respondents violate dominance, as predicted. These results contradict all theories that imply stochastic dominance as well as others (e.g., Machina, 1982) that predict the same choices in transparent and nontransparent contexts. The same conclusion applies to cancellation, as shown in the discussion of pseudocertainty. It appears that both cancellation and dominance have normative appeal, although neither one is descriptively valid.

The present results and analysis—particularly the role of transparency and the significance of framing—are consistent with the conception of bounded rationality originally presented by Herbert Simon (see, e.g., Simon, 1955, 1978; March, 1978; Nelson & Winter, 1982). Indeed, prospect theory is an attempt to articulate some of the principles of perception and judgment that limit the rationality of choice.

The introduction of psychological considerations (e.g., framing) both enriches and complicates the analysis of choice. Because the framing of decisions depends on the language of presentation, on the context of choice, and on the nature of the display, our treatment of the process is necessarily informal and incomplete. We have identified several common rules of framing, and we have demonstrated their effects on choice, but we have not provided a formal theory of framing. Furthermore, the present analysis does not account for all the observed failures of transitivity and invariance. Although some intransitivities (e.g., Tversky, 1969) can be explained by discarding small differences in the framing phase, and others (e.g., Raiffa, 1968, p. 75) arise from the combination of transparent and nontransparent comparisons, there are examples of cyclic preferences and context effects (see, e.g., Slovic, Fischhoff, & Lichtenstein, 1982; Slovic & Lichtenstein, 1983) that require additional explanatory mechanisms (e.g., multiple reference points and variable weights). An adequate account of choice cannot ignore these effects of framing and context, even if they are normatively distasteful and mathematically intractable.

Bolstering Assumptions

The assumption of rationality has a favored position in economics. It is accorded all the methodological privileges of a self-evident truth, a reasonable idealization, a tautology, and a null hypothesis. Each of these interpretations either puts the hypothesis of rational action beyond question or places the burden of proof squarely on any alternative analysis of belief and choice. The advantage of the rational model is compounded because no other theory of judgment and decision can ever match it in scope, power, and simplicity.

Furthermore, the assumption of rationality is protected by a formidable set of defenses in the form of bolstering assumptions that restrict the significance of any observed violation of the model. In particular, it is commonly assumed that substantial violations of the standard model are (i) restricted to insignificant choice problems, (ii) quickly eliminated by learning, or (iii) irrelevant to economics because of the corrective function of market forces. Indeed, incentives sometimes improve the quality of decisions, experienced decision makers often do better than novices, and the forces of arbitrage and competition can nullify some effects of error and illusion. Whether these factors ensure rational choices in any particular situation is an empirical issue, to be settled by observation, not by supposition.

It has frequently been claimed (see, e.g., Smith, 1985) that the observed failures of rational models are attributable to the cost of thinking and will thus be eliminated by proper incentives. Experimental findings provide little support for this view. Studies reported in the economic and psychological literature have shown that errors that are prevalent in responses to hypothetical questions persist even in the presence of significant monetary payoffs. In particular, elementary blunders of probabilistic reasoning (Grether, 1980; Tversky & Kahneman, 1983), major inconsistencies of choice (Grether & Plott, 1979; Slovic & Lichtenstein, 1983), and violations of stochastic dominance in nontransparent problems (see problem 2 above) are hardly reduced by incentives. The evidence that high stakes do not always improve decisions is not restricted to laboratory studies. Significant errors of judgment and choice can be documented in real-world decisions that involve high stakes and serious deliberation. The high rate of failures of small businesses, for example, is not easily reconciled with the assumptions of rational expectations and risk aversion.

Incentives do not operate by magic: they work by focusing attention and by prolonging deliberation. Consequently, they are more likely to prevent errors that arise from insufficient attention and effort than errors that arise from misperception or faulty intuition. The example of visual illusion is instructive. There is no obvious mechanism by which the mere introduction of incentives (without the added opportunity to make measurements) would reduce the illusion observed in figure 5.3, and the illusion vanishes—even in the absence of incentives—when the display is altered in figure 5.4. The corrective power of incentives depends on the nature of the particular error and cannot be taken for granted.

The assumption of the rationality of decision making is often defended by the argument that people will learn to make correct decisions and sometimes by the evolutionary argument that irrational decision makers will be driven out by rational ones. There is no doubt that learning and selection do take place and tend to improve efficiency. As in the case of incentives, however, no magic is involved. Effective learning takes place only under certain conditions: it requires accurate and immediate feedback about the relation between the situational conditions and the appropriate response. The necessary feedback is often lacking for the decisions made by managers, entrepreneurs, and politicians because (i) outcomes are commonly delayed and not easily attributable to a particular action; (ii) variability in the environment degrades the reliability of the feedback, especially where outcomes of low probability are involved; (iii) there is often no information about what the outcome would have been if another decision had been taken; and (iv) most important decisions are unique and therefore provide little opportunity for learning (see Einhorn & Hogarth, 1978). The conditions for organizational learning are hardly better. Learning surely occurs, for both individuals and organizations, but any claim that a particular error will be eliminated by experience must be supported by demonstrating that the conditions for effective learning are satisfied.

Finally, it is sometimes argued that failures of rationality in individual decision making are inconsequential because of the corrective effects of the market (Knez, Smith, & Williams, 1985). Economic agents are often protected from their own irrational predilections by the forces of competition and by the action of arbitrageurs, but there are situations in which this mechanism fails. Hausch, Ziemba, and Rubenstein (1981) have documented an instructive example: the market for win bets at the racetrack is efficient, but the market for bets on place and show is not. Bettors commonly underestimate the probability that the favorite will end up in second or third place, and this effect is sufficiently large to sustain a contrarian betting strategy with a positive expected value. This inefficiency is found in spite of the high incentives, of the unquestioned level of dedication and expertise among participants in racetrack markets, and of obvious opportunities for learning and for arbitrage.

Situations in which errors that are common to many individuals are unlikely to be corrected by the market have been analyzed by Haltiwanger and Waldman (1985) and by Russell and Thaler (1985). Furthermore, Akerlof and Yellen (1985) have presented their near-rationality theory, in which some prevalent errors in responding to economic changes (e.g., inertia or money illusion) will (i) have little effect on the individual (thereby eliminating the possibility of learning), (ii) provide no opportunity for arbitrage, and yet (iii) have large economic effects. The claim that the market can be trusted to correct the effect of individual irrationalities cannot be made without supporting evidence, and the burden of specifying a plausible corrective mechanism should rest on those who make this claim.

The main theme of this article has been that the normative and the descriptive analyses of choice should be viewed as separate enterprises. This conclusion suggests a research agenda. To retain the rational model in its customary descriptive role, the relevant bolstering assumptions must be validated. Where these assumptions fail, it is instructive to trace the implications of the descriptive analysis (e.g., the effects of loss aversion, pseudocertainty, or the money illusion) for public policy, strategic decision making, and macroeconomic phenomena (see Arrow, 1982; Akerlof & Yellen, 1985).

Acknowledgment

This work was supported by contract N00014–84-K-0615 from the Office of Naval Research to Stanford University. The present article reviews our work on decision making under risk from a new perspective, discussed primarily in the first and last sections. Most of the empirical demonstrations have been reported in earlier publications. Problems 3, 4, 7, 8, and 12 are published here for the first time.

Notes

1. All problems are presented in the text exactly as they were presented to the participants in the experiments.

2. If $p + q = 1$ and either $x > y > 0$ or $x < y < 0$, the value of a prospect is given by $v(y) + \pi(p) [v(x) - v(y)]$, so that decision weights are not applied to sure outcomes.

3. The extension of the present analysis to prospects with many (nonzero) outcomes involves two additional steps. First, we assume that continuous (or multivalued) distributions are approximated, in the framing phase, by discrete distributions with a relatively small number of outcomes. For example, a uniform distribution on the interval $(0, 90)$ may be represented by the discrete prospect $(0, 0.1; 10, 0.1; \ldots ; 90, 0.1)$. Second, in the multiple-outcome case the weighting function, $\pi_p(p_i)$, must depend on the probability vector p, not only on the component p_i, $i = 1, \ldots , n$. For example, Quiggin (1982) uses the function $\pi_p(p_i) = \pi(p_i)/[\pi(p_1) + \cdots + \pi(p_n)]$. As in the two-outcome case, the weighting function is assumed to satisfy subcertainty, $\pi_p(p_1) + \cdots + \pi_p(p_n) \leq 1$, and subproportionality.

4. In the modified version—problems 9'–11'—the probabilities of winning were generated by drawing a number from a bag containing 100 sequentially numbered tickets. In problem 10', the event associated with winning \$45 (drawing a number between one and 20) was included in the event associated with winning \$30 (drawing a number between one and 25). The sequential setup of problem 11 was replaced by the simultaneous play of two chance devices: the roll of a die (whose outcome determines whether the game is on) and the drawing of a numbered ticket from a bag. The possibility of regret now exists in all three problems, and problems 10' and 11' no longer differ in this respect because a decision maker would always know the outcomes of alternative choices. Consequently, regret theory cannot explain either the certainty effect (9' vs. 10') or the pseudocertainty effect (10' vs. 11') observed in the modified problems.

5. It is noteworthy that the conditional framing used in problems 11 and 12 (case 3) is much more effective in eliminating the common responses to Allais's paradox than the partition framing introduced by Savage (see, e.g., Slovic & Tversky, 1974). This is probably due to the fact that the conditional framing makes it clear that the critical options are identical—after eliminating the state whose outcome does not depend on one's choice (i.e., reaching the second stage in problem 11, an untreatable tumor in problem 12, case 3).

6. Because the present article focuses on prospects with known probabilities, we do not discuss the important violations of cancellation due to ambiguity (Ellsberg, 1961).

References

Akerlof, G. A., & Yellen, J. (1985). Can small deviations from rationality make significant differences to economic equilibria? *American Economic Review, 75,* 708–720.

Allais, M. (1953). Le comportement de l'homme rationnel devant le risque: Critique des postulats et axiomes de l'Ecole Américaine. *Econometrica, 21,* 503–546.

Allais, M. (1979). The foundations of a positive theory of choice involving risk and a criticism of the postulates and axioms of the American School. In M. Allais & O. Hagen (Eds.), *Expected utility hypotheses and the Allais paradox* (pp. 27–145). Dordrecht, the Netherlands: Reidel.

Arrow, K. J. (1982). Risk perception in psychology and economics. *Economic Inquiry, 20,* 1–9.

Bazerman, M. H. (1983). Negotiator judgment. *American Behavioral Scientist, 27,* 211–228.

Bell, D. E. (1982). Regret in decision making under uncertainty. *Operations Research, 30,* 961–981.

Bishop, R. C., & Heberlein, T. A. (1979). Measuring values of extra-market goods: Are indirect measures biased? *American Journal of Agricultural Economics, 61,* 926–930.

Chew, S. H. (1983). A generalization of the quasilinear mean with applications to the measurement of income inequality and decision theory resolving the Allais paradox. *Econometrica, 51,* 1065–1092.

Chew, S. H., & MacCrimmon, K. 1979. Alpha utility theory, lottery composition, and the Allais paradox. Working Paper no. 686. Vancouver, BC: University of British Columbia.

Clark, H. H., & Clark, E. V. (1977). *Psychology and language.* New York, NY: Harcourt Brace Jovanovich.

Einhorn, H. J., & Hogarth, R. M. (1978). Confidence in judgment: Persistence of the illusion of validity. *Psychological Review, 85,* 395–416.

Ellsberg, D. (1961). Risk, ambiguity, and the Savage axioms. *Quarterly Journal of Economics, 75,* 643–669.

Eraker, S. E., & Sox, H. C. (1981). Assessment of patients' preferences for therapeutic outcomes. *Medical Decision Making, 1,* 29–39.

Fischhoff, B. (1983). Predicting frames. *Journal of Experimental Psychology: Learning, Memory, and Cognition, 9,* 103–116.

Fishburn, P. C. (1982). Nontransitive measurable utility. *Journal of Mathematical Psychology, 26,* 31–67.

Fishburn, P. C. (1983). Transitive measurable utility. *Journal of Economic Theory, 31,* 293–317.

Fishburn, P. C. (1984). SSB utility theory and decision making under uncertainty. *Mathematical Social Sciences, 8,* 253–285.

Fishburn, P. C. (1985). Uncertainty aversion and separated effects in decision making under uncertainty. Working paper. Murray Hill, NJ: AT&T Bell Labs.

Fishburn, P. C., & Kochenberger, G. A. (1979). Two-piece von Neumann–Morgenstern utility functions. *Decision Sciences, 10,* 503–518.

Grether, D. M. (1980). Bayes rule as a descriptive model: The representativeness heuristic. *Quarterly Journal of Economics, 95,* 537–557.

Grether, D. M., & Plott, C. R. (1979). Economic theory of choice and the preference reversal phenomenon. *American Economic Review, 69,* 623–638.

Hagen, O. (1979). Towards a positive theory of preferences under risk. In M. Allais & O. Hagen (Eds.), *Expected utility hypotheses and the Allais paradox* (pp. 271–302). Dordrecht, the Netherlands: Reidel.

Haltiwanger, J., & Waldman, M. (1985). Rational expectations and the limits of rationality: An analysis of heterogeneity. *American Economic Review, 75*, 326–340.

Hammond, P. (1985). Consequential behavior in decision trees and expected utility. Institute for Mathematical Studies in the Social Sciences Working Paper no. 112. Stanford University.

Hansson, B. (1975). The appropriateness of the expected utility model. *Erkenntnis, 9*, 175–193.

Hausch, D. B., Ziemba, W. T., & Rubenstein, M. E. (1981). Efficiency of the market for racetrack betting. *Management Science, 27*, 1435–1452.

Hershey, J. C., & Schoemaker, P. J. H. (1980). Risk taking and problem context in the domain of losses: An expected utility analysis. *Journal of Risk and Insurance, 47*, 111–132.

Kahneman, D., Knetsch, J. L., & Thaler, R. H. (1986a). Fairness and the assumptions of economics. *Journal of Business, 59*, S285–S300.

Kahneman, D., Knetsch, J. L., & Thaler, R. (1986b). Fairness as a constraint on profit seeking: Entitlements in the market. *American Economic Review, 76*, 728–741.

Kahneman, D., & Tversky, A. (1979). Prospect theory: An analysis of decision under risk. *Econometrica, 47*, 263–291.

Kahneman, D., & Tversky, A. (1982). The psychology of preferences. *Scientific American, 246*, 160–173.

Kahneman, D., & Tversky, A. (1984). Choices, values, and frames. *American Psychologist, 39*, 341–350.

Knetsch, J. L., & Sinden, J. A. (1984). Willingness to pay and compensation demanded: Experimental evidence of an unexpected disparity in measures of value. *Quarterly Journal of Economics, 99*, 507–521.

Knez, P., Smith, V. L., & Williams, A. W. (1985). Individual rationality, market rationality and value estimation. *American Economic Review, 75*, 397–402.

Loomes, G., & Sugden, R. (1982). Regret theory: An alternative theory of rational choice under uncertainty. *Economic Journal (Oxford), 92*, 805–824.

Luce, R. D., & Krantz, D. H. (1971). Conditional expected utility. *Econometrica, 39*, 253–271.

Luce, R. D., & Narens, L. (1985). Classification of concatenation measurement structures according to scale type. *Journal of Mathematical Psychology, 29*, 1–72.

Machina, M. J. (1982). "Expected utility" analysis without the independence axiom. *Econometrica, 50*, 277–323.

March, J. G. (1978). Bounded rationality, ambiguity, and the engineering of choice. *Bell Journal of Economics, 9*, 587–608.

Markowitz, H. (1952). The utility of wealth. *Journal of Political Economy, 60*, 151–158.

McNeil, B. J., Pauker, S. G., Sox, H. C., Jr., & Tversky, A. (1982). On the elicitation of preferences for alternative therapies. *New England Journal of Medicine, 306*, 1259–1262.

Nelson, R. R., & Winter, S. G. (1982). *An evolutionary theory of economic change.* Cambridge, MA: Harvard University Press.

Payne, J. W., Laughhunn, D. J., & Crum, R. (1980). Translation of gambles and aspiration level effects in risky choice behavior. *Management Science, 26,* 1039–1060.

Quiggin, J. (1982). A theory of anticipated utility. *Journal of Economic Behavior & Organization, 3,* 323–343.

Raiffa, H. (1968). *Decision analysis: Introductory lectures on choices under uncertainty.* Reading, MA: Addison-Wesley.

Russell, T., & Thaler, R. (1985). The relevance of quasi-rationality in competitive markets. *American Economic Review, 75,* 1071–1082.

Savage, L. J. (1954). *The foundations of statistics.* New York, NY: Wiley.

Schelling, T. C. (1981). Economic reasoning and the ethics of policy. *Public Interest, 63,* 37–61.

Schmeidler, D. (1984). *Subjective probability and expected utility without additivity. Preprint Series no. 84.* Minneapolis, MN: University of Minnesota, Institute for Mathematics and Its Applications.

Schumpeter, J. A. (1954). *History of economic analysis.* New York, NY: Oxford University Press.

Segal, U. 1984. Nonlinear decision weights with the independence axiom. Working Paper in Economics no. 353. Los Angeles, CA: University of California, Los Angeles.

Simon, H. A. (1955). A behavioral model of rational choice. *Quarterly Journal of Economics, 69,* 99–118.

Simon, H. A. (1978). Rationality as process and as product of thought. *American Economic Review, 68,* 1–16.

Slovic, P., Fischhoff, B., & Lichtenstein, S. (1982). Response mode, framing, and information processing effects in risk assessment. In R. M. Hogarth (Ed.), *New directions for methodology of social and behavioral science: Question framing and response consistency* (pp. 21–36). San Francisco, CA: Jossey-Bass.

Slovic, P., & Lichtenstein, S. (1983). Preference reversals: A broader perspective. *American Economic Review, 73,* 596–605.

Slovic, P., & Tversky, A. (1974). Who accepts Savage's axiom? *Behavioral Science, 19,* 368–373.

Smith, V. L. (1985). Experimental economics [Reply]. *American Economic Review, 75,* 265–272.

Stigler, G. J., & Kindahl, J. K. (1970). *The Behavior of industrial prices.* New York, NY: National Bureau of Economic Research.

Thaler, R. H. (1980). Towards a positive theory of consumer choice. *Journal of Economic Behavior & Organization, 1,* 39–60.

Tversky, A. (1969). Intransitivity of preferences. *Psychological Review, 76,* 105–110.

Tversky, A. (1977). On the elicitation of preferences: Descriptive and prescriptive considerations. In D. E. Bell, R. L. Keeney, & H. Raiffa (Eds.), *Conflicting objectives in decisions* (pp. 209–222). New York, NY: Wiley.

Tversky, A., & Kahneman, D. (1981). The framing of decisions and the psychology of choice. *Science, 211*, 453–458.

Tversky, A., & Kahneman, D. (1983). Extensional versus intuitive reasoning: The conjunction fallacy in probability judgment. *Psychological Review, 90*, 293–315.

von Neumann, J., & Morgenstern, O. (1944). *Theory of games and economic behavior*. Princeton, NJ: Princeton University Press.

Weber, R. J. (1982). The Allais paradox, Dutch auctions, and alpha-utility theory. Working paper. Northwestern University.

Yaari, M. E. (1984). *Risk aversion without decreasing marginal utility. Report series in theoretical economics.* London, England: London School of Economics.

6 Discrepancy between Medical Decisions for Individual Patients and for Groups

Donald A. Redelmeier and Amos Tversky

Tension between health policy and medical practice exists in many situations. For example, regional variations in practice patterns persist despite extensive shared information,[1-3] there are substantial deviations from accepted guidelines daily in the care of patients,[4-7] and disproportionate amounts of care are given to selected individuals.[8-10] These observations indicate that decisions in the clinical arena, which focus on the individual patient, may be at variance with general medical policies, which are based on wider considerations. Our study investigated this discrepancy.

Imagine a patient presenting to a physician with a specific problem. Normally the physician treats each patient as a unique case and selects the treatment that seems best for that person. Over time, however, the physician may encounter many similar patients. Does the physician make a different judgment when a case is viewed as unique rather than as one of a group of comparable cases? There is evidence that people make different choices between financial gambles when they face single rather than repeated situations.[11-13] Furthermore, studies of both economic and medical decisions show that looking at a problem from different perspectives can change the relative weight given to its attributes and lead to different choices.[14-16]

We hypothesized that physicians give more weight to a patient's personal concerns when they consider the patient as an individual and more weight to general criteria of effectiveness when they consider the patient as part of a group. More specifically, we suggested that in viewing a patient as an individual rather than as a member of a group, physicians are more likely to do the following: recommend an additional test with a low cost and a possible benefit, examine a patient directly rather than follow progress by telephone, avoid troubling problems such as discussing organ donation, and recommend a therapy with a high probability of success but the chance of an adverse outcome. In this study we explored these issues to address the question: Do physicians make different judgments in evaluating an individual patient as compared with considering a group of similar patients? Our data suggest that they do, that the discrepancy is recognized by physicians trained in health-services research, and that lay people also make this distinction.

Methods

In our first experiment we invited practicing physicians to participate in a study of medical decision making. The questionnaire we used contained clinical scenarios describing problems in patient management about which reasonable physicians could disagree. Each physician was asked to select the most appropriate treatment.

We presented the problems in two versions, each from a different perspective. The individual version concerned the treatment of one patient. The aggregate version concerned the treatment of a group of comparable patients. In all other respects, the two versions contained the same information. For example, the individual version of one scenario was as follows.

The literature provides little information on the use of the telephone as an instrument of medical care. For example, H.B. is a young woman well known to her family physician and free from any serious illnesses. She contacts her family physician by phone because of 5 days of fever without any localizing symptoms. A tentative diagnosis of viral infection is made, symptomatic measures are prescribed, and she is told to stay "in touch." After about 36 hours she phones back reporting feeling about the same: no better, no worse, no new symptoms. The choice must be made between continuing to follow her a little longer by telephone or else telling her to come in now to be examined. Which management would you select for H.B.?

The aggregate version of this scenario was similar, except that we replaced all references to the individual patient with terms denoting a group of patients.

The literature provides little information on the use of the telephone as an instrument of medical care. For example, consider young women who are well known to their family physicians and free from any serious illnesses. They might contact their respective family physicians by phone because of 5 days of fever without any localizing symptoms. Frequently a tentative diagnosis of viral infection is made, symptomatic measures are prescribed, and they are told to stay "in touch." Suppose that after about 36 hours they phone back reporting feeling about the same: no better, no worse, no new symptoms. The choice must be made between continuing to follow them a little longer by telephone or else telling them to come in now to be examined. Which management strategy would you recommend?

Four groups of doctors participated in this part of the study: house staff in the Department of Medicine at Stanford University Hospital, physicians who were practicing full time in a regional health maintenance organization (HMO), academic physicians affiliated with Stanford's Department of Internal Medicine, and full-time physicians associated with a county medical center. Within each group we randomly assigned physicians to receive either the individual or the aggregate version of the questionnaire. We then compared their responses to the two versions using the Mann–Whitney test.[17]

In our second experiment we presented scenarios analogous to those in experiment 1 and asked participants to compare the two perspectives directly. For this questionnaire we surveyed a group of internists, psychiatrists, and pediatricians who had advanced training in both clinical medicine and health-services research. For each scenario the participants indicated whether they thought that physicians were more likely to recommend a particular action from the individual-patient perspective or the general-policy perspective. We presented, for example, the following scenario: "A 25-year-old man who rides a motorcycle is being seen for routine medical reasons. From which perspective do you think the option of discussing organ donation is more likely to be recommended?"

In our third experiment, we asked undergraduate students at Stanford to consider a hypothetical medical case that could be understood without technical knowledge. As in the first experiment, half the students were presented with the individual version, and half the aggregate version. Participants in all three experiments received the questionnaires, completed them at their leisure, and then returned them anonymously.

Results

Experiment 1

In the first experiment, 59 house officers returned completed questionnaires, as did 94 university-affiliated physicians, 75 HMO physicians, and 128 physicians associated with the county hospital. The overall rate of response was 78%. As expected, the two groups that had received the different versions of the questionnaire were similar in age, sex, experience, and rate of response. The four issues we have raised are discussed below.

Blood Test   To explore the first issue, we asked the physicians to consider the scenario of a college student presenting with fatigue, insomnia, and difficulty in concentrating. In addition to the usual evaluation we described an extra blood test that might detect a rare, treatable condition but that entailed a $20 cost, which the student would have to pay out of pocket. The physicians chose to perform the test more frequently when given the individual version, which referred to one patient, than when given the aggregate version, which referred to a group of patients (30% vs. 17%; $p < 0.005$). The difference was evident among the house staff (26% vs. 4%; $p < 0.05$), the HMO physicians (28% vs. 7%; $p < 0.10$), the academic physicians (40% vs. 19%; $p < 0.01$), and doctors at the county hospital (43% vs. 22%; $p < 0.05$).

Telephone Medicine   To explore the second, we asked the physicians to consider the scenario of an otherwise healthy young woman who calls her family doctor because of a persistent mild fever. The physicians recommended following by telephone, rather than asking the patient to come in for an examination, more frequently in the aggregate version than in the individual version (13% vs. 9%; $p < 0.005$). The difference was evident among the academic physicians (15% vs. 6%; $p < 0.01$) and the doctors at the county hospital (12% vs. 2%; $p < 0.05$), but not among the HMO physicians (14% vs. 24%; n.s.). The house staff were not presented with this scenario.

Experiment 2

In contrast with the physicians in experiment 1, who each evaluated only one version of a problem, the physicians in experiment 2 compared the aggregate and the individual perspectives directly. A total of 89 completed questionnaires were returned, representing a rate of response of 77%. The results confirmed the findings of our first experiment. In the case of the college student with fatigue, 81% of the respondents ($p < 0.005$) thought that the additional test would be recommended more frequently if considered from the individual rather than the aggregate perspective. In the case of the young woman with a fever, 87% of the respondents ($p < 0.005$) thought that the option of following by telephone would be selected more frequently from the group perspective.

Organ Donation   To explore the third issue, we also presented the health-service researchers with the scenario of a healthy motorcycle rider who was being seen for a minor medical problem. When asked about discussing organ donation, 93% of the respondents ($p < 0.005$) thought that it would be recommended more frequently from the aggregate perspective.

Adverse Outcomes   To explore the fourth issue, we presented the health-service researchers with a scenario of a woman with a blood condition. We described a medication, which could be added to her therapy, that sometimes improves longevity but sometimes makes things worse. The medication offered an 85% chance of adding two years to her life and a 15% chance of shortening it by two years. In this case, 59% of the respondents ($p < 0.10$) thought that the medication would be recommended more frequently from the individual perspective.

Experiment 3

This experiment tested whether the difference between the perspectives was also evident in the judgments of lay people. A total of 327 students were presented with the adverse-outcomes scenario, selected because it involved no technical knowledge of medicine. As in the first experiment, each student received either the individual or the aggregate version. In accordance with our previous finding, the medication was recommended more frequently by those given the individual version than by those given the aggregate version (62% vs. 42%; $p < 0.005$).

Discussion

Our results indicate that physicians make different decisions when evaluating an individual patient than when considering a group of comparable patients (experiment 1). This discrepancy is recognized as a professional norm (experiment 2) and is also found in the judgments of lay people (experiment 3). We explored four issues that highlight the discrepancy. From the individual as compared with the aggregate perspective, physicians are more likely to order an additional test, expend time directly assessing a patient, avoid raising some troubling issues, and recommend a therapy with a high probability of success but the chance of an adverse outcome.

The discrepancy between the aggregate and individual perspectives demonstrated in these experiments cannot be attributed to differences in either medical information or economic incentives; hence it is difficult to explain on normative grounds.[18,19] Our results are consistent with the notion that physicians give more weight to the personal concerns of patients when considering them as individuals and more weight to general criteria of effectiveness when considering them as a group. For example, the responses to our adverse-outcomes scenario suggest that small probabilities are taken less seriously when deciding about just one case. Such differences in giving weight to various aspects of a problem may help to explain why general principles, which reflect a group perspective, are not always followed in clinical practice, which proceeds on a case-by-case basis. As a consequence, the discrepancy between the aggregate and individual perspectives may create tension between health policy makers and medical practitioners even when the pertinent facts are accepted by both. Several characteristics of medical decision making may amplify the discrepancy between perspectives. Schelling has discussed the distinction between statistical lives and identified lives, emphasizing the higher value society places on the life of an identified person.[20] Fuchs has suggested a "technologic imperative" in doctor–patient relationships that reflects physicians' desires to do everything they have been trained to do in treating individual patients.[21] Evans has addressed the physician's conflict between being a perfect agent for the patient and being the protector of society.[22] Financial incentives, of course, may also contribute to the tension between policy and practice.[23,24]

Although the discrepancy between the aggregate and individual perspectives calls for resolution, we do not suggest discarding either perspective. The individual perspective emphasizes the particular concerns of the patient and is more in accord with the personal nature of the doctor–patient relationship. The aggregate perspective acknowledges the fact that over time doctors will treat many similar patients. Physicians and policy makers may wish to examine problems from both perspectives to ensure that treatment decisions are appropriate whether applied to one or to many patients. An awareness of the two perspectives may enhance clinical judgment and enrich health policy.

Acknowledgments

We are indebted to Tammy Tengs, Joan Esplin, Marcus Krupp, Edward Harris, Eliott Wolfe, and Patrick Kearns for assistance with the questionnaires; to Halsted Holman, Dianna Dutton, Alan Garber, Robert Wachter, and Mitchel Wilson for help in preparing the manuscript; and to our respondents for their thoughtful effort.

References

1. Chassin, M. R., Brook, R. H., Park, R. E., et al. (1986). Variations in the use of medical and surgical services by the Medicare population. *New England Journal of Medicine, 314,* 285–290.

2. Wennberg, J. (1986). Which rate is right? *New England Journal of Medicine, 314,* 310–311.

3. Iglehart, J. K. (Ed.). (1984). Variations in medical practice. *Health Affairs (Project Hope), 3*(2), 6–148.

4. Woo, B., Woo, B., Cook, E. F., Weisberg, M., & Goldman, L. (1985). Screening procedures in the asymptomatic adult: Comparison of physicians' recommendations, patients' desires, published guidelines, and actual practice. *Journal of the American Medical Association, 254,* 1480–1484.

5. Kosecoff, J., Kanouse, D. E., Rogers, W. H., McCloskey, L., Winslow, C. M., & Brook, R. H. (1987). Effects of the National Institutes of Health Consensus Development Program on physician practice. *Journal of the American Medical Association, 258,* 2708–2713.

6. Eddy, D. M. (1982). Clinical policies and the quality of clinical practice. *New England Journal of Medicine, 307,* 343–347.

7. Lomas, J., Anderson, G. M., Domnick-Pierre, K., Vayda, E., Enkin, M. W., & Hannah, W. J. (1989). Do practice guidelines guide practice? The effect of a consensus statement on the practice of physicians. *New England Journal of Medicine, 321,* 1306–1311.

8. Woolley, F. R. (1984). Ethical issues in the implantation of the total artificial heart. *New England Journal of Medicine, 310,* 292–296.

9. Bunker, J. P. (1976). When the medical interests of society are in conflict with those of the individual, who wins? *Pharos, 39*(1), 64–66.

10. Levinsky, N. G. (1984). The doctor's master. *New England Journal of Medicine, 311,* 1573–1575.

11. Samuelson, P. A. (1963). Risk and uncertainty: A fallacy of large numbers. *Scientia, 98,* 108–113.

12. Keren, G., & Wagenaar, W. A. (1987). Violation of expected utility theory in unique and repeated gambles. *Journal of Experimental Psychology: Learning, Memory, and Cognition, 13*, 382–391.

13. Montgomery, H., & Adelbratt, T. (1982). Gambling decisions and information about expected value. *Organizational Behavior and Human Performance, 29*, 39–57.

14. McNeil, B. J., Pauker, S. G., Sox, H. C., Jr., & Tversky, A. (1982). On the elicitation of preferences for alternative therapies. *New England Journal of Medicine, 306*, 1259–1262.

15. Eraker, S. A., & Sox, H. C., Jr. (1981). Assessment of patients' preferences for therapeutic outcomes. *Medical Decision Making, 1*, 29–39.

16. Tversky, A., & Kahneman, D. (1986). Rational choice and the framing of decisions. *Journal of Business, 59*, S251–S278.

17. Moses, L. E. (1986). *Think and explain with statistics*. Reading, MA: Addison-Wesley.

18. Sox, H. C., Jr., Blatt, M. A., Higgins, M. C., & Marton, K. I. (1988). *Medical decision making*. Boston, MA: Butterworths.

19. Raiffa, H. (1968). *Decision analysis*. Reading, MA: Addison-Wesley.

20. Schelling, T. C. (1968). The life you save may be your own. In S. B. Chase, Jr. (Ed.), *Problems in public expenditure analysis* (pp. 127–176). Washington, DC: Brookings Institution.

21. Fuchs, V. R. (1974). *Who shall live? Health, economics, and social choice*. New York, NY: Basic Books.

22. Evans, R. W. (1983). Health care technology and the inevitability of resource allocation and rationing decisions. *Journal of the American Medical Association, 249*, 2208–2219.

23. Bock, R. S. (1988). The pressure to keep prices high at a walk-in clinic: A personal experience. *New England Journal of Medicine, 319*, 785–787.

24. Scovern, H. (1988). Hired help: A physician's experiences in a for-profit staff-model HMO. *New England Journal of Medicine, 319*, 787–790.

7 Thinking through Uncertainty: Nonconsequential Reasoning and Choice

Eldar Shafir and Amos Tversky

Much of everyday thinking and decision making involves uncertainty about the objective state of the world and about our subjective moods and desires. We may be uncertain about the future state of the economy, our mood following an upcoming examination, or whether we will want to vacation in Hawaii during the holidays. Different states of the world, of course, often lead to different decisions. If we do well on the exam, we may feel that we deserve a break and want to go to Hawaii; if we do poorly, we may prefer to stay at home. When making decisions under uncertainty we need to consider the possible states of the world and their potential implications for our desires and actions. Uncertain situations may be thought of as disjunctions of possible states: either one state will obtain, or another. A student who is uncertain about her performance on an exam, for instance, faces a disjunction of outcomes: passing the exam or failing the exam. In deciding whether or not to plan a vacation in Hawaii, the student needs to consider whether she would want to go to Hawaii if she were to pass the exam, and whether she would want to go if she were to fail, as diagrammed in figure 7.1. (As is customary, decision nodes are denoted by squares; chance nodes are denoted by circles.)

Most conceptions of decision making under uncertainty—both normative and descriptive—are *consequentialist* in the sense that decisions are determined by an assessment of the potential consequences and their perceived likelihood. According to this view, the student's decision to buy the Hawaiian vacation will depend on her subjective value of staying and going in the event that she passes the exam and in the event that she fails, and on her subjective probability of passing and failing.[1] Choices based on a consequentialist evaluation of anticipated outcomes are expected to satisfy a basic axiom of decision under uncertainty known as Savage's sure-thing principle (Savage, 1954, p. 21). The sure-thing principle (henceforth STP) says that if we prefer x to y given any possible state of the world, then we should prefer x to y even when the exact state of the world is not known. In the context of figure 7.1, it implies that if the student prefers going to staying both if she passes and if she fails the exam, then she should prefer going to staying even when the exam's outcome is not

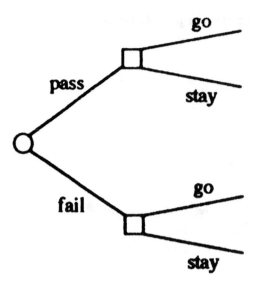

Figure 7.1
A tree diagram for the Hawaiian vacation problem.

known. STP is an important implication of the consequentialist view. It captures a fundamental intuition of what it means for a decision to be determined by the anticipated consequences. It is a cornerstone of expected utility theory, and it holds in other models that
impose less stringent criteria of rationality.

If, however, people do not always choose in a consequentialist manner, then STP may
sometimes be violated. For example, we have shown elsewhere that many people who chose
to purchase a vacation to Hawaii if they were to pass an exam *and* if they were to fail decided
to postpone buying the vacation in the disjunctive case, when the exam's outcome was not
known (Tversky & Shafir, 1992). Having passed the exam, the vacation is presumably seen
as a time of celebration following a successful semester; having failed the exam, the vacation
becomes a consolation and time of recovery. Not knowing the outcome of the exam, we suggest, the decision maker lacks a clear reason for going and, as a result, may prefer to wait and
learn the outcome before deciding to go, contrary to STP.

For another example of nonconsequential reasoning, imagine that you have agreed to
bet on a toss of a coin in which you had equal chances to win $200 or lose $100. Suppose
that the coin has been tossed, but that you do not know whether you have won or lost.
Would you now want to play this gamble a second time? Alternatively, how would you feel
about accepting the second gamble if you knew that you lost $100 on the first gamble? And

finally, would you play the second gamble having discovered that you won $200 on the first gamble? We have shown that, contrary to STP, a majority of respondents accepted the second gamble both after having won as well as after having lost the first, but a majority rejected the second gamble when the outcome of the first was not known (Tversky & Shafir, 1992). This pattern—accept when win, accept when lose, but reject when do not know—was the single most frequent pattern of preferences exhibited by our subjects. We have suggested that people have a good reason for accepting the second gamble following a gain (namely, "I am up and no matter what happens I cannot lose"), and that they have a compelling albeit different reason for accepting the second gamble following a loss (namely, "I am down and this is my chance to get out of the red"). But when the outcome of the first gamble is unknown, people do not know whether they are ahead and cannot lose or whether they are behind and need to recover their losses. In this condition, we have argued, they may have no clear reason for accepting the additional gamble, which, on its own, is not particularly attractive. We call the above pattern of preferences a *disjunction effect*. A disjunction effect occurs when people prefer *x* over *y* when they know that event *A* obtains, and they also prefer *x* over *y* when they know that event *A* does not obtain, but they prefer *y* over *x* when it is unknown whether or not *A* obtains. The disjunction effect amounts to a violation of STP, and hence of consequentialism.

In the present chapter we explore nonconsequential behavior in several reasoning and decision-making tasks. We suggest that various reasons and considerations are weighted differently in the presence of uncertainty than in its absence, giving rise to violations of STP. Our previous studies explored situations in which the reasons for a particular option (like going to Hawaii or taking the gamble) were more compelling once the uncertainty was resolved than when the outcome was uncertain. The present studies focus on scenarios in which arguments that seem appealing while the outcome is uncertain lose much of their force once the uncertainty is resolved. It is proposed that the shift in perspective induced by the resolution of uncertainty may shed light on several puzzling manifestations of nonconsequential behavior. In the first part of the chapter we explore one-shot Prisoner's Dilemmas, and a version of Newcomb's Problem played against a computer program. We then extend the analysis from decision making to reasoning. We suggest that nonconsequential reasoning plays an important role in Wason's selection task and then describe a scenario in which the U.S. financial markets seem to exhibit nonconsequential behavior. Finally, we explore the implications of the present findings on the analysis of thinking in the face of uncertainty and consider their relevance to the comparison between natural and artificial intelligence.

Games and Decisions

Prisoner's Dilemma

The theory of games provides an analysis of the interaction among players who act according to specific rules. One particular two-person game that has received enormous attention is the Prisoner's Dilemma, or PD for short. (For extensive discussion, see Rapoport & Chammah, 1965; Rapoport, 1988.) A typical PD is presented in figure 7.2. The cell entries indicate the payoffs (e.g., the number of points) received by each player. Thus, if both you and your opponent cooperate, each receives 75 points. However, if the other cooperates and you compete, you receive 85 points while the other receives 25, etc. What characterizes the PD is that regardless of the opponent's choice, each player fares better by competing than by cooperating; yet, if they both compete they do less well than if they had both cooperated. While many interesting strategies arise in the context of repeated games (see, e.g., Axelrod, 1984; Kreps & Wilson, 1982; Luce & Raiffa, 1957), the present discussion is confined to PD's that are played only once.

		OTHER	
		cooperates	competes
YOU	cooperate	You: 75 Other: 75	You: 25 Other: 85
	compete	You: 85 Other: 25	You: 30 Other: 30

Figure 7.2
A typical Prisoner's Dilemma. The cell entries indicate the number of points that you and the other player receive contingent on your choices.

This is the simplest and sharpest form of a dilemma. Because the opponent is encountered only once, there is no opportunity for conveying strategic messages, inducing reciprocity, developing a reputation, or otherwise influencing the other player's choice of strategy. Because regardless of what the other does on this single encounter you will receive more points if you compete than if you cooperate, the dominant strategy is to compete. Nevertheless, some—presumably on ethical grounds—choose to cooperate. When Douglas Hofstadter (1983) presented a problem of this kind to a group of experts, roughly a third chose cooperation. Similar rates of cooperation were observed in a number of experimental studies (see, e.g., Rapoport, Guyer, & Gordon, 1976; Rapoport, 1988). The philosopher Dan Dennett captured the guiding ethical motivation when he remarked: "I'd rather be the person who bought the Brooklyn Bridge than the person who sold it. Similarly, I'd feel better spending $3 gained by cooperating than $10 gained by defecting." Evidently, some people are willing to forego some gains in order to make the cooperative, ethical decision.

Our previous discussion of nonconsequential reasoning suggests an alternative interpretation of the cooperation observed in one-shot PD games. Once the player knows that the other has chosen either to compete or to cooperate, it is clear that competition will be more advantageous to him than cooperation. But as long as the other has not made his decision, mutual cooperation looms as an attractive solution for both players. Although each player cannot affect the other's decision, he may be tempted to do his best (in this case, cooperate) to bring about the mutually desired state. This reasoning, of course, no longer applies once the outcome has occurred. Voting behavior is a case in point. We know that our individual vote is unlikely to affect the outcome of elections. Nevertheless, many of us who would not bother to vote once the outcome has been determined are inclined to vote when the outcome of the elections is still pending. If this interpretation of cooperation in the PD game is correct, we expect a greater rate of cooperation in the disjunctive condition, when the other player's strategy is not known, than when the other player has chosen to compete or when the other has chosen to cooperate. This hypothesis is tested in the following study.

Method Eighty Princeton undergraduates were presented with PD games displayed on a computer screen one at a time, in the format given in figure 7.2. On each trial, they chose whether to compete or cooperate by pressing the appropriate button. Subjects responded at their own pace, and once they chose their strategy, the screen cleared and the next game was presented. Each subject was presented with 40 games, of which only six were PDs. Other two-person games (with different payoff structures) were interspersed among the PDs in order to force subjects to consider each game anew, rather than adopt a "standard" strategy. Subjects were told that these games were being played with other students currently on the computer system, and that the outcomes would be determined by their choice and that of a new participant in each game. Their choices would not be made available to anyone playing with them. Thus, subjects were playing a series of one-shot games, each against a different opponent. In addition, subjects were told that they had been randomly assigned to a bonus group: this meant that, occasionally, they would be given information about the other player's already-chosen strategy before they had to choose their own. This information appeared on the screen along with the game, so that subjects could use it in making their decision. Subjects were to be paid according to the number of points that they accumulated throughout the session. They were paid $6.00 on average, and the entire session lasted approximately 40 minutes. The complete instructions appear in the appendix.

We focus now on the six PD games that the subjects played. Each of these appeared three times throughout the session: once in the standard version where the other player's strategy was not known, a second time with the information that the other had competed, and a third time with the information that the other had cooperated. The standard version of each PD game appeared first, and the order of the other two was counterbalanced across subjects. The three versions of each game were separated by a number of other games in between. We refer to the three versions of each PD game as a PD "triad." The first 18 subjects were presented with four PD triads, and the remaining subjects played six PD triads each, yielding a total of 444 triads.

Results and Discussion   Subjects' responses to the PD triads are presented in table 7.1. Table 7.1A summarizes subjects' chosen strategies, over all 444 games, when the other player competes and when the other player cooperates. Table 7.1B shows these same subjects' chosen strategy in the disjunctive case, when the other player's strategy is not known. When informed that the other has chosen to compete, the great majority of subjects reciprocate by competing. To cooperate would mean to turn the other cheek and forfeit points. Of the 444 games in which subjects were informed that the other had chosen to compete (table 7.1A), only 3% resulted in cooperation. When informed that the other has chosen to cooperate, a larger percentage of subjects choose cooperation. This confirms the widespread sentiment that there is an ethical inclination to reciprocate when the other cooperates. Of the 444 games in which subjects were told that the other player had cooperated, 16% resulted in cooperation. Now what should subjects do when the other's strategy is not known? Since 3% cooperate when the other competes and 16% cooperate when the other cooperates, we would expect an intermediate rate of cooperation when the other's strategy is not known. Instead, of the 444 games in which the other's strategy was unknown (table 7.1B), a full 37% resulted in cooperation (the cooperation rates in the three versions are all significantly different, $p < 0.001$ in all cases). The increased tendency to cooperate when uncertain about the other's chosen strategy cannot be attributed to a moral imperative of the type articulated by

Table 7.1

Prisoner's Dilemma

		Other player competes		
		S competes	*S* cooperates	
A. Other's strategy known[a]				
Other player cooperates	*S* competes	364	7	371 (84%)
	S cooperates	66	7	73 (16%)
		430	14	444
		(97%)	(3%)	
B. Other's strategy not known[b]				
Other player cooperates	*S* competes	113 cooperate	3 cooperate	
		251 compete	4 compete	
	S cooperates	43 cooperate	5 cooperate	
		23 compete	2 compete	

[a]Joint distribution of subjects' (*S*) strategies when the other player competes and when the other player cooperates.

[b]Distribution of subjects' strategies when the other player's strategy is not known, broken down—as in A—according to subjects' choice of strategy when the other player competes and cooperates.

Dennett. Any account based on ethical considerations implies that the rate of cooperation should be highest when the other player is known to have cooperated, contrary to table 7.1.

As expected, competition was the most popular strategy in all conditions. Consequently, the single most frequent choice pattern was to compete in all three versions. The next most frequent pattern, however, representing 25% of all response triads (113 out of 444 triads in table 7.1B), was of the form: compete when the other competes, compete when the other cooperates, but cooperate when the other's strategy is not known. Sixty-five percent of the subjects exhibited such a disjunction effect on at least one of the six PD triads that they played. Of all triads yielding cooperation when the other player's strategy was unknown, 69% resulted in competition both when the other competed and when the other cooperated. This pattern is illustrated using the tree diagram of figure 7.3. The majority of subjects choose to compete at the upper branch (when the other cooperates) as well as at the lower branch (when the other competes). Contrary to STP, however, many cooperate when they do not know on which branch they are.

A behavioral pattern that violates a simple normative rule calls for both a positive analysis, which explains the specific factors that produce the observed response, and a negative analysis, which explains why the correct response is not made (Kahneman & Tversky, 1982). The conjunction fallacy (Tversky & Kahneman, 1983) is a case in point. The positive analysis of this phenomenon has invoked judgmental heuristics, such as availability and

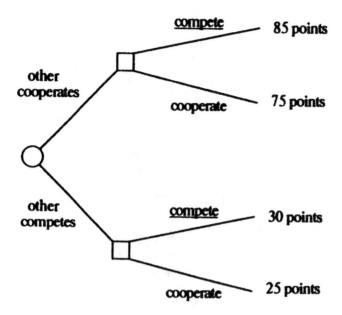

Figure 7.3
A tree diagram illustrating the Prisoner's Dilemma presented in figure 7.2. Decision nodes and chance nodes are denoted by squares and circles, respectively. Modal choices are underlined.

representativeness, whereas the negative analysis attributes conjunction errors to people's failure to detect the fact that one event is included in the other, or to their failure to appreciate the implication of this inclusion. Analogously, a negative analysis of the disjunction effect suggests that people do not evaluate appropriately all the relevant outcomes. This may occur because people sometimes fail to consider all the branches of the relevant decision tree, especially when the number of outcomes is large. Alternatively, people may consider all the relevant outcomes but, due to the presence of uncertainty, may not see their own preferences very clearly. Consider the Hawaii scenario described earlier. A person who has just taken the exam but does not know the outcome may feel, without specifically considering the implications of success and failure, that this is not the time to choose to go to Hawaii. Alternatively, the person might contemplate the outcomes, but—uncertain about which outcome will occur—may feel unsure about her own preferences. For example, she may feel confident about wanting to go to Hawaii if she passes the exam, but unsure about whether she would want to go in case she failed. Only when she focuses exclusively on the possibility of failing the exam does her preference for going to Hawaii become clear. A similar analysis applies to the present PD game. Not knowing the opponent's strategy, a player may realize that he wishes to compete if the other competes, but he may not be sure about his preference if the other were to cooperate. Having focused exclusively on the latter possibility, the player now sees more clearly that he wishes to compete in this case as well. The presence of uncertainty, we suggest, makes it difficult to focus sharply on any single branch; broadening the focus of attention results in a loss of acuity. The failure to appreciate the force of STP, therefore, is attributed to people's reluctance to consider all the outcomes, or to their reluctance to formulate a clear preference in the presence of uncertainty about those outcomes. This interpretation is consistent with the finding that, once people are made aware of their preferences given each possible outcome, STP is no longer violated (Tversky & Shafir, 1992).

Several factors may contribute to a positive analysis of the disjunction effect in the PD game. The game is characterized by the fact that an individually rational decision by each player results in an outcome that is not optimal collectively. Our subjects seem to exhibit a change of perspective that may be described as a shift from individual to collective rationality. Once the other's strategy is known, a player is "on her own." Only one column of the PD table is relevant (that which corresponds to the strategy chosen by the other), and the outcome of the game depends on her and her alone. The individually rational strategy, of course, is to compete. In the disjunctive condition, by contrast, all four cells of the table are in play. The outcome of the game depends on the collective decision of both players, and the collectively optimal decision is for both to cooperate. Thus, the pattern of behavior observed in the PD may be explained, in part at least, by the greater tendency to adopt the collective perspective in the disjunctive version of the game.[2] Note, incidentally, that collective—albeit uncoordinated—action is quite viable. To the extent that our nonconsequentialist subjects play against one another, they stand to receive more points (for reaching the cooperate–cooperate cell) than would be awarded to consequentialist subjects (for their compete–compete cell). The potential benefits of cooperation in social dilemmas are discussed by Dawes and Orbell (1995).

A consequentialist subject who chooses to compete both when the other competes and when the other cooperates should also compete when the other's decision—as is usually the case—is not known. Instead, uncertainty promotes a tendency to cooperate, which disappears once the other player's decision has been determined. It appears that many subjects did not appropriately evaluate each possible outcome and its implications. Rather, when the opponent's response was not known, many subjects preferred to cooperate, perhaps as a way of "inducing" cooperation from the other. Because subjects naturally assume that the other player—a fellow student—will approach the game in much the same way they do, whatever they decide to do, it seems, the other is likely to do the same. Along these lines, Messe and Sivacek (1979) have argued that people overestimate the likelihood that others will act the way they do in mixed-motive games. Such an attitude may lead subjects to cooperate in the hope of achieving joint cooperation and thereby obtaining the largest mutual benefit, rather than compete and risk joint competition. If they were able to coordinate a binding agreement, subjects would certainly agree on mutual cooperation. Being unable to secure a binding agreement in the PD game, subjects are nevertheless tempted to act in accord with the agreement that both players would have endorsed. Although they cannot actually affect the other's decision, subjects choose to "do their share" to bring about the mutually preferred state. This interpretation is consistent with the finding of Quattrone and Tversky (1984) that people often select actions that are diagnostic of favorable outcomes even though they do not cause those outcomes. A discussion of the relation between causal and diagnostic reasoning is resumed in the next section.

We have interpreted violations of STP in the above PD games as an indication that people do not evaluate the outcomes in a consequentialist manner. We now consider two alternative interpretations of the above findings. First, subjects might have cooperated in the disjunctive version of the game because they were afraid that their choices will be relayed to the other player before she had made her decision. This concern, of course, would not arise once the other's decision has already been made. Recall that subjects were specifically told that their choices would not be communicated to anyone playing with them. Nevertheless, they could have been suspicious. Post-experimental interviews, however, revealed that while a few subjects were suspicious about the actual, simultaneous presence of other players on the system, none were concerned that their choices would be surreptitiously divulged. It is unlikely that suspicion could account for subjects' strategies in the present experiment.

Second, it could be argued that the present results can be explained by the hypothesis that the tendency to compete increases as the experiment progresses. In order to observe subjects' untainted strategies in the standard prisoner's dilemmas, we presented these games before the known-outcome games. Hence, an increase in the tendency to compete as the experiment progressed could contribute to the observed pattern because the disjunctive problems—where cooperation was highest—generally occurred earlier in the experiment. However, no such temporal change was observed. The rates of cooperation in the first disjunction encountered (the sixth game played), the fourth disjunction (game number 15), and the last disjunction (game number 19) were 33%, 30%, and 40%, respectively. Similarly, the rate of cooperation when subjects were told that the other had cooperated averaged 13% for the first three occurrences and 21% for the last three. In effect, cooperation tended to increase as the experiment progressed, which would diminish the observed frequency of disjunction effects.

Recall that, like Hofstadter's experts, nearly 40% of our subjects chose to cooperate in a single-shot Prisoner's Dilemma. Once they discovered the other's strategy, however, nearly 70% of these cooperators chose to compete both when the other competed and when the other cooperated. These players followed a variant of Kant's Categorical Imperative: act in the way you wish others to act. They felt less compelled, however, to act in ways others have already acted. This pattern suggests that some of the cooperation observed in one-shot PD games may stem not from a moral imperative of the kind described by Dennett but, rather, from a combination of wishful thinking and nonconsequential evaluation. A similar analysis may apply to a related decision problem to which we turn next.

Newcomb's Problem

First published by Nozick (1969), Newcomb's Problem has since generated a lively philosophical debate that touches on the nature of rational decision. The standard version of the problem proceeds roughly as follows.

Suppose that you have two options: to take the contents of a closed box in front of you, or to take the contents of the closed box *plus* another, open box that you can see contains $1000 in cash. The closed box contains either one million dollars ($M) or nothing, depending on whether a certain being with miraculous powers of foresight, called the Predictor, has or has not placed $M there prior to the time at which you are to make your decision. You know that the Predictor will have placed the $M in the closed box if he has predicted that you will choose the closed box alone; he will have left the closed box empty if he has predicted that you will choose both boxes. You also know that almost everyone who has chosen both boxes found the closed box empty and received just $1000, whereas almost everyone who has chosen just the closed box has found $M in it. What is your choice?

A number of authors (e.g., Brams, 1975; Lewis, 1979; Sobel, 1991) have commented on the logical affinity of Newcomb's Problem with the Prisoner's Dilemma. In both cases, the outcome depends on the choice that you make and on that made by another being—the other player in the Prisoner's Dilemma, and the Predictor in Newcomb's Problem. In both cases, one option (competing or taking both boxes) dominates the other, yet the other option (cooperating or taking just one box) seems preferable if the being—the Predictor or the other player—knows what you will do, or will act like you.

The conflicting intuitions generated by Newcomb's Problem proceed roughly as follows (see Nozick, 1969, for a more complete treatment).

ARGUMENT 1 (FOR ONE BOX). If I choose both boxes, the Predictor, almost certainly, will have predicted this and will not have put the $M in the closed box, and so I will get only $1000. If I take only the closed box, the Predictor, almost certainly, will have predicted this and will have put the $M in that box, and so I will get $M. Thus, if I take both boxes I, almost certainly, will get $1000, and if I take just the closed box I, almost certainly, will get $M. Therefore, I should choose just the closed box.

ARGUMENT 2 (FOR TWO BOXES). The Predictor has already made his prediction and has already either put the $M in the closed box or has not. If the Predictor has already put the $M in the closed box, and I take both boxes, I get $M + $1000, whereas if I take only the closed box, I get only $M. If the Predictor has not put the $M in the closed box, and I take both boxes, I get $1000, whereas if I take only the closed box I get no money. Therefore, whether the $M is there or not, I get $1000 more by taking both boxes rather than only the closed box. So I should take both boxes.

When Martin Gardner (1973, 1974) published Newcomb's Problem in *Scientific American* and invited readers to send in their responses, roughly 70% of the readers who indicated a preference found Argument 1 more compelling and chose to take just the closed box, whereas 30% were driven by Argument 2 to take both boxes. Argument 2 relies on consequential reasoning reminiscent of STP, namely, whatever the state of the boxes, I will do better choosing both boxes than one only. Argument 1, however, is more problematic. While couched in terms of expected utility, it seems to suppose that what the Predictor will have predicted—although he has done so already—depends somehow on what I decide to do now. Excluding trickery, there are two interpretations of the Predictor's unusual powers. According to the first interpretation, the Predictor is simply an excellent judge of human character. Using some database (including, e.g., gender, background, and appearance), a Predictor might be able to predict the decision maker's response with remarkable success. If this interpretation is correct, then you have no reason to take just one box: however insightful the Predictor's forecast, you will do better if you take both boxes rather than one box only. The second interpretation is that the Predictor has truly supernatural powers of insight. If you are unwilling to dismiss this possibility, then you may be justified in deferring to the mysterious powers of the Predictor and taking just one box (cf. Bar-Hillel & Margalit, 1972). This puzzle has captured the imagination of many people. An interesting collection of articles on Newcomb's Problem and its relation to the Prisoner's Dilemma is provided in Campbell and Sowden (1985).

Like Gardner's readers, many people presented with Newcomb's problem opt for one box only, contrary to the consequential logic of Argument 2. The choice of the single box may result from a belief in the Predictor's supernatural abilities. Alternatively, it may reflect a nonconsequential evaluation of the options in question. To distinguish between these interpretations, we created a credible version of Newcomb's problem that involves no supernatural elements. The role of the predictor is played by a fictitious computer program, whose predictions of subjects' choices are based on a previously established database. The experiment proceeded as follows. Upon completing the PD study described in the previous section, subjects ($N = 40$) were presented with the following scenario, displayed on the computer screen:

You now have one more chance to collect additional points. A program developed recently at MIT was applied during this entire session to analyze the pattern of your preferences. Based on that analysis, the program has predicted your preference in this final problem.

20 points		?
Box A		Box B

Consider the two boxes above. Box A contains 20 points for sure. Box B may or may not contain 250 points. Your options are to:

(1) Choose both boxes (and collect the points that are in both).

(2) Choose Box B only (and collect only the points that are in Box B).

If the program predicted, based on observation of your previous preferences, that you will take both boxes, then it left Box B empty. However, if it predicted that you will take only Box B, then it put 250 points in that box. (So far, the program has been remarkably successful: 92% of the participants who chose only Box B found 250 points in it, as opposed to 17% of those who chose both boxes.)

To ensure that the program does not alter its guess after you have indicated your preference, please indicate to the person in charge whether you prefer both boxes or Box B only. After you indicate your preference, press any key to discover the allocation of points.

This scenario provides a believable version of Newcomb's Problem. While the computer program is quite successful, it is by no means infallible.[3] Also, any suspicion of backward causality has been removed: assuming the experimenter does not cheat in some sophisticated fashion (and our post-experimental interviews indicated that no subject thought he would), it is clear that the program's prediction has been made and can be observed at any point, without further feedback about the subject's decision. This problem has a clear "common cause" structure (see Eells, 1982): the subject's strategic tendencies in games of this kind, as observed in the preceding PD games, are supposedly predictive of both his preferred strategy in the next game and of the prediction made by the program. While the choice of a single box is diagnostic of the presence of 250 points in it, there can be no relevant causal influence between the two events. Under these conditions, there seems to be no defensible rationale for taking just one box. As Nozick (1969) points out, "if the actions or decisions . . . do not affect, help bring about, influence, and so on *which* state obtains, then whatever the conditional probabilities . . . , one should perform the dominant action," namely, take both boxes. In this situation, it would appear, people should choose both boxes because both boxes are better than one no matter what.

The results were as follows: 35% (14 of the 40 subjects) chose both boxes, whereas 65% preferred to take Box B only. The present scenario, which removed all supernatural elements from the original formulation of Newcomb's Problem, yielded roughly the same proportions of choices for one and for both boxes as those obtained by Gardner from the readers of *Scientific American*. What can be said about the majority of subjects who preferred to take just one box? Had they known for certain that the 250 points were in that box (and could see that 20 were in the other), they surely would have taken both rather than just one. And certainly, if they knew that the 250 points were not in that box, they would have taken both rather than just the one that is empty. These subjects, in other words, would have taken both boxes had they known that Box B is full, and they also would have taken both boxes had they known that Box B is empty. Consequentialist subjects should then choose both boxes even when it is not known whether Box B is full or empty. The majority, however, chose Box B alone when its contents were not known. Note that the hypothesis discussed earlier, which attributes the disjunction effect to subjects' failure to predict their own preferences, cannot account for the present finding. No subject would have had any difficulty predicting his preference for more rather than fewer points, had he considered the possible states of the unknown box. Evidently, many subjects do not consider separately the consequences of the program's predictions and as a result succumb to the temptation to choose the single box, which happens to be correlated with the higher prize.

Quasi-magical Thinking   Magical thinking refers to the erroneous belief that one can influence an outcome (e.g., the role of a die) by some symbolic or other indirect act (e.g., imagining a particular number) even though the act has no causal link to the outcome. We introduce the term quasi-magical thinking to describe cases in which people act as if they erroneously believe that their action influences the outcome, even though they do not really hold that belief. As in the Prisoner's Dilemma, the pattern of preferences observed in Newcomb's Problem may be described as quasi-magical thinking. When the program's prediction is known, the outcome depends entirely on the subject's decision and the obvious choice is to take both boxes. But as long as the program's prediction is not known and the eventual outcome depends on the behavior of both subject and program, there is a temptation to act as if one's decision could affect the program's prediction. As Gibbard and Harper (1978) suggest in an attempt to explain people's choice of a single box, "a person may . . . want to bring about an indication of a desired state of the world, even if it is known that the act that brings about the indication in no way brings about the desired state itself." Most people, of course, do not actually believe that they are able to alter the decision made by the program or the other player. Nevertheless, they feel compelled to "do their bit" in order to bring about the desired outcome. Another demonstration of such quasi-magical thinking was provided by Quattrone and Tversky (1984), whose subjects in effect "cheated" on a medical exam by selecting actions (e.g., holding their hand in very cold water for an extended period of time) that they believed were diagnostic of favorable outcomes (e.g., a strong heart) even though they must have known that their actions could not possibly produce the desired outcomes.

Quasi-magical thinking, we believe, underlies several phenomena related to self-deception and the illusion of control. Quattrone and Tversky (1984), for example, noted that Calvinists act as if their behavior will determine whether they will go to heaven or to hell, despite their belief in divine pre-determination, which entails that their fate has been determined prior to their birth. Several authors, notably Langer (1975), showed that people often behave as if they can exert control over chance events and, as a result, exhibit different attitudes and place larger bets when betting before rather than after a coin has been tossed (Rothbart & Snyder, 1970; Strickland, Lewicki, & Katz, 1966).[4] Most people, however, do not really believe that they can control the toss of a coin, nor that the choice of a single box in the Newcomb experiment can influence the program's already-made prediction. In these and other cases, people probably know that they cannot affect the outcome, but they act as if they could. It is told of Niels Bohr that, when asked by a journalist about a horse-shoe (purported to bring good luck) hanging over his door, he explained that he of course does not believe in such nonsense, but heard that it helped even if one did not believe.

It is exceedingly difficult, of course, to ascertain what people really believe. The preceding discussion suggests that we cannot always infer belief from action. People may behave as if they could influence uncontrollable events even though they do not actually believe in being able to do so. For example, dice players who throw softly for low numbers and hard for high numbers (Henslin, 1967) may not necessarily believe that the nature of the throw influences the outcome. People who exhibit superstitious behaviors, such as wearing a good luck charm or avoiding crossing a black cat's path, may not actually believe that their actions can affect the future. There is a sense in which quasi-magical thinking appears more rational than magical thinking because it does not commit one to patently absurd beliefs. However, quasi-magical thinking appears even more puzzling because it undermines the link between belief and action. Whereas magical thinking involves indefensible beliefs, quasi-magical thinking yields inexplicable actions. The presence of uncertainty, we suggest, is a major contributor to quasi-magical thinking; few people act as if they can undo an already certain event by performing an action that is diagnostic of an alternative event. In this vein, subjects in Quattrone and Tversky's (1984) experiment would have been less willing to keep their hands in painfully cold water if they knew that they had strong or weak hearts than when their "diagnosis" was uncertain. And Calvinists would perhaps do fewer good deeds if they knew that they had already been assigned to heaven, or to hell, than while their fate remains a mystery.

General Discussion

As demonstrated in the previous section, people often fail to consider the possible outcomes and consequences of uncertain events. The difficulties of thinking through uncertainty manifest themselves in a variety of situations: they encompass reasoning as well as decision-making tasks, and they are observed both inside and outside the laboratory. In the present section, we extend the analysis of nonconsequential evaluation to deductive reasoning and economic forecast.

Wason's Selection Task

One of the best known tasks in research on human reasoning is the selection task, devised by Wason (1966). In a typical version of the task, subjects are presented with four cards, each of which has a letter on one side and a number on the other. Only one side of each card is displayed. For example:

E	D	4	7

Subjects' task is to indicate which cards must be turned over to test the rule: "If there is a vowel on one side of the card, then there is an even number on the other side of the card." The simplicity of the problem is deceptive—the great majority of subjects fail to solve it.[5] Most select only the *E*, or the *E* and the *4* cards, whereas the correct choices are the *E* and the *7* cards. The difficulty of the selection task is puzzling, especially because people generally have no trouble evaluating the relevance of the items that may be hidden on the other side of each card. Wason and Johnson-Laird (1970; see also Wason, 1969) have commented on the discrepancy between subjects' ability to evaluate the relevance of potential outcomes (i.e., to understand the truth conditions of the rule) and their inappropriate selection of the relevant cards. Subjects, for example, understand that neither a vowel nor a consonant on the other side of the *4* card contributes to the possible falsification of the rule, but they choose to turn the *4* card when its other side is not known. Similarly, subjects understand that a consonant on the other side of the *7* card would not falsify the rule and that a vowel *would* falsify it, yet they neglect to turn the *7* card. The above pattern, which resembles a disjunction effect, arises when subjects who are easily able to evaluate the relevance of a specific outcome fail to apply this knowledge when facing a disjunction of outcomes. As Evans (1984, 458) notes, "this strongly confirms the view that card selections are not based upon any analysis of the consequences of turning the cards." Like the people who postpone the trip to Hawaii when the exam's outcome is not known, and those who cooperate in the disjunctive version of the Prisoner's Dilemma, subjects performing the selection task fail to consider the consequences of each of the events. Instead of considering the consequences of each particular kind of symbol on the other side of the card, they appear to remain behind a veil of uncertainty when the card's other side is not known.

Numerous studies have explored the elusive thought process that underlies subjects' performance on the selection task. Indeed, a complex pattern of content effects has emerged from a number of variations on the original task (see, e.g., Johnson-Laird, Legrenzi, & Legrenzi, 1972; Griggs & Cox, 1982; Wason, 1983; Evans, 1989, for a review; although see also Manktelow & Evans, 1979, for conflicting reports). To explain these findings, researchers have suggested verification biases (Johnson-Laird & Wason, 1970), matching biases (Evans & Lynch, 1973; Evans, 1984), memories of domain-specific experiences (Griggs & Cox, 1982;

Manktelow & Evans, 1979), pragmatic reasoning schemas (Cheng & Holyoak, 1985, 1989), and an innate propensity to look out for cheaters (Cosmides, 1989). What these explanations have in common is an account of performance on the selection task that fails to refer to formal reasoning. Instead, people are assumed to focus on items that have been explicitly mentioned, to apply pre-stored knowledge structures, or to remember relevant past experiences. "The inferential processes that occur in these cases," concludes Wason (1983, p. 69), "are not . . . instances of 'logical' reasoning." Thus, people find it relatively easy to reason logically about each isolated outcome, but a disjunction of outcomes leads them to suspend logical reasoning. This is reminiscent of the eight-year-olds studied by Osherson and Markman (1974–75) who, when asked about a concealed, single-color poker chip whether it is true that "Either the chip in my hand is yellow or it is not yellow?" responded "I don't know" because they could not see it. While most adults find the poker chip disjunction trivial, subtler disjunctions can lead to a temporary suspension of judgment.

The Disjunction Effect in Financial Markets One result of nonconsequential decision making is that people will sometimes seek information that has no impact on their decision. In the Hawaii problem described earlier, for example, subjects were willing in effect to pay for information that was not going to change their choice but—as we have interpreted it—was merely going to clarify their reasons for choosing. In a variation on the earlier PD experiment, we presented a new group of subjects with the same PD games, but this time, instead of being told the other's decision, subjects were offered, for a very small fee, the opportunity to learn the other's decision before making their own choice. The great majority of subjects chose to compete regardless of whether the opponent had decided to compete or to cooperate, but on 81% of the trials subjects first chose to pay to discover the opponent's decision. Although this behavior can be attributed to curiosity, we conjecture that people's willingness to pay for the information would have diminished had they realized that it would not affect their decision. Searching for information that has no impact on decision may be quite frequent in situations of uncertainty. For example, we may call to find out whether a beach hotel has a pool before making a reservation, despite the fact that we will end up going whether it has a pool or not. One intriguing case of a nonconsequential evaluation of information is provided by the following account regarding the U.S. financial markets.

In the weeks preceding the 1988 U.S. Presidential election, the financial markets in the U.S. remained relatively inactive and stable "because of caution before the Presidential election" (*New York Times*, Nov. 5, 1988). "Investors were reluctant to make major moves early in a week full of economic uncertainty and 7 days away from the Presidential election" (*Wall Street Journal*, Nov. 2, 1988). The market, reported the *Wall Street Journal*, was "killing time." "There is literally nothing going on, and there probably won't be at least until Wednesday," observed the head of a trading desk at Shearson Lehman Hutton, referring to the day following the election (*Wall Street Journal*, Nov. 8, 1988). "Once the uncertainty of the election is removed, investors could begin to develop a better feeling about the outlook for the economy, inflation and interest rates," remarked the president of an investment firm (*New York Times*, Nov. 2, 1988). "The outcome of the election had cast a decided cloud over the market in recent days. Its true direction is likely to surface rapidly in coming days," explained a portfolio strategist (*New York Times*, Nov. 9, 1988). And, in fact, immediately following the election, a clear direction surfaced. The dollar plunged sharply to its lowest level in 10 months, and stock and bond prices declined. During the week following Bush's victory the DOW Jones industrial average fell a total of 78 points.[6] "The post-election reality is setting in," explained the co-chairman of an investment committee at Goldman, Sachs & Co. (*Wall Street Journal*, Nov. 21, 1988). The dollar's decline, explained the analysts, "reflected continued worry about the U.S. trade and budget deficits," "the excitement of the election is over, the honeymoon is over, and economic reality has set back in" (*Wall Street Journal*, Nov. 10, 1988). The financial markets, said the front page of the *New York Times* on November 12, "had generally favored the election of Mr. Bush and had expected his victory, but in the three days since the election they have registered their concern about where he goes from here." Of course, the financial markets would likely have registered at least as much concern had Mr. Dukakis been elected. Most traders agree, wrote the *Wall Street Journal* on election day, "the stock market would drop significantly if Democratic candidate Michael Dukakis stages a come-from-behind victory." In fact, the market reacted to Bush's victory just as it would have reacted to Dukakis's. "When I walked in and looked at the screen," explained one trader after the election, "I thought Dukakis had won" (*New York Times*, Nov. 10, 1988).

After long days of inactivity preceding the election, the market declined immediately following Bush's victory, and certainly would have declined at least as much had Dukakis been the victor. Of course, a thorough analysis of the financial markets' behavior is likely to reveal numerous complications. There is, for example, the possibility that an unexpected margin of victory, a surprising last-minute outcome, could have contributed to the paradoxical effect. As it happens, however, "newspapers and television networks came about as close as polling specialists believe is possible to forecasting the results of [the] election" (*New York Times*, Nov. 10, 1988). In the week preceding the election, while some thought a Dukakis "surge" still possible, polls conducted by Gallup, ABC News/*Washington Post*, NBC/*Wall Street Journal*, and *New York Times*/CBS News predicted a Bush victory by an average margin of 9 percentage points, 1 point off the eventual 8-point margin. Similarly, the Democrats were expected to retain control of both the Congress (where they were predicted to pick up one or two seats) and the House of Representatives, which is precisely what occurred. The election results do not appear to have been a surprise. At least on the surface, this incident has all the makings of a disjunction effect: the markets were going to decline if Bush was elected, they were going to decline if Dukakis was elected, but they resisted any change until they knew which of the two had been elected. Being at the node of such a momentous disjunction seems to have stopped Wall Street from seriously addressing the consequences of the election. While either elected official would have led the financial markets to "register their concern about where he goes from here," the interim situation of uncertainty highlighted the need for "caution before the election." After all, how can we worry about "where he goes from here" before we know who is doing the going?

Concluding Comments

Patterns of decision and reasoning that violate STP were observed in simple contexts involving uncertainty. These patterns, we suggest, reflect a failure on the part of people to detect and apply this principle rather than a lack of appreciation for its normative appeal. When we first asked subjects to indicate their preferred course of action under each outcome and only then to make a decision in the disjunctive condition, the majority of subjects who opted for the same option under every outcome chose that option also when the precise outcome was not known (Tversky & Shafir, 1992). The frequency of disjunction effects, in other words, substantially diminishes when the logic of STP is made salient. Like other normative principles of decision making, STP is generally satisfied when its application is transparent, but is sometimes violated when it is not (Tversky & Kahneman, 1986).

A number of factors may contribute to the reluctance to think consequentially. Thinking through an event tree requires people to assume momentarily as true something that may in fact be false. People may be reluctant to make this assumption, especially when another plausible alternative (another branch of the tree) is readily available. It is apparently difficult to devote full attention to each of several branches of an event tree (see also Slovic & Fischhoff, 1977). As a result, people may be reluctant to entertain the various hypothetical branches. Furthermore, they may lack the motivation to traverse the tree simply because they presume, as is often the case, that the problem will not be resolved by separately evaluating the branches. We usually tend to formulate problems in ways that have sifted through the irrelevant disjunctions: those that are left are normally assumed to involve genuine conflict.

The disjunctive scenarios investigated in this chapter were relatively simple, involving just two possible outcomes. Disjunctions of multiple outcomes are more difficult to think through and, as a result, are more likely to give rise to nonconsequential reasoning. This is particularly true for economic, social, or political decisions, where the gravity and complexity of situations may conceal the fact that all possible outcomes are eventually—perhaps for different reasons—likely to lead to a similar decision. Critics of U.S. nuclear first-strike strategies, for example, have maintained that while every plausible array of Russian missiles argues against the viability of an American first-strike, American strategists have insisted on retaining that option while the exact array of Russian arsenals is not known. Of course, the strategies involved in such scenarios are exceedingly complex, but it is conceivable that a first-strike option appears attractive partly *because* the adversary's precise arsenals are not known.

Shortcomings in reasoning have typically been attributed to quantitative limitations of human beings as processors of information. "Hard problems" are typically characterized by reference to the "amount of knowledge required," the "memory load," or the "size of the search space" (cf. Kotovsky, Hayes, & Simon, 1985; Kotovsky & Simon, 1990). These limitations play a critical role in many problems. They explain why we cannot remember all the cards that have previously come up in a poker game, or why we are severely limited in the number of steps that we can plan ahead in a game of chess. Such limitations, however, are not sufficient to account for all that is difficult about thinking. In contrast to many complicated tasks that people perform with relative ease, the problems investigated in this paper are computationally very simple, involving a single disjunction of two well-defined states. The present studies highlight the discrepancy between logical complexity on the one hand and psychological difficulty on the other. In contrast with the "frame problem" (McCarthy & Hayes, 1969; Hayes, 1973), for example, which is trivial for people but exceedingly difficult for AI, the task of thinking through disjunctions is trivial for AI (which routinely implements "tree search" and "path finding" algorithms) but very difficult for people. The failure to reason consequentially may constitute a fundamental difference between natural and artificial intelligence.

Notes

1. The notion of consequentialism appears in the philosophical and decision theoretic literature in a number of different senses. See, e.g., Hammond (1988), Levi (1991), and Bacharach and Hurley (1991) for technical discussions.

2. A "collective action" interpretation of cooperative behavior in one-shot PD games is proposed by Hurley (1989, 1991). She interprets such behavior as "quite rational" because, according to her, it is motivated by "a concern to be part of, do one's part in, participate in . . . a valuable form of collective agency" (Hurley, 1989, p. 150). As with the ethical arguments mentioned earlier, however, this interpretation entails that subjects should certainly be inclined to cooperate when the other has cooperated, contrary to the present findings.

3. In retrospect, the remarkably simple program, "Put 250 points in Box B if the subject has produced at least two disjunction effects in the PD experiment; otherwise, leave Box B empty," would have rewarded 70% of the one-boxers and only 29% of the two-boxers with 250 points in Box B. More sophisticated rules could probably come closer to the alleged performance of the MIT program.

4. One may distinguish between uncertainty about the outcome of a future event and uncertainty about the outcome of an event that has already occurred. While the present study does not systematically differentiate between the two, Greene and Yolles (1990) present data that give reason to expect more nonconsequential reasoning in the former than the latter.

5. The success rate of initial choices in dozens of studies employing the basic form of the selection task (with "abstract" materials) typically ranges between 0 and somewhat over 20%. See Evans (1989) and Gilhooly (1988) for reviews.

6. Some believed that the central banks were actually involved in preventing the dollar from plummeting just before the U.S. presidential election (see, e.g., *Wall Street Journal*, Nov. 2–4, 1988).

Appendix: Instructions Given to Subjects in Prisoner's Dilemma Game

Welcome to the Intercollegiate Computer Game. The game will be conducted on an IBM PC. In this game you will be presented with situations involving you and one other player. Each situation will require that you make a strategic decision: to cooperate or to compete with the other player. The other player will have to make a similar decision.

Each situation will present a payoff-matrix that will determine how many points each of you earns depending on whether you compete or cooperate. One such matrix looks like the following.

	Other cooperates		Other competes	
You cooperate	You:	20	You:	5
	Other:	20	Other:	25
You compete	You:	25	You:	10
	Other:	5	Other:	10

According to this matrix, if you both cooperate you will both earn a considerable number of points (20 points each). If you cooperate and the other competes, the other will earn 25 points and you will earn only 5 points. Similarly, if you compete and the other cooperates, you will earn 25 points and the other will earn only 5 points. Finally, if you both choose to compete, you will earn only 10 points each.

You will be presented with numerous matrices of the kind shown above. In each case, you will be asked to indicate whether you choose to compete or to cooperate. As in the matrix above, you will frequently do rather well if you both cooperate, you will do worse if you both compete, and one will often do better than the other if one competes and the other cooperates.

You will be playing with other students who are currently on the computer system. For each new matrix you will be matched with a different person. Thus, you will never play against the same person more than once.

You have been arbitrarily assigned to the bonus group. A random bonus program will occasionally inform you of the strategy that the other player has already chosen.

Thus, for example, upon being presented with a new matrix, you may be told that the other player has chosen to compete. You are free to use the bonus information to help you choose your own strategy. (Your strategy will not be revealed to anyone who is playing with you.)

At the end of the game, the points that you accumulate will be converted (via a pre-determined algorithm) to actual money that will be paid to you. The more points you accumulate, the more money you will earn.

Of course, there are no "correct" choices. People typically find certain situations more conductive to cooperation and others to competition. The matrices differ significantly, and their outcomes depend both on your choice and on that of a different player at each turn. Please observe each matrix carefully and decide separately on your preferred strategy in each particular case. Also, be sure to note those cases where the bonus program informs you of the other player's choice. If you have any questions, please ask the person in charge. Otherwise, turn to the terminal and begin.

Acknowledgments

This research was supported by U.S. Public Health Service Grant 1-R29-MH46885 from the National Institute of Mental Health to the first author, by Grant 89–0064 from the Air Force Office of Scientific Research to the second author, and by a grant from the Hewlett Foundation to the Stanford Center on Conflict and Negotiation.

References

Axelrod, R. (1984). *The evolution of cooperation*. New York, NY: Basic Books.

Bacharach, M., & Hurley, S. (1991). Issues and advances in the foundations of decision theory. In M. Bacharach & S. Hurley (Eds.), *Foundations of decision theory: Issues and advances* (pp. 1–38). Oxford, England: Basil Blackwell.

Bar-Hillel, M., & Margalit, A. (1972). Newcomb's paradox revisited. *British Journal for the Philosophy of Science, 23*, 295–304.

Brams, S. J. (1975). Newcomb's Problem and Prisoner's Dilemma. *Journal of Conflict Resolution, 19*(4), 596–612.

Campbell, R., & Sowden, L. (Eds.). (1985). *Paradoxes of rationality and cooperation: Prisoner's Dilemma and Newcomb's Problem*. Vancouver, BC: University of British Columbia Press.

Cheng, P. W., & Holyoak, K. J. (1985). Pragmatic reasoning schemas. *Cognitive Psychology, 17*, 391–416.

Cheng, P. W., & Holyoak, K. J. (1989). On the natural selection of reasoning theories. *Cognition*, *33*, 285–313.

Cosmides, L. (1989). The logic of social exchange: Has natural selection shaped how humans reason? *Cognition*, *31*, 187–276.

Dawes, R. M., & Orbell, J. M. (1995). The potential benefit of optional play in a one-shot prisoner's dilemma game. In K. Arrow et al. (Eds.), *Barriers to conflict resolution* (pp. 62–85). New York, NY: Norton.

Eells, E. (1982). *Rational decision and causality*. Cambridge, England: Cambridge University Press.

Evans, J. St. B. T. (1984). Heuristic and analytic processes in reasoning. *British Journal of Psychology*, *75*, 451–468.

Evans, J. St B. T. (1989). *Bias in human reasoning: Causes and consequences*. Hillsdale, NJ: Lawrence Erlbaum Associates.

Evans, J. St. B. T., & Lynch, J. S. (1973). Matching bias in the selection task. *British Journal of Psychology*, *64*, 391–397.

Gardner, M. (1973). Free will revisited, with a mind-bending prediction paradox by William Newcomb. *Scientific American*, *229*(1), 104–108.

Gardner, M. (1974). Reflections on Newcomb's problem: A prediction and free-will dilemma. *Scientific American*, *230*(3), 102–109.

Gibbard, A., & Harper, W. L. (1978). Counterfactuals and two kinds of expected utility. In C. A. Hooker, J. J. Leach, & E. F. McClennen (Eds.), *Foundations and applications of decision theory* (Vol. 1, pp. 125–162). Dordrecht, the Netherlands: Reidel.

Gilhooly, K. J. (1988). *Thinking: Directed, undirected, and creative* (2nd ed.). San Diego, CA: Academic Press.

Greene, S. B., & Yolles, D. J. (1990). *Perceived determinacy of unknown outcomes*. Unpublished manuscript, Princeton University.

Griggs, R. A., & Cox, J. R. (1982). The elusive thematic-materials effect in Wason's selection task. *British Journal of Psychology*, *73*, 407–420.

Hammond, P. (1988). Consequentialist foundations for expected utility. *Theory and Decision*, *25*, 25–78.

Hayes, P. (1973). The frame problem and related problems in artificial intelligence. In A. Elithorn & D. Jones (Eds.), *Artificial and human thinking* (pp. 45–59). San Francisco, CA: Jossey-Bass.

Henslin, J. M. (1967). Craps and magic. *American Journal of Sociology*, *73*, 316–330.

Hofstadter, D. R. (1983, June). Dilemmas for superrational thinkers, leading up to a luring lottery. *Scientific American*. Reprinted in Hofstadter, D. R. (1985). *Metamagical themas: Questing for the essence of mind and pattern*. New York, NY: Basic Books.

Hurley, S. L. (1989). *Natural reasons: Personality and polity*. New York, NY: Oxford University Press.

Hurley, S. L. (1991). Newcomb's Problem, Prisoner's Dilemma, and collective action. *Synthese, 86*, 173–196.

Johnson-Laird, P. N., Legrenzi, P., & Legrenzi, S. M. (1972). Reasoning and a sense of reality. *British Journal of Psychology, 63*, 395–400.

Johnson-Laird, P. N., & Wason, P. C. (1970). A theoretical analysis of insight into a reasoning task. *Cognitive Psychology, 1*, 134–148.

Kahneman, D., & Tversky, A. (1982). On the study of statistical intuitions. *Cognition, 11*, 123–141.

Kotovsky, K., Hayes, J. R., & Simon, H. A. (1985). Why are some problems hard? Evidence from Tower of Hanoi. *Cognitive Psychology, 17*, 284–294.

Kotovsky, K., & Simon, H. A. (1990). What makes some problems really hard: Explorations in the problem space of difficulty. *Cognitive Psychology, 22*, 143–183.

Kreps, D., & Wilson, R. (1982). Reputations and imperfect information. *Journal of Economic Theory, 27*, 253–279.

Langer, E. J. (1975). The illusion of control. *Journal of Personality and Social Psychology, 32*, 311–328.

Levi, I. (1991). Consequentialism and sequential choice. In M. Bacharach & S. Hurley (Eds.), *Foundations of decision theory: Issues and advances* (pp. 92–122). Oxford, England: Basil Blackwell.

Lewis, D. (1979). Prisoner's Dilemma is a Newcomb Problem. *Philosophy & Public Affairs, 8*, 235–240.

Luce, R. D., & Raiffa, H. (1957). *Games and decisions.* New York, NY: Wiley.

Manktelow, K. I., & Evans, J. St. B. T. (1979). Facilitation of reasoning by realism: Effect or non-effect? *British Journal of Psychology, 70*, 477–488.

McCarthy, J., & Hayes, P. (1969). Some philosophical problems from the standpoint of Artificial Intelligence. In B. Meltzer & D. Michie (Eds.), *Machine intelligence* (pp. 463–502). New York, NY: American Elsevier.

Messe, L. A., & Sivacek, J. M. (1979). Predictions of others' responses in a mixed-motive game: Self-justification or false consensus? *Journal of Personality and Social Psychology, 37*(4), 602–607.

Nozick, R. (1969). Newcomb's problem and two principles of choice. In N. Rescher (Ed.), *Essays in honor of Carl G. Hempel* (pp. 114–146). Dordrecht, the Netherlands: Reidel.

Osherson, D. N., & Markman, E. (1974–75). Language and the ability to evaluate contradictions and tautologies. *Cognition, 3*(3), 213–226.

Quattrone, G. A., & Tversky, A. (1984). Causal versus diagnostic contingencies: On self-deception and on the voter's illusion. *Journal of Personality and Social Psychology, 46*(2), 237–248.

Rapoport, A. (1988). Experiments with n-person social traps I: Prisoner's Dilemma, weak Prisoner's Dilemma, Volunteer's Dilemma, and Largest Number. *Journal of Conflict Resolution, 32*(3), 457–472.

Rapoport, A., & Chammah, A. (1965). *Prisoner's Dilemma.* Ann Arbor, MI: University of Michigan Press.

Rapoport, A., Guyer, M. J., & Gordon, D. G. (1976). *The 2 2 game*. Ann Arbor, MI: University of Michigan Press.

Rothbart, M., & Snyder, M. (1970). Confidence in the prediction and postdiction of an uncertain event. *Canadian Journal of Behavioural Science, 2*, 38–43.

Savage, L. J. (1954). *The foundations of statistics*. New York, NY: Wiley & Sons.

Slovic, P., & Fischhoff, B. (1977). On the psychology of experimental surprises. *Journal of Experimental Psychology: Human Perception and Performance, 3*, 544–551.

Sobel, J. H. (1991). Some versions of Newcomb's Problem are Prisoner's Dilemmas. *Synthese, 86*, 197–208.

Strickland, L. H., Lewicki, R. J., & Katz, A. M. (1966). Temporal orientation and perceived control as determinants of risk-taking. *Journal of Experimental Social Psychology, 2*, 143–151.

Tversky, A., & Kahneman, D. (1983). Extensional versus intuitive reasoning: The conjunction fallacy in probability judgment. *Psychological Review, 90*, 293–315.

Tversky, A., & Kahneman, D. (1986). Rational choice and the framing of decisions. *Journal of Business, 59*(4, part 2), 251–278.

Tversky, A., & Shafir, E. (1992). The disjunction effect in choice under uncertainty. *Psychological Science, 3*, 305–309.

Wason, P. C. (1966). Reasoning. In B. M. Foss (Ed.), *New horizons in psychology* (Vol. 1, pp. 135–151). Harmandsworth, England: Penguin.

Wason, P. C. (1969). Structural simplicity and psychological complexity: Some thoughts on a novel problem. *Bulletin of the British Psychological Society, 22*, 281–284.

Wason, P. C. (1983). Realism and rationality in the selection task. In J. St B. T. Evans (Ed.), *Thinking and reasoning: Psychological approaches* (pp. 44–75). London, England: Routledge & Kegan Paul.

Wason, P. C., & Johnson-Laird, P. N. (1970). A conflict between selecting and evaluating information in an inferential task. *British Journal of Psychology, 61*, 509–515.

8 Loss Aversion in Riskless Choice: A Reference-Dependent Model

Amos Tversky and Daniel Kahneman

The standard models of decision making assume that preferences do not depend on current assets. This assumption greatly simplifies the analysis of individual choice and the prediction of trades: indifference curves are drawn without reference to current holdings, and the Coase theorem asserts that, except for transaction costs, initial entitlements do not affect final allocations. The facts of the matter are more complex. There is substantial evidence that initial entitlements do matter and that the rate of exchange between goods can be quite different depending on which is acquired and which is given up, even in the absence of transaction costs or income effects. In accord with a psychological analysis of value, reference levels play a large role in determining preferences. In the present paper we review the evidence for this proposition and offer a theory that generalizes the standard model by introducing a reference state.

The present analysis of riskless choice extends our treatment of choice under uncertainty (Kahneman & Tversky, 1979, 1984; Tversky & Kahneman, 1991), in which the outcomes of risky prospects are evaluated by a value function that has three essential characteristics. *Reference dependence:* the carriers of value are gains and losses defined relative to a reference point. *Loss aversion:* the function is steeper in the negative than in the positive domain; losses loom larger than corresponding gains. *Diminishing sensitivity:* the marginal value of both gains and losses decreases with their size. These properties give rise to an asymmetric S-shaped value function, concave above the reference point and convex below it, as illustrated in figure 8.1. In this article we apply reference dependence, loss aversion, and diminishing sensitivity to the analysis of riskless choice. To motivate this analysis, we begin with a review of selected experimental demonstrations.

Empirical Evidence

The examples discussed in this section are analyzed by reference to figure 8.2. In every case we consider two options x and y that differ on two valued dimensions and show how the

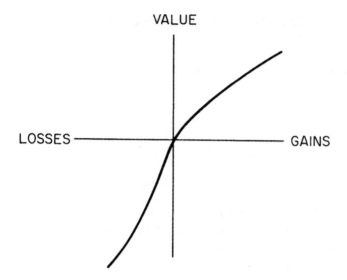

Figure 8.1
An illustration of a value function.

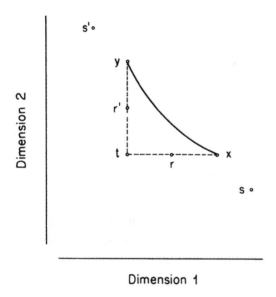

Figure 8.2
Multiple reference points for the choice between *x* and *y*.

choice between them is affected by the reference point from which they are evaluated. The common reason for these reversals of preference is that the relative weight of the differences between x and y on dimensions 1 and 2 varies with the location of the reference value on these attributes. Loss aversion implies that the impact of a difference on a dimension is generally greater when that difference is evaluated as a loss than when the same difference is evaluated as a gain. Diminishing sensitivity implies that the impact of a difference is attenuated when both options are remote from the reference point for the relevant dimension. This simple scheme serves to organize a large set of observations. Although isolated findings may be subject to alternative interpretations, the entire body of evidence provides strong support for the phenomenon of loss aversion.

a. Instant Endowment.   An immediate consequence of loss aversion is that the loss of utility associated with giving up a valued good is greater than the utility gain associated with receiving it. Thaler (1980) labeled this discrepancy the endowment effect because value appears to change when a good is incorporated into one's endowment. Kahneman, Knetsch, and Thaler (1990) tested the endowment effect in a series of experiments, conducted in a classroom setting. In one of these experiments a decorated mug (retail value of about $5) was placed in front of one third of the seats after students had chosen their places. All participants received a questionnaire. The form given to the recipients of a mug (the "sellers") indicated that "You now own the object in your possession. You have the option of selling it if a price, which will be determined later, is acceptable to you. For each of the possible prices below indicate whether you wish to (*x*) Sell your object and receive this price; (*y*) Keep your object and take it home with you." The subjects indicated their decision for prices ranging from $0.50 to $9.50 in steps of 50 cents. Some of the students who had not received a mug (the "choosers") were given a similar questionnaire informing them that they would have the option of receiving either a mug or a sum of money to be determined later. They indicated their preferences between a mug and sums of money ranging from $0.50 to $9.50.

The choosers and the sellers face precisely the same decision problem, but their reference states differ. As shown in figure 8.2, the choosers' reference state is *t*, and they face a positive choice between two options that dominate *t*: receiving a mug or receiving a sum in cash. The sellers evaluate the same options from *y*; they must choose between retaining the status quo (the mug) or giving up the mug in exchange for money. Thus, the mug is evaluated as a gain by the choosers and as a loss by the sellers. Loss aversion entails that the rate of exchange of the mug against money will be different in the two cases. Indeed, the median value of the mug was $7.12 for the sellers and $3.12 for the choosers in one experiment, $7.00 and $3.50 in another. The difference between these values reflects an endowment effect that is produced, apparently instantaneously, by giving an individual property rights over a consumption good.

The interpretation of the endowment effect may be illuminated by the following thought experiment.

Imagine that as a chooser you prefer $4 over a mug. You learn that most sellers prefer the mug to $6, and you believe that if you had the mug you would do the same. In light of this knowledge, would you now prefer the mug over $5?

If you do, it is presumably because you have changed your assessment of the pleasure associated with owning the mug. If you still prefer $4 over the mug—which we regard as a more likely response—this indicates that you interpret the effect of endowment as an aversion to giving up your mug rather than as an unanticipated increase in the pleasure of owning it.

b. Status Quo Bias.   The retention of the status quo is an option in many decision problems. As illustrated by the analysis of the sellers' problem in the example of the mugs, loss aversion induces a bias that favors the retention of the status quo over other options. In figure 8.2, a decision maker who is indifferent between x and y from t will prefer x over y from x and y over x from y. Samuelson and Zeckhauser (1988) introduced the term "status quo bias" for this effect of reference position.

Knetsch and Sinden (1984) and Knetsch (1989) have offered compelling experimental demonstrations of the status quo bias. In the latter study two undergraduate classes were required to answer a brief questionnaire. Students in one of the classes were immediately given a decorated mug as compensation; students in another class received a large bar of Swiss chocolate. At the end of the session students in both classes were shown the alternative gift and were allowed the option of trading the gift they had received for the other by raising a card with the word "Trade" written on it. Although the transaction cost associated with the change was surely slight, approximately 90% of the participants retained the gift they had received.

Samuelson and Zeckhauser (1988) documented the status quo bias in a wide range of decisions, including hypothetical choices about jobs, automobile color, financial investments, and policy issues. Alternative versions of each problem were presented to different subjects: each option was designated as the status quo in one of these versions; one (neutral) version did not single out any option. The number of options presented for each problem was systematically varied. The results were analyzed by regressing the proportions of subjects choosing an option designated as status quo $P(SQ)$, or an alternative to the status quo $P(ASQ)$, on the choice proportions for the same options in the neutral version $P(N)$. The results were well described by the equations,

$$P(SQ) = 0.17 + 0.83P(N) \quad \text{and} \quad P(ASQ) = 0.83P(N).$$

The difference (0.17) between $P(SQ)$ and $P(ASQ)$ is a measure of the status quo bias in this experiment.

Samuelson and Zeckhauser (1988) also obtained evidence of status quo bias in a field study of the choice of medical plans by Harvard employees. They found that a new medical plan is generally more likely to be chosen by new employees than by employees hired before that plan became available—in spite of the yearly opportunity to review the decision and the minimal cost of changing it. Furthermore, small changes from the status quo were favored over larger changes: enrollees who did transfer from the originally most popular Blue Cross/ Blue Shield plan tended to favor a new variant of that plan over other new alternatives. Samuelson and Zeckhauser also observed that the allocations of pension reserves to TIAA and CREF tend to be very stable from year to year, in spite of large variations in rate of return. They invoked the status quo bias as an explanation of brand loyalty and pioneer firm advantage, and noted that rational models that ignore status quo effects "will present excessively radical conclusions, exaggerating individuals' responses to changing economic variables and predicting greater instability than is observed in the world" (p. 47).

Loss aversion implies the status quo bias. As noted by Samuelson and Zeckhauser (1988), however, there are several factors, such as costs of thinking, transaction costs, and psychological commitment to prior choices that can induce a status quo bias even in the absence of loss aversion.

c. Improvements versus Tradeoffs.   Consider the evaluation of the options x and y in figure 8.2 from the reference points r and r'. When evaluated from r, option x is simply a gain (improvement) on dimension 1, whereas y combines a gain in dimension 2 with a loss in dimension 1. These relations are reversed when the same options are evaluated from r'. Considerations of loss aversion suggest that x is more likely to be preferred from r than from r'.

Ninety undergraduates took part in a study designed to test this hypothesis. They received written instructions indicating that some participants, selected at random, would receive a gift package. For half the participants (the dinner group) the gift consisted of "one free dinner at MacArthur Park Restaurant and a monthly Stanford calendar." For the other half (the photo group) the gift was "one 8 × 10 professional photo portrait and a monthly Stanford calendar." All subjects were informed that some of the winners, again selected at random, would be given an opportunity to exchange the original gift for one of the following options:

x: two free dinners at MacArthur Park Restaurant

y: one 8 × 10 professional photo portrait plus two 5 × 7 and three wallet size prints.

The subjects were asked to indicate whether they preferred to (i) keep the original gift, (ii) exchange it for x, or (iii) exchange it for y. If people are averse to giving up the reference gift, as implied by loss aversion, then the preference for a dinner-for-two (x) over multiple photos (y) should be more common among the subjects whose reference gift was a dinner-for-one (r) than among subjects whose reference gift was the single photo (r'). The results confirmed this prediction. Only ten participants chose to keep the original gift. Among the remaining subjects, option x was selected by 81% of the dinner group and by 52% of the photo group ($p < 0.01$).

d. Advantages and Disadvantages.   In our next demonstration a combination of a small gain and a small loss is compared with a combination of a larger gain and a larger loss. Loss aversion implies that the same difference between two options will be given greater weight if it is viewed as a difference between two disadvantages (relative to a reference state) than if it is viewed as a difference between two advantages. In the representation of figure 8.2, x is more likely to be preferred over y from s than from s' because the difference between x and y in dimension 1 involves disadvantages relative to s and advantages relative to s'. A similar argument applies to dimension 2. In a test of this prediction subjects answered one of two versions of the following question:

Imagine that as part of your professional training you were assigned to a part-time job. The training is now ending, and you must look for employment. You consider two possibilities. They are like your training job in most respects except for the amount of social contact and the convenience of commuting to and from work. To compare the two jobs to each other and to the present one, you have made up the following table:

	Social contact	Daily travel time
Present job	Isolated for long stretches	10 min.
Job x	Limited contact with others	20 min.
Job y	Moderately sociable	60 min.

The second version of this problem included the same options x and y, but a different reference job (s'), described by the following attributes: "much pleasant social interaction and 80 minutes of daily commuting time."

In the first version both options are superior to the current reference job on the dimension of social contact and both are inferior in commuting time. The different amounts of social contact in jobs x and y are evaluated as advantages (gains), whereas the commuting times are evaluated as disadvantages (losses). These relations are reversed in the second version. Loss aversion implies that a given difference between two options will generally have greater impact when it is evaluated as a difference between two losses (disadvantages) than when it is viewed as a difference between two gains (or advantages). This prediction was confirmed: Job x was chosen by 70% of the participants in version 1 and by only 33% of the participants in version 2 ($N = 106$, $p < 0.01$).

Reference Dependence

In order to interpret the reversals of preference that are induced by shifts of reference, we introduce, as a primitive concept, a preference relation indexed to a given reference state. As in the standard theory, we begin with a choice set $X = \{x, y, z, \ldots\}$ and assume, for simplicity, that it is isomorphic to the positive quadrant of the real plane, including its boundaries. Each option, $x = (x_1, x_2)$ in X, $x_1, x_2 \geq 0$, is interpreted as a bundle that offers x_1 units of good 1 and x_2 units of good 2, or as an activity characterized by its levels on two dimensions of value. The extension to more than two dimensions is straightforward.

A *reference structure* is a family of indexed preference relations, where $x \geq_r y$ is interpreted as x is weakly preferred to y from reference state r. The relations $>_r$ and $=_r$ correspond to strict preference and indifference, respectively. Throughout this article we assume that each $\geq_r$, $r \in X$, satisfies the standard assumptions of the classical theory. Specifically, we assume that $\geq_r$ is complete, transitive, and continuous; that is, $\{x: x \geq_r y\}$ and $\{x: y \geq_r x\}$ are closed for any y. Furthermore, each preference order is strictly monotonic in the sense that $x \geq_r y$ and $x \neq y$ imply that $x >_r y$. Under these assumptions each $\geq_r$ can be represented by a strictly increasing continuous utility function U_r (see, e.g., Varian, 1984; ch. 3).

Because the standard theory does not recognize the special role of the reference state, it implicitly assumes *reference independence*; that is, $x \geq_r y$ iff $x \geq_s y$ for all $x, y, r, s \in X$. This property, however, was consistently violated in the preceding experiments. To accommodate these observations, we describe individual choice not by a single preference order but by a family or a book of indexed preference orders $\{\geq_r: r \in X\}$. For convenience, we use the letters r, s to denote reference states and x, y to denote options, although they are all elements of X.

A treatment of reference-dependent choice raises two questions: what is the reference state, and how does it affect preferences? The present analysis focuses on the second question. We assume that the decision maker has a definite reference state in X, and we investigate its impact on the choice between options. The question of the origin and the determinants of the reference state lies beyond the scope of the present article. Although the reference state usually corresponds to the decision maker's current position, it can also be influenced by aspirations, expectations, norms, and social comparisons (Easterlin, 1974; van Praag, 1971; van de Stadt, Kapteyn, & van de Geer, 1985).

In the present section we first define loss aversion and diminishing sensitivity in terms of the preference orders $\geq_r$, $r \in X$. Next we introduce the notion of a decomposable reference function and characterize the concept of constant loss aversion. Finally, we discuss some empirical estimates of the coefficient of loss aversion.

Loss Aversion

The basic intuition concerning loss aversion is that losses (outcomes below the reference state) loom larger than corresponding gains (outcomes above the reference state). Because a shift of reference can turn gains into losses and vice versa, it can give rise to reversals of preference, as implied by the following definition.

A reference structure satisfies *loss aversion* (LA) if the following condition holds for all x, y, r, s in X. Suppose that $x_1 \geq r_1 > s_1 = y_1$, $y_2 > x_2$ and $r_2 = s_2$; see figure 8.3. Then $x =_s y$ implies that $x >_r y$; the same holds if the subscripts 1 and 2 are interchanged throughout. (Note that the relations $>$ and $=$ refer to the numerical components of the options, whereas $>_r$ and $=_r$ refer to the preference between options in reference state r.) Loss aversion implies that the slope of the indifference curve through y is steeper when y is evaluated from r than when it is evaluated from s. In other words, $U_r^*(y) > U_s^*(y)$, where $U_r^*(y)$ is the marginal rate of substitution of U_r at y.

To motivate the definition of loss aversion, it is instructive to restate it in terms of advantages and disadvantages, relative to a reference point r. An ordered pair $[x_i, r_i]$, $i = 1, 2$, is called an advantage or a disadvantage, respectively, if $x_i > r_i$, or $x_i < r_i$. We use brackets to distinguish between the pair $[x_i, r_i]$ and the two-dimensional option (x_1, x_2). Suppose that there exist real-valued functions v_1, v_2 such that $U_r(x)$ can be expressed as $U(v_1[x_1, r_1], v_2[x_2, r_2])$. To simplify matters, suppose that $x_1 = r_1$ and $x_2 > r_2$, as in figure 8.3. Hence, $x =_s y$ implies that

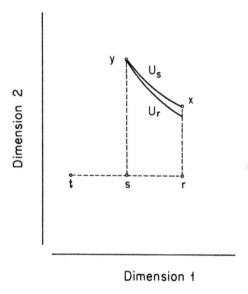

Figure 8.3
A graphic illustration of loss aversion.

the combination of the two advantages, $[x_1, s_1]$ and $[x_2, s_2]$, relative to the reference state s, has the same impact as the combination of the advantage $[y_2, s_2]$ and the null interval $[y_1, y_1]$. Similarly, $x >_r y$ implies that the combination of the advantage $[x_2, r_2]$ and the null interval $[x_1, x_1]$ has greater impact than the combination of the advantage $[y_2, r_2]$ and the disadvantage $[y_1, r_1]$. As the reference state shifts from s to r, therefore, the disadvantage $[y_1, r_1] = [s_1, r_1]$ enters into the evaluation of y, and the advantage $[x_1, s_1] = [r_1, s_1]$ is deleted from the evaluation of x. But because $[s_1, r_1]$ and $[r_1, s_1]$ differ by sign only, loss aversion implies that the introduction of a disadvantage has a bigger effect than the deletion of the corresponding advantage. A similar argument applies to the case where $x_1 > r_1 > s_1$.

The present notion of loss aversion accounts for the endowment effect and the status quo bias described in the preceding section. Consider the effect of different reference points on the preference between x and y, as illustrated in figure 8.2. Loss aversion entails that a decision maker who is indifferent between x and y from t will prefer x over y from x and y over x from y. That is, $x =_t y$ implies that $x >_x y$ and $y >_y x$. This explains the different valuations of a good by sellers and choosers and other manifestations of the status quo bias.

Diminishing Sensitivity

Recall that, according to the value function of figure 8.1, marginal value decreases with the distance from the reference point. For example, the difference between a yearly salary of $60,000 and a yearly salary of $70,000 has a bigger impact when current salary is $50,000 than when it is $40,000. A reference structure satisfies *diminishing sensitivity* (DS) if the following condition holds for all x, y, s, t in X. Suppose that $x_1 > y_1$, $y_2 > x_2$, $s_2 = t_2$, and either $y_1 \geq s_1 \geq t_1$ or $t_1 \geq s_1 \geq x_1$; see figure 8.3. Then $y =_s x$ implies that $y \geq_t x$; the same holds if the subscripts 1 and 2 are interchanged throughout. *Constant sensitivity* is satisfied if the same hypotheses imply that $y =_t x$. DS states that the sensitivity to a given difference on a dimension is smaller when the reference point is distant than when it is near. It follows from DS that the slope of the indifference curve through x is steeper when evaluated from s than from t, or $U_s^*(x) > U_t^*(x)$. It is important to distinguish between the present notion of diminishing sensitivity, which pertains to the effect of the reference state, and the standard assumption of diminishing marginal utility. Although the two hypotheses are conceptually similar, they are logically independent. In particular, diminishing sensitivity does not imply that the indifference curves are concave below the reference point.

Each reference state r partitions X into four quadrants defined by treating r as the origin. A pair of options, x and y, belong to the same quadrant with respect to r whenever $x_i \geq r_i$ iff $y_i \geq r_i$, $i = 1, 2$. A reference structure satisfies *sign dependence* if for all x, y, r, s in X $x \geq_r y$ iff $x \geq_s y$ whenever (i) x and y belong to the same quadrant with respect to r and with respect to s, and (ii) r and s belong to the same quadrant with respect to x and with respect to y. This condition

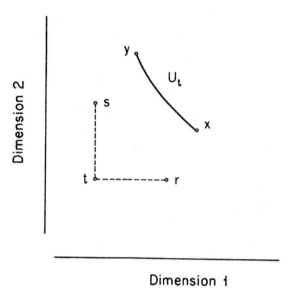

Figure 8.4
An illustration of reference-dependent preferences.

implies that reference independence can be violated only when a change in reference turns a gain into a loss or vice versa. It is easy to verify that sign dependence is equivalent to constant sensitivity. Although sign dependence may not hold in general, it serves as a useful approximation whenever the curvature induced by the reference state is not very pronounced.

The assumption of diminishing (or constant) sensitivity allows us to extend the implications of loss aversion to reference states that do not coincide with x or y on either dimension. Consider the choice between x and y in figure 8.4. Note that r is dominated by x but not by y, whereas s is dominated by y but not by x. Let t be the meet of r and s; that is, $t_i = \min(r_i, s_i)$, $i = 1, 2$. It follows from loss aversion and diminishing sensitivity that if $x =_t y$, then $x >_r y$ and $y >_s x$. Thus, x is more likely to be chosen over y when evaluated from r than when evaluated from s. This proposition is illustrated by our earlier observation that a gift was more attractive when evaluated as a moderate improvement on one attribute than when evaluated as a combination of a large improvement and a loss (see example c above).

Consider two exchangeable individuals (i.e., hedonic twins), each of whom holds position t, with low status and low pay; see figure 8.4. Suppose that both are indifferent between position x (very high status, moderate pay) and position y (very high pay, moderate status). Imagine now that both individuals move to new positions, which become their respective reference points; one individual moves to r (high status, low pay), and the other moves to s (high pay, low status). LA and DS imply that the person who moved to r now prefers x, whereas the person who moved to s now prefers y because they are reluctant to give up either salary or status.

Constant Loss Aversion

The present section introduces additional assumptions that constrain the relation among preference orders evaluated from different reference points. A reference structure $(X, \geq_r)$, $r \in X$, is *decomposable* if there exists a real-valued function U, increasing in each argument, such that for each $r \in X$, there exist increasing functions $R_i: X_i \to$ Reals, $i = 1, 2$ satisfying

$$U_r(x_1, x_2) = U(R_1(x_1), R_2(x_2)).$$

The functions R_i are called the reference functions associated with reference state r. In this model the effect of the reference point is captured by separate monotonic transformations of the two axes. Decomposability has testable implications. For example, suppose that U_r is additive; that is, $U_r(x_1, x_2) = R_1(x_1) + R_2(x_2)$. It follows then that, for any $s \in X$, U_s is also additive although the respective scales may not be linearly related.

In this section we focus on a special case of decomposability in which the reference functions assume an especially simple form. A reference structure $(X, \geq_r)$ satisfies *constant loss aversion* if there exist functions $u_i: X_i \to$ Reals, constants $\lambda_i > 0$, $i = 1, 2$, and a function U such that $U_r(x_1, x_2) = U(R_1(x_1), R_2(x_2))$, where

$$R_i(x_i) = \begin{cases} u_i(x_i) - u_i(r_i) & \text{if } x_i \geq r_i \\ (u_i(x_i) - u_i(r_i))/\lambda_i & \text{if } x_i < r_i. \end{cases}$$

Thus, the change in the preference order induced by a shift of reference is described in terms of two constants, λ_1 and λ_2, which can be interpreted as the coefficients of loss aversion for dimensions 1 and 2, respectively. Figure 8.5 illustrates constant loss aversion, with $\lambda_1 = 2$ and $\lambda_2 = 3$. For simplicity, we selected a linear utility function, but this is not essential.

Although we do not have an axiomatic characterization of constant loss aversion in general, we characterize below the special case where U is additive, called additive constant loss aversion. This case is important because additivity serves as a good approximation in many contexts. Indeed, some of the commonly used utility functions (e.g., Cobb-Douglas, or CES) are additive. Recall that a family of indifference curves is additive if the axes can be monotonically transformed so that the indifference curves become parallel straight lines. The following cancellation condition, also called the Thomsen condition, is both necessary and sufficient for additivity in the present context (Debreu, 1960; Krantz, Luce, Suppes, & Tversky, 1971).

For all $x_1, y_1, z_1 \in X_1$, $x_2, y_2, z_2 \in X_2$, and $r \in X$, if $(x_1, z_2) \geq_r (z_1, y_2)$ and $(z_1, x_2) \geq_r (y_1, z_2)$, then $(x_1, x_2) \geq_r (y_1, y_2)$.

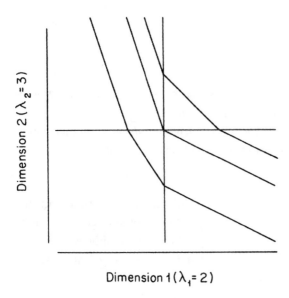

Figure 8.5
A set of indifference curves illustrating constant loss aversion.

Assuming cancellation for each $\geq_r$, we obtain an additive representation for each reference state. In order to relate the separate additive representations to each other, we introduce the following axiom. Consider w, w', x, x', y, y', z, z' in X that (i) belong to the same quadrant with respect to r as well as with respect to s, and (ii) satisfy $w_1 = w'_1$, $x_1 = x'_1$, $y_1 = y'_1$, $z_1 = z'_1$ and $x_2 = z_2$, $w_2 = y_2$, $x'_2 = z'_2$, $w'_2 = y'_2$; see figure 8.6. A reference structure $(X, \geq_r)$, $r \in X$, satisfies *reference interlocking* if, assuming (i) and (ii) above, $w =_r x$, $y =_r z$, and $w' =_s x'$ imply that $y' =_s z'$. Essentially the same condition was invoked by Tversky, Sattath, and Slovic (1988) in the treatment of preference reversals, and by Wakker (1989) and Tversky and Kahneman (1991) in the analysis of decision under uncertainty.

To appreciate the content of reference interlocking, note that, in the presence of additivity, indifference can be interpreted as a matching of an interval on one dimension to an interval on the second dimension. For example, the observation $w =_r x$ indicates that the interval $[x_1, w_1]$ on the first dimension matches the interval $[w_2, x_2]$ on the second dimension. Similarly, $y =_r z$ indicates that $[z_1, y_1]$ matches $[y^2, z^2]$. But because $[w_2, x_2]$ and $[y_2, z_2]$ are identical by construction (see figure 8.6), we conclude that $[x_1, w_1]$ matches $[z_1, y_1]$. In this manner we can match two intervals on the *same* dimension by matching each of them to an interval on the *other* dimension. Reference interlocking states that if two intradimensional intervals are matched as gains, they are also matched as losses. It is easy to verify that reference interlocking follows from additive constant loss aversion. Furthermore, the following theorem

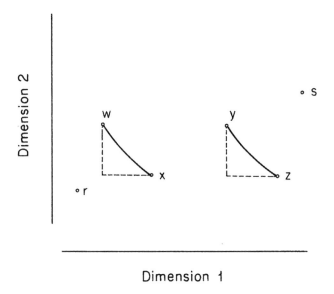

Figure 8.6
A graphic illustration of reference interlocking.

shows that in the presence of cancellation and sign dependence, reference interlocking is not only necessary but it is also sufficient for additive constant loss aversion.

THEOREM. A reference structure $(X \geq_r)$, $r \in X$, satisfies additive constant loss aversion iff it satisfies cancellation, sign dependence, and reference interlocking.

The proof of the theorem is presented in the appendix. An estimate of the coefficients of loss aversion can be derived from an experiment described earlier, in which two groups of subjects assigned a monetary value to the same consumption good: sellers who were given the good and the option of selling it, and choosers who were given the option of receiving the good or a sum of money (Kahneman, Knetsch, & Thaler, 1990). The median value of the mug for sellers was \$7.12 and \$7.00 in two separate replications of the experiments; choosers valued the same object at \$3.12 and \$3.50. According to the present analysis, the sellers and the choosers differ only in that the former evaluate the mug as a loss, the latter as a gain. If the value of money is linear in that range, the coefficient of loss aversion for the mug in these experiments was slightly greater than two.

There is an intriguing convergence between this estimate of the coefficient of loss aversion and estimates derived from decisions under risk. Such estimates can be obtained by observing the ratio G/L that makes an even chance to gain G or lose L just acceptable. We have observed a ratio of just over 2:1 in several experiments. In one gambling experiment with real payoffs, for example, a 50–50 bet to win $25 or lose $10 was barely acceptable, yielding a ratio of 2.5:1. Similar values were obtained from hypothetical choices regarding the acceptability of larger gambles, over a range of several hundred dollars (Tversky & Kahneman, 1991). Although the convergence of estimates should be interpreted with caution, these findings suggest that a loss aversion coefficient of about two may explain both risky and riskless choices involving monetary outcomes and consumption goods.

Recall that the coefficient of loss aversion could vary across dimensions, as illustrated in figure 8.5. We surmise that the coefficient of loss aversion associated with different dimensions reflects the importance or prominence of these dimensions (Tversky, Sattath, & Slovic, 1988). For example, loss aversion appears to be more pronounced for safety than for money (Viscusi, Magat, & Huber, 1987), and more pronounced for income than for leisure.

Implications of Loss Aversion

Loss aversion is an important component of a phenomenon that has been much discussed in recent years: the large disparity often observed between the minimal amount that people are willing to accept (WTA) to give up a good they own and the maximal amount they would be willing to pay (WTP) to acquire it. Other potential sources of this discrepancy include income effect, strategic behavior, and the legitimacy of transactions. The buying-selling discrepancy was initially observed in hypothetical questions involving public goods (see Cummings, Brookshire, & Schulze, 1986, for a review), but it has also been confirmed in real exchanges (Heberlein & Bishop, 1985; Kahneman, Knetsch, & Thaler, 1990; Loewenstein, 1988). It also survived, albeit reduced, in experiments that attempted to eliminate it by the discipline of market experience (Brookshire & Coursey, 1987; Coursey, Hovis, & Schulze, 1987; see also Knetsch & Sinden, 1984, 1987). Kahneman, Knetsch, and Thaler (1990) showed that the disparate valuations of consumption goods by owners and by potential buyers inhibit trade. They endowed half the participants with a consumption good (e.g., a mug) and set up a market for that good. Because the mugs were allocated at random, standard theory predicts that half the sellers should trade their mugs to buyers who value them more. The actual volume of trade was consistently observed to be about half the predicted amount. Control experiments in which subjects traded tokens redeemable for cash produced nearly perfect efficiency and no disparity between the values assigned by buyers and sellers.

A trade involves two dimensions, and loss aversion may operate on one or both. Thus, the present analysis suggests two ways in which loss aversion could contribute to the disparity between WTA and WTP. The individual who states WTA for a good considers giving it up; the individual who states WTP for that good considers acquiring it. If there is loss aversion for the good, the owner will be reluctant to sell. If the buyer views the money spent on the purchase as a loss, there will be reluctance to buy. The relative magnitude of the two effects can be esti-mated by comparing sellers and buyers to choosers, who are given a choice between the good and cash, and are therefore not susceptible to loss aversion. Results of several comparisons indicated that the reluctance to sell is much greater than the reluctance to buy (Kahneman, Knetsch, & Thaler, 1990). The buyers in these markets do not appear to value the money they give up in a transaction as a loss. These observations are consistent with the standard theory of consumer choice, in which the decision of whether or not to purchase a good is treated as a choice between it and other goods that could be purchased instead.

Loss aversion is certainly not involved in the exchange of a $5 bill for $5 because the transaction is evaluated by its net outcome. Similarly, reluctance to sell is surely absent in routine commercial transactions, in which goods held for sale have the status of tokens for money. However, the present analysis implies that asymmetric evaluations of gains and losses will affect the responses of both buyers and sellers to changes of price of profit, relative to the reference levels established in prior transactions (Kahneman, Knetsch, & Thaler, 1986; Winer, 1986). The response to changes is expected to be more intense when the changes are unfavorable (losses) than when they are for the better. Putler (1988) developed an analysis of demand that incorporates an asymmetric effect of price increases and decreases. He tested the model by estimating separate demand elasticities for increases and for decreases in the retail price of shell eggs, relative to a reference price estimated from the series of earlier prices. The estimated elasticities were −1.10 for price increases and −0.45 for price decreases, indi-cating that price increases have a significantly greater impact on consumer decisions. (This analysis assumes that the availability of substitutes eliminates loss aversion in the response to the reduced consumption of eggs.) A similar result was observed in scanner-panel data in the coffee market (Kalwani, Yim, Rinne, & Sugita, 1990). The reluctance to accept losses may also affect sellers: a study of the stock market indicated that the volume of trade tends to be higher when prices are rising than when prices are falling (Shefrin & Statman, 1985).

Loss aversion can complicate negotiations. Experimental evidence indicates that negotia-tors are less likely to achieve agreement when the attributes over which they bargain are framed as losses than when they are framed as gains (Bazerman & Carroll, 1987). This result is expected if people are more sensitive to marginal changes in the negative domain. Fur-thermore, there is a natural asymmetry between the evaluations of the concessions that one makes and the concessions offered by the other party; the latter are normally evaluated as gains, whereas the former are evaluated as losses. The discrepant evaluations of concessions significantly reduce the region of agreement in multi-issue bargaining.

A marked asymmetry in the responses to favorable or unfavorable changes of prices or profits was noted in a study of the rules that govern judgments of the fairness of actions that set prices or wages (Kahneman, Knetsch, & Thaler, 1986). In particular, most people reject as highly unfair price increases that are not justified by increased costs and cuts in wages that are not justified by a threat of bankruptcy. However, the customary norms of economic fairness do not absolutely require the firm to share the benefits of reduced costs or increased profits with its customers or its employees. In contrast to economic analysis, which does not distinguish losses from forgone gains, the standards of fairness draw a sharp distinction between actions that impose losses on others and actions (or failures to act) that do not share benefits. A study of court decisions documented a similar distinction in the treatment of losses and forgone gains; in cases of negligence, for example, compensation is more likely to be awarded for out-of-pocket costs than for unrealized profits (Cohen & Knetsch, 1990).

Because actions that are perceived as unfair are often resisted and punished, considerations of fairness have been invoked as one of the explanations of wage stickiness and of other cases in which markets clear only sluggishly (Kahneman, Knetsch, & Thaler, 1986; Okun, 1981; Olmstead & Rhode, 1985). For example, the difference in the evaluation of losses and of forgone gains implies a corresponding difference in the reactions to a wage cut and to a failure to increase wages when such an increase would be feasible. The terms of previous contracts define the reference levels for collective as well as for individual bargaining; in the bargaining context the aversion to losses takes the form of an aversion to concessions. The rigidity induced by loss aversion may result in inefficient labor contracts that fail to respond adequately to changing economic circumstances and technological developments. As a consequence, new firms that bargain with their workers without the burden of previous agreements may gain a competitive advantage.

Is loss aversion irrational? This question raises a number of difficult normative issues. Questioning the values that decision makers assign to outcomes requires a criterion for the evaluation of preferences. The actual experience of consequences provides such a criterion: the value assigned to a consequence in a decision context can be justified as a prediction of the quality of the experience of that consequence (Kahneman & Snell, 1990). Adopting this predictive stance, the value function of figure 8.1, which was initially drawn to account for the pattern of risky choices, can be interpreted as a prediction of the psychophysics of hedonic experience. The value function appropriately reflects three basic facts: organisms habituate to steady states, the marginal response to changes is diminishing, and pain is more urgent than pleasure. The asymmetry of pain and pleasure is the ultimate justification of loss aversion in choice. Because of this asymmetry a decision maker who seeks to maximize the experienced utility of outcomes is well advised to assign greater weight to negative than to positive consequences.

The demonstrations discussed in the first part of this paper compared choices between the same two objective states, evaluated from different reference points. The effects of reference levels on decisions can only be justified by corresponding effects of these reference levels on the experience of consequences. For example, a bias in favor of the status quo can be justified if the disadvantages of any change will be experienced more keenly than its advantages. However, some reference levels that are naturally adopted in the context of decision are irrelevant to the subsequent experience of outcomes, and the impact of such reference levels on decisions is normatively dubious. In evaluating a decision that has long-term consequences, for example, the initial response to these consequences may be relatively unimportant, if adaptation eventually induces a shift of reference. Another case involves principal–agent relations: the principal may not wish the agent's decisions to reflect the agent's aversion to losses, because the agent's reference level has no bearing on the principal's experience of outcomes. We conclude that there is no general answer to the question about the normative status of loss aversion or of other reference effects, but there is a principled way of examining the normative status of these effects in particular cases.

Appendix

THEOREM. A reference structure $(X, \geq_r)$, $r \in X$, satisfies additive constant loss aversion iff it satisfies cancellation, sign dependence, and reference interlocking.

Proof. Necessity is straightforward. To establish sufficiency, note that, under the present assumptions, cancellation implies additivity (Debreu, 1960; Krantz et al., 1971). Hence, for any $r \in X$ there exist continuous functions $R_i: X_i \to$ Reals, unique up to a positive linear transformation, such that $R(x) = R_1(x_1) + R_2(x_2)$ represents $\geq_r$. That is, for any $x, y \in X$, $x \geq_r y$ iff $R(x) \geq R(y)$. We next establish the following two lemmas.

LEMMA 1. Let A be a set of options that belong to the same quadrant with respect to r and with respect to s. Then there exist $\lambda_i > 0$ such that for all x, y in A,

$$R_i(y_i) - R_i(x_i) = (S_i(y_i) - S_i(x_i)) / \lambda_i, \quad i = 1, 2.$$

Proof. We wish to show that for all $r, s, w, x, y, z \in X$,

$$R_i(z_i) - R_i(y_i) = R_i(x_i) - R_i(w_i) \quad \text{implies that}$$

$$S_i(z_i) - S_i(y_i) = S_i(x_i) - S_i(w_i), \quad i = 1, 2.$$

This proposition follows from continuity, additivity, and reference interlocking whenever the *i*-intervals in question can be matched by intervals on the other dimension. If such matching is not possible, we use continuity to divide these *i*-intervals into sufficiently small subintervals that could be matched by intervals on the other dimension. Because equality of R_i differences implies equality of S_i differences, Lemma 1 follows from continuity and additivity.

LEMMA 2. Suppose that $r, s \in X$, with $s_1 < r_1$ and $s_2 = r_2$. Let S be a representation of $\geq_s$ satisfying $S_1(s_1) = 0$. If sign dependence and reference interlocking hold, then there exist $\lambda_1 > 0$, $\lambda_2 = 1$, such that $R^*(x) = R_1^*(x_1) + R_2^*(x_2)$ represents $\geq_r$, where

$$R_1^*(x_1) = \begin{cases} S_1(x_1) - S_1(r_1) & \text{if } x_1 \geq r_1 \\ (S_1(x_1) - S_1(r_1)) / \lambda_1 & \text{if } s_1 \leq x_1 \leq r_1 \\ S_1(x_1) - S_1(r) / \lambda_1 & \text{if } x_1 \leq s_1 \end{cases}$$

and $R_2^*(x_2) = S_2(x_2) - S_2(r_2) / \lambda_2$. The same holds if the indices 1 and 2 are interchanged throughout.

Proof. By sign dependence $\geq_r$ and $\geq_s$ coincide for all pairs of elements of $\{x \in X: x_1 \geq r_1, x_2 \geq r_2\}$ and of $\{x \in X: x_1 \geq r_1, x_2 \leq r_2\}$. To prove that $\geq_r$ and $\geq_s$ also coincide on their union, suppose that y belongs to the former set and z belongs to the latter. It suffices to show that $y =_r z$ implies that $y =_s z$. By monotonicity and continuity there exists w such that $y =_r w =_r z$ and $w_2 = r_2 = s_2$. Because w belongs to the intersection of the two sets, $y =_r w$ implies that $y =_s w$ and $z =_r w$ implies that $z =_s w$; hence, $y =_s z$.

Therefore, we can select the scales so that $R_i = S_i$, $i = 1, 2$, on $\{x \in X: x_1 \geq r_1\}$. Next we show that $R^*(x) + S(r) = R(x)$. We consider each dimension separately. For $i = 2$, $R_2^*(x_2) + S_2(r_2) = S_2(x_2)$. We show that $S_2(x_2) = R_2(x_2)$. Select an $x_1 \geq r_1$. By construction, $S(x) = R(x)$—hence $S_2(x_2) = R_2(x_2)$.

For $i = 1$, if $x_1 \geq r_1$, we get $R_1^*(x_1) + S_1(r_1) = S_1(x_1)$ and $R_1(x_1) = S_1(x_1)$, by construction. Hence

$$R_1^*(x_1) + S_1(r_1) = S_1(x_1) = R_1(x_1).$$

For $s_1 < x_1 < r_1$, we want to show that there exists λ_1 such that

$$R_1(x_1) = S_1(r_1) + (S_1(x_1) - S_1(r_1)) / \lambda_1, \quad \text{or}$$

$$R_1(x_1) - R_1(r_1) = (S_1(x_1) - S_1(r_1)) / \lambda_1,$$

which follows from Lemma 1.

For $x_1 \leq s_1$, $\geq_r$ and $\geq_s$ coincide, by sign dependence—hence, $R_1 = \alpha S_1 + \beta$, $\alpha > 0$. Because $R_2 = S_2$, $a = 1$, and because $S_1(s_1) = 0$, $\beta = R_1(s_1)$—hence $R_1(x_1) = S_1(x_1) + R_1(s_1)$. Consequently,

$$R_1(x_1) - R_1^*(x_1) = S_1(x_1) + R_1(s_1) - (S_1(x_1) - S_1(r_1) / \lambda_1)$$
$$= R_1(s_1) + S_1(r_1) / \lambda_1.$$

It suffices to show that this expression equals $S_1(r_1)$. Consider the case $s_1 < x_1 < r_1$, by continuity at s_1,

$$R_1(s_1) - R_1(r_1) = (S_1(s_1) - S_1(r_1)) / \lambda_1; \quad \text{hence,}$$

$R_1(s_1) + S_1(r_1) / \lambda_1 = R_1(r_1)$

$\qquad = S_1(r_1)$, by construction,

which completes the proof of Lemma 2.

Next we show that λ_i, $i = 1, 2$, is independent of r. Select $r, s, t \in X$ such that $r_2 = s_2 = t_2$ and $s_1 < r_1 < t_1$. By the previous lemma there exist R^* and T^*, defined in terms of S, with constants $\lambda^{(r)}$ and $\lambda^{(t)}$, respectively. Because $\geq_r$ and $\geq_t$ coincide on $\{x \in X: x_1 \leq r_1\}$, by sign dependence, $\lambda^{(r)}$ $= \lambda^{(t)}$. The same argument applies when indices 1 and 2 are interchanged and when $r_1 < s_1$.

To establish sufficiency for the general case, consider $r, s \in X$, with $r_1 > s_1$, $r_2 \leq s_2$, and $t = (r_1, s_2)$. By applying the previous (one-dimensional) construction twice, once for (s, t) and then for (t, r), we obtain the desired result.

Acknowledgments

This paper has benefited from the comments of Kenneth Arrow, Peter Diamond, David Krantz, Matthew Rabin, and Richard Zeckhauser. We are especially grateful to Shmuel Sattath and Peter Wakker for their helpful suggestions. This work was supported by Grants No. 89–0064 and 88–0206 from the Air Force Office of Scientific Research and the Sloan Foundation.

References

Bazerman, M., & Carroll, J. S. (1987). Negotiator cognition. In B. Staw & L. L. Cummings (Eds.), *Research in organizational behavior* (Vol. 9, pp. 247–288). Greenwich, CT: JAI Press.

Brookshire, D. S., & Coursey, D. L. (1987). Measuring the value of a public good: An empirical of elicitation procedures. *American Economic Review, 77*, 554–566.

Cohen, D., & Knetsch, J. L. (1990). Judicial choice and disparities between measures of economic values. Working paper. Burnaby, BC: Simon Fraser University.

Coursey, D. L., Hovis, J. L., & Schulze, W. D. (1987). The disparity between willingness to accept and willingness to pay measures of value. *Quarterly Journal of Economics, 102*, 679–690.

Cummings, R. G., Brookshire, D. S., & Schulze, W. D. (Eds.). (1986). *Valuing environmental goods.* Totowa, NJ: Rowman and Allanheld.

Debreu, G. (1960). Topological methods in cardinal utility theory. In K. J. Arrow, S. Karlin, & P. Suppes (Eds.), *Mathematical methods in the social sciences* (pp. 16–26). Stanford, CA: Stanford University Press.

Easterlin, R. A. (1974). Does economic growth improve the human lot? Some empirical evidence. In P. A. David & M. W. Reder (Eds.), *Nations and households in economic growth* (pp. 89–125). New York, NY: Academic Press.

Heberlein, T. A., & Bishop, R. C. (1985). Assessing the validity of contingent valuation: Three field experiments. Paper presented at the International Conference on Man's Role in Changing the Global Environment, Venice, Italy.

Kahneman, D., Knetsch, J. L., & Thaler, R. (1986). Fairness as a constraint on profit seeking: Entitlements in the market. *American Economic Review, 76*, 728–741.

Kahneman, D., Knetsch, J. L., & Thaler, R. (1990). Experimental tests of the endowment effect and the Coase theorem. *Journal of Political Economy, 98*, 1325–1348.

Kahneman, D., & Snell, J. (1990). Predicting utility. In R. Hogarth (Ed.), *Insights in decision making* (pp. 295–310). Chicago, IL: University of Chicago Press.

Kahneman, D., & Tversky, A. (1979). Prospect theory: An analysis of decision under risk. *Econometrica, 47*, 263–291.

Kahneman, D., & Tversky, A. (1984). Choices, values and frames. *American Psychologist, 39*, 341–350.

Kalwani, M. U., Yim, C. K., Rinne, H. J., & Sugita, Y. (1990). A price expectations model of customer brand choice. *JMR, Journal of Marketing Research, 27*, 251–262.

Knetsch, J. L. (1989). The endowment effect and evidence of nonreversible indifference curves. *American Economic Review, 79*, 1277–1284.

Knetsch, J. L., & Sinden, J. A. (1984). Willingness to pay and compensation demanded: Experimental evidence of an unexpected disparity in measures of value. *Quarterly Journal of Economics, 99*, 507–521.

Knetsch, J. L., & Sinden, J. A. (1987). The persistence of evaluation disparities. *Quarterly Journal of Economics, 102*, 691–695.

Krantz, D. H., Luce, R. D., Suppes, P., & Tversky, A. (1971). *Foundations of measurement* (Vol. I). New York, NY: Academic Press.

Loewenstein, G. (1988). Frames of mind in intertemporal choice. *Management Science, 34*, 200–214.

Okun, A. (1981). *Prices and quantities: A macroeconomic analysis.* Washington, DC: The Brookings Institution.

Olmstead, A. L., & Rhode, P. (1985). Rationing without government: the West Coast gas famine of 1920. *American Economic Review, 75*, 1044–1055.

Putler, D. S. (1988). Reference price effects and consumer behavior. Unpublished manuscript. Economic Research Service, U.S. Department of Agriculture, Washington, DC.

Samuelson, W., & Zeckhauser, R. (1988). Status quo bias in decision making. *Journal of Risk and Uncertainty, 1*, 7–59.

Shefrin, H., & Statman, M. (1985). The disposition to sell winners too early and ride losers too long: Theory and evidence. *Journal of Finance, 40*, 777–790.

Thaler, R. (1980). Toward a positive theory of consumer choice. *Journal of Economic Behavior & Organization, 1*, 39–60.

Tversky, A., Sattath, S., & Slovic, P. (1988). Contingent weighting in judgment and choice. *Psychological Review, 95*, 371–384.

Tversky, A., & Kahneman, D. (1991). Advances in prospect theory: Cumulative representation of uncertainty. Unpublished manuscript, Stanford University, Stanford, CA.

van de Stadt, H., Kapteyn, A., & van de Geer, S. (1985). The relativity of utility: Evidence from panel data. *Review of Economics and Statistics, 67*, 179–187.

van Praag, B. M. S. (1971). The individual welfare function of income in Belgium: An empirical investigation. *European Economic Review, 20*, 337–369.

Varian, H. R. (1984). *Microeconomic Analysis*. New York, NY: Norton.

Viscusi, W. K., Magat, W. A., & Huber, J. (1987). An investigation of the rationality of consumer valuations of multiple health risks. *Rand Journal of Economics, 18*, 465–479.

Wakker, P. P. (1989). *Additive representations of preferences: A new foundation of decision analysis*. Dordrecht, the Netherlands: Kluwer Academic Publishers.

Winer, R. S. (1986). A reference price model of brand choice for frequently purchased products. *Journal of Consumer Research, 13*, 250–256.

9 Preference and Belief: Ambiguity and Competence in Choice under Uncertainty

Chip Heath and Amos Tversky

The uncertainty we encounter in the world is not readily quantified. We may feel that our favorite football team has a good chance to win the championship match, that the price of gold will probably go up, and that the incumbent mayor is unlikely to be reelected, but we are normally reluctant to assign numerical probabilities to these events. However, to facilitate communication and enhance the analysis of choice, it is often desirable to quantify uncertainty. The most common procedure for quantifying uncertainty involves expressing belief in the language of chance. When we say that the probability of an uncertain event is 30%, for example, we express the belief that this event is as probable as the drawing of a red ball from a box that contains 30 red and 70 green balls. An alternative procedure for measuring subjective probability seeks to infer the degree of belief from preference via expected utility theory. This approach, pioneered by Ramsey (1931) and further developed by Savage (1954) and by Anscombe and Aumann (1963), derives subjective probability from preferences between bets. Specifically, the subjective probability of an uncertain event E is said to be p if the decision maker is indifferent between the prospect of receiving x if E occurs (and nothing otherwise) and the prospect of receiving x if a red ball is drawn from a box that contains a proportion p of red balls.

The Ramsey scheme for measuring belief and the theory on which it is based were challenged by Daniel Ellsberg (1961; see also Fellner, 1961) who constructed a compelling demonstration of what has come to be called an ambiguity effect, although the term *vagueness* may be more appropriate. The simplest demonstration of this effect involves two boxes: one contains 50 red balls and 50 green balls, whereas the second contains 100 red and green balls in unknown proportion. You draw a ball blindly from a box and guess its color. If your guess is correct, you win $20; otherwise you get nothing. On which box would you rather bet? Ellsberg argued that people prefer to bet on the 50/50 box rather than on the box with the unknown composition, even though they have no color preferences and so are indifferent between betting on red or on green in either box. This pattern of preferences, which was later confirmed in many experiments, violates the additivity of subjective probability because it implies that the sum of the probabilities of red and of green is higher in the 50/50 box than in the unknown box.

Ellsberg's (1961) work has generated a great deal of interest for two reasons. First, it provides an instructive counterexample to (subjective) expected utility theory within the context of games of chance. Second, it suggests a general hypothesis that people prefer to bet on clear rather than on vague events, at least for moderate and high probability. For small probability, Ellsberg suggested, people may prefer vagueness to clarity. These observations present a serious problem for expected utility theory and other models of risky choice because, with the notable exception of games of chance, most decisions in the real world depend on uncertain events whose probabilities cannot be precisely assessed. If people's choices depend not only on the degree of uncertainty but also on the precision with which it can be assessed, then the applicability of the standard models of risky choice is severely limited. Indeed, several authors have extended the standard theory by invoking nonadditive measures of belief (e.g., Fishburn, 1988; Schmeidler, 1989) or second-order probability distributions (e.g., Gärdenfors & Sahlin, 1982; Skyrm, 1980) in order to account for the effect of ambiguity. The normative status of these models is a subject of lively debate. Several authors, notably Ellsberg (1963), maintain that aversion to ambiguity can be justified on normative grounds, although Raiffa (1961) has shown that it leads to incoherence.

Ellsberg's (1963) example, and most of the subsequent experimental research on the response to ambiguity or vagueness, was confined to chance processes, such as drawing a ball from a box, or problems in which the decision maker is provided with a probability estimate. The potential significance of ambiguity, however, stems from its relevance to the evaluation of evidence in the real world. Is ambiguity aversion limited to games of chance and stated probabilities, or does it also hold for judgmental probabilities? We found no answer to this question in the literature, but there is evidence that casts some doubt on the generality of ambiguity aversion.

For example, Budescu, Weinberg, and Wallsten (1988) compared the cash equivalents given by subjects for gambles whose probabilities were expressed numerically, graphically, or verbally. In the graphical display, probabilities were presented as the shaded area of a circle. In the verbal form, probabilities were described by expressions such as "very likely" or "highly improbable." Because the verbal and the graphical forms are more ambiguous than the numerical form, ambiguity aversion implies a preference for the numerical display. This prediction was not confirmed. Subjects priced the gambles roughly the same in all three displays. In a different experimental paradigm, Cohen and Hansel (1959) and Howell (1971) investigated subjects' choices between compound gambles involving both skill and chance components. For example, in the latter experiment the subject had to hit a target with a dart (where the subject's hit rate equaled 75%) as well as spin a roulette wheel so that it would land on a marked section composing 40% of the area. Success involves a 75% skill compo-nent and 40% chance component with an overall probability of winning of $0.75 \times 0.4 = 0.3$. Howell varied the skill and chance components of the gambles, holding the overall prob-ability of winning constant. Because the chance level was known to the subject whereas the skill level was not, ambiguity aversion implies that subjects would shift as much uncertainty as possible to the chance component of the gamble. In contrast, 87% of the choices reflect a preference for skill over chance. Cohen and Hansel (1959) obtained essentially the same result.

The Competence Hypothesis

The preceding observations suggest that the aversion to ambiguity observed in a chance setup (involving aleatory uncertainty) does not readily extend to judgmental problems (involving espistemic uncertainty). In this article, we investigate an alternative account of uncertainty preferences, called the competence hypothesis, which applies to both chance and evidential problems. We submit that the willingness to bet on an uncertain event depends not only on the estimated likelihood of that event and the precision of that estimate; it also depends on one's general knowledge or understanding of the relevant context. More specifically, we propose that—holding judged probability constant—people prefer to bet in a context where they consider themselves knowledgeable or competent than in a context where they feel ignorant or uninformed. We assume that our feeling of competence[1] in a given context is determined by what we know relative to what can be known. Thus, it is enhanced by general knowledge, familiarity, and experience, and is diminished, for example, by calling attention to relevant information that is not available to the decision maker, especially if it is available to others.

There are both cognitive and motivational explanations for the competence hypothesis. People may have learned from lifelong experience that they generally do better in situations they understand than in situations where they have less knowledge. This expectation may carry over to situations where the chances of winning are no longer higher in the familiar than in the unfamiliar context. Perhaps the major reason for the competence hypothesis is motivational rather than cognitive. We propose that the consequences of each bet include, besides the monetary payoffs, the credit or blame associated with the outcome. Psychic pay-offs of satisfaction or embarrassment can result from self-evaluation or from an evaluation by others. In either case, the credit and the blame associated with an outcome depend, we suggest, on the attributions for success and failure. In the domain of chance, both success and failure are attributed primarily to luck. The situation is different when a person bets on his or her judgment. If the decision maker has limited understanding of the problem at hand, failure will be attributed to ignorance, whereas success is likely to be attributed to chance. In contrast, if the decision maker is an "expert," success is attributable to knowledge, whereas failure can sometimes be attributed to chance.

We do not wish to deny that in situations where experts are supposed to know all the facts, they are probably more embarrassed by failure than are novices. However, in situations that call for an educated guess, experts are sometimes less vulnerable than novices because they can better justify their bets, even if they do not win. In betting on the winner of a football game, for example, people who consider themselves experts can claim credit for a correct prediction and treat an incorrect prediction as an upset. People who do not know much about football, by contrast, cannot claim much credit for a correct prediction (because they are guessing), and they are exposed to blame for an incorrect prediction (because they are ignorant).

Competence or expertise, therefore, helps people take credit when they succeed and sometimes provides protection against blame when they fail. Ignorance or incompetence, however, prevents people from taking credit for success and exposes them to blame in case of failure. As a consequence, we propose, the balance of credit to blame is most favorable for bets in one's area of expertise, intermediate for chance events, and least favorable for bets in an area where one has only limited knowledge. This account provides an explanation of the competence hypothesis in terms of the asymmetry of credit and blame induced by knowledge or competence.

The preceding analysis readily applies to Ellsberg's example. People do not like to bet on the unknown box, we suggest, because there is information, namely the proportion of red and green balls in the box, that is knowable in principle but unknown to them. The presence of such data makes people feel less knowledgeable and less competent and reduces the attractiveness of the corresponding bet. A closely related interpretation of Ellsberg's example has been offered by Frisch and Baron (1988). The competence hypothesis is also consistent with the finding of Curley, Yates, and Abrams (1986) that the aversion to ambiguity is enhanced by anticipation that the contents of the unknown box will be shown to others.

Essentially the same analysis applies to the preference for betting on the future rather than on the past. Rothbart and Snyder (1970) asked subjects to roll a die and bet on the outcome either before the die was rolled or after the die was rolled but before the result was revealed. The subjects who predicted the outcome before the die was rolled expressed greater confidence in their guesses than the subjects who predicted the outcome after the die roll ("postdiction"). The former group also bet significantly more money than the latter group. The authors attributed this phenomenon to magical thinking or the illusion of control, namely the belief that one can exercise some control over the outcome before, but not after, the roll of the die. However, the preference to bet on future rather than past events is observed even when the illusion of control does not provide a plausible explanation, as illustrated by the following problem in which subjects were presented with a choice between the two bets:

1. A stock is selected at random from the *Wall Street Journal*. You guess whether it will go up or down tomorrow. If you're right, you win $5.

2. A stock is selected at random from the *Wall Street Journal*. You guess whether it went up or down yesterday. You cannot check the paper. If you're right, you win $5.

Sixty-seven percent of the subjects ($N = 184$) preferred to bet on tomorrow's closing price. (10% of the participants, selected at random, actually played their chosen bet.) Because the past, unlike the future, is knowable in principle, but not to them, subjects prefer the future bet where their relative ignorance is lower. Similarly, Brun and Teigen (1990) observed that subjects preferred to guess the result of a die roll, the sex of a child, or the outcome of a soccer game before the event rather than afterward. Most of the subjects found guessing before the event more "satisfactory if right" and less "uncomfortable if wrong." In prediction, only the future can prove you wrong; in postdiction, you could be wrong right now. The same argument applies to Ellsberg's problem. In the 50/50 box, a guess could turn out to be wrong only after drawing the ball. In the unknown box, however, the guess may turn out to be mistaken even before the drawing of the ball—if it turns out that the majority of balls in the box are of the opposite color. It is noteworthy that the preference to bet on future rather than on past events cannot be explained in terms of ambiguity because, in these problems, the future is as ambiguous as the past.

Simple chance events, such as drawing a ball from a box with a known composition, involve no ambiguity; the chances of winning are known precisely. If betting preferences between equiprobable events are determined by ambiguity, people should prefer to bet on chance over their own vague judgments (at least for moderate and high probability). In contrast, the attributional analysis described above implies that people will prefer betting on their judgment over a matched chance event when they feel knowledgeable and competent, but not otherwise. This prediction is confirmed by the finding that people prefer betting on their skill rather than on chance. It is also consistent with the observation of March and Shapira (1987) that many top managers, who consistently bet on highly uncertain business propositions, resist the analogy between business decisions and games of chance.

We have argued that the present attributional analysis can account for the available evidence on uncertainty preferences, whether or not they involve ambiguity. These include (i) the preference for betting on the known rather than on the unknown box in Ellsberg's problem, (ii) the preference to bet on future rather than on past events, and (iii) the preference for betting on skill rather than on chance. Furthermore, the competence hypothesis implies a *choice—judgment discrepancy*, namely a preference to bet on A rather than on B even though B is judged to be at least as probable as A. In the following series of experiments, we test the competence hypothesis and investigate the choice—judgment discrepancy. In experiment 1 we offer people the choice between betting on their judged probabilities for general knowledge items or on a matched chance lottery. Experiments 2 and 3 extend the test by studying real-world events and eliciting an independent assessment of knowledge. In experiment 4, we sort subjects according to their area of expertise and compare their willingness to bet on their expert category, a nonexpert category, and chance. Finally, in experiment 5, we test the competence hypothesis in a pricing task that does not involve probability judgment. The relations between belief and preference are discussed in the last section of the article.

Experiment 1: Betting on Knowledge

Subjects answered 30 knowledge questions in two different categories, such as history, geography, or sports. Four alternative answers were presented for each question, and the subjects first selected a single answer and then rated their confidence in that answer on a scale from 25% (pure guessing) to 100% (absolute certainty). Participants were given detailed instructions about the use of the scale and the notion of calibration. Specifically, they were instructed to use the scale so that a confidence rating of 60%, say, would correspond to a hit rate of 60%. They were also told that these ratings would be the basis for a money-making game and warned that both underconfidence and overconfidence would reduce their earnings.

After answering the questions and assessing confidence, subjects were given an opportunity to choose between betting on their answers or on a lottery in which the probability of winning was equal to their stated confidence. For a confidence rating of 75%, for example, subjects were given the choice between (i) betting that their answer was correct, or (ii) betting on a 75% lottery, defined by drawing a numbered chip in the range 1–75 from a bag filled with 100 numbered poker chips. For half of the questions, lotteries were directly equated to confidence ratings. For the other half of the questions, subjects chose between the complement of their answer (betting that an answer other than the one they choose is correct) or the complement of their confidence rating. Thus, if subjects chose answer A with confidence of 65%, they could choose between betting that one of the remaining answers B, C, or D is correct, or betting on a 100% − 65% = 35% lottery.

Two groups of subjects participated in the experiment. One group ($N = 29$) included psychology students who received course credit for participation. The second group ($N = 26$) was recruited from introductory economics classes and performed the experiment for cash earnings. To determine the subjects' payoffs, ten questions were selected at random, and the subjects played out the bets they had chosen. If subjects chose to gamble on their answer, they collected $1.50 if their answer was correct. If subjects chose to bet on the chance lottery, they drew a chip from the bag and collected $1.50 if the number on the chip fell in the proper range. Average earnings for the experiment were around $8.50.

Paid subjects took more time than unpaid subjects in selecting their answers and assessing confidence; they were slightly more accurate. Both groups exhibited overconfidence: the paid subjects answered correctly 47% of the questions and their average confidence was 60%. The unpaid subjects answered correctly 43% of the questions and their average confidence was 53%. We first describe the results of the simple lotteries; the complementary (disjunctive) lotteries are discussed later.

The results are summarized by plotting the percentage of choices (C) that favor the judgment bet over the lottery as a function of judged probability (P). Before discussing the actual data, it is instructive to examine several contrasting predictions, implied by five alternative hypotheses, which are displayed in figure 9.1.

The upper panel of figure 9.1 displays the predictions of three hypotheses in which C is independent of P. According to expected utility theory, decision makers will be indifferent between betting on their judgment and betting on a chance lottery; hence C should equal 50% throughout. Ambiguity aversion implies that people will prefer to bet on a chance event whose probability is well defined rather than on their judged probability, which is inevitably vague; hence C should fall below 50% everywhere. The opposite hypothesis, called chance aversion, predicts that people will prefer to bet on their judgment rather than on a matched chance lottery; hence C should exceed 50% for all P. In contrast to the flat predictions displayed in the upper panel, the two hypotheses in the lower panel imply that C depends on P. The regression hypothesis states that the decision weights, which control choice, will be regressive relative to stated probabilities. Thus, C will be relatively high for small probabilities and relatively low for high probabilities. This prediction also follows from the theory proposed by Einhorn and Hogarth (1985), who put forth a particular process model based on mental simulation, adjustment, and anchoring. The predictions of this model, however, coincide with the regression hypothesis.

Finally, the competence hypothesis implies that people will tend to bet on their judgment when they feel knowledgeable and on the chance lottery when they feel ignorant. Because higher stated probability generally entails higher knowledge, C will be an increasing function of P except at 100% where the chance lottery amounts to a sure thing.

The results of the experiment are summarized in table 9.1 and figure 9.2. Table 9.1 presents, for three different ranges of P, the percentage of paid and nonpaid subjects who bet on their answers rather than on the matched lottery. Recall that each question had four possible answers, so the lowest confidence level is 25%. Figure 9.2 displays the overall percentage of choices C that favored the judgment bet over the lottery as a function of judged probability P.[2] The graph shows that subjects chose the lottery when P was low or moderate (below 65%)

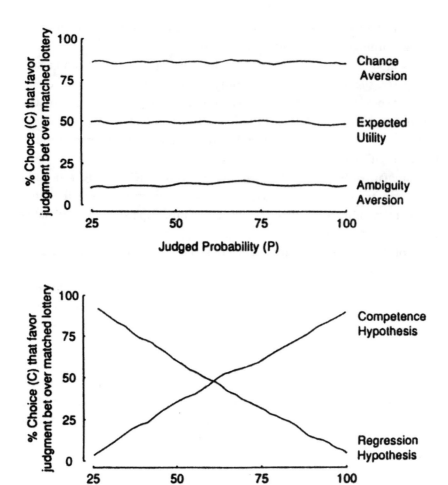

Figure 9.1
Five contrasting predictions of the results of an uncertainty preference experiment.

Table 9.1
Percentage of Paid and Nonpaid Subjects Who Preferred the Judgment Bet over the Lottery for Low, Medium, and High P (the Number of Observations Are Given in Parentheses)

	$25 \leq P \leq 50$	$50 < P < 75$	$75 \leq P \leq 100$
Paid	29	42	55
	(278)	(174)	(168)
Nonpaid	22	43	69
	(394)	(188)	(140)

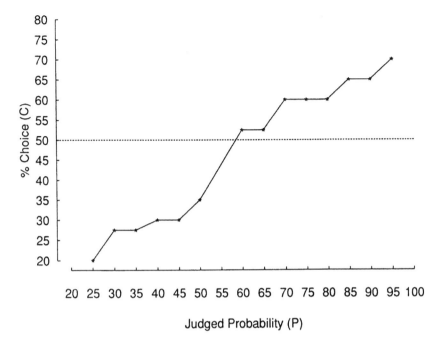

Figure 9.2
Percentage of choice (*C*) that favor a judgment bet over a matched lottery as a function of judged probability (*P*) in experiment 1.

and that they chose to bet on their answers when *P* was high. The pattern of results was the same for the paid and for the nonpaid subjects, but the effect was slightly stronger for the latter group. These results confirm the prediction of the competence hypothesis and reject the four alternative accounts, notably the ambiguity aversion hypothesis implied by second-order probability models (e.g., Gärdenfors & Sahlin, 1982) and the regression hypothesis implied by the model of Einhorn and Hogarth (1985).

To obtain a statistical test of the competence hypothesis, we computed, separately for each subject, the binary correlation coefficient (ϕ) between choice (judgment bet vs. lottery) and judged probability (above median vs. below median). The median judgment was 0.65. Seventy-two percent of the subjects yielded positive coefficients, and the average ϕ was 0.30 ($t(54) = 4.3$, $p < 0.01$). To investigate the robustness of the observed pattern, we replicated the experiment with one major change. Instead of constructing chance lotteries whose probabilities matched the values stated by the subjects, we constructed lotteries in which the probability of winning was either 6% higher or 6% lower than the subjects' judged probability. For high-knowledge questions ($P \geq 75\%$), the majority of responses (70%) favored

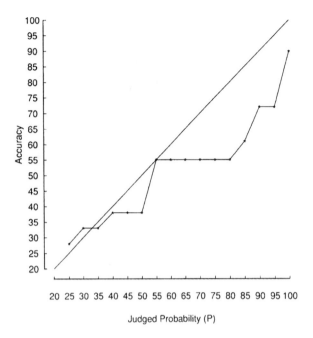

Figure 9.3
Calibration curve for experiment 1.

the judgment bet over the lottery even when the lottery offered a (6%) higher probability of winning. Similarly, for low-confidence questions ($P \geq 50\%$), the majority of responses (52%) favored the lottery over the judgment bet even when the former offered a lower (6%) probability of winning.

Figure 9.3 presents the calibration curve for the data of experiment 1. The figure shows that, on the whole, people are reasonably well calibrated for low probability but exhibit substantial overconfidence for high probability. The preference for the judgment bet over the lottery for high probability, therefore, cannot be justified on an actuarial basis.

The analysis of the complementary bets, where subjects were asked in effect to bet that their chosen answer was incorrect, revealed a very different pattern. Across subjects, the judgment bet was favored 40.5% of the time, indicating a statistically significant preference for the chance lottery ($t(54) = 3.8$, $p < 0.01$). Furthermore, we found no systematic relation between C and P, in marked contrast to the monotonic relation displayed in figure 9.2. In accord with our attributional account, this result suggests that people prefer to bet on their beliefs rather than against them. These data, however, may also be explained by the hypothesis that people prefer to bet on simple rather than on disjunctive hypotheses.

Experiment 2: Football and Politics

Our next experiment differs from the previous one in three respects. First, it concerns the prediction of real-world future events rather than the assessment of general knowledge. Second, it deals with binary events so that the lowest level of confidence is 0.5 rather than 0.25 as in the previous experiment. Third, in addition to judgments of probability, subjects also rated their level of knowledge for each prediction.

A group of 20 students predicted the outcomes of 14 football games each week for five consecutive weeks. For each game, subjects selected the team that they thought would win the game and assessed the probability of their chosen team winning. The subjects also assessed, on a five-point scale, their knowledge about each game. Following the rating, subjects were asked whether they preferred to bet on the team they chose or on a matched chance lottery. The results summarized in figure 9.4 confirm the previous finding. For both high and low knowledge (defined by a median split on the knowledge rating scale), C was an increasing function of P. Moreover, C was greater for high knowledge than for low knowledge at any $P > 0.5$. Only 5% of the subjects produced negative correlations between C and P, and the average ϕ coefficient was 0.33 ($t(77) = 8.7$, $p < 0.01$).

We next took the competence hypothesis to the floor of the Republican National Convention in New Orleans in August 1988. The participants were volunteer workers at the convention. They were given a one-page questionnaire that contained instructions and an answer sheet. Thirteen states were selected to represent a cross-section of different geographical areas as well to include the most important states in terms of electoral votes. The participants ($N = 100$) rated the probability of Bush carrying each of the 13 states in the November 1988 election on a scale from 0 (Bush is certain to lose) to 100 (Bush is certain to win). As in the football experiment, the participants rated their knowledge of each state on a five-point scale and indicated whether they would rather bet on their prediction or on a chance lottery. The results, summarized in figure 9.5, show that C increased with P for both levels of knowledge, and that C was greater for high knowledge than for low knowledge at all levels of P. When asked about their home state, 70% of the participants selected the judgment bet over the lottery. Only 5% of the subjects yielded negative correlations between C and P, and the average ϕ coefficient was 0.42 ($t(99) = 13.4$, $p < 0.01$).

The results displayed in figures 9.4 and 9.5 support the competence hypothesis in the prediction of real-world events: in both tasks, C increases with P, as in experiment 1. In that study, however, probability and knowledge were perfectly correlated; hence the choice—judgment discrepancy could be attributed to a distortion of the probability scale in the judgement task. This explanation does not apply to the results of the present experiment, which exhibits an independent effect of rated knowledge. As seen in figures 9.4 and 9.5, the preference for the judgment bet over the chance lottery is greater for high-knowledge items than

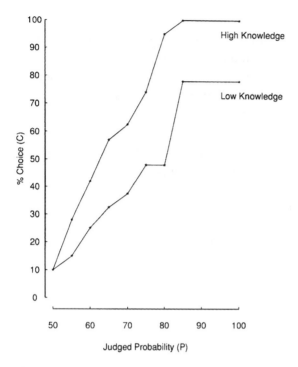

Figure 9.4
Percentage of choices (C) that favor a judgment bet over a matched lottery as a function of judged probability (P), for high- and low-knowledge items in the football prediction task (experiment 2).

for low-knowledge items for all levels of judged probability. It is noteworthy that the strategy of betting on judgment was less successful than the strategy of betting on chance in both datasets. The former strategy yielded hit rates of 64% and 78% for football and election, respectively, whereas the latter strategy yielded hit rates of 73% and 80%. The observed tendency to select the judgment bet, therefore, does not yield better performance.

Experiment 3: Long Shots

The preceding experiments show that people often prefer to bet on their judgment than on a matched chance event, even though the former is more ambiguous than the latter. This effect, summarized in figures 9.2, 9.4, and 9.5, was observed at the high end of the probability scale. These data could perhaps be explained by the simple hypothesis that people prefer the judgment bet when the probability of winning exceeds 0.5 and the chance lottery when the probability of winning is below 0.5. To test this hypothesis, we sought high-knowledge items in which the probability of winning is low, so the subject's best guess is unlikely to be

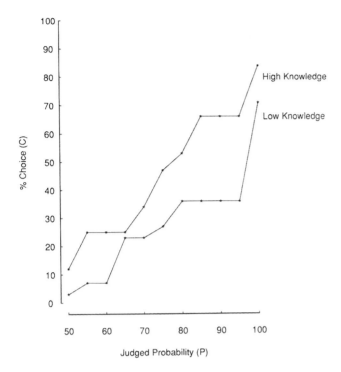

Figure 9.5
Percentage of choices (C) that favor a judgment bet over a matched lottery as a function of judged probability (P), for high- and low-knowledge items in experiment 2 (election data).

true. In this case, the above hypothesis implies a preference for the chance lottery, whereas the competence hypothesis implies a preference for the judgment bet. These predictions are tested in the following experiment.

One hundred and eight students were presented with open-ended questions about 12 future events (e.g., what movie will win this year's Oscar for best picture? What football team will win the next Super Bowl? In what class next quarter will you have the highest grade?). They were asked to answer each question, to estimate the chances that their guess will turn out to be correct, and to indicate whether they have high or low knowledge of the relevant domain. The use of open-ended questions eliminates the lower bound of 50% imposed by the use of dichotomous predictions in the previous experiment. After the subjects completed these tasks, they were asked to consider, separately for each question, whether they would rather bet on their prediction or on a matched chance lottery.

On average, the subjects answered 10 out of 12 questions. Table 9.2 presents the percentage (C) of responses that favor the judgment bet over the chance lottery for high- and

Table 9.2
Percentage of Choices (C) That Favor a Judgment Bet over a Matched
Lottery for High- and Low-rated Knowledge and for Judged Probabil-
ity below and above 0.5 (the Number of Responses Are Given in
Parentheses)

Rated knowledge	Judged probability	
	$p < 0.5$	$p \geq 0.5$
Low	36	58
	(593)	(128)
High	61	69
	(151)	(276)

low-knowledge items, and for judged probabilities below or above 0.5. The number of
responses in each cell is given in parentheses. The results show that, for high-knowledge
items, the judgment bet was preferred over the chance lottery regardless of whether P was
above or below one-half ($p < 0.01$ in both cases), as implied by the competence hypothesis.
Indeed, the discrepancy between the low- and high-knowledge conditions was greater for $p <$
0.5 than for $p \geq 0.5$. Evidently, people prefer to bet on their high-knowledge predictions even
when the predictions are unlikely to be correct.

Experiment 4: Expert Prediction

In the preceding experiments, we used the subjects' ratings of specific items to define high
and low knowledge. In this experiment, we manipulate knowledge or competence by sorting
subjects according to their expertise. To this end, we asked 110 students in an introductory
psychology class to assess their knowledge of politics and of football on a nine-point scale.
All subjects who rated their knowledge of the two areas on opposite sides of the midpoint
were asked to take part in the experiment. Twenty-five subjects met this criterion, and all
but two agreed to participate. They included 12 political "experts" and 11 football "experts"
defined by their strong area. To induce the subjects to give careful responses, we gave them
detailed instructions including a discussion of calibration, and we employed the Brier scoring rule (see, e.g., Lichtenstein et al., 1982) designed to motivate subjects to give their best
estimates. Subjects earned about $10, on average.

The experiment consisted of two sessions. In the first session, subjects made predictions
for a set of 40 future events (20 political events and 20 football games). All the events were
resolved within five weeks of the date of the initial session. The political events concerned
the winner of the various states in the 1988 presidential election. The 20 football games
included 10 professional and 10 college games. For each contest (politics or football), subjects

Table 9.3
Ranking Data for Expert Study

Type of bet	Rank			
	1st	2nd	3rd	Mean rank
High-knowledge	192	85	68	1.64
Chance	74	155	116	2.12
Low-knowledge	79	105	161	2.23

chose a winner by circling the name of one of the contestants and then assessed the probability that their prediction would come true (on a scale from 50% to 100%).

Using the results of the first session, 20 triples of bets were constructed for each participant. Each triple included three matched bets with the same probability of winning generated by (i) a chance device, (ii) the subject's prediction in his or her strong category, and (iii) the subject's prediction in his or her weak category. Obviously, some events appeared in more than one triple. In the second session, subjects ranked each of the 20 triples of bets. The chance bets were defined as in experiment 1 with reference to a box containing 100 numbered chips. Subjects were told that they would actually play their choices in each of the triples. To encourage careful ranking, subjects were told that they would play 80% of their first choices and 20% of their second choices.

The data are summarized in table 9.3 and in figure 9.6, which plots the attractiveness of the three types of bets (mean rank order) against judged probability. The results show a clear preference for betting on the strong category. Across all triples, the mean ranks were 1.64 for the strong category, 2.12 for the chance lottery, and 2.23 for the weak category. The difference among the ranks is highly significant ($p < 0.001$) by the Wilcoxon rank-sum test. In accord with the competence hypothesis, people prefer to bet on their judgment in their area of competence but prefer to bet on chance in an area in which they are not well informed. As expected, the lottery became more popular than the high-knowledge bet only at 100%. This pattern of result is inconsistent with an account based on ambiguity or second-order probabilities because both the high- and low-knowledge bets are based on vague judgmental probabilities whereas the chance lotteries have clear probabilities. Ambiguity aversion could explain why low-knowledge bets are less attractive than either the high-knowledge bet or the chance bet, but it cannot explain the major finding of this experiment that the vague high-knowledge bets are preferred to the clear chance bets.

A noteworthy feature of figure 9.6, which distinguishes it from the previous graphs, is that preferences are essentially independent of P. Evidently, the competence effect is fully captured in this case by the contrast between the categories; hence the added knowledge implied by the judged probability has little or no effect on the choice among the bets.

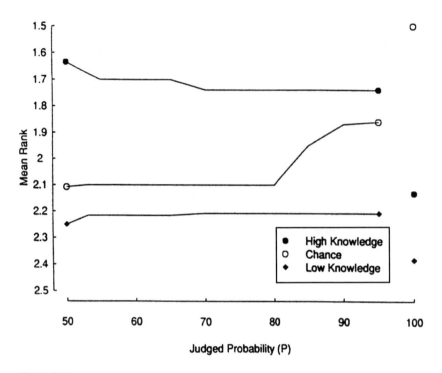

Figure 9.6
Ranking data for high-knowledge, low-knowledge, and chance bets as a function of P in experiment 4.

Figure 9.7 presents the average calibration curves for experiment 4, separately for the high- and low-knowledge categories. These graphs show that judgments were generally over-confident: subjects' confidence exceeded their hit rate. Furthermore, the overconfidence was more pronounced in the high-knowledge category than in the low-knowledge category. As a consequence, the ordering of bets did not mirror judgmental accuracy. Summing across all triples, betting on the chance lottery would win 69% of the time, betting on the novice category would win 64% of the time, and betting on the expert category would win only 60% of the time. By betting on the expert category therefore the subjects are losing, in effect, 15% of their expected earnings.

The preference for knowledge over chance is observed not only for judgments of prob-ability for categorical events (win, loss), but also for probability distributions over numerical variables. Subjects ($N = 93$) were given an opportunity to set 80% confidence intervals for a variety of quantities (e.g., average SAT score for entering freshmen at Stanford; driving dis-tance from San Francisco to Los Angeles). After setting confidence intervals, subjects were given the opportunity to choose between (i) betting that their confidence interval contained

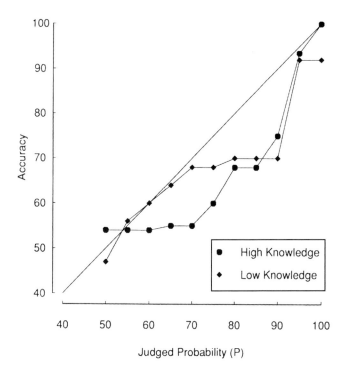

Figure 9.7
Calibration curves for high- and low-knowledge categories in experiment 4.

the true value, or (ii) an 80% lottery. Subjects preferred betting on the confidence interval in the majority of cases, although this strategy paid off only 69% of the time because the confidence intervals they set were generally too narrow. Again, subjects paid a premium of nearly 15% to bet on their judgment.

Experiment 5: Complementary Bets

The preceding experiments rely on judgments of probability to match the chance lottery and the judgment bet. To control for possible biases in the judgment process, out last test of the competence hypothesis is based on a pricing task that does not involve probability judgment. This experiment also provides an estimate of the premium that subjects are paying in order to bet on high-knowledge items.

Sixty-eight students were instructed to state their cash equivalent (reservation price) for each of 12 bets. They were told that one pair of bets would be chosen and a few students, selected at random, would play the bet for which they stated the higher cash equivalent. (For a discussion of this payoff scheme, see Tversky, Slovic, & Kahneman, 1990.) All bets in this experiment offered a prize of $15 if a given proposition were true, and nothing otherwise. Complementary propositions were presented to different subjects. For example, half the subjects were asked to price a bet that paid $15 if the air distance between New York and San Francisco is more than 2500 miles, and nothing otherwise. The half of the subjects were asked to price the complementary bet that paid $15 if the air distance between New York and San Francisco is less than 2500 miles, and nothing otherwise.

To investigate uncertainty preferences, we paired high- and low-knowledge propositions. For example, we assumed that the subjects know more about the air distance between New York and San Francisco than about the air distance between Beijing and Bangkok. We also assumed that our respondents (Stanford students) know more about the percentage of undergraduate students who receive on-campus housing at Stanford than at the University of Nevada, Las Vegas. As before, we refer to these propositions as high- and low-knowledge items, respectively. Note that the selection of the stated value of the uncertain quantity (e.g., air distance, percentage of students) controls a subject's confidence in the validity of the proposition in question, independent of his or her general knowledge about the subject matter. Twelve pairs of complementary propositions were constructed, and each subject evaluated one of the four bets defined by each pair. In the air-distance problem, for example, the four propositions were d(SF, NY) > 2500, d(SF, NY) < 2500, d(Be, Ba) > 3000, and d(Be, Ba) < 3000, where d(SF, NY) and d(Be, Ba) denote, respectively, the distances between San Francisco and New York and between Beijing and Bangkok.

Note that according to expected value, the average cash equivalent for each pair of complementary bets should be $7.50. Summing across all 12 pairs of complementary bets, subjects paid on average $7.12 for the high-knowledge bets and only $5.96 for the low-knowledge bets ($p < 0.01$). Thus, people were paying, in effect, a competence premium of nearly 20% in order to bet on the more familiar propositions. Furthermore, the average price for the (complementary) high-knowledge bets was greater than that for the low-knowledge bets in 11 out of 12 problems. For comparison, the average cash equivalent for a coin toss to win $15 was $7. In accord with our previous findings, the chance lottery is valued above the low-knowledge bets but not above the high-knowledge bets.

We next test the competence hypothesis against expected utility theory. Let H and $\bar{H}$ denote two complimentary high-knowledge propositions, and let L and $\bar{L}$ denote the corresponding low-knowledge propositions. Suppose a decision maker prefers betting on H over L and on $\bar{H}$ over $\bar{L}$. This pattern is inconsistent with expected utility theory because it implies that $P(H) > P(L)$ and $P(\bar{H}) > P(\bar{L})$, contrary to the additivity assumption $P(H) + P(\bar{H}) = P(L) + P(\bar{L}) = 1$. If, by contrast, high-knowledge bets are preferred to low-knowledge bets, such a pattern is likely to arise. Because the four propositions (H, $\bar{H}$, L, $\bar{L}$) were evaluated by four different groups of subjects, we employ a between-subject test of additivity. Let $M(H_i)$ be the median price for the high-knowledge proposition H_i, etc. The responses in problem i violate additivity, in the direction implied by the competence hypothesis, whenever $M(H_i) > M(L_i)$ and $M(\bar{H}_i) \geq M(\bar{L}_i)$.

Five of the 12 pairs of problems exhibited this pattern indicating a preference for the high-knowledge bets, and none of the pairs exhibited the opposite pattern. For example, the median price for betting on the proposition "more than 85% of undergraduates at Stanford receive on-campus housing" was $7.50, and the median cash equivalent for betting on the complementary proposition was $10. In contrast, the median cash equivalent for betting on the proposition "more than 70% of undergraduates at UNLV receive on-campus housing" was $3, and the median value for the complementary bet was $7. The majority of respondents, therefore, were willing to pay more to bet on either side of a high-knowledge item than on either side of a low-knowledge item.

The preceding analysis, based on medians, can be extended as follows. For each pair of propositions (H_i, L_i), we computed the proportion of comparisons in which the cash equivalent of H_i exceeded the cash equivalent of L_i, denoted $P(H_i > L_i)$. We also computed $P(\bar{H}_i > \bar{L}_i)$ for the complementary propositions. All ties were excluded. Under expected utility theory,

$$P(H_i > L_i) + P(\bar{H}_i > \bar{L}_i) = P(L_i > H_i) + P(\bar{L}_i > \bar{H}_i) = 1$$

because the additivity of probability implies that for every comparison that favors H_i over L_i, there should be another comparison that favors $\bar{L}_i$ over $\bar{H}_i$. On the other hand, if people prefer the high-knowledge bets, as implied by the competence hypothesis, we expect

$$P(H_i > L_i) + P(\bar{H}_i > \bar{L}_i) > P(L_i > H_i) + P(\bar{L}_i > \bar{H}_i).$$

Among the 12 pairs of complementary propositions, the above inequality was satisfied in 10 cases, the opposite inequality was satisfied in one case, and equality was observed in one case, indicating a significant violation of additivity in the direction implied by the competence hypothesis ($p < 0.01$ by sign test). These findings confirm the competence hypothesis in a test that does not rely on judgments of probability or on a comparison of a judgment bet to a matched lottery. Hence, the present results cannot be attributed to a bias in the judgment process or in the matching of high- and low-knowledge items.

Discussion

The experiments reported in this article establish a consistent and pervasive discrepancy between judgments of probability and choice between bets. Experiment 1 demonstrates that the preference for the knowledge bet over the chance lottery increases with judged confidence. Experiments 2 and 3 replicate this finding for future real-world events and demonstrate a knowledge effect independent of judged probability. In experiment 4, we sort subjects into their strong and weak areas and show that people like betting on their strong category and dislike betting on their weak category; the chance bet is intermediate between the two. This pattern cannot be explained by ambiguity or by second-order probability because chance is unambiguous, whereas judgmental probability is vague. Finally, experiment 5 confirms the prediction of the competence hypothesis in a pricing task that does not rely on probability matchings and shows that people are paying a premium of nearly 20% for betting on high-knowledge items.

These observations are consistent with our attributional account, which holds that knowledge induces an asymmetry in the internal balance of credit and blame. Competence, we suggest, allows people to claim credit when they are right, and its absence exposes people to blame when they are wrong. As a consequence, people prefer the high-knowledge bet over the matched lottery, and they prefer the matched lottery over the low-knowledge bet. This account explains other instances of uncertainty preferences reported in the literature, notably the preference for clear over vague probabilities in a chance setup (Ellsberg, 1961), the preference to bet on the future over the past (Rothbart & Snyder, 1970; Brun & Teigen, 1990), the preference for skill over chance (Cohen & Hansel, 1959; Howell, 1971), and the enhancement of ambiguity aversion in the presence of knowledgeable others (Curley, Yates, & Abrams, 1986). The robust finding that, in their area of competence, people prefer to bet on their (vague) beliefs over a matched chance event indicates that the impact of knowledge or competence outweighs the effect of vagueness.

In experiments 1–4 we used probability judgments to establish belief and choice data to establish preference. Furthermore, we have interpreted the choice–judgment discrepancy as a preference effect. In contrast, it could be argued that the choice–judgment discrepancy is attributable to a judgmental bias, namely underestimation of the probabilities of high-knowledge items and overestimation of the probabilities of low-knowledge items. This interpretation, however, is not supported by the available evidence. First, it implies less overconfidence for high-knowledge than for low-knowledge items contrary to fact (see figure 9.7). Second, judgments of probability cannot be dismissed as inconsequential because in the presence of a scoring rule, such as the one used in experiment 4, these judgments represent another form of betting. Finally, a judgmental bias cannot explain the results of experiment 5, which demonstrates preferences for betting on high-knowledge items in a pricing task that does not involve probability judgment.

The distinction between preference and belief lies at the heart of Bayesian decision theory. The standard interpretation of this theory assumes that (i) the expressed beliefs (i.e., probability judgments) of an individual are consistent with an additive probability measure, (ii) the preferences of an individual are consistent with the expectation principle and thus give rise to a (subjective) probability measure derived from choice, and (iii) the two measures of subjective probability—obtained from judgment and from choice—are consistent. Note that points 1 and 2 are logically independent. Allais's counterexample, for instance, violates 2 but not 1. Indeed, many authors have introduced nonadditive decision weights, derived from preferences, to accommodate the observed violations of the expectation principle (see, e.g., Kahneman & Tversky, 1979). These decision weights, however, need not reflect the decision maker's beliefs. A person may believe that the probability of drawing the ace of spades from a well-shuffled deck is 1/52, yet in betting on this event he or she may give it a higher weight. Similarly, Ellsberg's example does not prove that people regard the clear event as more probable than the corresponding vague event; it only shows that people prefer to bet on the clear event. Unfortunately, the term *subjective probability* has been used in the literature to describe decision weights derived from preference as well as direct expressions of belief. Under the standard interpretation of the Bayesian theory, the two concepts coincide. As we go beyond this theory, however, it is essential to distinguish between the two.

Manipulations of Ambiguity

The distinction between belief and preference is particularly important for the interpretation of ambiguity effects. Several authors have concluded that, when the probability of winning is small or when the probability of losing is high, people prefer ambiguity to clarity (Curley & Yates, 1989; Einhorn & Hogarth, 1985; Hogarth & Kunreuther, 1989). However, this interpretation can be challenged because, as will be shown below, the data may reflect differences in belief rather than uncertainty preferences. In this section, we investigate the experimental procedures used to manipulate ambiguity and argue that they tend to confound ambiguity with perceived probability.

Perhaps the simplest procedure for manipulating ambiguity is to vary the decision maker's confidence in a given probability estimate. Hogarth and his collaborators have used two versions of this procedure. Einhorn and Hogarth (1985) presented the subject with a probability estimate, based on the "judgement of independent observers," and varied the degree of confidence attached to that estimate. Hogarth and Kunreuther (1989) "endowed" the subject with his or her "best estimate of the probability" of a given event and manipulated ambiguity by varying the degree of confidence associated with this estimate. If we wish to interpret people's willingness to bet on these sorts of events as ambiguity seeking or ambiguity aversion, however, we must first verify that the manipulation of ambiguity did not affect the perceived probability of the events.

To investigate this question, we first replicated the manipulation of ambiguity used by Hogarth and Kunreuther (1989). One group of subjects ($N = 62$), called the high-confidence group, received the following information:

Imagine that you head a department in a large insurance company. The owner of a small business comes to you seeking insurance against a $100,000 loss, which could result from claims concerning a defective product. You have considered the manufacturing process, the reliabilities of the machines used, and evidence contained in the business records. After considering the evidence available to you, your best estimate of the probability of a defective product is .01. Given the circumstances, you feel confident about the precision of this estimate. Naturally you will update your estimate as you think more about the situation or receive additional information.

A second group of subjects ($N = 64$), called the low-confidence group, received the same information, except that the phrase "you feel confident about the precision of this estimate" was replaced by "you experience considerable uncertainty about the precision of this estimate." All subjects were then asked:

Do you expect that the new estimate will be (Check one):

Above 0.01 _____

Below 0.01 _____

Exactly 0.01 _____

The two groups were also asked to evaluate a second case in which the stated probability of a loss was 0.90. If the stated value (0.01 or 0.90) is interpreted as the mean of the respective second-order probability distribution, then a subject's expectation for the updated estimate should coincide with the current "best estimate." Furthermore, if the manipulation of confidence affects ambiguity but not perceived probability, there should be no difference between the responses of the high-confidence and the low-confidence groups. The data presented in table 9.4, under the heading *Your probability*, clearly violate these assumptions. The distributions of responses in the low-confidence condition are considerably more skewed than the distributions in the high-confidence condition. Furthermore, the skewness is positive for 0.01 and negative for 0.90. Telling subjects that they "experience considerable uncertainty" about their best estimate produces a regressive shift: the expected probability of loss is above 0.01 in the first problem and below 0.90 in the second. The interaction between confidence (high—low) and direction (above—below) is statistically significant ($p < 0.01$).

We also replicated the procedure employed by Einhorn and Hogarth (1985) in which subjects were told that "independent observers have stated that the probability of a defective product is .01." Subjects ($N = 52$) in the high-confidence group were told that "you could feel confident about the estimate," whereas subjects ($N = 52$) in the low-confidence group were told that "you could experience considerable uncertainty about the estimate." Both groups were then asked whether their best guess of the probability of experiencing a loss is above 0.01, below 0.01, or exactly 0.01. The two groups also evaluated a second case in which the probability of loss was 0.90. The results presented in table 9.4, under the heading

Table 9.4

Subjective Assessments of Stated Probabilities of 0.01 and 0.90 under High-confidence and Low-confidence Instructions (the Entries are the Percentage of Subjects Who Chose Each of the Three Responses)

Stated value	Response	Your probability		Others' estimate	
		High confidence	Low confidence	High confidence	Low confidence
0.01	Above 0.01	45	75	46	80
	Exactly 0.01	34	11	15	6
	Below 0.01	21	14	39	14
0.90	Above 0.90	29	28	42	26
	Exactly 0.90	42	14	23	12
	Below 0.90	29	58	35	62

Others' estimate, reveal the pattern observed above. In the high-confidence condition, the distributions of responses are fairly symmetric, but in the low-confidence condition the distributions exhibit positive skewness at 0.01 and negative skewness at 0.90. Again, the interaction between confidence (high–low) and direction (above–below) is statistically significant ($p < 0.01$).

These results indicate that the manipulations of confidence influenced not only the ambiguity of the event in question but also its perceived probability: they increased the perceived probability of the highly unlikely event and decreased the perceived probability of the likely event. A regressive shift of this type is not at all unreasonable and can even be rationalized by a suitable prior distribution. As a consequence of the shift in probability, the bet on the vaguer estimate should be more attractive when the probability of loss is high (0.90) and less attractive when the probability of loss is low (0.01). This is exactly the pattern of preferences observed by Einhorn and Hogarth (1985) and by Hogarth and Kunreuther (1989), but it does not entail either ambiguity seeking or ambiguity aversion because the events differ in perceived probability, not only in ambiguity.

The results of table 9.4 and the findings of Hogarth and his collaborators can be explained by the hypothesis that subjects interpret the stated probability value as the median (or the mode) of a second-order probability distribution. If the second-order distributions associated with extreme probabilities are skewed toward 0.5, the mean is less extreme than the median, and the difference between them is greater when ambiguity is high than when it is low. Consequently, the mean of the second-order probability distribution, which controls choice in the Bayesian model, will be more regressive (i.e., closer to 0.5) under low confidence than under high confidence.

Table 9.5

Percentage of Subjects Who Favored the Clear Event and the Vague Event in Judgment and in Choice

			Choice	
	Probability (win/lose)	Judgment $N = 72$	Win $100 $N = 58$	Lose $100 $N = 58$
Low	0.05	28	12	66
	[0, 0.1]	47	74	22
Medium	0.5	38	60	60
	[0, 1]	22	26	21
High	0.9	50	50	22
	[0.8, 1]	21	34	47

Note: The sum of the two values in each condition is less than 100%; the remaining responses expressed equivalence. In the choice task, the low probabilities were 0.075 and [0, 0.15]. *N* denotes sample size. (Based on Parayre and Kahneman.)

The potential confounding of ambiguity and degree of belief arises even when ambiguity is manipulated by information regarding a chance process. Unlike Ellsberg's comparison of the 50/50 box with the unknown box, where symmetry precludes a bias in one direction or another, similar manipulations of ambiguity in asymmetric problems could produce a regressive shift, as demonstrated in an unpublished study by Parayre and Kahneman.[3]

These investigators compared a clear event, defined by the proportion of red balls in a box, with a vague event defined by the range of balls of the designated color. For a vague event [0.8, 1], subjects were informed that the proportion of red balls could be anywhere between 0.8 and 1, compared with 0.9 for the clear event. Table 9.5 presents both choice and judgment data for three probability levels: low, medium, and high. In accord with previous work, the choice data show that subjects preferred to bet on the vague event when the probability of winning was low and when the probability of losing was high, and they preferred to bet on the clear event in all other cases. The novel feature of the Parayre and Kahneman experiment is the use of a perceptual rating scale based on a judgment of length, which provides a nonnumerical assessment of probability. Using this scale, the investigators showed that the judged probabilities were regressive. That is, the vague low-probability event [0, 0.10] was judged as more probable than the clear event, 0.05, and the vague high-probability event [0.8, 1] was judged as less probable than the clear event, 0.9. For the medium probability, there was no significant difference in judgment between the vague event [0, 1] and the clear event, 0.5. These results, like the data of table 9.4, demonstrate that the preference for betting on the ambiguous event (observed at the low end for positive bets and at the high end for negative bets) could reflect a regressive shift in the perception of probability rather than a preference for ambiguity.

Concluding Remarks

The findings regarding the effect of competence and the relation between preferences and beliefs challenge the standard interpretation of choice models that assumes independence of preference and belief. The results are also at variance with post-Bayesian models that invoke second-order beliefs to explain the effects of ambiguity or partial knowledge. Moreover, our results call into question the basic idea of defining beliefs in terms of preferences. If willingness to bet on an uncertain event depends on more than the perceived likelihood of that event and the confidence in that estimate, it is exceedingly difficult—if not impossible—to derive underlying beliefs from preferences between bets.

Besides challenging existing models, the competence hypothesis might help explain some puzzling aspects of decisions under uncertainty. It could shed light on the observation that many decision makers do not regard a calculated risk in their area of competence as a gamble (see, e.g., March & Shapira, 1987). It might also help explain why investors are sometimes willing to forego the advantage of diversification and concentrate on a small number of companies (Blume, Crockett, & Friend, 1974) with which they are presumably familiar. The implications of the competence hypothesis to decision making at large are left to be explored.

Acknowledgments

This work was supported by Grant 89–0064 from The Air Force Office of Scientific Research to Stanford University. Funding for experiment 1 was provided by SES 8420240 to Ray Battalio. We have benefited from discussions with Max Bazerman, Daniel Ellsberg, Richard Gonzales, Robin Hogarth, Linda Ginzel, Daniel Kahneman, and Eldar Shafir.

Notes

1. We use the tern *competence* in a broad sense that includes skill, as well as knowledge or understanding.

2. In this and all subsequent figures, we plot the isotone regression of C on P—that is, the best-fitting monotone function in the least squares sense (see Barlow et al., 1972).

3. We are grateful to Parayre and Kahneman for providing us with these data.

References

Anscombe, F. J., & Aumann, R. J. (1963). A definition of subjective probability. *Annals of Mathematical Statistics, 34*, 199–205.

Barlow, R. E., et al. (1972). *Statistical inference under order restrictions: The theory and application of isotonic regression*. New York, NY: John Wiley.

Blume, M. E., Crockett, J., & Friend, I. (1974). Stock ownership in the United States: Characteristics and trends. *Survey of Current Business, 54*, 16–40.

Brun, W., & Teigen, K. (1990). Prediction and postdiction preferences in guessing. *Journal of Behavioral Decision Making, 3*, 17–28.

Budescu, D., Weinberg, S., & Wallsten, T. (1988). Decisions based on numerically and verbally expressed uncertainties. *Journal of Experimental Psychology: Human Perception and Performance, 14*(2), 281–294.

Cohen, J., & Hansel, M. (1959). Preferences for different combinations of chance and skill in gambling. *Nature, 183*, 841–843.

Curley, S., & Yates, J. F. (1989). An empirical evaluation of descriptive models of ambiguity reactions in choice situations. *Journal of Mathematical Psychology, 33*, 397–427.

Curley, S., Yates, J. F., & Abrams, R. (1986). Psychological sources of ambiguity avoidance. *Organizational Behavior and Human Decision Processes, 38*, 230–256.

Einhorn, H., & Hogarth, R. (1985). Ambiguity and uncertainty in probabilistic inference. *Psychological Review, 93*, 433–461.

Ellsberg, D. (1961). Risk, ambiguity, and the savage axioms. *Quarterly Journal of Economics, 75*, 643–669.

Ellsberg, D. (1963). Risk, ambiguity, and the savage axioms: Reply. *Quarterly Journal of Economics, 77*, 336–342.

Fellner, W. (1961). Distortion of subjective probabilities as a reaction to uncertainty. *Quarterly Journal of Economics, 75*, 670–689.

Fishburn, P. (1988). *Nonlinear preference and utility theory*. Baltimore, MD: Johns Hopkins University Press.

Frisch, D., & Baron, J. (1988). Ambiguity and rationality. *Journal of Behavioral Decision Making, 1*, 149–157.

Gärdenfors, P., & Sahlin, N.-E. (1982). Unreliable probabilities, risk taking, and decision making. *Synthese, 53*(3), 361–386.

Hogarth, R., & Kunreuther, H. (1988). *Pricing insurance and warranties: Ambiguity and correlated risks*. Unpublished manuscript, University of Chicago and University of Pennsylvania.

Hogarth, R., & Kunreuther, H. (1989). Risk, ambiguity, and insurance. *Journal of Risk and Uncertainty, 2*, 5–35.

Howell, W. (1971). Uncertainty from internal and external sources: A clear case of overconfidence. *Journal of Experimental Psychology, 89*(2), 240–243.

Kahneman, D., & Tversky, A. (1979). Prospect theory: An analysis of decision under risk. *Econometrica, 47*, 263–291.

Lichtenstein, S., Fischhoff, B., & Phillips, L. (1982). Calibration of probabilities: The state of the art to 1980. In D. Kahneman, P. Slovic, & A. Tversky (Eds.), *Judgment under uncertainty: Heuristics and biases* (pp. 306–334). New York, NY: Cambridge University Press.

March, J., & Shapira, Z. (1987). Managerial perspectives on risk and risk taking. *Management Science, 33*(11), 1404–1418.

Raiffa, H. (1961). Risk, ambiguity, and the savage axioms: Comment. *Quarterly Journal of Economics, 75,* 690–694.

Ramsey, F. (1931). Truth and probability. In F. P. Ramsey (Ed.), *The foundations of mathematics and other logical essays* (pp. 156–198). New York, NY: Harcourt, Brace and Co.

Rothbart, M., & Snyder, M. (1970). Confidence in the prediction and postdiction of an uncertain outcome. *Canadian Journal of Behavioural Science, 2*(1), 38–43.

Savage, L. (1954). *The foundations of statistics.* New York, NY: Wiley.

Schmeidler, D. (1989). Subjective probability and expected utility without additivity. *Econometrica, 57*(3), 571–587.

Skyrm, B. (1980). Higher order degrees of belief. In D. H. Mellor (Ed.), *Prospects for pragmatism: Essays in memory of F. P. Ramsey* (pp. 109–137). Cambridge, England: Cambridge University Press.

Tversky, A., Slovic, P., & Kahneman, D. (1990). The causes of preference reversal. *American Economic Review, 80,* 204–217.

10   Belief in the Law of Small Numbers

Amos Tversky and Daniel Kahneman

"Suppose you have run an experiment on 20 subjects, and have obtained a significant result which confirms your theory ($z = 2.23$, $p < 0.05$, two-tailed). You now have cause to run an additional group of 10 subjects. What do you think the probability is that the results will be significant, by a one-tailed test, separately for this group?"

If you feel that the probability is somewhere around 0.85, you may be pleased to know that you belong to a majority group. Indeed, that was the median answer of two small groups that were kind enough to respond to a questionnaire distributed at meetings of the Mathematical Psychology Group and of the American Psychological Association.

By contrast, if you feel that the probability is around 0.48, you belong to a minority. Only 9 of our 84 respondents gave answers between 0.40 and 0.60. However, 0.48 happens to be a much more reasonable estimate than 0.85.[1]

Apparently, most psychologists have an exaggerated belief in the likelihood of successfully replicating an obtained finding. The sources of such beliefs, and their consequences for the conduct of scientific inquiry, are what this chapter is about. Our thesis is that people have strong intuitions about random sampling, that these intuitions are wrong in fundamental respects, that these intuitions are shared by naive subjects and by trained scientists, and that they are applied with unfortunate consequences in the course of scientific inquiry.

We submit that people view a sample randomly drawn from a population as highly representative, that is, similar to the population in all essential characteristics. Consequently, they expect any two samples drawn from a particular population to be more similar to one another and to the population than sampling theory predicts, at least for small samples.

The tendency to regard a sample as a representation is manifest in a wide variety of situations. When subjects are instructed to generate a random sequence of hypothetical tosses of a fair coin, for example, they produce sequences where the proportion of heads in any short segment stays far closer to 0.50 than the laws of chance would predict (Tune, 1964). Thus, each segment of the response sequence is highly representative of the "fairness" of the coin. Similar effects are observed when subjects successively predict events in a randomly generated series, as in probability learning experiments (Estes, 1964) or in other sequential games of chance. Subjects act as if *every* segment of the random sequence must reflect the true proportion: if the sequence has strayed from the population proportion, a corrective bias in the other direction is expected. This has been called the gambler's fallacy.

The heart of the gambler's fallacy is a misconception of the fairness of the laws of chance. The gambler feels that the fairness of the coin entitles him to expect that any deviation in one direction will soon be canceled by a corresponding deviation in the other. Even the fairest of coins, however, given the limitations of its memory and moral sense, cannot be as fair as the gambler expects it to be. This fallacy is not unique to gamblers. Consider the following example:

The mean IQ of the population of eighth graders in a city is *known* to be 100. You have selected a random sample of 50 children for a study of educational achievements. The first child tested has an IQ of 150. What do you expect the mean IQ to be for the whole sample?

The correct answer is 101. A surprisingly large number of people believe that the expected IQ for the sample is still 100. This expectation can be justified only by the belief that a random process is self-correcting. Idioms such as "errors cancel each other out" reflect the image of an active self-correcting process. Some familiar processes in nature obey such laws: a deviation from a stable equilibrium produces a force that restores the equilibrium. The laws of chance, in contrast, do not work that way: deviations are not canceled as sampling proceeds, they are merely diluted.

Thus far, we have attempted to describe two related intuitions about chance. We proposed a representation hypothesis according to which people believe samples to be very similar to one another and to the population from which they are drawn. We also suggested that people believe sampling to be a self-correcting process. The two beliefs lead to the same consequences. Both generate expectations about characteristics of samples, and the variability of these expectations is less than the true variability, at least for small samples.

The law of large numbers guarantees that very large samples will indeed be highly representative of the population from which they are drawn. If, in addition, a self-corrective tendency is at work, then small samples should also be highly representative and similar to one another. People's intuitions about random sampling appear to satisfy the law of small numbers, which asserts that the law of large numbers applies to small numbers as well.

Consider a hypothetical scientist who lives by the law of small numbers. How would his belief affect his scientific work? Assume our scientist studies phenomena whose magnitude is small relative to uncontrolled variability, that is, the signal-to-noise ratio in the messages he receives from nature is low. Our scientist could be a meteorologist, a pharmacologist, or perhaps a psychologist.

If he believes in the law of small numbers, the scientist will have exaggerated confidence in the validity of conclusions based on small samples. To illustrate, suppose he is engaged in studying which of two toys infants will prefer to play with. Of the first five infants studied, four have shown a preference for the same toy. Many a psychologist will feel some confidence at this point, that the null hypothesis of no preference is false. Fortunately, such a conviction is not a sufficient condition for journal publication, although it may do for a book. By a quick computation, our psychologist will discover that the probability of a result as extreme as the one obtained is as high as $\frac{3}{8}$ under the null hypothesis.

To be sure, the application of statistical hypothesis testing to scientific inference is beset with serious difficulties. Nevertheless, the computation of significance levels (or likelihood ratios, as a Bayesian might prefer) forces the scientist to evaluate the obtained effect in terms of a *valid* estimate of sampling variance rather than in terms of his subjective biased estimate. Statistical tests, therefore, protect the scientific community against overly hasty rejections of the null hypothesis (i.e., type I error) by policing its many members who would rather live by the law of small numbers. However, there are no comparable safeguards against the risk of failing to confirm a valid research hypothesis (i.e., type II error).

Imagine a psychologist who studies the correlation between need for achievement and grades. When deciding on sample size, he may reason as follows: "What correlation do I expect? $r = .35$. What N do I need to make the result significant? (Looks at table.) $N = 33$. Fine, that's my sample." The only flaw in this reasoning is that our psychologist has forgotten about sampling variation, possibly because he believes that any sample must be highly representative of its population. However, if his guess about the correlation in the population is correct, the correlation in the sample is about as likely to lie below or above 0.35. Hence, the likelihood of obtaining a significant result (i.e., the power of the test) for $N = 33$ is about 0.50.

In a detailed investigation of statistical power, J. Cohen (1962, 1969) has provided plausible definitions of large, medium, and small effects and an extensive set of computational aids to the estimation of power for a variety of statistical tests. In the normal test for a difference between two means, for example, a difference of 0.25σ is small, a difference of 0.50σ is medium, and a difference of 1σ is large, according to the proposed definitions. The mean IQ difference between clerical and semiskilled workers is a medium effect. In an ingenious study of research practice, J. Cohen (1962) reviewed all the statistical analyses published in one volume of the *Journal of Abnormal and Social Psychology* and computed the likelihood of detecting each of the three sizes of effect. The average power was 0.18 for the detection of small effects, 0.48 for medium effects, and 0.83 for large effects. If psychologists typically expect medium effects and select sample size as in the above example, the power of their studies should indeed be about 0.50.

Cohen's analysis shows that the statistical power of many psychological studies is ridiculously low. This is a self-defeating practice: it makes for frustrated scientists and inefficient research. The investigator who tests a valid hypothesis but fails to obtain significant results cannot help but regard nature as untrustworthy or even hostile. Furthermore, as Overall (1969) has shown, the prevalence of studies deficient in statistical power is not only wasteful but actually pernicious: it results in a large proportion of invalid rejections of the null hypothesis among published results.

Because considerations of statistical power are of particular importance in the design of replication studies, we probed attitudes concerning replication in our questionnaire.

Suppose one of your doctoral students has completed a difficult and time-consuming experiment on 40 animals. He has scored and analyzed a large number of variables. His results are generally inconclusive, but one before-after comparison yields a highly significant $t = 2.70$, which is surprising and could be of major theoretical significance.

Considering the importance of the result, its surprisal value, and the number of analyses that your student has performed, would you recommend that he replicate the study before publishing? If you recommend replication, how many animals would you urge him to run?

Among the psychologists to whom we put these questions there was overwhelming sentiment favoring replication: it was recommended by 66 out of 75 respondents, probably because they suspected that the single significant result was due to chance. The median recommendation was for the doctoral student to run 20 subjects in a replication study. It is instructive to consider the likely consequences of this advice. If the mean and the variance in the second sample are actually identical to those in the first sample, then the resulting value of t will be 1.88. Following the reasoning of note 1, the student's chance of obtaining a significant result in the replication is only slightly above one-half (for $p = 0.05$, one-tail test). Because we had anticipated that a replication sample of 20 would appear reasonable to our respondents, we added the following question:

Assume that your unhappy student has in fact repeated the initial study with 20 additional animals and has obtained an insignificant result in the same direction, $t = 1.24$. What would you recommend now? Check one: [the numbers in parentheses refer to the number of respondents who checked each answer]

(a) He should pool the results and publish his conclusion as fact. (0)

(b) He should report the results as a tentative finding. (26)

(c) He should run another group of [median 20] animals. (21)

(d) He should try to find an explanation for the difference between the two groups. (30)

Note that regardless of one's confidence in the original finding, its credibility is surely enhanced by the replication. Not only is the experimental effect in the same direction in the two samples but the magnitude of the effect in the replication is fully two-thirds of that in the original study. In view of the sample size (20), which our respondents recommended, the replication was about as successful as one is entitled to expect. The distribution of responses, however, reflects continued skepticism concerning the student's finding following the recommended replication. This unhappy state of affairs is a typical consequence of insufficient statistical power.

In contrast to Responses b and c, which can be justified on some grounds, the most popular response, Response d, is indefensible. We doubt that the same answer would have been obtained if the respondents had realized that the difference between the two studies does not even approach significance. (If the variances of the two samples are equal, t for the difference is 0.53.) In the absence of a statistical test, our respondents followed the representation hypothesis: as the difference between the two samples was larger than they expected, they viewed it as worthy of explanation. However, the attempt to "find an explanation for the difference between the two groups" is in all probability an exercise in explaining noise.

Altogether our respondents evaluated the replication rather harshly. This follows from the representation hypothesis: if we expect all samples to be very similar to one another, then almost all replications of a valid hypothesis should be statistically significant. The harshness of the criterion for successful replication is manifest in the responses to the following question:

An investigator has reported a result that you consider implausible. He ran 15 subjects and reported a significant value, $t = 2.46$. Another investigator has attempted to duplicate his procedure, and he obtained a nonsignificant value of t with the same number of subjects. The direction was the same in both sets of data.

You are reviewing the literature. What is the highest value of t in the second set of data that you would describe as a failure to replicate?

The majority of our respondents regarded $t = 1.70$ as a failure to replicate. If the data of two such studies ($t = 2.46$ and $t = 1.70$) are pooled, the value of t for the combined data is about 3.00 (assuming equal variances). Thus, we are faced with a paradoxical state of affairs, in which the same data that would increase our confidence in the finding when viewed as part of the original study shake our confidence when viewed as an independent study. This double standard is particularly disturbing because, for many reasons, replications are usually considered as independent studies, and hypotheses are often evaluated by listing confirming and disconfirming reports.

Contrary to a widespread belief, a case can be made that a replication sample should often be larger than the original. The decision to replicate a once obtained finding often expresses a great fondness for that finding and a desire to see it accepted by a skeptical community. Because that community unreasonably demands that the replication be independently significant, or at least that it approach significance, one must run a large sample. To illustrate, if the unfortunate doctoral student whose thesis was discussed earlier assumes the validity of his initial result ($t = 2.70$, $N = 40$), and if he is willing to accept a risk of only 0.10 of obtaining a t lower than 1.70, he should run approximately 50 animals in his replication study. With a somewhat weaker initial result ($t = 2.20$, $N = 40$), the size of the replication sample required for the same power rises to about 75.

That the effects discussed thus far are not limited to hypotheses about means and variances is demonstrated by the responses to the following question:

You have run a correlational study, scoring 20 variables on 100 subjects. Twenty-seven of the 190 correlation coefficients are significant at the 0.05 level, and 9 of these are significant beyond the 0.01 level. The mean absolute level of the significant correlations is 0.31, and the pattern of results is very reasonable on theoretical grounds. How many of the 27 significant correlations would you expect to be significant again in an exact replication of the study where $N = 40$?

With $N = 40$, a correlation of about 0.31 is required for significance at the 0.05 level. This is the mean of the significant correlations in the original study. Thus, only about half of the originally significant correlations (i.e., 13 or 14) would remain significant with $N = 40$. In addition, of course, the correlations in the replication are bound to differ from those in the original study. Hence, by regression effects, the initially significant coefficients are most likely to be reduced. Thus, 8 to 10 repeated significant correlations from the original 27 is probably a generous estimate of what one is entitled to expect. The median estimate of our respondents is 18. This is more than the number of repeated significant correlations that will be found if the correlations are recomputed for 40 subjects randomly selected from the original 100! Apparently, people expect more than a mere duplication of the original statistics in the replication sample; they expect a duplication of the significance of results, with little regard for sample size. This expectation requires a ludicrous extension of the representation hypothesis; even the law of small numbers is incapable of generating such a result.

The expectation that patterns of results are replicable almost in their entirety provides the rationale for a common, though much deplored practice. The investigator who computes all correlations among three indexes of anxiety and three indexes of dependency will often report and interpret with great confidence the single significant correlation obtained. His confidence in the shaky finding stems from his belief that the obtained correlation matrix is highly representative and readily replicable.

In review, we have seen that the believer in the law of small numbers practices science as follows:

1. He gambles his research hypotheses on small samples without realizing that the odds against him are unreasonably high. He overestimates power.

2. He has undue confidence in early trends (e.g., the data of the first few subjects) and in the stability of observed patterns (e.g., the number and identity of significant results). He overestimates significance.

3. In evaluating replications, his or others', he has unreasonably high expectations about the replicability of significant results. He underestimates the breadth of confidence intervals.

4. He rarely attributes a deviation of results from expectations to sampling variability because he finds a causal "explanation" for any discrepancy. Thus, he has little opportunity to recognize sampling variation in action. His belief in the law of small numbers, therefore, will forever remain intact.

Our questionnaire elicited considerable evidence for the prevalence of the belief in the law of small numbers.[2] Our typical respondent is a believer, regardless of the group to which he belongs. There were practically no differences between the median responses of audiences at a mathematical psychology meeting and at a general session of the American Psychological Association convention, although we make no claims for the representativeness of either sample. Apparently, acquaintance with formal logic and with probability theory does not extinguish erroneous intuitions. What, then, can be done? Can the belief in the law of small numbers be abolished or at least controlled?

Research experience is unlikely to help much because sampling variation is all too easily "explained." Corrective experiences are those that provide neither motive nor opportunity for spurious explanation. Thus, a student in a statistics course may draw repeated samples of a given size from a population and learn the effect of sample size on sampling variability from personal observation. We are far from certain, however, that expectations can be corrected in this manner because related biases, such as the gambler's fallacy, survive considerable contradictory evidence.

Even if the bias cannot be unlearned, students can learn to recognize its existence and take the necessary precautions. Because the teaching of statistics is not short on admonitions, a warning about biased statistical intuitions may not be out of place. The obvious precaution is computation. The believer in the law of small numbers has incorrect intuitions about significance level, power, and confidence intervals. Significance levels are usually computed and reported, but power and confidence limits are not. Perhaps they should be.

Explicit computation of power, relative to some reasonable hypothesis, for instance, Cohen's (1962, 1969) small, large, and medium effects, should surely be carried out before any study is done. Such computations will often lead to the realization that there is simply no point in running the study unless, for example, sample size is multiplied by four. We refuse to believe that a serious investigator will knowingly accept a 0.50 risk of failing to confirm a valid research hypothesis. In addition, computations of power are essential to the interpretation of negative results, that is, failures to reject the null hypothesis. Because readers' intuitive estimates of power are likely to be wrong, the publication of computed values does not appear to be a waste of either readers' time or journal space.

In the early psychological literature, the convention prevailed of reporting, for example, a sample mean as $M \pm PE$, where PE is the probable error (i.e., the 50% confidence interval around the mean). This convention was later abandoned in favor of the hypothesis-testing formulation. A confidence interval, however, provides a useful index of sampling variability, and it is precisely this variability that we tend to underestimate. The emphasis on significance levels tends to obscure a fundamental distinction between the size of an effect and its statistical significance. Regardless of sample size, the size of an effect in one study is a reasonable estimate of the size of the effect in replication. In contrast, the estimated significance level in a replication depends critically on sample size. Unrealistic expectations concerning the replicability of significance levels may be corrected if the distinction between size and significance is clarified and if the computed size of observed effects is routinely reported. From this point of view, at least, the acceptance of the hypothesis-testing model has not been an unmixed blessing for psychology.

The true believer in the law of small numbers commits his multitude of sins against the logic of statistical inference in good faith. The representation hypothesis describes a cognitive or perceptual bias, which operates regardless of motivational factors. Thus, while the hasty rejection of the null hypothesis is gratifying, the rejection of a cherished hypothesis is aggravating, yet the true believer is subject to both. His intuitive expectations are governed by a consistent misperception of the world rather than by opportunistic wishful thinking. Given some editorial prodding, he may be willing to regard his statistical intuitions with proper suspicion and replace impression formation by computation whenever possible.

Notes

1. The required estimate can be interpreted in several ways. One possible approach is to follow common research practice, where a value obtained in one study is taken to define a plausible alternative to the null hypothesis. The probability requested in the question can then be interpreted as the power of the second test (i.e., the probability of obtaining a significant result in the second sample) against the alternative hypothesis defined by the result of the first sample. In the special case of a test of a mean with known variance, one would compute the power of the test against the hypothesis that the population mean equals the mean of the first sample. Because the size of the second sample is half that of the first, the computed probability of obtaining $z \geq 1.645$ is only 0.473. A theoretically more justifiable approach is to interpret the requested probability within a Bayesian framework and compute it relative to some appropriately selected prior distribution. Assuming a uniform prior, the desired posterior probability is 0.478. Clearly, if the prior distribution favors the null hypothesis, as is often the case, the posterior probability will be even smaller.

2. W. Edwards (1968, 25) has argued that people fail to extract sufficient information or certainty from probabilistic data; he called this failure conservatism. Our respondents can hardly be described as conservative. Rather, in accord with the representation hypothesis, they tend to extract more certainty from the data than the data, in fact, contain.

References

Cohen, J. (1962). The statistical power of abnormal-social psychological research. *Journal of Abnormal and Social Psychology, 65*, 145–153.

Cohen, J. (1969). *Statistical power analysis in the behavioral sciences*. New York, NY: Academic Press.

Edwards, W. (1968). Conservatism in human information processing. In B. Kleinmuntz (Ed.), *Formal representation of human judgment* (pp. 17–52). New York, NY: Wiley.

Estes, W. K. (1964). Probability learning. In A. W. Melton (Ed.), *Categories of human learning* (pp. 89–128). New York, NY: Academic Press.

Overall, J. E. (1969). Classical statistical hypothesis testing within the context of Bayesian theory. *Psychological Bulletin, 71*, 285–292.

Tune, G. S. (1964). Response preferences: A review of some relevant literature. *Psychological Bulletin, 61*, 286–302.

11   The Weighing of Evidence and the Determinants of Confidence

Dale Griffin and Amos Tversky

The weighing of evidence and the formation of belief are basic elements of human thought. The question of how to evaluate evidence and assess confidence has been addressed from a normative perspective by philosophers and statisticians; it has also been investigated experimentally by psychologists and decision researchers. One of the major findings that has emerged from this research is that people are often more confident in their judgments than is warranted by the facts. Overconfidence is not limited to lay judgment or laboratory experiments. The well-publicized observation that more than two-thirds of small businesses fail within 4 years (Dun & Bradstreet, 1967) suggests that many entrepreneurs overestimate their probability of success (Cooper, Woo, & Dunkelberg, 1988). With some notable exceptions, such as weather forecasters (Murphy & Winkler, 1977) who receive immediate frequentistic feedback and produce realistic forecasts of precipitation, overconfidence has been observed in judgments of physicians (Lusted, 1977), clinical psychologists (Oskamp, 1965), lawyers (Wagenaar & Keren, 1986), negotiators (Neale & Bazerman, 1990), engineers (Kidd, 1970), and security analysts (Staël von Holstein, 1972). As one critic described expert prediction, "often wrong but rarely in doubt."

Overconfidence is common but not universal. Studies of calibration have found that with very easy items, overconfidence is eliminated, and underconfidence is often observed (Lichtenstein, Fischhoff, & Phillips, 1982). Furthermore, studies of sequential updating have shown that posterior probability estimates commonly exhibit conservatism or underconfidence (Edwards, 1968). In the present paper, we investigate the weighting of evidence and propose an account that explains the pattern of overconfidence and underconfidence observed in the literature.[1]

The Determinants of Confidence

The assessment of confidence or degree of belief in a given hypothesis typically requires the integration of different kinds of evidence. In many problems, it is possible to distinguish between the strength, or extremeness, of the evidence and its weight, or predictive validity. When we evaluate a letter of recommendation for a graduate student written by a former teacher, we may wish to consider two separate aspects of the evidence: (i) how positive or warm is the letter? and (ii) how credible or knowledgeable is the writer? The first question refers to the strength or extremeness of the evidence, whereas the second question refers to its weight or credence. Similarly, suppose we wish to evaluate the evidence for the hypothesis that a coin is biased in favor of heads rather than in favor of tails. In this case, the proportion of heads in a sample reflects the strength of evidence for the hypothesis in question, and the size of the sample reflects the credence of these data. The distinction between the strength of evidence and its weight is closely related to the distinction between the size of an effect (e.g., a difference between two means) and its reliability (e.g., the standard error of the difference). Although it is not always possible to decompose the impact of evidence into the separate contributions of strength and weight, there are many contexts in which they can be varied independently. A strong or a weak recommendation may come from a reliable or an unreliable source, and the same proportion of heads can be observed in a small or large sample.

Statistical theory and the calculus of chance prescribe rules for combining strength and weight. For example, probability theory specifies how sample proportion and sample size combine to determine posterior probability. The extensive experimental literature on judgment under uncertainty indicates that people do not combine strength and weight in accord with the rules of probability and statistics. Rather, intuitive judgments are overly influenced by the degree to which the available evidence is representative of the hypothesis in question (Dawes, 1988; Kahneman, Slovic, & Tversky, 1982; Nisbett & Ross, 1980). If people were to rely on representativeness alone, their judgments (e.g., that a person being interviewed will be a successful manager) would depend only on the strength of their impression (e.g., the degree to which the individual in question "looks like" a successful manager) with no regard for other factors that control predictive validity. In many situations, however, it appears that people do not neglect these factors altogether. Instead, we propose, people focus on the strength of the evidence—as they perceive it—and then make some adjustment in response to its weight.

In evaluating a letter of recommendation, we suggest, people first attend to the warmth of the recommendation and then make allowance for the writer's limited knowledge. Similarly, when judging whether a coin is biased in favor of heads or in favor of tails, people focus on the proportion of heads in the sample and then adjust their judgment according to the number of tosses. Because such an adjustment is generally insufficient (Slovic & Lichtenstein, 1971; Tversky & Kahneman, 1974), the strength of the evidence tends to dominate its weight in comparison to an appropriate statistical model. Furthermore, the tendency to focus on the strength of the evidence leads people to underutilize other variables that control predictive validity, such as base rate and discriminability. This treatment combines judgment by representativeness, which is based entirely on the strength of an impression, with an anchoring and adjustment process that takes the weight of the evidence into account, albeit insufficiently. The role of anchoring in impression formation has been addressed by Quattrone (1982).

This hypothesis implies a distinctive pattern of overconfidence and underconfidence. If people are highly sensitive to variations in the extremeness of evidence and not sufficiently sensitive to variations in its credence or predictive validity, then judgments will be overconfident when strength is high and weight is low, and they will be underconfident when weight is high and strength is low. As is shown below, this hypothesis serves to organize and summarize much experimental evidence on judgment under uncertainty.

Consider the prediction of success in graduate school on the basis of a letter of recommendation. If people focus primarily on the warmth of the recommendation with insufficient regard for the credibility of the writer, or the correlation between the predictor and the criterion, they will be overconfident when they encounter a glowing letter based on casual contact, and they will be underconfident when they encounter a moderately positive letter from a highly knowledgeable source. Similarly, if people's judgments regarding the bias of a coin are determined primarily by the proportion of heads and tails in the sample with insufficient regard for sample size, then they will be overconfident when they observe an extreme proportion in a small sample and underconfident when they observe a moderate proportion in a large sample.

In this article, we test the hypothesis that overconfidence occurs when strength is high and weight is low, and underconfidence occurs when weight is high and strength is low. The first three experiments are concerned with the evaluation of statistical hypotheses, where strength of evidence is defined by sample proportion. In the second part of the paper, we extend this hypothesis to more complex evidential problems and investigate its implications for judgments of confidence.

Evaluating Statistical Hypotheses

Study 1: Sample Size

We first investigate the relative impact of sample proportion (strength) and sample size (weight) in an experimental task involving the assessment of posterior probability. We presented 35 students with the following instructions:

Imagine that you are spinning a coin, and recording how often the coin lands heads and how often the coin lands tails. Unlike tossing, which (on average) yields an equal number of heads and tails, spinning a coin leads to a bias favoring one side or the other because of slight imperfections on the rim of the

Table 11.1

Stimuli and Responses for Study 1

Number of heads (h)	Number of tails (t)	Sample size (n)	Posterior probability $P(H \mid D)$	Median confidence (%)
2	1	3	0.60	63.0
3	0	3	0.77	85.0
3	2	5	0.60	60.0
4	1	5	0.77	80.0
5	0	5	0.88	92.5
5	4	9	0.60	55.0
6	3	9	0.77	66.9
7	2	9	0.88	77.0
9	8	17	0.60	54.5
10	7	17	0.77	59.5
11	6	17	0.88	64.5
19	14	33	0.88	60.0

coin (and an uneven distribution of mass). Now imagine that you know this bias is 3/5. It tends to land on one side 3 out of 5 times. But you do not know if this bias is in favor of heads or in favor of tails.

Subjects were then given various samples of evidence differing in sample size (from 3 to 33) and in the number of heads (from 2 to 19). All samples contained a majority of heads, and subjects were asked to estimate the probability (from 0.5 to 1) that the bias favored heads (H) rather than tails (T). Subjects received all 12 combinations of sample proportion and sample size shown in table 11.1. They were offered a prize of $20 for the person whose judgments most closely matched the correct values.

Table 11.1 also presents, for each sample of data (D), the posterior probability for hypothesis H (a 3:2 bias in favor of heads) computed according to Bayes' Rule. Assuming equal prior probabilities, Bayes' Rule yields

$$\log\left(\frac{P(H \mid D)}{P(T \mid D)}\right) = n\left(\frac{h-t}{n}\right)\log\left(\frac{.6}{.4}\right),$$

where h and t are the number of heads and tails, respectively, and $n = h + t$ denotes sample size. The first term on the right-hand side, n, represents the weight of evidence. The second term, the difference between the proportion of heads and tails in the sample, represents the strength of the evidence for H against T. The third term, which is held constant in this study, is the discriminability of the two hypotheses, corresponding to d' in signal detection theory. Plotting equal-support lines for strength and weight in logarithmic coordinates yields a family of parallel straight lines with a slope of −1, as illustrated by the dotted lines in figure

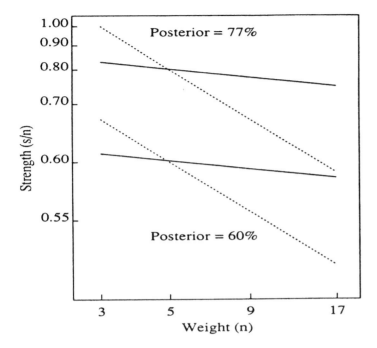

Figure 11.1
Equal support lines for strength and sample size.

11.1. (To facilitate interpretation, the strength dimension is defined as h/n, which is linearly related to $(h − t)/n$.) Each line connects all datasets that provide the same support for hypothesis H. For example, a sample size of 9 with 6 heads and 3 tails and a sample size of 17 with 10 heads and 7 tails yield the same posterior probability (0.77) for H over T. Thus, the point (9, 6/9) and the point (17, 10/17) both lie on the upper line. Similarly, the lower line connects the datasets that yield a posterior probability of 0.60 in favor of H (see table 11.1).

To compare the observed judgments with Bayes' Rule, we first transformed each probability judgment into log odds and then, for each subject as well as the median data, regressed the logarithm of these values against the logarithms of strength, $(h − t)/n$, and of weight, n, separately for each subject. The regressions fit the data quite well: multiple R was 0.95 for the median data and 0.82 for the median subject. According to Bayes' Rule, the regression weights for strength and weight in this metric are equal (see figure 11.1). In contrast, the regression coefficient for strength was larger than the regression coefficient for weight for 30 out of 35 subjects ($p < 0.001$ by sign test). Across subjects, the median ratio of these coefficients was 2.2 to 1 in favor of strength.[2] For the median data, the observed regression weight for strength (0.81) was almost 3 times larger than that for weight (0.31).

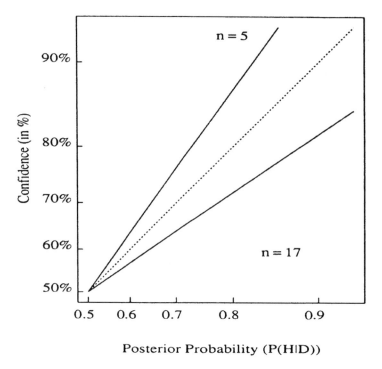

Figure 11.2
Sample size and confidence.

The equal-support lines obtained from the regression analysis are plotted in figure 11.1 as solid lines. The comparison of the two sets of lines highly reveals two noteworthy observations. First, the intuitive lines are much shallower than the Bayesian lines, indicating that the strength of evidence dominates its weight. Second, for a given level of support (e.g., 60% or 77%), the Bayesian and the intuitive lines cross, indicating overconfidence where strength is high and weight is low, and underconfidence where strength is low and weight is high. As is seen later, the crossing point is determined primarily by the discriminability of the competing hypotheses (d').

Figure 11.2 plots the median confidence for a given sample of evidence as a function of the (Bayesian) posterior probability for two separate sample sizes. The best-fitting lines were calculated using the log odds metric. If the subjects were Bayesian, the solid lines would coincide with the dotted line. Instead, intuitive judgments based on the small sample ($N = 5$) were overconfident, whereas the judgments based on the larger sample ($N = 17$) were underconfident.

The results described in table 11.1 are in general agreement with previous results that document the nonnormative nature of intuitive judgment (for reviews see, e.g., Kahneman, Slovic, & Tversky, 1982; von Winterfeldt & Edwards, 1986). Moreover, they help reconcile apparently inconsistent findings. Edwards and his colleagues (e.g., Edwards, 1968), who used a sequential updating paradigm, argued that people are conservative in the sense that they do not extract enough information from sample data. By contrast, Tversky and Kahneman (1971), who investigated the role of sample size in researchers' confidence in the replicability of their results, concluded that people (even those trained in statistics) make radical inferences on the basis of small samples. Figures 11.1 and 11.2 suggest how the dominance of sample proportion over sample size could produce both findings. In some updating experiments conducted by Edwards, subjects were exposed to large samples of data typically of moderate strength. This is the context in which we expect underconfidence or conservatism. The situations studied by Tversky and Kahneman, however, involve moderately strong effects based on fairly small samples. This is the context in which overconfidence is likely to prevail. Both conservatism and overconfidence, therefore, can be generated by a common bias in the weighting of evidence, namely the dominance of strength over weight.

As was noted earlier, the tendency to focus on the strength of the evidence leads people to neglect or underweight other variables, such as the prior probability of the hypothesis in question or the discriminability of the competing hypotheses. These effects are demonstrated in the following two studies. All three studies reported in this section employ a within-subject design, in which both the strength of the evidence and the mitigating variable (e.g., sample size) are varied within subjects. This procedure may underestimate the dominance of strength because people tend to respond to whatever variable is manipulated within a study whether or not it is normative to do so (Fischhoff & Bar-Hillel, 1984). Indeed, the neglect of sample size and base-rate information has been most pronounced in between-subject comparisons (Kahneman & Tversky, 1972).

Study 2: Base Rate

Considerable research has demonstrated that people tend to neglect background data (e.g., base rates) in the presence of specific evidence (Kahneman, Slovic, & Tversky, 1982; Bar-Hillel, 1983). This neglect can lead either to underconfidence or overconfidence, as is shown below. We asked 40 students to imagine that they had three different foreign coins, each with a known bias of 3:2. As in study 1, subjects did not know if the bias of each coin was in favor of heads (H) or in favor of tails (T). The subjects' prior probabilities of the two hypotheses (H and T) were varied. For one-half of the subjects, the probability of H was 0.50 for one type of coin, 0.67 for a second type of coin, and 0.90 for a third type of coin. For the other half of the subjects, the prior probabilities of H were 0.50, 0.33, and 0.10. Subjects were presented

Table 11.2
Stimuli and Responses for Study 2

Number of heads (out of 10)	Prior probability (base rate)	Posterior probability $P(H \mid D)$	Median confidence (%)
5	9:1	0.90	60.0
6	9:1	0.95	70.0
7	9:1	0.98	85.0
8	9:1	0.99	92.5
9	9:1	0.996	98.5
5	2:1	0.67	55.0
6	2:1	0.82	65.0
7	2:1	0.91	71.0
8	2:1	0.96	82.5
9	2:1	0.98	90.0
5	1:1	0.50	50.0
6	1:1	0.69	60.0
7	1:1	0.84	70.0
8	1: 1	0.92	80.0
9	1:1	0.96	90.0
5	1:2	0.33	33.0
6	1:2	0.53	50.0
7	1:2	0.72	57.0
8	1:2	0.85	77.0
9	1:2	0.93	90.0
5	1:9	0.10	22.5
6	1:9	0.20	45.0
7	1:9	0.36	60.0
8	1:9	0.55	80.0
9	1:9	0.74	85.0

with samples of size 10, which included from 5 to 9 heads. They were then asked to give their confidence (in %) that the coin under consideration was biased in favor of heads. Again, a $20 prize was offered for the person whose judgments most closely matched the correct values. Table 11.2 summarizes the sample data, the posterior probability for each sample, and subjects' median confidence judgments. It is clear that our subjects overweighted strength of evidence and underweighted the prior probability.

Figure 11.3 plots median judgments of confidence as a function of (Bayesian) posterior probability for high (0.90) and low (0.10) prior probabilities of H. The figure also displays the best-fitting lines for each condition. It is evident from the figure that subjects were overconfident in the low base rate condition and underconfident in the high base rate condition.

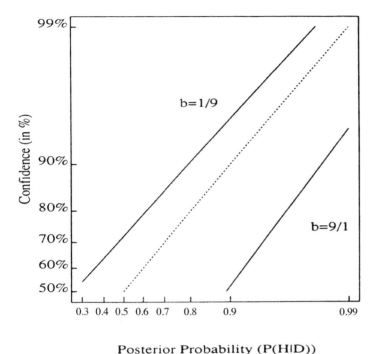

Figure 11.3
Base rate and confidence.

These results are consistent with Grether's (1980, 1990) studies on the role of the representativeness heuristic in judgments of posterior probability. Unlike the present study, where both prior probabilities and data were presented in numerical form, Grether's procedure involved random sampling of numbered balls from a bingo cage. He found that subjects overweighted the likelihood ratio relative to prior probability, as implied by representativeness, and that monetary incentives reduced but did not eliminate base rate neglect. Grether's results, like those found by Camerer (1990) in his extensive study of market trading, contradict the claim of Gigerenzer, Hell, and Blank (1988) that explicit random sampling eliminates base rate neglect. Evidence that explicit random sampling alone does not reduce base rate neglect is presented in Griffin (1991).

Our analysis implies that people are prone to overconfidence when the base rate is low and to underconfidence when the base rate is high. Dunning, Griffin, Milojkovic, and Ross (1990) observed this pattern in a study of social prediction. In their study, each subject interviewed a target person before making predictions about the target's preferences and behavior (e.g., "If this person were offered a free subscription, which magazine would he choose:

Playboy or *New York Review of Books*?"). The authors presented each subject with the empirically derived estimates of the base rate frequency of the responses in question (e.g., that 68% of prior respondents preferred *Playboy*). To investigate the effect of empirical base rates, Dunning et al. analyzed separately the predictions that agreed with the base rate (i.e., "high" base rate predictions) and the predictions that went against the base rate (i.e., "low" base rate predictions). Overconfidence was much more pronounced when base rates were low (confidence = 72%, accuracy = 49%) than when base rates were high (confidence = 79%, accuracy = 75%). Moreover, for items with base rates that exceeded 75%, subjects' predictions were actually underconfident. This is exactly the pattern implied by the hypothesis that subjects evaluate the probability that a given person would prefer *Playboy* over the *New York Review of Books* on the basis of their impression of that person with little or no regard for the empirical base rate, that is, the relative popularity of the two magazines in the target population.

Study 3: Discriminability
When we consider the question of which of two hypotheses is true, confidence should depend on the degree to which the data fit one hypothesis better than the other. However, people seem to focus on the strength of evidence for a given hypothesis and neglect how well the same evidence fits an alternate hypothesis. The Barnum effect is a case in point. It is easy to construct a personality sketch that will impress many people as a fairly accurate description of their own characteristics because they evaluate the description by the degree to which it fits their personality with little or no concern for whether it fits others just as well (Forer, 1949). To explore this effect in a chance setup, we presented 50 students with evidence about two types of foreign coins. Within each type of coin, the strength of evidence (sample proportion) varied from 7/12 heads to 10/12 heads. The two types of coins differed in their characteristic biases. Subjects were instructed:

Imagine that you are spinning a foreign coin called a *quinta*. Suppose that half of the quintas (the "X" type) have a 0.6 bias toward heads (that is, heads comes up on 60% of the spins for X-quintas) and half of the quintas (the "Y" type) have a 0.75 bias toward tails (that is, tails comes up on 75% of the spins for Y-quintas). Your job is to determine if this is an X-quinta or a Y-quinta.

They then received the samples of evidence displayed in table 11.3. After they gave their confidence that each sample came from an X-quinta or a Y-quinta, subjects were asked to make the same judgments for A-libnars (which have a 0.6 bias toward heads) and B-libnars (which have a 0.5 chance of heads). The order of presentation of coins was counterbalanced.

Table 11.3 summarizes the sample data, the posterior probability for each sample, and subjects' median confidence judgments. The comparison of the confidence judgments to the Bayesian posterior probabilities indicates that our subjects focused primarily on the degree to which the data fit the favored hypothesis with insufficient regard for how well

Table 11.3
Stimuli and Responses for Study 3

Number of heads (out of 12)	Separation of hypotheses (d')	Posterior probability $P(H \mid D)$	Median confidence (%)
7	0.6 vs 0.5	0.54	55.0
8	0.6 vs 0.5	0.64	66.0
9	0.6 vs 0.5	0.72	75.0
10	0.6 vs 0.5	0.80	85.0
7	0.6 vs 0.25	0.95	65.0
8	0.6 vs 0.25	0.99	70.0
9	0.6 vs 0.25	0.998	80.0
10	0.6 vs 0.25	0.999	90.0

they fit the alternate hypothesis (Fischhoff & Beyth-Marom, 1983). Figure 11.4 plots subjects' median confidence judgments against the Bayesian posterior probability for both low-discriminability and high-discriminability comparisons. When the discriminability between the hypotheses was low (when the coin's bias was either 0.6 or 0.5) subjects were slightly overconfident, but when the discriminability between the hypotheses was high (when the bias was either 0.6 or 0.25) subjects were grossly underconfident.

In the early experimental literature on judgments of posterior probability, most studies (e.g., Peterson, Schneider, & Miller, 1965) examined symmetric hypotheses that were highly discriminable (e.g., 3:2 versus 2:3) and found consistent underconfidence. In accord with our hypothesis, however, studies that included pairs of hypotheses of low discriminability found overconfidence. For example, Peterson and Miller (1965) found overconfidence in posterior probability judgments when the respective ratios were 3:2 and 3:4, and Phillips and Edwards (1966) found overconfidence when the ratios were 11:9 and 9:11.

Confidence in Knowledge

The preceding section shows that people are more sensitive to the strength of evidence than to its weight. Consequently, people are overconfident when strength is high and weight is low and underconfident when strength is low and weight is high. This conclusion, we propose, applies not only to judgments about chance processes such as coin spinning, but also to judgments about uncertain events such as who will win an upcoming election, or whether a given book will make the best-seller list. When people assess the probability of such events they evaluate, we suggest, their impression of the candidate or the book. These impressions may be based on a casual observation or on extensive knowledge of the preferences of voters

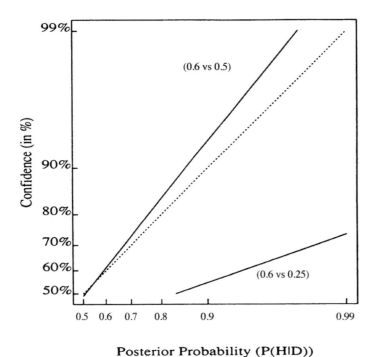

Figure 11.4
Discriminability and confidence.

and readers. In an analogy to a chance setup, the extremeness of an impression may be compared to sample proportion, and the credence of an impression may correspond to the size of the sample or to the discriminability of the competing hypotheses. If people focus on the strength of the impression with insufficient appreciation of its weight, then the pattern of overconfidence and underconfidence observed in the evaluation of chance processes should also be present in evaluations of nonstatistical evidence.

In this section, we extend this hypothesis to complex evidential problems where strength and weight cannot be readily defined. We first compare the prediction of self and of others. Next, we show how the present account gives rise to the "difficulty effect." Finally, we explore the determinants of confidence in general-knowledge questions and relate the confidence-frequency discrepancy to the illusion of validity.

Study 4: Self versus Other

In this study, we ask people to predict their own behavior, about which they presumably know a great deal, and the behavior of others, about which they know less. If people base their confidence primarily on the strength of their impression with insufficient regard for its weight, we expect more overconfidence in the prediction of others than in the prediction of self.

Fourteen pairs of same-sex students, who did not know each other, were asked to predict each other's behavior in a task involving risk. They were first given 5 minutes to interview each other, and then they sat at individual computer terminals where they predicted their own and their partner's behavior in a Prisoner's Dilemma–type game called "The Corporate Jungle." On each trial, participants had the option of "merging" their company with their partner's company (i.e., cooperating) or "taking over" their partner's company (i.e., competing). If one partner tried to merge and the other tried to take over, the cooperative merger took a steep loss and the corporate raider made a substantial gain. However, if both partners tried a takeover on the same trial, they both suffered a loss. There were 20 payoff matrices, some designed to encourage cooperation and some designed to encourage competition.

Subjects were asked to predict their own behavior for 10 of the payoff matrices and the behavior of the person they had interviewed for the other 10. The order of the two tasks was counterbalanced, and each payoff matrix appeared an equal number of times in each task. In addition to predicting cooperation or competition for each matrix, subjects indicated their confidence in each prediction (on a scale from 50% to 100%). Shortly after the completion of the prediction task, subjects played 20 trials against their opponents, without feedback, and received payment according to the outcomes of the 20 trials.

The analysis is based on 25 subjects who completed the entire task. Overall, subjects were almost equally confident in their self-predictions ($M = 84\%$) and in their predictions of others ($M = 83\%$), but they were considerably more accurate in predicting their own behavior ($M = 81\%$) than in predicting the behavior of others ($M = 68\%$). Thus, people exhibited considerable overconfidence in predictions of others but were relatively well calibrated in predicting themselves (see figure 11.5).

In some circumstances, where the strength of evidence is not extreme, the prediction of one's own behavior may be underconfident. In the case of a job choice, for example, underconfidence may arise if a person has good reasons for taking job A and good reasons for taking job B, but fails to appreciate that even a small advantage for job A over B would generally lead to the choice of A. If confidence in the choice of A over B reflects the balance of arguments for the two positions (Koriat, Lichtenstein, & Fischhoff, 1980), then a balance of 2 to 1 would produce confidence of about 2/3, although the probability of choosing A over B is likely to be higher. Over the past few years, we have discreetly approached colleagues faced with a choice between job offers and asked them to estimate the probability that they will choose one job over another. The average confidence in the predicted choice was a modest 66%, but only 1 of the 24 respondents chose the opinion to which he or she initially

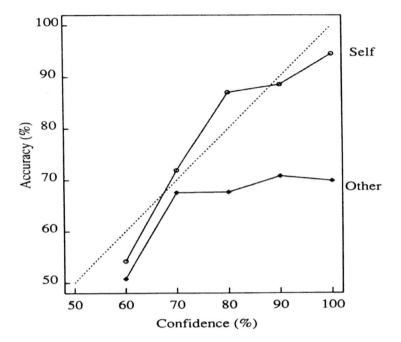

Figure 11.5
Predicting self and other.

assigned a lower probability, yielding an overall accuracy rate of 96%. It is noteworthy that there are situations in which people exhibit overconfidence even in predicting their own behavior (Vallone, Griffin, Lin, & Ross, 1990). The key variable, therefore, is not the target of prediction (self versus other) but rather the relation between the strength and the weight of the available evidence.

The tendency to be confident about the prediction of the behavior of others, but not of one's own behavior, has intriguing implications for the analysis of decision making. Decision analysts commonly distinguish between decision variables that are controlled by the decision maker and state variables that are not under his or her control. The analysis proceeds by determining the values of decision variables (i.e., decide what you want) and assigning probabilities to state variables (e.g., the behavior of others). Some decision analysts have noted that their clients often wish to follow an opposite course: determine or predict (with certainty) the behavior of others and assign probabilities to their own choices. After all, the behavior of others should be predictable from their traits, needs, and interests, whereas our own behavior is highly flexible and contingent on changing circumstances (Jones & Nisbett, 1972).

The Effect of Difficulty

The preceding analysis suggests that people assess their confidence in one of two competing hypotheses on the basis of their balance of arguments for and against this hypothesis, with insufficient regard for the quality of the data. This mode of judgment gives rise to overconfidence when people form a strong impression on the basis of limited knowledge and to underconfidence when people form a moderate impression on the basis of extensive data.

The application of this analysis to general knowledge questions is complicated by the fact that strength and weight cannot be experimentally controlled as in studies 1–3. However, in an analogy to a chance setup, let us suppose that the balance of arguments for a given knowledge problem can be represented by the proportion of red and white balls in a sample. The difficulty of the problem can be represented by the discriminability of the two hypotheses, that is, the difference between the probabilities of obtaining a red ball under each of the two competing hypotheses. Naturally, the greater the difference, the easier the task, that is, the higher the posterior probability of the more likely hypothesis on the basis of any given sample. Suppose confidence is given by the balance of arguments, that is, the proportion of red balls in the sample. What is the pattern of results predicted by this model?

Figure 11.6 displays the predicted results (for a sample size of 10) for three pairs of hypotheses that define three levels of task difficulty: an "easy" task where the probability of getting red balls under the competing hypotheses are 0.50 and 0.40, respectively; a "difficult" task, where the probabilities are 0.50 and 0.45; and an "impossible" task, where the probability of drawing a red ball is 0.5 under both hypotheses. We have chosen nonsymmetric hypotheses for our example to allow for an initial bias that is often observed in calibration data.

It is instructive to compare the predictions of this model to the results of Lichtenstein and Fischhoff (1977) who investigated the effect of task difficulty (see figure 11.7). Their "easy" items (accuracy = 85%) produced underconfidence through much of the confidence range, their "difficult" items (accuracy = 61%) produced overconfidence through most of the confidence range, and their "impossible" task (discriminating European from American handwriting, accuracy = 51%) showed dramatic overconfidence throughout the entire range.

A comparison of figures 11.6 and 11.7 reveals that our simple chance model reproduces the pattern of results observed by Lichtenstein and Fischhoff (1977): slight underconfidence for very easy items, consistent overconfidence for difficult items, and dramatic overconfidence for "impossible" items. This pattern follows from the assumption that judged confidence is controlled by the balance of arguments for the competing hypotheses. The present account, therefore, can explain the observed relation between task difficulty and overconfidence (see Ferrell & McGoey, 1980).

The difficulty effect is one of the most consistent findings in the calibration literature (Lichtenstein & Fischhoff, 1977; Lichtenstein, Fischhoff, & Phillips, 1982; Yates, 1990). It is

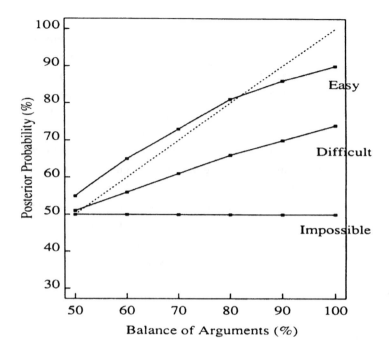

Figure 11.6
Predicted calibration for item difficulty.

observed not only in general knowledge questions, but also in clinical diagnoses (Oskamp, 1962), predictions of future events (contrast Fischhoff & MacGregor, 1982, versus Wright & Wisudha, 1982), and letter identification (Keren, 1988). Moreover, the difficulty effect may contribute to other findings that have been interpreted in different ways. For example, Keren (1987) showed that world-class bridge players were well calibrated, whereas amateur players were overconfident. Keren interpreted this finding as an optimism bias on the part of the amateur players. In addition, however, the professionals were significantly more accurate than the amateurs in predicting the outcome of bridge hands, and the difference in difficulty could have contributed to the difference in overconfidence.

The difficulty effect can also explain the main finding of a study by Gigerenzer, Hoffrage, and Kleinbolting (1991). In this study, subjects in one group were presented with pairs of cities and asked to choose the city with the larger population and indicate their confidence in each answer. The items were randomly selected from a list of all large West German cities. Subjects in a second group were presented with general knowledge questions (e.g., Was the zipper invented before or after 1920?) and instructed to choose the correct answer and assess their confidence in that answer. Judgments about the population of cities were fairly

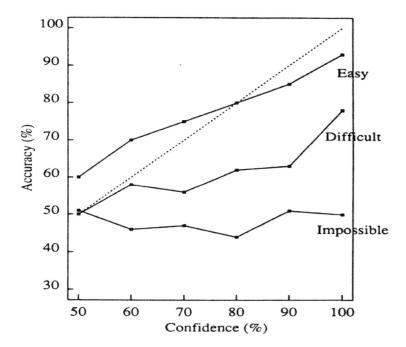

Figure 11.7
Calibration plots for item difficulty.

well calibrated, but responses to the general knowledge questions exhibited overconfidence. However, the two tasks were not equally difficult: average accuracy was 72% for the city judgments and only 53% for the general knowledge questions. Hence, the presence of overconfidence in the latter but not in the former could be entirely due to the difficulty effect, documented by Lichtenstein and Fischhoff (1977). Indeed, when Gigerenzer et al. (1991) selected a set of city questions that were matched in difficulty to the general knowledge questions, the two domains yielded the same degree of overconfidence. The authors did not acknowledge the fact that their study confounded item generation (representative versus selective) with task difficulty (easy versus hard). Instead, they interpret their data as confirmation for their theory that overconfidence in individual judgments is a consequence of item selection and that it disappears when items are randomly sampled from some natural environment. This prediction is tested in the following study.

Study 5: The Illusion of Validity

In this experiment, subjects compared pairs of American states on several attributes reported in the *1990 World Almanac*. To ensure representative sampling, we randomly selected 30 pairs of American states from the set of all possible pairs of states. Subjects were presented with pairs of states (e.g., Alabama, Oregon) and asked to choose the state that was higher on a particular attribute and to assess the probability that their answer was correct. According to Gigerenzer et al. (1991), there should be no overconfidence in these judgments because the states were randomly selected from a natural reference class. In contrast, our account suggests that the degree of overconfidence depends on the relation between the strength and weight of the evidence. More specifically, overconfidence will be most pronounced when the weight of evidence is low and the strength of evidence is high. This is likely to arise in domains in which people can readily form a strong impression even though these impressions have low predictive validity. For example, an interviewer can form a strong impression of the quality of the mind of a prospective graduate student even though these impressions do not predict the candidate's performance (Dawes, 1979).

The use of natural stimuli precludes the direct manipulation of strength and weight. Instead, we used three attributes that vary in terms of the strength of impression that subjects are likely to form and the amount of knowledge they are likely to have. The three attributes were the number of people in each state (population), the high-school graduation rate in each state (education), and the difference in voting rates between the last two presidential elections in each state (voting). We hypothesized that the three attributes would yield different patterns of confidence and accuracy. First, we expected people to be more knowledgeable about population than about either education or voting. Second, we expected greater confidence in the prediction of education than in the prediction of voting because people's images or stereotypes of the various states are more closely tied to the former than the latter. For example, people are likely to view one state as more "educated" than another if it has more famous universities or if it is associated with more cultural events. Because the correlations between these cues and high-school graduation rates are very low, however, we expected greater overconfidence for education than for population or voting. Thus, we expected high accuracy and high confidence for population, low accuracy and low confidence for voting, and low accuracy and higher confidence for education.

To test these hypotheses, 298 subjects each evaluated half (15) of the pairs of states on one of the attributes. After subjects had indicated their confidence for each of the 15 questions, they were asked to estimate how many of the 15 questions they had answered correctly. They were reminded that by chance alone the expected number of correct answers was 7.5.

Table 11.4 presents mean judgments of confidence, accuracy, and estimated frequency of correct answers for each of the three attributes. Judgments of confidence exhibited significant overconfidence ($p < 0.01$) for all three attributes, contradicting the claim that "If the set of general-knowledge tasks is randomly sampled from a natural environment, we expect overconfidence to be zero" (Gigerenzer et al., 1991, p. 512). Evidently there is a great deal more to overconfidence than the biased selection of items.

Table 11.4
Confidence and Accuracy for Study 6

	Population N = 93	Voting N = 77	Education N = 118
Confidence	74.7	59.7	65.6
Accuracy	68.2	51.2	49.8
Conf-Acc	6.5	8.5	15.8
Frequency	51.3	36.1	41.2

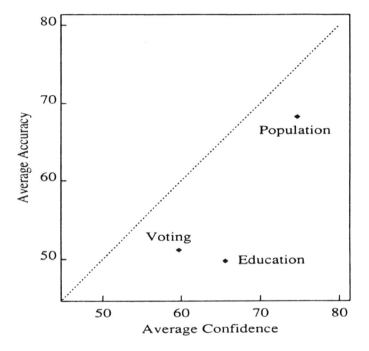

Figure 11.8
Confidence and accuracy for three attributes.

The observed pattern of confidence and accuracy is consistent with our hypothesis, as can be seen in figure 11.8. This figure plots average accuracy against average confidence, across all subjects and items, for each of the three attributes. For population, people exhibited considerable accuracy and moderate overconfidence. For voting, accuracy was at chance level, but overconfidence was again moderate. For education, too, accuracy was at chance level, but overconfidence was massive.

The present results indicate that overconfidence cannot be fully explained by the effect of difficulty. Population and voting produced comparable levels of overconfidence (6.5 versus

8.5, $t < 1$, n.s.) despite a large difference in accuracy (68.2 versus 51.2, $p < 0.001$). However, there is much greater overconfidence in judgments about education than about voting (15.8 versus 8.5, $p < 0.01$) even though their level of accuracy was nearly identical (49.8 versus 51.2, $t < 1$, n.s.).

This analysis may shed light on the relation between overconfidence and expertise. When predictability is reasonably high, experts are generally better calibrated than lay people. Studies of race oddsmakers (Griffith, 1949; Hausch, Ziemba, & Rubinstein, 1981; McGlothlin, 1956) and expert bridge players (Keren, 1987) are consistent with this conclusion. When predictability is very low, however, experts may be more prone to overconfidence than novices. If the future state of a mental patient, the Russian economy, or the stock market cannot be predicted from present data, then experts who have rich models of the system in question are more likely to exhibit overconfidence than lay people who have a very limited understanding of these systems. Studies of clinical psychologists (e.g., Oskamp, 1965) and stock market analysts (e.g., Yates, 1990) are consistent with this hypothesis.

Frequency versus Confidence

We now turn to the relation between people's confidence in the validity of their individual answers and their estimates of the overall hit rate. A sportscaster, for example, can be asked to assess his confidence in the prediction of each game as well as the number of games he expects to predict correctly. According to the present account, these judgments are not expected to coincide because they are based on different evidence. A judgment of confidence in a particular case, we propose, depends primarily on the balance of arguments for and against a specific hypothesis; for example, the relative strength of two opposing teams. Estimated frequency of correct prediction, by contrast, is likely to be based on a general evaluation of the difficulty of the task, the knowledge of the judge, or past experience with similar problems. Thus, the overconfidence observed in average judgments of confidence need not apply to global judgments of expected accuracy. Indeed, table 11.4 shows that estimated frequencies were substantially below the actual frequencies of correct prediction. In fact, the latter estimates were below chance for two of the three attributes.[3] Similar results have been observed by other investigators (e.g., Gigerenzer et al., 1991; May, 1986; Sniezek & Switzer, 1989). Evidently, people can maintain a high degree of confidence in the validity of specific answers even when they know that their overall hit rate is not very high.[4] This phenomenon has been called the "illusion of validity" (Kahneman & Tversky, 1973): people often make confident predictions about individual cases on the basis of fallible data (e.g., personal interviews or projective tests) even when they know that these data have low predictive validity (Dawes, Faust, & Meehl, 1989).

The discrepancy between estimates of frequency and judgments of confidence is an inter-esting finding but it does not undermine the significance of overconfidence in individual items. The latter phenomenon is important because people's decisions are commonly based on their confidence in their assessment of individual events, not on their estimates of their overall hit rate. For example, an extensive survey of new business owners (Cooper, Woo, & Dunkelberg, 1988) revealed that entrepreneurs were, on average, highly optimistic (i.e., over-confident) about the success of their specific new ventures even when they were reasonably realistic about the general rule of failure for ventures of that kind. We suggest that decisions to undertake new ventures are based primarily on beliefs about individual events, rather than about overall base rates. The tendency to prefer an individual or "inside" view rather than a statistical or "outside" view represents one of the major departures of intuitive judgment from normative theory (Kahneman & Lovallo, 1994; Kahneman & Tversky, 1982).

Finally, note that people's performance on the frequency task leaves much to be desired. The degree of underestimation in judgments of frequency was comparable, on average, to the degree of overconfidence in individual judgments of probability (see table 11.4). Further-more, the correlation across subjects between estimated and actual frequency was negligible for all three attributes (+.10 for population, −0.10 for voting, and +.15 for education). These observations do not support the view that people estimate their hit rate correctly, and that the confidence–frequency discrepancy is merely a manifestation of their inability to evaluate the probability of unique events. Research on overconfidence has been criticized by some authors on the grounds that it applies a frequentistic criterion (the rate of correct prediction) to a nonfrequentistic or subjective concept of probability. This objection, however, overlooks the fact that a Bayesian expects to be calibrated (Dawid, 1982); hence, the theory of subjec-tive probability permits the comparison of confidence and accuracy.

Concluding Remarks

The preceding study demonstrated that the overconfidence observed in calibration exper-iments is not an artifact of item selection or a byproduct of test difficulty. Furthermore, overconfidence is not limited to the prediction of discrete events; it has consistently been observed in the assessment of uncertain quantities (Alpert & Raiffa, 1982).

The significance of overconfidence to the conduct of human affairs can hardly be over-stated. Although overconfidence is not universal, it is prevalent, often massive, and difficult to eliminate (Fischhoff, 1982). This phenomenon is significant not only because it demon-strates the discrepancy between intuitive judgments and the laws of chance, but primarily because confidence controls action (Heath & Tversky, 1991). It has been argued (see, e.g., Taylor & Brown, 1988) that overconfidence—like optimism—is adaptive because it makes people feel good and moves them to do things that they would not have done otherwise. These benefits, however, may be purchased at a high price. Overconfidence in the diagnosis of a patient, the outcome of a trial, or the projected interest rate could lead to inappropriate medical treatment, bad legal advice, and regrettable financial investments. It can be argued that people's willingness to engage in military, legal, and other costly battles would be reduced if they had a more realistic assessment of their chances of success. We doubt that the benefits of overconfidence outweigh its costs.

Acknowledgments

This work was supported by an NSERC research grant to the first author and by Grant 89–0064 from the Air Force Office of Scientific Research to the second author. The paper has benefited from discussions with Robyn Dawes, Baruch Fischhoff, and Daniel Kahneman.

Notes

1. A person is said to exhibit overconfidence if she overestimates the probability of her favored hypothesis. The appropriate probability estimate may be determined empirically (e.g., by a person's hit rate) or derived from an appropriate model.

2. To explore the effect of the correlation between strength and weight, we replicated our experiment with another set of stimuli that were selected to have a smaller correlation between the two independent variables ($r = -0.27$ as compared to $r = -0.64$). The results for this set of stimuli were remarkably similar to those reported in the text; that is, the regression weights for the median data yielded a ratio of nearly 2 to 1 in favor of strength.

3. One possible explanation for this puzzling observation is that subjects reported the number of items they knew with certainty, without correction for guessing.

4. This is the statistical version of the paradoxical statement "I believe in all of my beliefs, but I believe that some of my beliefs are false."

References

Alpert, M., & Raiffa, H. (1982). A progress report on the training of probability assessors. In D. Kahneman, P. Slovic, & A. Tversky (Eds.), *Judgment under uncertainty: Heuristics and biases* (pp. 294–305). Cambridge, England: Cambridge University Press.

Bar-Hillel, M. (1983). The base rate fallacy controversy. In R. W. Scholz (Ed.), *Decision making under uncertainty* (pp. 39–61). Amsterdam, the Netherlands: North-Holland.

Camerer, C. (1990). Do markets correct biases in probability judgment? Evidence from market experiments. In L. Green & J. H. Kagel (Eds.), *Advances in behavioral economics* (Vol. 2, pp. 126–172). Santa Barbara, CA: Praeger.

Cooper, A. C., Woo, C. Y., & Dunkelberg, W. C. (1988). Entrepreneurs' perceived chances for success. *Journal of Business Venturing, 3*, 97–108.

Dawes, R. M. (1979). The robust beauty of improper linear models in decision making. *American Psychologist, 34*, 571–582.

Dawes, R. M. (1988). *Rational choice in an uncertain world.* New York, NY: Harcourt Brace Jovanovich.

Dawes, R. M., Faust, D., & Meehl, P. E. (1989). Clinical versus actuarial judgment. *Science, 243*, 1668–1674.

Dawid, A. P. (1982). The well-calibrated Bayesian. *Journal of the American Statistical Association, 77*, 605–613.

Dun & Bradstreet. (1967). *Patterns of success in managing a business.* New York, NY: Dun & Bradstreet.

Dunning, D., Griffin, D. W., Milojkovic, J., & Ross, L. (1990). The overconfidence effect in social prediction. *Journal of Personality and Social Psychology, 58*, 568–581.

Edwards, W. (1968). Conservatism in human information processing. In B. Kleinmuntz (Ed.), *Formal representation of human judgment* (pp. 17–52). New York, NY: Wiley.

Ferrell, W. R., & McGoey, P. J. (1980). A model of calibration for subjective probabilities. *Organizational Behavior and Human Performance, 26*, 32–53.

Fischhoff, B. (1982). Debiasing. In D. Kahneman, P. Slovic, & A. Tversky (Eds.), *Judgment under uncertainty: Heuristics and biases* (pp. 422–444). New York, NY: Cambridge University Press.

Fischhoff, B., & Bar-Hillel, M. (1984). Focusing techniques: A shortcut to improving probability judgments? *Organizational Behavior and Human Performance, 34*, 175–194.

Fischhoff, B., & Beyth-Marom, R. (1983). Hypothesis evaluation from a Bayesian perspective. *Psychological Review, 90*, 239–260.

Fischhoff, B., & MacGregor, D. (1982). Subjective confidence in forecasts. *Journal of Forecasting, 1*, 155–172.

Forer, B. (1949). The fallacy of personal validation: A classroom demonstration of gullibility. *Journal of Abnormal and Social Psychology, 44*, 118–123.

Gigerenzer, G., Hell, W., & Blank, H. (1988). Presentation and content: The use of base rates as a continuous variable. *Journal of Experimental Psychology: Human Perception and Performance, 14*, 513–525.

Gigerenzer, G., Hoffrage, U., & Kleinbolting, H. (1991). Probabilistic mental models: A Brunswikian theory of confidence. *Psychological Review, 98*, 506–528.

Grether, D. M. (1980). Bayes' rule as a descriptive model: The representativeness heuristic. *Quarterly Journal of Economics, 95*, 537–557.

Grether, D. M. (1990). *Testing Bayes' rule and the representativeness heuristic: Some experimental evidence* (Social Science Working Paper 724). Pasadena, CA: Division of the Humanities and Social Sciences, California Institute of Technology.

Griffin, D. W. (1991). *On the use and neglect of base rates.* Unpublished manuscript, Department of Psychology, University of Waterloo.

Griffith, R. M. (1949). Odds adjustments by American horse-race bettors. *American Journal of Psychology, 62,* 290–294.

Hausch, D. B., Ziemba, W. T., & Rubinstein, M. (1981). Efficiency of the market for racetrack betting. *Management Science, 27,* 1435–1452.

Heath, F., & Tversky, A. (1991). Preference and belief: Ambiguity and competence in choice under uncertainty. *Journal of Risk and Uncertainty, 4,* 5–28.

Jones, E. E., & Nisbett, R. E. (1972). *The actor and the observer: Divergent perceptions of the causes of behavior.* Morristown, NJ: General Learning Press.

Kahneman, D., & Lovallo, D. (1994). Timid decisions and bold forecasting: A cognitive perspective on risk taking. In R. Rumelt, P. Schendel, & D. Teece (Eds.), *Fundamental issues in strategy* (pp. 71–96). Cambridge, MA: Harvard Business School Press.

Kahneman, D., Slovic, P., & Tversky, A. (1982). *Judgment under uncertainty: Heuristics and biases.* Cambridge, England: Cambridge University Press.

Kahneman, D., & Tversky, A. (1972). Subjective probability: A judgment of representativeness. *Cognitive Psychology, 3,* 430–454.

Kahneman, D., & Tversky, A. (1973). On the psychology of prediction. *Psychological Review, 80,* 237–251.

Kahneman, D., & Tversky, A. (1982). Intuitive prediction: Biases and corrective procedures. In D. Kahneman, P. Slovic, & A. Tversky (Eds.), *Judgment under uncertainty: Heuristics and biases* (pp. 414–421). Cambridge, England: Cambridge University Press.

Keren, G. (1987). Facing uncertainty in the game of bridge: A calibration study. *Organizational Behavior and Human Decision Processes, 39,* 98–114.

Keren, G. (1988). On the ability of monitoring non-veridical perceptions and uncertain knowledge: Some calibration studies. *Acta Psychologica, 67,* 95–119.

Kidd, J. B. (1970). The utilization of subjective probabilities in production planning. *Acta Psychologica, 34,* 338–347.

Koriat, A., Lichtenstein, S., & Fischhoff, B. (1980). Reasons for confidence. *Journal of Experimental Psychology. Human Learning and Memory, 6,* 107–118.

Lichtenstein, S., & Fischhoff, B. (1977). Do those who know more also know more about how much they know? The calibration of probability judgments. *Organizational Behavior and Human Performance, 20,* 159–183.

Lichtenstein, S., Fischhoff, B., & Phillips, L. D. (1982). Calibration of probabilities: The state of the art to 1980. In D. Kahneman, P. Slovic, & A. Tversky (Eds.), *Judgment under uncertainty: Heuristics and biases* (pp. 306–334). Cambridge, England: Cambridge University Press.

Lusted, L. B. (1977). *A study of the efficacy of diagnostic radiologic procedures: Final report on diagnostic efficacy*. Chicago, IL: Efficacy Study Committee of the American College of Radiology.

May, R. S. (1986). Inferences, subjective probability and frequency of correct answers: A cognitive approach to the overconfidence phenomenon. In B. Brehmer, H. Jungermann, P. Lourens, & G. Sevo'n (Eds.), *New directions in research on decision making* (pp. 175–189). Amsterdam, the Netherlands: North-Holland.

McGlothlin, W. H. (1956). Stability of choices among uncertain alternatives. *American Journal of Psychology, 69*, 604–615.

Murphy, A. H., & Winkler, R. L. (1977). Can weather forecasters formulate reliable probability forecasts of precipitation and temperature? *National Weather Digest, 2*, 2–9.

Neale, M. A., & Bazerman, M. H. (1990, forthcoming). *Cognition and rationality in negotiation*. New York, NY: The Free Press.

Nisbett, R. E., & Ross, L. (1980). *Human inference: Strategies and shortcomings of human judgment*. Englewood Cliffs, NJ: Prentice-Hall.

Oskamp, S. (1962). The relationship of clinical experience and training methods to several criteria of clinical prediction. *Psychological Monographs, 76*(28), 1–28.

Oskamp, S. (1965). Overconfidence in case-study judgments. *Journal of Consulting Psychology, 29*, 261–265.

Peterson, C. R., & Miller, A. J. (1965). Sensitivity of subjective probability revision. *Journal of Experimental Psychology, 70*, 117–121.

Peterson, C. R., Schneider, R. J., & Miller, A. J. (1965). Sample size and the revision of subjective probabilities. *Journal of Experimental Psychology, 69*, 522–527.

Phillips, L. D., & Edwards, W. (1966). Conservatism in a simple probability inference task. *Journal of Experimental Psychology, 72*, 346–354.

Quattrone, G. A. (1982). Overattribution and unit formation: When behavior engulfs the person. *Journal of Personality and Social Psychology, 42*, 593–607.

Slovic, P., & Lichtenstein, S. (1971). Comparison of Bayesian and regression approaches to the study of information processing in judgment. *Organizational Behavior and Human Performance, 6*, 649–744.

Sniezek, J. A., & Switzer, F. S. (1989). *The over-underconfidence paradox: High Pi's but poor unlucky me*. Paper presented at the Judgment and Decision Making Society annual meeting in Atlanta, Georgia.

Staël von Holstein, C.-A. S. (1972). Probabilistic forecasting: An experiment related to the stock market. *Organizational Behavior and Human Performance, 8*, 139–158.

Taylor, S. E., & Brown, J. D. (1988). Illusion and well-being: A social psychological perspective on mental health. *Psychological Bulletin, 103*, 193–210.

Tversky, A., & Kahneman, D. (1971). The belief in the law of small numbers. *Psychological Bulletin, 76*, 105–110.

Tversky, A., & Kahneman, D. (1974). Judgment under uncertainty: Heuristics and biases. *Science, 185*, 1124–1131.

Vallone, R. P., Griffin, D. W., Lin, S., & Ross, L. (1990). The overconfident prediction of future actions and outcomes by self and others. *Journal of Personality and Social Psychology, 58*, 582–592.

von Winterfeldt, D., & Edwards, W. (1986). *Decision analysis and behavioral research*. New York, NY: Cambridge University Press.

Wagenaar, W. A., & Keren, G. (1986). Does the expert know? The reliability of predictions and confidence ratings of experts. In E. Hollnagel, G. Maneini, & D. Woods (Eds.), *Intelligent decision support in process environments* (pp. 87–107). Berlin: Springer.

Wright, G., & Wisudha, A. (1982). Distribution of probability assessments for almanac and future event questions. *Scandinavian Journal of Psychology, 23*, 219–224.

Yates, J. F. (1990). *Judgment and decision making*. Englewood Cliffs, NJ: Prentice-Hall.

12 Ambiguity Aversion and Comparative Ignorance

Craig R. Fox and Amos Tversky

Introduction

One of the fundamental problems of modern decision theory is the analysis of decisions under ignorance or ambiguity, where the probabilities of potential outcomes are neither specified in advance nor readily assessed on the basis of the available evidence. This issue was addressed by Knight (1921), who distinguished between *measurable uncertainty* or *risk*, which can be represented by precise probabilities, and *unmeasurable uncertainty*, which cannot. Furthermore, he suggested that entrepreneurs are compensated for bearing unmeasurable uncertainty as opposed to risk. Contemporaneously, Keynes (1921) distinguished between *probability*, representing the balance of evidence in favor of a particular proposition, and the *weight of evidence*, representing the quantity of evidence supporting that balance. He then asked, "If two probabilities are equal in degree, ought we, in choosing our course of action, to prefer that one which is based on a greater body of knowledge?" (p. 313). The distinction between clear and vague probabilities has been rejected by proponents of the subjectivist school. Although Savage (1954) acknowledged that subjective probabilities are commonly vague, he argued that vagueness has no role in a rational theory of choice.

Interest in the problem of decision under ignorance was revived by a series of papers and commentaries published in the early sixties in this *Journal*. The most influential of these papers, written by Ellsberg (1961), presented compelling examples in which people prefer to bet on known rather than on unknown probabilities (see also Fellner, 1961). Ellsberg's simplest example, known as the "two-color" problem, involves two urns each containing red and black balls. Urn 1 contains 50 red and 50 black balls, whereas urn 2 contains 100 red and black balls in an unknown proportion. Suppose that a ball is drawn at random from an urn and one receives $100 or nothing depending on the outcome. Most people seem indifferent between betting on red or on black for either urn, yet they prefer to bet on the 50–50 urn rather than on the urn with the unknown composition. This pattern of preferences is inconsistent with expected utility theory because it implies that the subjective probabilities of black and of red are greater in the 50–50 urn than in the unknown urn, and therefore cannot sum to one for both urns.

Essentially the same problem was discussed by Keynes (1921) some 40 years earlier: "In the first case we know that the urn contains black and white balls in equal proportions; in the second case the proportion of each color is unknown, and each ball is as likely to be black as white. It is evident that in either case the probability of drawing a white ball is $\frac{1}{2}$, but that the weight of the argument in favor of this conclusion is greater in the first case" (p. 75). In the spirit of Knight and Keynes, Ellsberg (1961) argued that people's willingness to act in the presence of uncertainty depends not only on the perceived probability of the event in question but also on its vagueness or ambiguity. Ellsberg characterized ambiguity as "a quality depending on the amount, type, and 'unanimity' of information, and giving rise to one's degree of 'confidence' in an estimate of relative likelihoods" (p. 657).

The preference for the clear over the vague bet has been demonstrated in many experiments using several variations of Ellsberg's original problems (for a comprehensive review of the literature, see Camerer & Weber [1992]). As noted above, these observations provide evidence against the descriptive validity of expected utility theory. Furthermore, many authors have attempted to justify the preference for risk over ambiguity on normative grounds, although Raiffa (1961) has argued that ambiguity can be reduced to risk by tossing a coin to decide whether to guess red or black.

Ambiguity aversion has attracted much attention because, with the notable exception of games of chance, decision makers usually do not know the precise probabilities of potential outcomes. The decisions to undertake a business venture, to go to court, or to undergo medical treatment are commonly made in the absence of a clear idea of the chances that these actions will be successful. The question arises, then, whether the ambiguity aversion demonstrated using the Ellsberg urn applies to such decisions. In other words, is the preference for clear over vague probabilities confined to the domain of chance, or does it extend to uncertain beliefs based on world knowledge?

To answer this question, Heath and Tversky (1991) conducted a series of experiments comparing people's willingness to bet on their uncertain beliefs with their willingness to bet on clear chance events. Contrary to ambiguity aversion, they found that people prefer to bet on their vague beliefs in situations where they feel especially competent or knowledgeable, although they prefer to bet on chance when they do not. In one study, subjects were asked to choose among bets based on three sources of uncertainty: the results in various states of the 1988 presidential election, the results of various professional football games, and the results of random draws from an urn with a known composition. Subjects who were preselected for their knowledge of politics and lack of knowledge of football preferred betting on political events rather than on chance events that they considered equally probable. However, these subjects preferred betting on chance events rather than on sports events that they considered equally probable. Analogously, subjects who were preselected for their knowledge of football and lack of knowledge of politics exhibited the opposite pattern, preferring football to chance and chance to politics. Another finding that is consistent with Heath and Tversky's competence hypothesis but not with ambiguity aversion is people's preference to bet on their physical skills (e.g., throwing darts) rather than on matched chance events despite the fact that the perceived probability of success is vague for skill and clear for chance (Cohen & Hansel, 1959; Howell, 1971).

If ambiguity aversion is driven by the feeling of incompetence, as suggested by the preceding discussion, the question arises as to what conditions produce this state of mind. We propose that people's confidence is undermined when they contrast their limited knowledge about an event with their superior knowledge about another event, or when they compare themselves with more knowledgeable individuals. Moreover, we argue that this contrast between states of knowledge is the predominant source of ambiguity aversion. When evaluating an uncertain event in isolation, people attempt to assess its likelihood—as a good Bayesian would—paying relatively little attention to second-order characteristics such as vagueness or weight of evidence. However, when people compare two events about which they have different levels of knowledge, the contrast makes the less familiar bet less attractive or the more familiar bet more attractive. The main implication of this account, called the *comparative ignorance hypothesis*, is that ambiguity aversion will be present when subjects evaluate clear and vague prospects jointly, but it will greatly diminish or disappear when they evaluate each prospect in isolation.

A review of the experimental literature reveals a remarkable fact: virtually every test of ambiguity aversion to date has employed a within-subjects design in which respondents compared clear and vague bets, rather than a between-subjects design in which different respondents evaluated each bet. This literature, therefore, does not answer the question of whether ambiguity aversion exists in the absence of a contrast between clear and vague bets. In the following series of studies we test the hypothesis that ambiguity aversion holds in a comparative context (or a within-subjects design) but that it is reduced or eliminated in a noncomparative context (or a between-subjects design).

Experiments

Study 1

The following hypothetical problem was presented to 141 undergraduates at Stanford University. It was included in a questionnaire consisting of several unrelated items that subjects completed for class credit.

Imagine that there is a bag on the table (*Bag A*) filled with exactly 50 red poker chips and 50 black poker chips, and a second bag (*Bag B*) filled with 100 poker chips that are red and black, but you do not know their relative proportion. Suppose that you are offered a ticket to a game that is to be played as follows: First, you are to guess a color (red or black). Next, without looking, you are to draw a poker chip out of one of the bags. If the color that you draw is the same as the one you predicted, then you will win $100; otherwise you win nothing. What is the most that you would pay for a ticket to play such a game for each of the bags? ($0–$100)

Bag A	Bag B
50 red chips	? red chips
50 black chips	? black chips
100 total chips	100 total chips

The most that I would be willing to pay for a ticket to *Bag A* (50 red; 50 black) is: ___
The most that I would be willing to pay for a ticket to *Bag B* (? red; ? black) is: ___

Approximately half the subjects performed the comparative task described above; the order in which the two bets were presented was counterbalanced. The remaining subjects performed a noncomparative task: approximately half evaluated the clear bet alone, and the remaining subjects evaluated the vague bet alone.

Mean willingness to pay for each bet is presented in table 12.1. As in all subsequent tables, standard errors (in parentheses) and sample sizes (*N*) are listed below the means. The data support our hypothesis. In the comparative condition, there is strong evidence of ambiguity aversion: subjects were willing to pay on average $9.51 more for the clear bet than for the vague bet ($t(66) = 6.00$, $p < 0.001$). However, in the noncomparative condition, there is no trace of ambiguity aversion as subjects paid slightly less for the clear bet than for the vague bet ($t(72) = -0.12$, n.s.). This interaction is significant ($z = 2.42$, $p < 0.01$).

Study 2

Our next study tested the comparative ignorance hypothesis with real money at stake. Subjects were recruited via signs posted in the psychology building at Stanford University, promising a chance to win up to $20 for participation in a brief study. We recruited 110 students, faculty, and staff; six subjects were excluded because of inconsistent responses.

Table 12.1
Results of Study 1

	Clear bet		Vague bet	
Comparative	$24.34		$14.85	
	(2.21)	N = 67	(1.80)	N = 67
Noncomparative	$17.94		$18.42	
	(2.50)	N = 35	(2.87)	N = 39

Subjects were run individually. Participants in the comparative condition priced both the clear bet and the vague bet. Half the subjects in the noncomparative condition priced the clear bet alone; the other half priced the vague bet alone. The clear bet involved a draw from a bag containing one red ping-pong ball and one green ping-pong ball. The vague bet involved a draw from a bag containing two ping-pong balls, each of which could be either red or green. Subjects were first asked to guess the color of the ball to be drawn. Next, they were asked to make a series of choices between receiving $20 if their guess is correct (and nothing otherwise) or receiving $X for sure. Subjects marked their choices on a response sheet that listed the various sure amounts ($X) in descending order from $19.50 to $0.50 in steps of 50 cents. They were informed that some participants would be selected at random to play for real money. For these subjects, one choice would be selected at random, and the subjects would either receive $X or play the bet, depending on the preference they had indicated. This procedure is incentive-compatible because subjects can only make themselves worse off by misrepresenting their preferences.

Cash equivalents were estimated by the midpoint between the lowest amount of money that was preferred to the uncertain bet and the highest amount of money for which the bet was preferred. Mean cash equivalents are listed in table 12.2. The procedural variations introduced in this study (real bets, monetary incentive, individual administration) did not affect the pattern of results. In the comparative condition, subjects priced the clear bet $1.21 higher on average than the vague bet ($t(51) = 2.70$, $p < 0.01$). However, in the noncomparative condition, subjects priced the vague bet slightly above the clear bet ($t(50) = -0.61$, n.s.). Again, the interaction is significant ($z = 1.90$, $p < 0.05$).

Two comments regarding the interpretation of studies 1 and 2 are in order. First, subjects in both the comparative and noncomparative conditions were clearly aware of the fact that they did not know the composition of the vague urn. Only in the comparative task, however, did this fact influence their prices. Hence, ambiguity aversion seems to require a direct comparison between the clear and the vague bet; an awareness of missing information is not sufficient (cf. Frisch & Baron, 1988). Second, it is noteworthy that in both studies 1 and 2,

Table 12.2
Results of Study 2

	Clear bet		Vague bet	
Comparative	$9.74		$8.53	
	(0.49)	N = 52	(0.58)	N = 52
Noncomparative	$7.58		$8.04	
	(0.62)	N = 26	(0.43)	N = 26

the comparative context enhanced the attractiveness of the clear bet somewhat more than it diminished the attractiveness of the vague bet. The comparative ignorance hypothesis, however, makes no prediction about the relative magnitude of these effects.

Study 3

In addition to the two-color problem described above, Ellsberg (1961) introduced a three-color problem, depicted in table 12.3. Consider an urn that contains ten white balls and twenty balls that are red and blue in unknown proportion. In decision 1 subjects are asked to choose between f_1, winning on white $(p = \frac{1}{3})$; or g_1, winning on red $(0 \le p \le \frac{2}{3})$. In decision 2 subjects are asked to choose between f_2, winning on either white or blue $(\frac{1}{3} \le p \le 1)$, or g_2, winning on either red or blue $(p = \frac{2}{3})$. As suggested by Ellsberg, people typically favor f_1 over g_1 in decision 1 and g_2 over f_2 in decision 2, contrary to the independence axiom of expected utility theory.

From the standpoint of the comparative ignorance hypothesis, this problem differs from the two-color problem because here the description of the bets (especially f_2) involves both clear and vague probabilities. Consequently, we expect some ambiguity aversion even in a noncomparative context in which each subject evaluates only one bet. However, we expect a stronger effect in a comparative context in which each subject evaluates both the clear and vague bets. The present study tests these predictions.

Subjects were 162 first-year law students at Willamette University who completed a short questionnaire in a classroom setting. Three subjects who violated dominance were excluded from the analysis. Subjects were informed that some people would be selected at random to be paid on the basis of their choices. The instructions included a brief description of an incentive-compatible payoff scheme (based on Becker, DeGroot, & Marschak, 1964). Subjects were asked to state their minimum selling price for the bets displayed in table 12.3. In the comparative condition, subjects priced all four bets. In the noncomparative condition,

Table 12.3
Ellsberg's Three-Color Problem

		10 balls	20 balls	
	Bet	white	red	blue
Decision 1	f_1	$50	0	0
	g_1	0	$50	0
Decision 2	f_2	$50	0	$50
	g_2	0	$50	$50

approximately half the subjects priced the two complementary clear bets (f_1 and g_2), and the remaining subjects priced the two complementary vague bets (f_2 and g_1). The order of the bets was counterbalanced.

Let $c(f)$ be the stated price of bet f. As expected, most subjects in the comparative condition priced the clear bets above the vague bets. In particular, we observed $c(f_1) > c(g_1)$ for 28 subjects, $c(f_1) = c(g_1)$ for 17 subjects, and $c(f_1) < c(g_1)$ for 8 subjects ($p < 0.01$). Similarly, we observed $c(g_2) > c(f_2)$ for 36 subjects, $c(g_2) = c(f_2)$ for 12 subjects, and $c(g_2) < c(f_2)$ for 5 subjects ($p < 0.001$). Moreover, the pattern implied by ambiguity aversion (i.e., $c(f_1) \geq c(g_1)$ and $c(f_2) \leq c(g_2)$), where at least one inequality is strict) was exhibited by 62% of the subjects.

In order to contrast the comparative and the noncomparative conditions, we have added for each subject the selling prices of the two complementary clear bets (i.e., $c(f_1) + c(g_2)$) and the selling prices of the two complementary vague bets (i.e., $c(g_1) + c(f_2)$). Obviously, for subjects in the noncomparative condition, we can compute only one such sum. These sums measure the attractiveness of betting on either side of the clear and of the vague bets. The means of these sums are presented in table 12.4. The results conform to expectation. In the comparative condition, subjects priced clear bets \$10.68 higher on average than vague bets ($t(52) = 6.23, p < 0.001$). However, in the noncomparative condition, the difference was only \$3.85 ($t(104) = 0.82$, n.s.). This interaction is marginally significant ($z = 1.37, p < 0.10$).

Inspection of the individual bets reveals that for the more probable bets, f_2 and g_2, there was a strong preference for the clear over the vague in the comparative condition ($c(g_2) = \$33.75, c(f_2) = \$24.66, t(52) = 5.85, p < 0.001$) and a moderate preference for the clear over the vague in the noncomparative condition ($c(g_2) = \$31.67, c(f_2) = \$26.71, t(104) = 2.05, p < 0.05$). However, for the less probable bets, f_1 and g_1, we found no significant differences between selling prices for clear and vague bets in either the comparative condition ($c(g_1) = \$20.26, c(f_1) = \$21.85, t(52) = 1.05$, n.s.) or the noncomparative condition ($c(g_1) = \$21.13, c(f_1) = \$20.02, t(104) = 0.43$, n.s.). The aggregate pattern displayed in table 12.4, therefore, is driven primarily by the more probable bets.

Table 12.4
Results of Study 3

	Clear bet		Vague bet	
Comparative	\$55.60		\$44.92	
	(2.66)	N = 53	(3.27)	N = 53
Noncomparative	\$51.69		\$47.85	
	(2.94)	N = 54	(3.65)	N = 52

Study 4

In the preceding three studies, uncertainty was generated using a chance device (i.e., drawing a ball from an urn with a known or an unknown composition). Our next study tests the comparative ignorance hypothesis using natural events. Specifically, we asked subjects to price hypothetical bets contingent on future temperature in a familiar city (San Francisco) and an unfamiliar city with a similar climate (Istanbul). Ambiguity aversion suggests that our subjects (who were living near San Francisco) should prefer betting on San Francisco temperature, with which they were highly familiar, to betting on Istanbul temperature, with which they were not.

Subjects were asked how much they would be willing to pay to bet on each side of a proposition that offered a fixed prize if the temperature in a given city is above or below a specified value. The exact wording was as follows.

Imagine that you have been offered a ticket that will pay you $100 if the afternoon high temperature in [San Francisco/Istanbul] is *at least* 60 degrees Fahrenheit one week from today. What is the most you would be willing to pay for such a ticket?
    The most I would be willing to pay is $___

Imagine that you have been offered a ticket that will pay you $100 if the afternoon high temperature in [San Francisco/Istanbul] is *less than* 60 degrees Fahrenheit one week from today. What is the most you would be willing to pay for such a ticket?
    The most I would be willing to pay is $___

In the noncomparative condition one group of subjects priced the above two bets for San Francisco, and a second group of subjects priced the same two bets for Istanbul. In the comparative condition, subjects performed both tasks, pricing all four bets. The order of the events (less than 60 degrees/at least 60 degrees) and of the cities was counterbalanced. To minimize order effects, all subjects were asked before answering the questions to consider their best guess of the afternoon high temperature in the city or cities on which they were asked to bet.

Subjects were 189 pedestrians on the University of California at Berkeley campus who completed a five-minute survey (that included a few unrelated items) in exchange for a California lottery ticket. Ten subjects who violated dominance were excluded from the analysis. There were no significant order effects. Let $c(SF \geq 60)$ denote willingness to pay for the prospect "Win $100 if the high temperature in San Francisco one week from today is at least 60 degrees," etc. As in Study 3 we added for each subject his or her willingness to pay for both sides of complementary bets. In particular, we computed $c(SF \geq 60) + c(SF < 60)$ for the San Francisco bets and $c(Ist \geq 60) + c(Ist < 60)$ for the Istanbul bets. Table 12.5 presents the means of these sums. The results again support our hypothesis. In the comparative condition subjects were willing to pay on average $15.84 more to bet on familiar San Francisco

Table 12.5
Results of Study 4

	San Francisco bets		Istanbul bets	
Comparative	$40.53		$24.69	
	(4.27)	N = 90	(3.09)	N = 90
Noncomparative	$39.89		$38.37	
	(5.06)	N = 44	(6.10)	N = 45

temperature than on unfamiliar Istanbul temperature ($t(89)$ = 5.05, $p < 0.001$). However, in the noncomparative condition subjects were willing to pay on average a scant $1.52 more to bet on San Francisco than on Istanbul ($t(87)$ = 0.19, n.s.). This interaction is significant ($z = 1.68$, $p < 0.05$).

The same pattern holds for the individual bets. In the comparative condition, $c(SF \geq 60)$ = $22.74 and $c(Ist \geq 60)$ = $15.21 ($t(89)$ = 3.13, $p < 0.01$). Similarly, $c(SF < 60)$ = $17.79 and $c(Ist < 60)$ = $9.49 ($t(89)$ = 4.25, $p < 0.001$). In the noncomparative condition, however, $c(SF \geq 60)$ = $21.95 and $c(Ist \geq 60)$ = $21.07 ($t(87)$ = 0.17, n.s.). Similarly, $c(SF < 60)$ = $17.94 and $c(Ist < 60)$ = $17.29 ($t(87)$ = 0.13, n.s.). Thus, subjects in the comparative condition were willing to pay significantly more for either side of the San Francisco proposition than they were willing to pay for the corresponding sides of the Istanbul proposition. However, no such pattern is evident in the noncomparative condition. Note that unlike the effect observed in studies 1 and 2, the present effect is produced by the reduction in the attractiveness of the less familiar bet.

Study 5

We have interpreted the results of the preceding studies in terms of comparative ignorance. Alternatively, it might be argued that these results can be explained at least in part by the more general hypothesis that the difference between cash equivalents of prospects evaluated in isolation will be enhanced by a direct comparison between them. Such enhancement would apply whether or not the prospects in question involve different sources of uncertainty that vary with respect to familiarity or ambiguity.

To test this hypothesis, we recruited 129 Stanford undergraduates to answer a one-page questionnaire. Subjects were asked to state their maximum willingness to pay for hypothetical bets that offered $100 if the daytime high temperature in Palo Alto (where Stanford is located) on a particular day falls in a specified range. The two bets were described as follows:

[A] Imagine that you have been offered a ticket that will pay you $100 if the afternoon high temperature *two weeks* from today in Palo Alto is *more than* 70 degrees Fahrenheit. What is the most you would be willing to pay for such a ticket?

The most I would be willing to pay is $___

Table 12.6
Results of Study 5

	Bet A		Bet B	
Comparative	$25.77		$6.42	
	(3.68)	$N = 47$	(1.84)	$N = 47$
Noncomparative	$23.07		$5.32	
	(3.42)	$N = 42$	(1.27)	$N = 40$

[B] Imagine that you have been offered a ticket that will pay you $100 if the afternoon high temperature *three weeks* from today in Palo Alto is *less than* 65 degrees Fahrenheit. What is the most you would be willing to pay for such a ticket?

The most I would be willing to pay is $___

Subjects in the comparative condition evaluated both [A] and [B] (the order was counter-balanced). Approximately half the subjects in the noncomparative condition evaluated [A] alone, and the remaining subjects evaluated [B] alone.

Because Palo Alto temperature in the springtime (when the study was conducted) is more likely to be above 70 degrees than below 65 degrees, we expected bet [A] to be generally more attractive than bet [B]. The enhancement hypothesis, therefore, implies that the difference between $c(A)$ and $c(B)$ will be greater in the comparative than in the noncomparative condition. The mean values of $c(A)$ and $c(B)$ are presented in table 12.6. The results do not support the enhancement hypothesis. In this study, $c(A)$ was greater than $c(B)$. However, the difference $c(A) - c(B)$ was roughly the same in the two conditions (interaction $z = 0.32$, n.s). In fact, there were no significant differences between the comparative and noncomparative conditions in the cash equivalents of either prospect ($t(87) = 0.53$ for A, n.s.; $t(85) = 0.48$ for B, n.s.). This pattern contrasts sharply with the results of the preceding studies (see especially table 12.5), which reveal substantially larger differences between stated prices in the comparative than in the noncomparative conditions. We conclude that the comparative ignorance effect observed in studies 1–4 cannot be explained by the more general enhancement hypothesis.

Study 6

The comparative ignorance hypothesis attributes ambiguity aversion to the contrast between states of knowledge. In the first four studies we provided subjects with a comparison between more and less familiar events. In our final study we provided subjects with a comparison between themselves and more knowledgeable individuals.

Subjects were undergraduates at San Jose State University. The following hypothetical problem was included in a questionnaire containing several unrelated items that subjects completed for class credit.

Kaufman Broad Homes (KBH) is one of the largest home sellers in America. Their stock is traded on the New York Stock Exchange.

[1] Do you think that KBH stock will close higher or lower Monday than it did yesterday? (Circle one)

• KBH will close higher.
• KBH will close the same or lower.

[2] Which would you prefer? (Circle one)

• receive $50 for sure
• receive $150 if my prediction about KBH is correct.

Subjects in the noncomparative condition ($N = 31$) answered the above questions. Subjects in the comparative condition ($N = 32$) answered the same questions with the following additional item inserted between questions 1 and 2.

We are presenting this survey to undergraduates at San Jose State University, graduate students in economics at Stanford University, and to professional stock analysts.

Subjects were then asked to rate their knowledge of the item on a scale from 0 to 10.

The present account implies that the suggested comparison to more knowledgeable individuals (i.e., graduate students in economics and professional stock analysts) will undermine the subjects' sense of competence and consequently decrease their willingness to bet on their own judgment. The results support this prediction. The uncertain prospect of winning $150 was preferred to the sure payment of $50 by 68% of subjects in the noncomparative condition and by only 41% of subjects in the comparative condition ($\chi^2(1) = 4.66$, $p < 0.05$).

We replicated this effect using a different subject population (undergraduates at Stanford University enrolled in an introductory psychology course) and a different uncertain event. The following hypothetical problem was included in a questionnaire that contained several unrelated items that was completed for class credit.

[1] Do you think that the inflation rate in Holland over the past 12 months is greater than or less than 3.0%? (Circle one)

• *less than* 3.0%
• *at least* 3.0%

[2] Which of the following do your prefer? (Circle one)

• receive $50 for sure
• receive $150 if I am right about the inflation rate.

As before, subjects in the noncomparative condition ($N = 39$) evaluated the items above, and subjects in the comparative condition ($N = 37$) answered the same questions with the following additional item inserted between questions [1] and [2].

We are presenting this survey to undergraduates in Psych 1, graduate students in economics, and to professional business forecasters.

Subjects were then asked to rate their knowledge of the item on a scale from 0 to 10.

The uncertain prospect was preferred to the sure payment by 38% of subjects in the non-comparative condition and by only 11% of subjects in the comparative condition ($\chi^2(1)$ = 7.74, $p < 0.01$). Thus, the tendency to bet on a vague event is reduced by a suggested comparison to more knowledgeable individuals. Note that the results of this study, obtained by the mere mention of a more expert population, should be distinguished from the finding of Curley, Yates, and Abrams (1986) that ambiguity aversion is enhanced when people anticipate that their decision will be evaluated by their peers.

Market Experiments

Before we turn to the implications of the present findings, the question arises whether the effects of ambiguity and comparative ignorance persist when decision makers are given an opportunity to make multiple decisions in a market setting that provides incentives and immediate feedback. A positive answer to this question has been provided by Sarin and Weber (1993), who compared subjects' bids for clear and for vague bets in several experimental markets using sealed bid and double oral auctions. In one series of studies involving graduate students of business administration from Cologne University, the clear bet paid 100 Deutsche Marks (DM) if a yellow ball was drawn from an opaque urn containing ten yellow and ten white tennis balls, and nothing otherwise. The vague bet was defined similarly except that the subject did not know the proportion of yellow and white balls, which was sampled from a uniform distribution. In some studies, subjects traded both clear and vague bets in each market. In other studies, subjects traded clear bets in some markets and vague bets in other markets. Thus, all subjects evaluated both clear and vague bets. The comparative ignorance hypothesis predicts that (1) the clear bet will be generally priced above the vague bet, and (2) the discrepancy between the prices will be more pronounced when clear and vague bets are traded jointly than when they are traded separately. The data support both predictions. The difference between the average market price of the clear and the vague bets across both auction types (for the last trading period in experiments 11 through 14) was more than DM 20 in the joint markets and less than DM 5 in the separate markets. This effect was especially pronounced in the double oral auctions where there was no difference between the market price of the clear and the vague bets in the separate markets and a substantial difference (DM 18.5) in the joint markets. Evidently, market setting is not sufficient to eliminate the effects of ambiguity and comparative ignorance.

Discussion

The preceding studies provide support for the comparative ignorance hypothesis, according to which ambiguity aversion is driven primarily by a comparison between events or between individuals, and it is greatly reduced or eliminated in the absence of such a comparison. We hasten to add that the distinction between comparative and noncomparative assessment refers to the state of mind of the decision maker, which we have attempted to control through the experimental context. Of course, there is no guarantee that subjects in the comparative conditions actually performed the suggested comparison, or that subjects in the noncomparative conditions did not independently generate a comparison. In Ellsberg's two-color problem, for example, people who are presented with the vague urn alone may spontaneously invoke a comparison to a 50–50 urn, especially if they have previously encountered such a problem. However, the consistent results observed in the preceding studies suggest that the experimental manipulation was successful in inducing subjects to make a comparison in one condition but not in the other.

The comparative ignorance hypothesis suggests that when people price an uncertain prospect in isolation (e.g., receive $100 if Istanbul temperature one week from today exceeds 60 degrees), they pay little or no attention to the quality or precision of their assessment of the likelihood of the event in question. However, when people are asked to price this prospect in the context of another prospect (e.g., receive $100 if San Francisco temperature one week from today exceeds 60 degrees), they become sensitive to the contrast in their knowledge regarding the two events, and as a result price the less familiar or vaguer prospect lower than the more familiar or clearer prospect (see, e.g., Heath & Tversky, 1991; Keppe & Weber, 1995). Similarly, an uncertain prospect becomes less attractive when people are made aware that the same prospect will also be evaluated by more knowledgeable individuals. Thus, ambiguity aversion represents a reluctance to act on inferior knowledge, and this inferiority is brought to mind only through a comparison with superior knowledge about other domains or of other people.

Theoretical Implications

The comparative ignorance effect violates the principle of procedure invariance, according to which strategically equivalent elicitation procedures should produce the same preference order (cf. Tversky, Sattath, & Slovic, 1988). In the preceding studies, the vague and clear bets were equally valued when priced in isolation, yet the latter was strictly preferred to the former when the two bets were priced jointly. Like other instances of preference reversal (see, e.g., Tversky & Thaler, 1990), a particular attribute (in this case knowledge of probabilities) looms larger in comparative than in noncomparative evaluation. However, the most noteworthy finding is not the illustration of a new variety of preference reversal, but rather the conclusion that the Ellsberg phenomenon is an inherently comparative effect.

This discrepancy between comparative and noncomparative evaluation raises the question of which preference should be considered more rational. On the one hand, it could be argued that the comparative judgment reflects people's "true" preferences and in the absence of comparison, people fail to properly discount for their ignorance. On the other hand, it might be argued that the noncomparative judgments are more rational, and that subjects are merely intimidated by a comparison with superior knowledge. As we see it, there is no compelling argument to favor one interpretation over the other. The rational theory of choice (or more specifically, the principle of procedure invariance) requires that the comparative and noncomparative evaluations will coincide, but the theory does not provide a method for reconciling inconsistent preferences.

What are the implications of the present findings for the analysis of individual decision making? To answer this question, it is important to distinguish two phenomena that have emerged from the descriptive study of decision under uncertainty: source preference and source sensitivity (Tversky & Fox, 1995; Tversky & Wakker, 1995). Source preference refers to the observation that choices between prospects depend not only on the degree of uncertainty but also on the source of uncertainty (e.g., San Francisco temperature versus Istanbul temperature). Source preference is demonstrated by showing that a person prefers to bet on a proposition drawn from one source than on a proposition drawn from another source, and also prefers to bet against the first proposition than against the second (e.g., $c(SF \geq 60) > c(Ist \geq 60)$ and $c(SF < 60) > c(Ist < 60)$; see study 4 above). We have interpreted ambiguity aversion as a special case of source preference, in which risk is preferred to uncertainty, as in Ellsberg's examples.[1]

Source sensitivity refers to nonadditivity of decision weights. In particular, the descriptive analysis of decision under risk indicates that the impact of a given event on the value of a prospect is greater when it turns an impossibility into a possibility or a possibility into a certainty than when it merely makes an uncertain event more or less probable (Kahneman & Tversky, 1979). For example, increasing the probability of winning a fixed prize from 0 to 0.1 or 0.9 to 1.0 has a greater impact than increasing the probability from, say, 0.3 to 0.4. Tversky and Fox (1995) have further shown that this pattern, called bounded subadditivity, is more pronounced for uncertainty than for chance (i.e., for vague than for clear probabilities). In other words, people are less sensitive to uncertainty to chance, regardless of whether or not they prefer uncertainty than to chance. Thus, source preference and source sensitivity are logically independent.

The present experiments show that source preference, unlike source sensitivity, is an inherently comparative phenomenon, and it does not arise in an independent evaluation of uncertain prospects. This suggests that models based on decision weights or nonadditive probabilities (e.g., Quiggin, 1982; Gilboa, 1987; Schmeidler, 1989; Tversky & Wakker, 1995) can accommodate source sensitivity, but they do not provide a satisfactory account of source preference because they do not distinguish between comparative and noncomparative evaluation. One might attempt to model the comparative ignorance effect using a contingent weighting approach (Tversky, Sattath, & Slovic, 1988) in which the weight associated with an event depends on whether it is evaluated in a comparative or noncomparative context. The major difficulties with this, or any other attempt to model the comparative ignorance effect, is that it requires prior specification of the decision maker's sense of his or her competence regarding the event in question and the salience of alternative states of knowledge. Although these variables can be experimentally manipulated, as we did in the preceding studies, they cannot easily be measured and incorporated into a formal model.

Despite the difficulties in modeling comparative ignorance, it could have significant economic implications. For example, an individual who is knowledgeable about the computer industry but not about the energy industry may exhibit ambiguity aversion in choosing whether to invest in a high-tech startup or an oil exploration, but not when each investment is evaluated independently. Furthermore, the present account suggests that the order in which the two investments are considered could affect their valuation. In particular, the less familiar investment might be valued more when it is considered before rather than after the more familiar investment.[2] In light of the present analysis, recent attempts to model ambiguity aversion in financial markets (e.g., Dow & Ribeiro da Costa Werlang, 1991; Epstein & Wang, 1994) may be incomplete because they do not distinguish between comparative and noncomparative evaluation. In particular, such models are likely to overestimate the degree of ambiguity aversion in settings in which uncertain prospects are evaluated in isolation (cf. Sarin & Weber, 1993). The role of comparative ignorance in economic transactions awaits further empirical investigation.

Acknowledgments

This work was supported by grants SES-9109535 and SBR-9408684 from the National Science Foundation. It has benefited from discussion with Martin Weber.

Notes

1. Some authors have interpreted as ambiguity aversion the finding that people prefer to bet on a more reliable rather than on a less reliable estimate of a given probability p (e.g., Einhorn & Hogarth, 1985). This demonstration, however, does not establish source preference because it does not also consider the complements of the events in question. Hence, the above finding can be attributed to the fact that the

subjective probability associated with the less reliable estimate of p is less extreme (i.e., closer to 0.5) than that associated with the more reliable estimate of p (see Heath & Tversky, 1991, Table 4). More generally, the oft-cited conclusion that people are ambiguity-averse for high probabilities and ambiguity-seeking for small probabilities is questionable because the demonstrations on which it is based do not properly control for variations in subjective probability.

2. Unpublished data, collected by Fox and Weber, showed that an unfamiliar prospect was priced lower when evaluated after a familiar prospect than when evaluated before that prospect.

References

Becker, G., DeGroot, M., & Marschak, J. (1964). Measuring utility by a single-response sequential method. *Behavioral Science, 9*, 226–232.

Camerer, C., & Weber, M. (1992). Recent developments in modeling preferences: Uncertainty and ambiguity. *Journal of Risk and Uncertainty, 5*, 325–370.

Cohen, J., & Hansel, M. (1959). Preferences for different combinations of chance and skill in gambling. *Nature, 183*, 841–843.

Curley, S. P., Yates, J. F., & Abrams, R. A. (1986). Psychological sources of ambiguity avoidance. *Organizational Behavior and Human Decision Processes, 38*, 230–256.

Dow, J., & Ribeiro da Costa Werlang, S. (1991). Uncertainty aversion, risk aversion, and the optimal choice of portfolio. *Econometrica, 60*, 197–204.

Einhorn, H. J., & Hogarth, R. M. (1985). Ambiguity and uncertainty in probabilistic inference. *Psychological Review, 93*, 433–461.

Ellsberg, D. (1961). Risk, ambiguity and the savage axioms. *Quarterly Journal of Economics, 75*, 643–669.

Epstein, L. G., & Wang, T. (1994). Intertemporal asset pricing under Knightian uncertainty. *Econometrica, 62*, 283–322.

Fellner, W. (1961). Distortion of subjective probabilities as a reaction to uncertainty. *Quarterly Journal of Economics, 75*, 670–689.

Frisch, D., & Baron, J. (1988). Ambiguity and rationality. *Journal of Behavioral Decision Making, 1*, 149–157.

Gilboa, I. (1987). Expected utility with purely subjective non-additive probabilities. *Journal of Mathematical Economics, 16*, 65–88.

Heath, C., & Tversky, A. (1991). Preference and belief: Ambiguity and competence in choice under uncertainty. *Journal of Risk and Uncertainty, 4*, 5–28.

Howell, W. (1971). Uncertainty from internal and external sources: A clear case of overconfidence. *Journal of Experimental Psychology, 81*, 240–243.

Kahneman, D., & Tversky, A. (1979). Prospect theory: An analysis of decision under risk. *Econometrica, 47,* 263–291.

Keppe, H.-J., & Weber, M. (1995). Judged knowledge and ambiguity aversion. *Theory and Decision, 39,* 51–77.

Keynes, J. M. (1921). *A treatise on probability.* London, England: Macmillan.

Knight, F. H. (1921). *Risk, uncertainty, and profit.* Boston, MA: Houghton Mifflin.

Quiggin, J. (1982). A theory of anticipated utility. *Journal of Economic Behavior & Organization, 3,* 323–343.

Raiffa, H. (1961). Risk ambiguity and the savage axioms: Comment. *Quarterly Journal of Economics, 75,* 690–694.

Sarin, R. K., & Weber, M. (1993). Effects of ambiguity in market experiments. *Management Science, 39,* 602–615.

Savage, L. J. (1954). *The foundation of statistics.* New York, NY: John Wiley & Sons.

Schmeidler, D. (1989). Subjective probability and expected utility without additivity. *Econometrica, 57,* 571–587.

Tversky, A., & Fox, C. R. (1995). Weighing risk and uncertainty. *Psychological Review, 102,* 269–283.

Tversky, A., Sattath, S., & Slovic, P. (1988). Contingent weighting in judgment and choice. *Psychological Review, 95,* 371–384.

Tversky, A., & Thaler, R. (1990). Preference reversals. *Journal of Economic Perspectives, 4,* 201–211.

Tversky, A., & Wakker, P. (1995). Risk attitudes and decision weights. *Econometrica, 63,* 1255–1280.

13 Support Theory: A Nonextensional Representation of Subjective Probability

Amos Tversky and Derek J. Koehler

Both laypeople and experts are often called on to evaluate the probability of uncertain events such as the outcome of a trial, the result of a medical operation, the success of a business venture, or the winner of a football game. Such assessments play an important role in deciding, respectively, whether to go to court, undergo surgery, invest in the venture, or bet on the home team. Uncertainty is usually expressed in verbal terms (e.g., unlikely or probable), but numerical estimates are also common. Weather forecasters, for example, often report the probability of rain (Murphy, 1985), and economists are sometimes required to estimate the chances of recession (Zarnowitz, 1985). The theoretical and practical significance of subjective probability has inspired psychologists, philosophers, and statisticians to investigate this notion from both descriptive and prescriptive standpoints.

Indeed, the question of whether degree of belief can, or should be, represented by the calculus of chance has been the focus of a long and lively debate. In contrast to the Bayesian school, which represents degree of belief by an additive probability measure, there are many skeptics who question the possibility and wisdom of quantifying subjective uncertainty and are reluctant to apply the laws of chance to the analysis of belief. Besides the Bayesians and the skeptics, there is a growing literature on what might be called revisionist models of subjective probability. These include the Dempster–Shafer theory of belief (Dempster, 1967; Shafer, 1976), Zadeh's (1978) possibility theory, and the various types of upper and lower probabilities (e.g., see Suppes, 1974; Walley, 1991). Recent developments have been reviewed by Dubois and Prade (1988), Gilboa and Schmeidler (1994), and Mongin (1994). Like the Bayesians, the revisionists endorse the quantification of belief, using either direct judgments or preferences between bets, but they find the calculus of chance too restrictive for this purpose. Consequently, they replace the additive measure, used in the classical theory, with a nonadditive set function satisfying weaker requirements.

A fundamental assumption that underlies both the Bayesian and the revisionist models of belief is the extensionality principle: Events with the same extension are assigned the same probability. However, the extensionality assumption is descriptively invalid because alternative descriptions of the same event often produce systematically different judgments. The following three examples illustrate this phenomenon and motivate the development of a descriptive theory of belief that is free from the extensionality assumption.

1. Fischhoff, Slovic, and Lichtenstein (1978) asked car mechanics, as well as laypeople, to assess the probabilities of different causes of a car's failure to start. They found that the mean probability assigned to the residual hypothesis—"The cause of failure is something other than the battery, the fuel system, or the engine"—increased from 0.22 to 0.44 when the hypothesis was broken up into more specific causes (e.g., the starting system, the ignition system). Although the car mechanics, who had an average of 15 years of experience, were surely aware of these possibilities, they discounted hypotheses that were not explicitly mentioned.

2. Tversky and Kahneman (1983) constructed many problems in which both probability and frequency judgments were not consistent with set inclusion. For example, one group of subjects was asked to estimate the number of seven-letter words in four pages of a novel that end with *ing*. A second group was asked to estimate the number of seven-letter words that end with _*n*_. The median estimate for the first question (13.4) was nearly three times higher than that for the second (4.7), presumably because it is easier to think of seven-letter words ending with *ing* than to think of seven-letter words with *n* in the sixth position. It appears that most people who evaluated the second category were not aware of the fact that it includes the first.

3. Violations of extensionality are not confined to probability judgments; they are also observed in the evaluation of uncertain prospects. For example, Johnson, Hershey, Meszaros, and Kunreuther (1993) found that subjects who were offered (hypothetical) health insurance that covers hospitalization for any disease or accident were willing to pay a higher premium than subjects who were offered health insurance that covers hospitalization for any reason. Evidently, the explicit mention of disease and accident increases the perceived chances of hospitalization and, hence, the attractiveness of insurance.

These observations, like many others described later in this article, are inconsistent with the extensionality principle. We distinguish two sources of nonextensionality. First, extensionality may fail because of memory limitation. As illustrated in example 2, a judge cannot be expected to recall all of the instances of a category, even when he or she can recognize them without error. An explicit description could remind people of relevant cases that might otherwise slip their minds. Second, extensionality may fail because different descriptions of the same event may call attention to different aspects of the outcome and thereby affect their relative salience. Such effects can influence probability judgments even when they do not bring to mind new instances or new evidence.

The common failures of extensionality, we suggest, represent an essential feature of human judgment, not a collection of isolated examples. They indicate that probability judgments are attached not to events but to descriptions of events. In this article, we present a theory in which the judged probability of an event depends on the explicitness of its description. This treatment, called *support theory*, focuses on direct judgments of probability, but it is also applicable to decision under uncertainty. The basic theory is introduced and characterized in the next section. The experimental evidence is reviewed in the subsequent section. In the final section, we extend the theory to ordinal judgments, discuss upper and lower indicators of belief, and address descriptive and prescriptive implications of the present development.

Support Theory

Let T be a finite set including at least two elements, interpreted as states of the world. We assume that exactly one state obtains but it is generally not known to the judge. Subsets of T are called *events*. We distinguish between events and descriptions of events, called *hypotheses*. Let H be a set of hypotheses that describe the events in T. Thus, we assume that each hypothesis $A \in$ H corresponds to a unique event $A' \subset$ T. This is a many-to-one mapping because different hypotheses, say A and B, may have the same extension (i.e., $A' = B'$). For example, suppose one rolls a pair of dice. The hypotheses "The sum is 3" and "The product is 2" are different descriptions of the same event; namely, one die shows 1 and the other shows 2. We assume that H is finite and that it includes at least one hypothesis for each event. The following relations on H are induced by the corresponding relations on T. A is *elementary* if $A' \in$ T. A is *null* if $A' = \varnothing$. A and B are *exclusive* if $A' \cap B' = \varnothing$. If A and B are in H, and they are exclusive, then their explicit disjunction, denoted $A \vee B$, is also in H. Thus, H is closed under exclusive disjunction. We assume that $\vee$ is associative and commutative and that $(A \vee B)' = A' \cup B'$.

A key feature of the present formulation is the distinction between explicit and implicit disjunctions. A is an *implicit disjunction*, or simply an implicit hypothesis, if it is neither elementary nor null, and it is not an explicit disjunction (i.e., there are no exclusive non-null B, C in H such that $A = B \vee C$). For example, suppose A is "Ann majors in a natural science," B is "Ann majors in a biological science," and C is "Ann majors in a physical science." The explicit disjunction, $B \vee C$ ("Ann majors in either a biological or a physical science"), has the same extension as A (i.e., $A' = (B \vee C)' = B' \cup C'$), but A is an implicit hypothesis because it is not an explicit disjunction. Note that the explicit disjunction $B \vee C$ is defined for any exclusive $B, C \in$ H, whereas a coextensional implicit disjunction may not exist because some events cannot be naturally described without listing their components.

An *evaluation frame* (A, B) consists of a pair of exclusive hypotheses: The first element A is the *focal* hypothesis that the judge evaluates, and the second element B is the *alternative* hypothesis. To simplify matters, we assume that when A and B are exclusive, the judge perceives them as such, but we do not assume that the judge can list all of the constituents of an implicit disjunction. In terms of the above example, we assume that the judge knows, for instance, that genetics is a biological science, that astronomy is a physical science, and that the biological and the physical sciences are exclusive. However, we do not assume that the judge can list all of the biological or the physical sciences. Thus, we assume recognition of inclusion but not perfect recall.

We interpret a person's probability judgment as a mapping P from an evaluation frame to the unit interval. To simplify matters we assume that $P(A, B)$ equals zero if and only if A is null and that it equals one if and only if B is null; we assume that A and B are not both null. Thus, $P(A, B)$ is the judged probability that A rather than B holds, assuming that one and only one of them is valid. Obviously, A and B may each represent an explicit or an implicit disjunction. The extensional counterpart of $P(A, B)$ in the standard theory is the conditional probability $P(A' \mid A' \cup B')$. The present treatment is nonextensional because it assumes that probability judgment depends on the descriptions A and B, not just on the events A' and B'. We wish to emphasize that the present theory applies to the hypotheses entertained by the judge, which do not always coincide with the given verbal descriptions. A judge presented with an implicit disjunction may, nevertheless, think about it as an explicit disjunction, and vice versa.

Support theory assumes that there is a ratio scale s (interpreted as degree of support) that assigns to each hypothesis in H a nonnegative real number such that, for any pair of exclusive hypotheses $A, B \in$ H,

$$P(A, B) = \frac{s(A)}{s(A) + s(B)}. \tag{1}$$

If B and C are exclusive, A is implicit, and $A' = (B \vee C)'$, then

$$s(A) \leq s(B \vee C) = s(B) + s(C). \tag{2}$$

Equation 1 provides a representation of subjective probability in terms of the support of the focal and the alternative hypotheses. Equation 2 states that the support of an implicit disjunction A is less than or equal to that of a coextensional explicit disjunction $B \vee C$ that equals the sum of the support of its components. Thus, support is additive for explicit disjunctions and subadditive for implicit ones.

The subadditivity assumption, we suggest, represents a basic principle of human judgment. When people assess their degree of belief in an implicit disjunction, they do not normally unpack the hypothesis into its exclusive components and add their support, as required by extensionality. Instead, they tend to form a global impression that is based primarily on the most representative or available cases. Because this mode of judgment is selective rather than exhaustive, unpacking tends to increase support. In other words, we propose that the support of a summary representation of an implicit hypothesis is generally less than the sum of the support of its exclusive components. Both memory and attention may contribute to this effect. Unpacking a category (e.g., death from an unnatural cause) into its components (e.g., homicide, fatal car accidents, drowning) might remind people of possibilities that would not have been considered otherwise. Moreover, the explicit mention of an outcome tends to enhance its salience and hence its support. Although this assumption may fail in some circumstances, the overwhelming evidence for subadditivity, described in the next section, indicates that these failures represent the exception rather than the rule.

The support associated with a given hypothesis is interpreted as a measure of the strength of evidence in favor of this hypothesis that is available to the judge. The support may be based on objective data (e.g., the frequency of homicide in the relevant population) or on a subjective impression mediated by judgmental heuristics, such as representativeness, availability, or anchoring and adjustment (Kahneman, Slovic, & Tversky, 1982). For example, the hypothesis "Bill is an accountant" may be evaluated by the degree to which Bill's personality matches the stereotype of an accountant, and the prediction "An oil spill along the eastern coast before the end of next year" may be assessed by the ease with which similar accidents come to mind. Support may also reflect reasons or arguments recruited by the judge in favor of the hypothesis in question (e.g., if the defendant were guilty, he would not have reported the crime). Because judgments based on impressions and reasons are often nonextensional, the support function is nonmonotonic with respect to set inclusion. Thus, $s(B)$ may exceed $s(A)$ even though $A' \supset B'$. Note, however, that $s(B)$ cannot exceed $s(B \vee C)$. For example, if the support of a category is determined by the availability of its instances, then the support of the hypothesis that a randomly selected word ends with *ing* can exceed the support of the hypothesis that the word ends with _n_. Once the inclusion relation between the categories is made transparent, the _n_ hypothesis is replaced by "*ing* or any other _n_," whose support exceeds that of the *ing* hypothesis.

The present theory provides an interpretation of subjective probability in terms of relative support. This interpretation suggests that, in some cases, probability judgment may be predicted from independent assessments of support. This possibility is explored later. The following discussion shows that, under the present theory, support can be derived from probability judgments, much as utility is derived from preferences between options.

Consequences

Support theory has been formulated in terms of the support function s, which is not directly observable. We next characterize the theory in terms of the observed index P. We first exhibit four consequences of the theory and then show that they imply equations 1 and 2. An immediate consequence of the theory is *binary complementarity:*

$$P(A, B) + P(B, A) = 1. \tag{3}$$

A second consequence is *proportionality:*

$$\frac{P(A, B)}{P(B, A)} = \frac{P(A, B \vee C)}{P(B, A \vee C)}, \tag{4}$$

provided that A, B, and C are mutually exclusive and B is not null. Thus, the "odds" for A against B are independent of the additional hypothesis C.

To formulate the next condition, it is convenient to introduce the probability ratio $R(A, B) = P(A, B)/P(B, A)$, which is the odds for A against B. Equation 1 implies the following *product rule:*

$$R(A, B)R(C, D) = R(A, D)R(C, B), \tag{5}$$

provided that A, B, C, and D are not null and the four pairs of hypotheses in equation 5 are pairwise exclusive. Thus, the product of the odds for A against B and for C against D equals the product of the odds for A against D and for C against B. To see the necessity of the product rule, note that, according to equation 1, both sides of equation 5 equal $s(A)s(C)/s(B)s(D)$. Essentially the same condition has been used in the theory of preference trees (Tversky & Sattath, 1979).

Equations 1 and 2 together imply the *unpacking principle*. Suppose B, C, and D are mutually exclusive, A is implicit, and $A' = (B \vee C)'$. Then

$$P(A, D) \leq P(B \vee C, D) = P(B, C \vee D) + P(C, B \vee D). \tag{6}$$

The properties of s entail the corresponding properties of P: Judged probability is additive for explicit disjunctions and subadditive for implicit disjunctions. In other words, unpacking an implicit disjunction may increase, but not decrease, its judged probability. Unlike equations 3–5, which hold in the standard theory of probability, the unpacking principle (equation 6) generalizes the classical model. Note that this assumption is at variance with lower probability models, including Shafer's (1976), which assume extensionality and superadditivity (i.e., $P(A' \cup B') \geq P(A') + P(B')$ if $A' \cap B' = \emptyset$.

There are two conflicting intuitions that yield nonadditive probability. The first intuition, captured by support theory, suggests that unpacking an implicit disjunction enhances the salience of its components and consequently increases support. The second intuition, captured by Shafer's (1976) theory, among others, suggests that—in the face of partial ignorance—the judge holds some measure of belief "in reserve" and does not distribute it among all elementary hypotheses, as required by the Bayesian model. Although Shafer's theory is based on a logical rather than a psychological analysis of belief, it has also been interpreted by several authors as a descriptive model. Thus, it provides a natural alternative to be compared with the present theory.

Whereas proportionality (equation 4) and the product rule (equation 5) have not been systematically tested before, a number of investigators have observed binary complementarity (equation 3) and some aspects of the unpacking principle (equation 6). These data, as well as several new studies, are reviewed in the next section. The following theorem shows that the above conditions are not only necessary but also sufficient for support theory. The proof is given in the appendix.

THEOREM 1   Suppose $P(A, B)$ is defined for all exclusive $A, B \in H$ and that it vanishes if and only if A is null. Equations 3–6 hold if and only if there exists a nonnegative ratio scale s on H that satisfies equations 1 and 2.

The theorem shows that if probability judgments satisfy the required conditions, it is possible to scale the support or strength of evidence associated with each hypothesis without assuming that hypotheses with the same extension have equal support. An ordinal generalization of the theory, in which P is treated as an ordinal rather than a cardinal scale, is presented in the final section. In the remainder of this section, we introduce a representation of subadditivity and a treatment of conditioning.

Subadditivity

We extend the theory by providing a more detailed representation of subadditivity. Let A be an implicit hypothesis with the same extension as the explicit disjunction of the elementary hypotheses $A_1, \ldots, A_n$; that is, $A' = (A_1 \vee \cdots \vee A_n)'$. Assume that any two elementary hypotheses, B and C, with the same extension have the same support; that is, $B', C' \in T$ and $B' = C'$ implies $s(B) = s(C)$. It follows that, under this assumption, we can write

$$s(A) = w_{1A}s(A_1) + \cdots + w_{nA}s(A_n), \quad 0 \le w_{iA} \le 1, i = 1, \ldots, n. \tag{7}$$

In this representation, the support of each elementary hypothesis is "discounted" by its respective weight, which reflects the degree to which the judge attends to the hypothesis in question. If $w_{iA} = 1$ for all i, then $s(A)$ is the sum of the support of its elementary hypotheses, as in an explicit disjunction. By contrast, $w_{jA} = 0$ for some j indicates that A_j is effectively ignored. Finally, if the weights add to one, then $s(A)$ is a weighted average of the $s(A_i)$, $1 \le i \le n$. We hasten to add that equation 7 should not be interpreted as a process of deliberate discounting in which the judge assesses the support of an implicit disjunction by discounting the assessed support of the corresponding explicit disjunction. Instead, the weights are meant to represent the result of an assessment process in which the judge evaluates A without explicitly unpacking it into its elementary components. It should also be kept in mind that elementary hypotheses are defined relative to a given sample space. Such hypotheses may be broken down further by refining the level of description.

Note that whereas the support function is unique, except for a unit of measurement, the "local" weights w_{iA} are not uniquely determined by the observed probability judgments. These data, however, determine the "global" weights w_A defined by

$$s(A) = w_A[s(A_1) + \cdots + s(A_n)], \quad 0 \le w_A \le 1. \tag{8}$$

The global weight w_A, which is the ratio of the support of the corresponding implicit (A) and explicit ($A_1 \vee \cdots \vee A_n$) disjunctions, provides a convenient measure of the degree of subadditivity induced by A. The degree of subadditivity, we propose, is influenced by several factors, one of which is the interpretation of the probability scale. Specifically, subadditivity is expected to be more pronounced when probability is interpreted as a propensity of an individual case than when it is equated with, or estimated by, relative frequency. Kahneman and Tversky (1979, 1982) referred to these modes of judgment as singular and distributional, respectively, and argued that the latter is usually more accurate than the former[1] (see also Reeves & Lockhart, 1993). Although many events of interest cannot be interpreted in frequentistic terms, there are questions that can be framed in either a distributional or a singular mode. For example, people may be asked to assess the probability that an individual, selected at random from the general population, will die as a result of an accident. Alternatively, people may be asked to assess the percentage (or relative frequency) of the population that will die as a result of an accident. We propose that the implicit disjunction "accident" is more readily unpacked into its components (e.g., car accidents, plane crashes, fire, drowning, poisoning) when the judge considers the entire population rather than a single person. The various causes of death are all represented in the population's mortality statistics but not in the death of a single person. More generally, we propose that the tendency to unpack an implicit disjunction is stronger in the distributional than in the singular mode. Hence, a frequentistic formulation is expected to produce less discounting (i.e., higher ws) than a formulation that refers to an individual case.

Conditioning

Recall that $P(A, B)$ is interpreted as the conditional probability of A, given A or B. To obtain a general treatment of conditioning, we enrich the hypothesis set H by assuming that if A and B are distinct elements of H, then their conjunction, denoted AB, is also in H. Naturally, we assume that conjunction is associative and commutative and that $(AB)' = A' \cap B'$. We also assume distributivity, that is, $A(B \vee C) = AB \vee AC$. Let $P(A, B \mid D)$ be the judged probability that A rather than B holds, given some data D. In general, new evidence (i.e., a different state of information) gives rise to a new support function s_D that describes the revision of s in light of D. In the special case in which the data can be described as an element of H, which merely restricts the hypotheses under consideration, we can represent conditional probability by

$$P(A, B \mid D) = \frac{s(AD)}{s(AD) + s(BD)},$$ (9)

provided that A and B are exclusive but $A \vee B$ and D are not.

Several comments on this form are in order. First, note that if s is additive, then equation 9 reduces to the standard definition of conditional probability. If s is subadditive, as we have assumed throughout, then judged probability depends not only on the description of the focal and the alternative hypotheses but also on the description of the evidence D. Suppose $D' = (D_1 \vee D_2)'$, D_1 and D_2 are exclusive, and D is implicit. Then

$$P(A, B \mid D_1 \vee D_2) = \frac{s(AD_1 \vee D_2)}{s(AD_1 \vee AD_2) + s(BD_1 \vee BD_2)}.$$

But because $s(AD) \leq s(AD_1 \vee AD_2)$ and $s(BD) \leq s(BD_1 \vee BD_2)$ by subadditivity, the unpacking of D may favor one hypothesis over another. For example, the judged probability that a woman earns a very high salary given that she is a university professor is likely to increase when "university" is unpacked into "law school, business school, medical school, or any other school" because of the explicit mention of high-paying positions. Thus, equation 9 extends the application of subadditivity to the representation of evidence. As we show later, it also allows us to compare the impact of different bodies of evidence, provided they can be described as elements of H.

Consider a collection of $n \geq 3$ mutually exclusive and exhaustive (non-null) hypotheses, $A_1 \ldots A_n$, and let $\bar{A}_i$ denote the negation of A_i that corresponds to an implicit disjunction of the remaining hypotheses. Consider two items of evidence, $B, C \in$ H, and suppose that each A_i is more compatible with B than with C in the sense that $s(BA_i) \geq s(CA_i)$, $1 \leq i \leq n$. We propose that B induces more subadditivity than C so that $s(B\bar{A}_i)$ is discounted more heavily than $s(C\bar{A}_i)$ (i.e., $w_{B\bar{A}_i} \leq w_{C\bar{A}_i}$; see equation 7). This assumption, called *enhancement*, suggests that the assessments of $P(A_i, \bar{A}_i \mid B)$ will be generally higher than those of $P(A_i, \bar{A}_i \mid C)$. More specifically, we propose that the sum of the probabilities of $A_i \ldots A_n$, each evaluated by different judges,[2] is no smaller under B than under C. That is,

$$\sum_{i=1}^{n} P(A_i, \bar{A}_i \mid B) \geq \sum_{i=1}^{n} P(A_i, \bar{A}_i \mid C).$$ (10)

Subadditivity implies that both sums are greater than or equal to one. The preceding inequality states that the sum is increased by evidence that is more compatible with the hypotheses under study. It is noteworthy that enhancement suggests that people are inappropriately responsive to the prior probability of the data, whereas base-rate neglect indicates that people are not sufficiently responsive to the prior probability of the hypotheses. The following schematic example illustrates an implication of enhancement and compares it with other models.

Suppose that a murder was committed by one (and only one) of several suspects. In the absence of any specific evidence, assume that all suspects are considered about equally likely to have committed the crime. Suppose further that a preliminary investigation has uncovered a body of evidence (e.g., motives and opportunities) that implicates each of the suspects to roughly the same degree. According to the Bayesian model, the probabilities of all of the suspects remain unchanged because the new evidence is nondiagnostic. In Shafer's theory of belief functions, the judged probability that the murder was committed by one suspect rather than by another generally increases with the amount of evidence; thus, it should be higher after the investigation than before. Enhancement yields a different pattern: The binary probabilities (i.e., of one suspect against another) are expected to be approximately one half, both before and after the investigation, as in the Bayesian model. However, the probability that the murder was committed by a particular suspect (rather than by any of the others) is expected to increase with the amount of evidence. Experimental tests of enhancement are described in the next section.

Data

In this section, we discuss the experimental evidence for support theory. We show that the interpretation of judged probability in terms of a normalized subadditive support function provides a unified account of several phenomena reported in the literature; it also yields new predictions that have not been tested heretofore. This section consists of four parts. In the first part, we investigate the effect of unpacking and examine factors that influence the degree of subadditivity. In the second, we relate probability judgments to direct ratings of evidence strength. In the third, we investigate the enhancement effect and compare alternative models of belief. In the final part, we discuss the conjunction effect, hypothesis generation, and decision under uncertainty.

Studies of Unpacking

Recall that the unpacking principle (equation 6) consists of two parts: additivity for explicit disjunctions and subadditivity for implicit disjunctions, which jointly entail nonextensionality. (Binary complementarity [equation 3] is a special case of additivity.) Because each part alone is subject to alternative interpretations, it is important to test additivity and subadditivity simultaneously. For this reason, we first describe several new studies that have tested both parts of the unpacking principle within the same experiment, and then we review previous research that provided the impetus for the present theory.

Study 1: Causes of Death   Our first study followed the seminal work of Fischhoff et al. (1978) on fault trees, using a task similar to that studied by Russo and Kolzow (1992). We asked Stanford undergraduates ($N = 120$) to assess the likelihood of various possible causes of death. The subjects were informed that each year approximately 2 million people in the United States (nearly 1% of the population) die from different causes, and they were asked to estimate the probability of death from a variety of causes. Half of the subjects considered a single person who had recently died and assessed the probability that he or she had died from each in a list of specified causes. They were asked to assume that the person in question had been randomly selected from the set of people who had died the previous year. The other half, given a frequency judgment task, assessed the percentage of the 2 million deaths in the previous year attributable to each cause. In each group, half of the subjects were promised that the five most accurate subjects would receive $20 each.

Each subject evaluated one of two different lists of causes, constructed such that he or she evaluated either an implicit hypothesis (e.g., death resulting from natural causes) or a coextensional explicit disjunction (e.g., death resulting from heart disease, cancer, or some other natural cause), but not both. The full set of causes considered is listed in table 13.1. Causes of death were divided into natural and unnatural types. Each type had three components, one of which was further divided into seven subcomponents. To avoid very small probabilities, we conditioned these seven subcomponents on the corresponding type of death (i.e., natural or unnatural). To provide subjects with some anchors, we informed them that the probability or frequency of death resulting from respiratory illness is about 7.5% and the probability or frequency of death resulting from suicide is about 1.5%.

Table 13.1 shows that, for both probability and frequency judgments, the mean estimate of an implicit disjunction (e.g., death from a natural cause) is smaller than the sum of the mean estimates of its components (heart disease, cancer, or other natural causes), denoted Σ (natural causes). Specifically, the former equals 58%, whereas the latter equals 22% + 18% + 33% = 73%. All eight comparisons in table 13.1 are statistically significant ($p < 0.05$) by Mann–Whitney U test. (We used a nonparametric test because of the unequal variances involved when comparing a single measured variable with a sum of measured variables.)

Throughout this article, we use the ratio of the probabilities assigned to coextensional explicit and implicit hypotheses as a measure of subadditivity. The ratio in the preceding example is 1.26. This index, called the *unpacking factor*, can be computed directly from probability judgments, unlike w, which is defined in terms of the support function. Subadditivity

Table 13.1

Mean Probability and Frequency Estimates for Causes of Death in Study 1, Comparing Evaluations of Explicit Disjunctions with Coextensional Implicit Disjunctions

Hypothesis	Mean estimate (%)		Actual %
	Probability	Frequency	
Three-component			
P(heart disease)	22	18	34.1
P(cancer)	18	20	23.1
P(other natural cause)	33	29	35.2
$\sum$(natural cause)	73	67	92.4
P(natural cause)	58	56	
Σ/P	1.26	1.20	
P(accident)	32	30	4.4
P(homicide)	10	11	1.1
P(other unnatural cause)	11	12	2.1
$\sum$(unnatural cause)	53	53	7.6
P(unnatural cause)	32	39	
Σ/P	1.66	1.36	
Seven-component			
P(respiratory cancer | natural)	12	11	7.1
P(digestive cancer | natural)	8	7	5.9
P(genitourinary cancer | natural)	5	3	2.7
P(breast cancer | natural)	13	9	2.2
P(urinary cancer | natural)	7	3	1.0
P(leukemia | natural)	8	6	1.0
P(other cancer | natural)	17	10	5.1
$\sum$(cancer|natural)	70	49	25.0
P(cancer | natural)	32	24	
Σ/P	2.19	2.04	
P(auto accident | unnatural)	33	33	30.3
P(firearm accident | unnatural)	7	12	1.3
P(accidental fall | unnatural)	6	4	7.9
P(death in fire | unnatural)	4	5	2.6
P(drowning | unnatural)	5	4	2.6
P(accidental poisoning | unnatural)	4	3	3.9
P(other accident | unnatural)	24	17	9.2
$\sum$(accident|unnatural)	83	78	57.9
P(accident | unnatural)	45	48	
Σ/P	1.84	1.62	

Note: Actual percentages were taken from the 1990 *U.S. Statistical Abstract*. Σ = sum of mean estimates.

is indicated by an unpacking factor greater than 1 and a value of w less than 1. It is noteworthy that subadditivity, by itself, does not imply that explicit hypotheses are overestimated or that implicit hypotheses are underestimated relative to an appropriate objective criterion. It merely indicates that the former are judged as more probable than the latter.

In this study, the mean unpacking factors were 1.37 for the three-component hypotheses and 1.92 for the seven-component hypotheses, indicating that the degree of subadditivity increased with the number of components in the explicit disjunction. An analysis of medians rather than means revealed a similar pattern, with somewhat smaller differences between packed and unpacked versions. Comparison of probability and frequency tasks showed, as expected, that subjects gave higher and thus more subadditive estimates when judging probabilities than when judging frequencies ($F(12, 101) = 2.03$, $p < 0.05$). The average unpacking factors were 1.74 for probability and 1.56 for frequency.

The judgments generally overestimated the actual values, obtained from the 1990 *U.S. Statistical Abstract*. The only clear exception was heart disease, which had an actual probability of 34% but received a mean judgment of 20%. Because subjects produced higher judgments of probability than of frequency, the former exhibited greater overestimation of the actual values, but the correlation between the estimated and actual values (computed separately for each subject) revealed no difference between the two tasks. Monetary incentives did not improve the accuracy of people's judgments.

The following design provides a more stringent test of support theory and compares it with alternative models of belief. Suppose A_1, A_2, and B are mutually exclusive and exhaustive; $A' = (A_1 \vee A_2)'$; A is implicit; and $\bar{A}$ is the negation of A. Consider the following observable valucs:

$\alpha = P(A, B)$;

$\beta = P(A_1 \vee A_2, B)$;

$\gamma_1 = P(A_1; A_2 \vee B)$, $\gamma_2 = P(A_2, A_1 \vee B)$, $\gamma = \gamma_1 + \gamma_2$;   and

$\delta_1 = P(A_1, \bar{A}_1)$, $\delta_2 = (A_2, \bar{A}_2)$, $\delta = \delta_1 + \delta_2$.

Different models of belief imply different orderings of these values:

support theory, $\alpha \leq \beta = \gamma \leq \delta$;

Bayesian model, $\alpha = \beta = \gamma = \delta$;

belief function, $\alpha = \beta \geq \gamma = \delta$;   and

regressive model, $\alpha = \beta \leq \gamma = \delta$.

Support theory predicts $\alpha \leq \beta$ and $\gamma \leq \delta$ due to the unpacking of the focal and residual hypotheses, respectively; it also predicts $\beta = \gamma$ due to the additivity of explicit disjunctions.

The Bayesian model implies $\alpha = \beta$ and $\gamma = \delta$, by extensionality, and $\beta = \gamma$, by additivity. Shafer's theory of belief functions also assumes extensionality, but it predicts $\beta \geq \gamma$ because of super-additivity. The above data, as well as numerous studies reviewed later, demonstrate that $\alpha < \delta$, which is consistent with support theory but inconsistent with both the Bayesian model and Shafer's theory.

The observation that $\alpha < \delta$ could also be explained by a *regressive model* that assumes that probability judgments satisfy extensionality but are biased toward 0.5 (e.g., see Erev, Wallsten, & Budescu, 1994). For example, the judge might start with a "prior" probability of 0.5 that is not revised sufficiently in light of the evidence. Random error could also produce regressive estimates. If each individual judgment is biased toward 0.5, then β, which consists of a single judgment, would be less than γ, which is the sum of two judgments. However, this model predicts no difference between α and β, each of which consists of a single judgment, or between γ and δ, each of which consists of two. Thus, support theory and the regressive model make different predictions about the source of the difference between α and δ. Support theory predicts subadditivity for implicit disjunctions (i.e., $\alpha \leq \beta$ and $\gamma \leq \delta$) and additivity for explicit disjunctions (i.e., $\beta = \gamma$), whereas the regressive model assumes extensionality (i.e., $\alpha = \beta$ and $\gamma = \delta$) and subadditivity for explicit disjunctions (i.e., $\beta \leq \gamma$).

To contrast these predictions, we asked different groups (of 25 to 30 subjects each) to assess the probability of various unnatural causes of death. All subjects were told that a person had been randomly selected from the set of people who had died the previous year from an unnatural cause. The hypotheses under study and the corresponding probability judgments are summarized in table 13.2. The first row, for example, presents the judged probability β that death was caused by an accident or a homicide rather than by some other unnatural cause. In accord with support theory, $\delta = \delta_1 + \delta_2$ was significantly greater than $\gamma = \gamma_1 + \gamma_2$ ($p < 0.05$ by Mann–Whitney U test), but γ was not significantly greater than β,

Table 13.2
Mean and Median Probability Estimates for Various Causes of Death

Probability judgments	Mean	Median
$\beta = P$(accident or homicide, OUC)	64	70
$\gamma_1 = P$(accident, homicide or OUC)	53	60
$\gamma_2 = P$(homicide, accident or OUC)	16	10
$\gamma = \gamma_1 + \gamma_2$	69	70
$\delta^1 = P$(accident, OUC)	56	65
$\delta^2 = P$(homicide, OUC)	24	18
$\delta = \delta_1 + \delta_2$	80	83

Note: OUC = other unnatural causes.

contrary to the prediction of the regressive model. Nevertheless, we do not rule out the possibility that regression toward 0.5 could yield $\beta < \gamma$, which would contribute to the discrepancy between α and $d\delta$. A generalization of support theory that accommodates such a pattern is considered in the final section.

Study 2: Suggestibility and Subadditivity Before turning to additional demonstrations of unpacking, we discuss some methodological questions regarding the elicitation of probability judgments. It could be argued that asking a subject to evaluate a specific hypothesis conveys a subtle (or not so subtle) suggestion that the hypothesis is quite probable. Subjects, therefore, might treat the fact that the hypothesis has been brought to their attention as information about its probability. To address this objection, we devised a task in which the assigned hypotheses carried no information so that any observed subadditivity could not be attributed to experimental suggestion.

Stanford undergraduates ($N = 196$) estimated the percentage of U.S. married couples with a given number of children. Subjects were asked to write down the last digit of their telephone numbers and then to evaluate the percentage of couples having exactly that many children. They were promised that the three most accurate respondents would be awarded $10 each. As predicted, the total percentage attributed to the numbers 0 through 9 (when added across different groups of subjects) greatly exceeded 1. The total of the means assigned by each group was 1.99, and the total of the medians was 1.80. Thus, subadditivity was very much in evidence, even when the selection of focal hypothesis was hardly informative. Subjects overestimated the percentage of couples in all categories, except for childless couples, and the discrepancy between the estimated and the actual percentages was greatest for the modal couple with 2 children. Furthermore, the sum of the probabilities for 0, 1, 2, and 3 children, each of which exceeded 0.25, was 1.45. The observed subadditivity, therefore, cannot be explained merely by a tendency to overestimate very small probabilities.

Other subjects ($N = 139$) were asked to estimate the percentage of U.S. married couples with "less than 3," "3 or more," "less than 5," or "5 or more" children. Each subject considered exactly one of the four hypotheses. The estimates added to 97.5% for the first pair of hypotheses and to 96.3% for the second pair. In sharp contrast to the subadditivity observed earlier, the estimates for complementary pairs of events were roughly additive, as implied by support theory. The finding of binary complementarity is of special interest because it excludes an alternative explanation of subadditivity according to which the evaluation of evidence is biased in favor of the focal hypothesis.

Subadditivity in Expert Judgments Is subadditivity confined to novices, or does it also hold for experts? Redelmeier, Koehler, Liberman, and Tversky (1993) explored this question in the context of medical judgments. They presented physicians at Stanford University

(N = 59) with a detailed scenario concerning a woman who reported to the emergency room with abdominal pain. Half of the respondents were asked to assign probabilities to two specified diagnoses (gastroenteritis and ectopic pregnancy) and a residual category (none of the above); the other half assigned probabilities to five specified diagnoses (including the two presented in the other condition) and a residual category (none of the above). Subjects were instructed to give probabilities that summed to one because the possibilities under consideration were mutually exclusive and exhaustive. If the physicians' judgments conform to the classical theory, then the probability assigned to the residual category in the two-diagnosis condition should equal the sum of the probabilities assigned to its unpacked components in the five-diagnosis condition. Consistent with the predictions of support theory, however, the judged probability of the residual in the two-diagnosis condition (mean = 0.50) was significantly lower than that of the unpacked components in the five-diagnosis condition (mean = 0.69; $p < 0.005$; Mann–Whitney U test).

In a second study, physicians from Tel Aviv University (N = 52) were asked to consider several medical scenarios consisting of a one-paragraph statement including the patient's age, gender, medical history, presenting symptoms, and the results of any tests that had been conducted. One scenario, for example, concerned a 67-year-old man who arrived in the emergency room suffering a heart attack that had begun several hours earlier. Each physician was asked to assess the probability of one of the following four hypotheses: patient dies during this hospital admission (A), patient is discharged alive but dies within 1 year (B), patient lives more than 1 but less than 10 years (C), or patient lives more than 10 years (D). Throughout this article, we refer to these as *elementary judgments* because they pit an elementary hypothesis against its complement, which is an implicit disjunction of all of the remaining elementary hypotheses. After assessing one of these four hypotheses, all respondents assessed $P(A, B)$, $P(B, C)$, and $P(C, D)$ or the complementary set. We refer to these as *binary judgments* because they involve a comparison of two elementary hypotheses.

As predicted, the elementary judgments were substantially subadditive. The means of the four groups in the preceding example were 14% for A, 26% for B, 55% for C, and 69% for D, all of which overestimated the actual values reported in the medical literature. In problems like this, when individual components of a partition are evaluated against the residual, the denominator of the unpacking factor is taken to be 1; thus, the unpacking factor is simply the total probability assigned to the components (summed over different groups of subjects). In this example, the unpacking factor was 1.64. In sharp contrast, the binary judgments (produced by two different groups of physicians) exhibited near-perfect additivity, with a mean total of 100.5% assigned to complementary pairs.

Further evidence for subadditivity in expert judgment has been provided by Fox, Rogers, and Tversky (1994), who investigated 32 professional options traders at the Pacific Stock Exchange. These traders made probability judgments regarding the closing price of Microsoft stock on a given future date (e.g., that it will be less than $88 per share). Microsoft stock is traded at the Pacific Stock Exchange, and the traders are commonly concerned with the prediction of its future value. Nevertheless, their judgments exhibited the predicted pattern of subadditivity and binary complementarity. The average unpacking factor for a fourfold partition was 1.47, and the average sum of complementary binary events was 0.98. Subadditivity in expert judgments has been documented in other domains by Fischhoff et al. (1978), who studied auto mechanics, and by Dube-Rioux and Russo (1988), who studied restaurant managers.

Review of Previous Research   We next review other studies that have provided tests of support theory. Tversky and Fox (1994) asked subjects to assign probabilities to various intervals in which an uncertain quantity might fall, such as the margin of victory in the upcoming Super Bowl or the change in the Dow Jones Industrial Average over the next week. When a given event (e.g., "Buffalo beats Washington") was unpacked into individually evaluated components (e.g., "Buffalo beats Washington by less than 7 points" and "Buffalo beats Washington by at least 7 points"), subjects' judgments were substantially subadditive. Figure 13.1

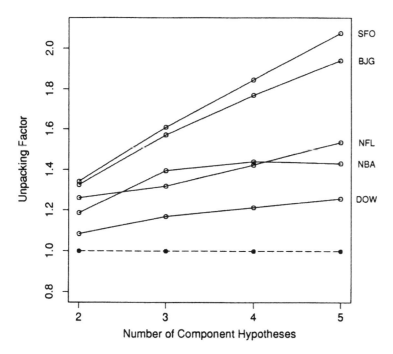

Figure 13.1
Unpacking factors from Tversky and Fox's (1994) data. SFO = San Francisco temperature; BJG = Beijing temperature; NFL = 1991 National Football League Super Bowl; NBA = National Basketball Association playoff; DOW = weekly change in Dow Jones index.

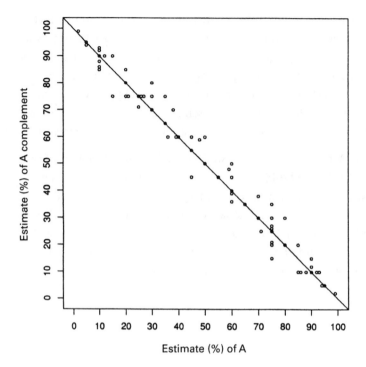

Figure 13.2
A test of binary complementarity based on Tversky and Fox (1994).

plots the unpacking factor obtained in this study as a function of the number of component hypotheses in the explicit disjunction. Judgments for five different types of events are shown: future San Francisco temperature (SFO), future Beijing temperature (BJG), the outcome of the Super Bowl of the National Football League (NFL), the outcome of a playoff game of the National Basketball Association (NBA), and weekly change in the Dow Jones index (DOW). Recall that an unpacking factor greater than 1 (i.e., falling above the dashed line in the plot) indicates subadditivity. The results displayed in figure 13.1 reveal consistent subadditivity for all sources that increases with the number of components in the explicit disjunction.

Figure 13.2 plots the median probabilities assigned to complementary hypotheses. (Each hypothesis is represented twice in the plot, once as the focal hypothesis and once as the complement.) As predicted by support theory, judgments of intervals representing complementary pairs of hypotheses were essentially additive, with no apparent tendency toward either subadditivity or superadditivity.

Further evidence for binary complementarity comes from an extensive study conducted by Wallsten, Budescu, and Zwick (1992),[3] who presented subjects with 300 propositions

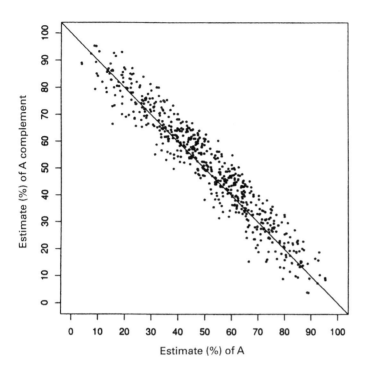

Figure 13.3
A test of binary complementarity based on Wallsten, Budescu, and Zwick (1992).

concerning world history and geography (e.g., "The Monroe Doctrine was proclaimed before the Republican Party was founded") and asked them to estimate the probability that each was true. True and false (complementary) versions of each proposition were presented on different days. Figure 13.3 plots the mean probabilities assigned to each of the propositions in both their true and false versions using the format of figure 13.2. Again, the judgments are additive (mean = 1.02) through the entire range.

We next present a brief summary of the major findings and list both current and previous studies supporting each conclusion.

SUBADDITIVITY   Unpacking an implicit hypothesis into its component hypotheses increases its total judged probability, yielding subadditive judgments. Tables 13.3 and 13.4 list studies that provide tests of the unpacking condition. For each experiment, the probability assigned to the implicit hypothesis and the total probability assigned to its components in the explicit disjunction are listed along with the resulting unpacking factor. All of the listed studies used an experimental design in which the implicit disjunction and the components of the explicit disjunction were evaluated independently, either by separate groups of subjects or by the

Table 13.3

Results of Experiments Using Qualitative Hypotheses: Average Probability Assigned to Coextensional Implicit and Explicit Disjunctions and the Unpacking Factor Measuring the Degree of Subadditivity

Study and topic	n	Explicit P	Implicit P	Unpacking factor
Fischhoff, Slovic, & Lichtenstein (1978)				
Car failure, experiment 1	4	0.54	0.18	3.00
Car failure, experiment 5	2	0.27	0.20	1.35
Car failure, experiment 6 (experts)	4	0.44	0.22	2.00
Mehle, Gettys, Manning, Baca, & Fisher (1981): college majors	6	0.27	0.18	1.50
Russo & Kolzow (1992)				
Causes of death	4	0.55	0.45	1.22
Car failure	4	0.55	0.27	2.04
Koehler & Tversky (1993)				
College majors	4	1.54	1.00[a]	1.54
College majors	5	2.51	1.00[a]	2.51
Study 1: causes of death	3	0.61	0.46	1.33
	7	0.70	0.37	1.86
Study 4: crime stories	4	1.71	1.00[a]	1.71
Study 5: college majors	4	1.76	1.00[a]	1.76

Note: The number of components in the explicit disjunction is denoted by n. Numbered studies with no citation refer to the present article.

[a] Because the components partition the space, it is assumed that a probability of 1.00 would have been assigned to the implicit disjunction.

same subjects but with a substantial number of intervening judgments. The probabilities are listed as a function of the number of components in the explicit disjunction and are collapsed over all other independent variables. Table 13.3 lists studies in which subjects evaluated the probability of qualitative hypotheses (e.g., the probability that Bill W. majors in psychology), and table 13.4 lists studies in which subjects evaluated quantitative hypotheses (e.g., the probability that a randomly selected adult man is between 6 ft. and 6 ft. 2 in. tall).

The tables show that the observed unpacking factors are, without exception, greater than one, indicating consistent subadditivity. The fact that subadditivity is observed both for qualitative and for quantitative hypotheses is instructive. Subadditivity in assessments of qualitative hypotheses can be explained, in part at least, by the failure to consider one or more component hypotheses when the event in question is described in an implicit form. The subadditivity observed in judgments of quantitative hypotheses, however, cannot be explained as a retrieval failure. For example, Teigen (1974b, experiment 2) found that the

Table 13.4

Results of Experiments Using Quantitative Hypotheses: Average Probability Assigned to Coextensional Implicit and Explicit Disjunctions and the Unpacking Factor Measuring the Degree of Subadditivity

Study and topic	n	Explicit P	Implicit P	Unpacking factor
Teigen (1974b)				
Experiment 1: binomial outcomes	2	0.66	0.38	1.73
	3	0.84	0.38	2.21
	5	1.62	1.00[a]	1.62
	9	2.25	1.00[a]	2.25
Teigen (1974b)				
Experiment 2: heights of students	2	0.58	0.36	1.61
	4	1.99	0.76	2.62
	5	2.31	0.75	3.07
	6	2.55	1.00[a]	2.55
Teigen (1974a)				
Experiment 2: binomial outcomes	11	4.25	1.00[a]	4.25
Olson (1976)				
Experiment 1: gender distribution	2	0.13	0.10	1.30
	3	0.36	0.21	1.71
	5	0.68	0.40	1.70
	9	0.97	0.38	2.55
Peterson and Pitz (1988)				
Experiment 3: baseball victories	3	1.58	1.00[a]	1.58
Tversky and Fox (1994):	2	0.77	0.62	1.27
uncertain quantities	3	1.02	0.72	1.46
	4	1.21	0.79	1.58
	5	1.40	0.84	1.27
Study 2: number of children	10	1.99	1.00[a]	1.99

Note: The number of components in the explicit disjunction is denoted by n. Numbered study with no citation refers to the present article.

[a] Because the components partition the space, it is assumed that a probability of 1.00 would have been assigned to the implicit disjunction.

judged proportion of college students whose heights fell in a given interval increased when that interval was broken into several smaller intervals that were assessed separately. Subjects evaluating the implicit disjunction (i.e., the large interval), we suggest, did not overlook the fact that the interval included several smaller intervals; rather, the unpacking manipulation enhanced the salience of these intervals and, hence, their judged probability. Subadditivity, therefore, is observed even in the absence of memory limitations.

NUMBER OF COMPONENTS   The degree of subadditivity increases with the number of components in the explicit disjunction. This follows readily from support theory: Unpacking an implicit hypothesis into exclusive components increases its total judged probability, and additional unpacking of each component should further increase the total probability assigned to the initial hypothesis. Tables 13.3 and 13.4 show, as expected, that the unpacking factor generally increases with the number of components (see also figure 13.1).

BINARY COMPLEMENTARITY   The judged probabilities of complementary pairs of hypotheses add to one. Table 13.5 lists studies that have tested this prediction. We considered only studies in which the hypothesis and its complement were evaluated independently, either by different subjects or by the same subjects but with a substantial number of intervening judgments. (We provide the standard deviations for the experiments that used the latter

Table 13.5
Results of Experiments Testing Binary Complementarity: Average Total Probability Assigned to Complementary Pairs of Hypotheses, Between-Subjects Standard Deviations, and the Number of Subjects in the Experiment

Study and topic	Mean total P	SD	N
Wallsten, Budescu, & Zwick (1992): general knowledge	1.02	0.06	23
Tversky & Fox (1994)			
NBA playoff	1.00	0.07	27
Super Bowl	1.02	0.07	40
Dow Jones	1.00	0.10	40
San Francisco temperature	1.02	0.13	72
Beijing temperature	0.99	0.14	45
Koehler & Tversky (1993): college majors[a]	1.00		170
Study 2: number of children[a]	0.97		139
Study 4: crime stories[a]	1.03		60
Study 5: college majors[a]	1.05		115

Note: Numbered studies with no citation refer to the present article. NBA = National Basketball Association.

[a] A given subject evaluated either the event or its complement, but not both.

design.) Table 13.5 shows that such judgments generally add to one. Binary complementarity indicates that people evaluate a given hypothesis relative to its complement. Moreover, it rules out alternative interpretations of subadditivity in terms of a suggestion effect or a confirmation bias. These accounts imply a bias in favor of the focal hypothesis yielding $P(A, B)$ + $P(B, A) > 1$, contrary to the experimental evidence. Alternatively, one might be tempted to attribute the subadditivity observed in probability judgments to subjects' lack of knowledge of the additivity principle of probability theory. This explanation, however, fails to account for the observed subadditivity in frequency judgments (in which additivity is obvious) and for the finding of binary complementarity (in which additivity is consistently satisfied).

The combination of binary complementarity and subadditive elementary judgments, implied by support theory, is inconsistent with both Bayesian and revisionist models. The Bayesian model implies that the unpacking factor should equal one because the unpacked and packed hypotheses have the same extension. Shafer's theory of belief functions and other models of lower probability require an unpacking factor of less than one because they assume that the subjective probability (or belief) of the union of disjoint events is generally greater than the sum of the probabilities of its exclusive constituents. Furthermore, the data cannot be explained by the dual of the belief function (called the plausibility function) or, more generally, by an upper probability (e.g., see Dempster, 1967) because this model requires that the sum of the assessments of complementary events exceed unity, contrary to the evidence. Indeed, if $P(A, B) + P(B, A) = 1$ (see table 13.5), then both upper and lower probability reduce to the standard additive model. The experimental findings, of course, do not invalidate the use of upper and lower probability, or belief functions, as formal systems for representing uncertainty. However, the evidence reviewed in this section indicates that these models are inconsistent with the principles that govern intuitive probability judgments.

PROBABILITY VERSUS FREQUENCY   Of the studies discussed earlier and listed in tables 13.3 and 13.4, some (e.g., Fischhoff et al., 1978) used frequency judgments and others (e.g., Teigen, 1974a, 1974b) used probability judgments. The comparison of the two tasks, summarized in table 13.6, confirms the predicted pattern: Subadditivity holds for both probability and frequency judgments, and the former are more subadditive than the latter.

Scaling Support

In the formal theory developed in the preceding section, the support function is derived from probability judgments. Is it possible to reverse the process and predict probability judgments from direct assessments of evidence strength? Let $\hat{s}(A)$ be the rating of the strength of evidence for hypothesis A. What is the relation between such ratings and the support estimated from probability judgments? Perhaps the most natural assumption is that the two scales are monotonically related; that is, $\hat{s}(A) \geq \hat{s}(B)$ if and only if (iff) $s(A) \geq s(B)$. This assumption

Table 13.6
Results of Experiments Comparing Probability and Frequency Judgments: Unpacking Factor Computed from Mean Probability Assigned to Coextensional Explicit and Implicit Disjunctions

		Unpacking factor	
Study and topic	n	Probability	Frequency
Teigen (1974b)			
Experiment 1: binomial outcomes	2	1.73	1.26
	5	2.21	1.09
	9	2.25	1.24
Teigen (1974b)			
Experiment 2: heights of students	6	2.55	1.68
Koehler & Tversky (1993): college majors	4	1.72	1.37
Study 1: causes of death	3	1.44	1.28
	7	2.00	1.84

Note: The number of components in the explicit disjunction is denoted by n. Numbered studies with no citation refer to the present article.

implies, for example, that $P(A, B) \geq \frac{1}{2}$ iff $\hat{s}(A) \geq \hat{s}(B)$, but it does not determine the functional form relating $\hat{s}$ and s. To further specify the relation between the scales, it may be reasonable to assume, in addition, that support ratios are also monotonically related. That is, $\hat{s}(A)/\hat{s}(B) \geq \hat{s}(C)/\hat{s}(D)$ iff $s(A)/s(B) \geq s(C)/s(D)$.

It can be shown that if the two monotonicity conditions are satisfied, and both scales are defined, say, on the unit interval, then there exists a constant $k > 0$ such that the support function derived from probability judgments and the support function assessed directly are related by a power transformation of the form $s = \hat{s}^k$. This gives rise to the *power model*

$$R(A, B) = P(A, B)/P(B, A) = [\hat{s}(A)/\hat{s}(B)]^k,$$

yielding

$$\log R(A, B) = k \log[\hat{s}(A)/\hat{s}(B)].$$

We next use this model to predict judged probability from independent assessments of evidence strength obtained in two studies.

Study 3: Basketball Games   Subjects ($N = 88$) were NBA fans who subscribe to a computer news group. We posted a questionnaire to this news group and asked readers to complete and return it by electronic mail within 1 week. In the questionnaire, subjects assessed the probability that the home team would win in each of 20 upcoming games. These 20 outcomes constituted all possible matches among five teams (Phoenix, Portland, Los Angeles Lakers,

Golden State, and Sacramento) from the Pacific Division of the NBA, constructed such that, for each pair of teams, two games were evaluated (one for each possible game location). Use of this "expert" population yielded highly reliable judgments, as shown, among other things, by the fact that the median value of the correlation between an individual subject's ratings and the set of mean judgments was 0.93.

After making their probability judgments, subjects rated the strength of each of the five teams. The participants were instructed as follows:

First, choose the team you believe is the strongest of the five, and set that team's strength to 100. Assign the remaining teams ratings in proportion to the strength of the strongest team. For example, if you believe that a given team is half as strong as the strongest team (the team you gave a 100), give that team a strength rating of 50.

We interpreted these ratings as a direct assessment of support.

Because the strength ratings did not take into account the home court effect, we collapsed the probability judgments across the two possible locations of the match. The slope of the regression line predicting log $R(A, B)$ from log $[\hat{s}(A)/\hat{s}(B)]$ provided an estimate of k for each subject. The median estimate of k was 1.8, and the mean was 2.2; the median R^2 for this analysis was 0.87. For the aggregate data, k was 1.9 and the resulting R^2 was 0.97. The scatterplot in figure 13.4 exhibits excellent correspondence between mean prediction based on team strength and mean judged probability. This result suggests that the power model can be used to predict judged probability from assessments of strength that make no reference to chance or uncertainty. It also reinforces the psychological interpretation of s as a measure of evidence strength.

Study 4: Crime Stories   This study was designed to investigate the relation between judged probability and assessed support in a very different context and to explore the enhancement effect, described in the next subsection. To this end, we adapted a task introduced by Teigen (1983) and Robinson and Hastie (1985) and presented subjects with two criminal cases. The first was an embezzlement at a computer-parts manufacturing company involving four suspects (a manager, a buyer, an accountant, and a seller). The second case was a murder that also involved four suspects (an activist, an artist, a scientist, and a writer). In both cases, subjects were informed that exactly one suspect was guilty. In the low-information condition, the four suspects in each case were introduced with a short description of their role and possible motive. In the high-information condition, the motive of each suspect was strengthened. In a manner resembling the typical mystery novel, we constructed each case so that all the suspects seemed generally more suspicious as more evidence was revealed.

Subjects evaluated the suspects after reading the low-information material and again after reading the high-information material. Some subjects ($N = 60$) judged the probability that

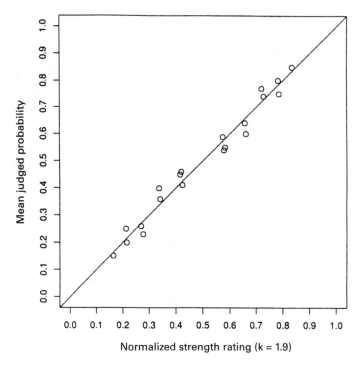

Figure 13.4
Judged probability for basketball games as a function of normalized strength ratings.

a given suspect was guilty. Each of these subjects made two elementary judgments (that a particular suspect was guilty) and three binary judgments (that suspect A rather than suspect B was guilty) in each case. Other subjects ($N = 55$) rated the suspiciousness of a given suspect, which we took as a direct assessment of support. These subjects rated two suspects per case by providing a number between 0 (indicating that the suspect was "not at all suspicious") and 100 (indicating that the suspect was "maximally suspicious") in proportion to the suspiciousness of the suspect.

As in the previous study, we assumed binary complementarity and estimated k by a logarithmic regression of $R(A, B)$ against the suspiciousness ratio. For these data, k was estimated to be 0.84, and R^2 was 0.65. Rated suspiciousness, therefore, provides a reasonable predictor of the judged probability of guilt. However, the relation between judged probability and assessed support was stronger in the basketball study than in the crime study. Furthermore, the estimate of k was much smaller in the latter than in the former. In the basketball study, a team that was rated twice as strong as another was judged more than twice as likely to win; in the crime stories, however, a character who was twice as suspicious as another was judged less than twice as likely to be guilty. This difference may be due to the fact that the judgments of team strength were based on more solid data than the ratings of suspiciousness.

In the preceding two studies, we asked subjects to assess the overall support for each hypothesis on the basis of all the available evidence. A different approach to the assessment of evidence was taken by Briggs and Krantz (1992; see also Krantz, Ray, & Briggs, 1990). These authors demonstrated that, under certain conditions, subjects can assess the degree to which an isolated item of evidence supports each of the hypotheses under consideration. They also proposed several rules for the combination of independent items of evidence, but they did not relate assessed support to judged probability.

The Enhancement Effect

Recall that assessed support is noncompensatory in the sense that evidence that increases the support of one hypothesis does not necessarily decrease the support of competing hypotheses. In fact, it is possible for new evidence to increase the support of all elementary hypotheses. We have proposed that such evidence will enhance subadditivity. In this section, we describe several tests of enhancement and compare support theory with the Bayesian model and with Shafer's theory.

We start with an example discussed earlier, in which one of several suspects has committed a murder. To simplify matters, assume that there are four suspects who, in the absence of specific evidence (low information), are considered equally likely to be guilty. Suppose further evidence is then introduced (high information) that implicates each of the suspects to roughly the same degree, so that they remain equally probable. Let L and H denote, respectively, the evidence available under low- and high-information conditions. Let $\bar{A}$ denote the negation of A, that is, "Suspect A is not guilty." According to the Bayesian model, then, $P(A, B \mid H) = P(A, B \mid L) = \frac{1}{2}$, $P(A, \bar{A} \mid H) = P(A, \bar{A} \mid L) = \frac{1}{4}$, and so forth.

In contrast, Shafer's (1976) belief-function approach requires that the probabilities assigned to each of the suspects add to less than one and suggests that the total will be higher in the presence of direct evidence (i.e., in the high-information condition) than in its absence. As a consequence, $\frac{1}{2} \geq P(A, B \mid H) \geq P(A, B \mid L)$, $\frac{1}{4} \geq P(A, \bar{A} \mid H) \geq P(A, \bar{A} \mid L)$, and so forth. In other words, both the binary and the elementary judgments are expected to increase as more evidence is encountered. In the limit, when no belief is held in reserve, the binary judgments approach one half and the elementary judgments approach one fourth.

The enhancement assumption yields a different pattern, namely $P(A, B \mid H) = P(A, B \mid L) = \frac{1}{2}$, $P(A, \bar{A} \mid H) \geq P(A, \bar{A} \mid L) \geq \frac{1}{4}$, and so forth. As in the Bayesian model, the binary judgments are one half; in contrast to that model, however, the elementary judgments are expected to exceed one fourth and to be greater under high- than under low-information conditions. Although both support theory and the belief-function approach yield greater elementary judgments under high- than under low-information conditions, support theory predicts that they will exceed one fourth in both conditions, whereas Shafer's theory requires that these probabilities be less than or equal to one fourth.

The assumption of equally probable suspects is not essential for the analysis. Suppose that initially the suspects are not equally probable, but the new evidence does not change the binary probabilities. Here, too, the Bayesian model requires additive judgments that do not differ between low- and high-information conditions; the belief-function approach requires superadditive judgments that become less superadditive as more information is encountered; and the enhancement assumption predicts subadditive judgments that become more subadditive with the addition of (compatible) evidence.

Evaluating Suspects   With these predictions in mind, we turn to the crime stories of study 4. Table 13.7 displays the mean suspiciousness ratings and elementary probability judgments of each suspect in the two cases under low- and high-information conditions. The table shows that, in all cases, the sums of both probability judgments and suspiciousness ratings exceed one. Evidently, subadditivity holds not only in probability judgment but also in ratings of evidence strength or degree of belief (e.g., that a given subject is guilty). Further examination of the suspiciousness ratings shows that all but one of the suspects increased in suspiciousness as more information was provided. In accord with our prediction, the

Table 13.7

Mean Suspiciousness Rating and Judged Probability of Each Suspect under Low- and High-Information Conditions

Case and suspect	Suspiciousness		Probability	
	Low information	High information	Low information	High information
Case 1: Embezzlement				
Accountant	41	53	40	45
Buyer	50	58	42	48
Manager	47	51	48	59
Seller	32	48	37	42
Total	170	210	167	194
Case 2: Murder				
Activist	32	57	39	57
Artist	27	23	37	30
Scientist	24	43	34	40
Writer	38	60	33	54
Total	122	184	143	181

judged probability of each of these suspects also increased with the added information, indicating enhanced subadditivity (see equation 10). The one exception was the artist in the murder case, who was given an alibi in the high-information condition and, as one would expect, subsequently decreased both in suspiciousness and in probability. Overall, both the suspiciousness ratings and the probability judgments were significantly greater under high- than under low-information conditions ($p < 0.001$ for both cases by t test).

From a normative standpoint, the support (i.e., suspiciousness) of all the suspects could increase with new information, but an increase in the probability of one suspect should be compensated for by a decrease in the probability of the others. The observation that new evidence can increase the judged probability of all suspects was made earlier by Robinson and Hastie (1985; Van Wallendael & Hastie, 1990). Their method differed from ours in that each subject assessed the probability of all suspects, but this method too produced substantial subadditivity, with a typical unpacking factor of about two. These authors rejected the Bayesian model as a descriptive account and proposed Shafer's theory as one viable alternative. As was noted earlier, however, the observed subadditivity is inconsistent with Shafer's theory, as well as the Bayesian model, but it is consistent with the present account.

In the crime stories, the added evidence was generally compatible with all of the hypotheses under consideration. Peterson and Pitz (1988, experiment 3), however, observed a similar effect with mixed evidence, which favored some hypotheses but not others. Their subjects were asked to assess the probability that the number of games won by a baseball team in a season fell in a given interval on the basis of one, two, or three cues (team batting average, earned run average, and total home runs during that season). Unbeknownst to subjects, they were asked, over a large number of problems, to assign probabilities to all three components in a partition (e.g., less than 80 wins, between 80 and 88 wins, and more than 88 wins). As the number of cues increased, subjects assigned a greater probability, on average, to all three intervals in the partition, thus exhibiting enhanced subadditivity. The unpacking factors for these data were 1.26, 1.61, and 1.86 for one, two, and three cues, respectively. These results attest to the robustness of the enhancement effect, which is observed even when the added evidence favors some, but not all, of the hypotheses under study.

Study 5: College Majors   In this study, we tested enhancement by replacing evidence rather than by adding evidence as in the previous study. Following Mehle, Gettys, Manning, Baca, and Fisher (1981), we asked subjects ($N = 115$) to assess the probability that a social science student at an unspecified Midwestern university majored in a given field. Subjects were told that, in this university, each social science student has one and only one of the following four majors: economics, political science, psychology, and sociology.

Subjects estimated the probability that a given student had a specified major on the basis of one of four courses the student was said to have taken in his or her second year. Two of the courses (statistics and Western civilization) were courses typically taken by social science majors; the other two (French literature and physics) were courses not typically taken by social science majors. This was confirmed by an independent group of subjects ($N = 36$) who evaluated the probability that a social science major would take each one of the four courses. Enhancement suggests that the typical courses will yield more subadditivity than the less typical courses because they give greater support to each of the four majors.

Each subject made both elementary and binary judgments. As in all previous studies, the elementary judgments exhibited substantial subadditivity (mean unpacking factor = 1.76), whereas the binary judgments were essentially additive (mean unpacking factor = 1.05). In the preceding analyses, we have used the unpacking factor as an overall measure of subadditivity associated with a set of mutually exclusive hypotheses. The present experiment also allowed us to estimate w (see equation 8), which provides a more refined measure of subadditivity because it is estimated separately for each of the implicit hypotheses under study. For each course, we first estimated the support of each major from the binary judgments and then estimated w for each major from the elementary judgments using the equation

$$P(A, \overline{A}) = \frac{s(A)}{s(A) + w_{\overline{A}}[s(B) + s(C) + s(D)]},$$

where A, B, C, and D denote the four majors.

This analysis was conducted separately for each subject. The average value of w across courses and majors was 0.46, indicating that a major received less than half of its explicit support when it was included implicitly in the residual. Figure 13.5 shows the median value of w (over subjects) for each major, plotted separately for each of the four courses. In accord with enhancement, the figure shows that the typical courses, statistics and Western civilization, induced more subadditivity (i.e., lower w) than the less typical courses, physics and French literature. However, for any given course, w was roughly constant across majors. Indeed, a two-way analysis of variance yielded a highly significant effect of course ($F(3, 112) = 31.4$, $p < 0.001$), but no significant effect of major ($F(3, 112) < 1$).

Implications

To this point, we have focused on the direct consequences of support theory. We conclude this section by discussing the conjunction effect, hypothesis generation, and decision under uncertainty from the perspective of support theory.

The Conjunction Effect   Considerable research has documented the conjunction effect, in which a conjunction AB is judged more probable than one of its constituents A. The effect is strongest when an event that initially seems unlikely (e.g., a massive flood in North America in which more than 1,000 people drown) is supplemented by a plausible cause or

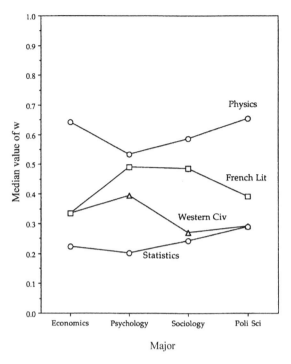

Figure 13.5
Median value of *w* for predictions of college majors, plotted separately for each course. Lit = literature; Civ = civilization; Poli Sci = political science.

qualification (e.g., an earthquake in California causing a flood in which more than 1,000 people drown), yielding a conjunction that is perceived as more probable than the initially implausible event of which it is a proper subset (Tversky & Kahneman, 1983). Support theory suggests that the implicit hypothesis *A* is not unpacked into the coextensional disjunction $AB \vee A\bar{B}$ of which the conjunction is one component. As a result, evidence supporting *AB* is not taken to support *A*. In the flood problem, for instance, the possibility of a flood caused by an earthquake may not come readily to mind; thus, unless it is mentioned explicitly, it does not contribute any support to the (implicit) flood hypothesis. Support theory implies that the conjunction effect would be eliminated in these problems if the implicit disjunction were unpacked before its evaluation (e.g., if subjects were reminded that a flood might be caused by excessive rainfall or by structural damage to a reservoir caused by an earthquake, an engineering error, sabotage, etc.).

The greater tendency to unpack either the focal or the residual hypothesis in a frequentistic formulation may help explain the finding that conjunction effects are attenuated, though not eliminated, when subjects estimate frequency rather than probability. For example, the proportion of subjects who judged the conjunction "*X* is over 55 years old and has had at least one heart attack" as more probable than the constituent event "*X* has had at least one heart attack" was significantly greater in a probabilistic formulation than in a frequentistic formulation (Tversky & Kahneman, 1983).

It might be instructive to distinguish two different unpacking operations. In *conjunctive unpacking*, an (implicit) hypothesis (e.g., nurse) is broken down into exclusive conjunctions (e.g., male nurse and female nurse). Most, but not all, initial demonstrations of the conjunction effect were based on conjunctive unpacking. In *categorical unpacking*, a superordinate category (e.g., unnatural death) is broken down into its "natural" components (e.g., car accident, drowning, and homicide). Most of the demonstrations reported in this article are based on categorical unpacking. A conjunction effect using categorical unpacking has been described by Bar-Hillel and Neter (1993), who found numerous cases in which a statement (e.g., "Daniela's major is literature") was ranked as more probable than a more inclusive implicit disjunction (e.g., "Daniela's major is in humanities"). These results held both for subjects' direct estimates of probabilities and for their willingness to bet on the relevant events.

Hypothesis Generation   All of the studies reviewed thus far asked subjects to assess the probability of hypotheses presented to them for judgment. There are many situations, however, in which a judge must generate hypotheses as well as assess their likelihood. In the current treatment, the generation of alternative hypotheses entails some unpacking of the residual hypothesis and, thus, is expected to increase its support relative to the focal hypothesis. In the absence of explicit instructions to generate alternative hypotheses, people are less likely to unpack the residual hypothesis and thus will tend to overestimate specified hypotheses relative to those left unspecified.

This implication has been confirmed by Gettys and his colleagues (Gettys, Mehle, & Fisher, 1986; Mehle et al., 1981), who have found that, in comparison with veridical values, people generally tend to overestimate the probability of specified hypotheses presented to them for evaluation. Indeed, overconfidence that one's judgment is correct (e.g., Lichtenstein, Fischhoff, & Phillips, 1982) may sometimes arise because the focal hypothesis is specified, whereas its alternatives often are not. Mehle et al. (1981) used two manipulations to encourage unpacking of the residual hypothesis: One group of subjects was provided with exemplar members of the residual, and another was asked to generate its own examples. Both manipulations improved performance by decreasing the probability assigned to specified alternatives and increasing that assigned to the residual. These results suggest that the effects of hypothesis generation are due to the additional hypotheses it brings to mind because simply providing hypotheses to the subject has the same effect. Using a similar manipulation, Dube-Rioux and Russo (1988) found that generation of alternative hypotheses increased the judged probability of the residual relative to that of specified categories and attenuated the effect of omitting a category. Examination of the number of instances generated by the subjects showed that, when enough instances were produced, the effect of category omission was eliminated altogether.

Now consider a task in which subjects are asked to generate a hypothesis (e.g., to guess which film will win the best picture Oscar at the next Academy Awards ceremony) before assessing its probability. Asking subjects to generate the most likely hypothesis might actually lead them to consider several candidates in the process of settling on the one they prefer. This process amounts to a partial unpacking of the residual hypothesis, which should decrease the judged probability of the focal hypothesis. Consistent with this prediction, a recent study (Koehler, 1994) found that subjects asked to generate their own hypotheses assigned them a lower probability of being true than did other subjects presented with the same hypotheses for evaluation. The interpretation of these results—that hypothesis generation makes alternative hypotheses more salient—was tested by two further manipulations. First, providing a closed set of specified alternatives eliminated the difference between the generation and evaluation conditions. In these circumstances, the residual should be represented in the same way in both conditions. Second, inserting a distracter task between hypothesis generation and probability assessment was sufficient to reduce the salience of alternatives brought to mind by the generation task, increasing the judged probability of the focal hypothesis.

Decision under Uncertainty This article has focused primarily on numerical judgments of probability. In decision theory, however, subjective probabilities are generally inferred from preferences between uncertain prospects rather than assessed directly. It is natural to inquire, then, whether unpacking affects people's decisions as well as their numerical judgments. There is considerable evidence that it does. For example, Johnson et al. (1993) observed that subjects were willing to pay more for flight insurance that explicitly listed certain events covered by the policy (e.g., death resulting from an act of terrorism or mechanical failure) than for a more inclusive policy that did not list specific events (e.g., death from any cause).

Unpacking can affect decisions in two ways. First, as has been shown, unpacking tends to increase the judged probability of an uncertain event. Second, unpacking can increase an event's impact on the decision, even when its probability is known. For example, Tversky and Kahneman (1986) asked subjects to choose between two lotteries that paid different amounts depending on the color of a marble drawn from a box. (As an inducement to consider the options with care, subjects were informed that one tenth of the participants, selected at random, would actually play the gambles they chose.) Two different versions of the problem were used, which differed only in the description of the outcomes. The fully unpacked version 1 was as follows:

Box A:	90% white	6% red	1% green	1% blue	2% yellow
	$0	win $45	win $30	lose $15	lose $15
Box B:	90% white	6% red	1% green	1% blue	2% yellow
	$0	win $45	win $30	lose $15	lose $15

It is not difficult to see that box B dominates box A; indeed, all subjects chose box B in this version. Version 2 combined the two outcomes resulting in a loss of $15 in box A (i.e., blue and yellow) and the two outcomes resulting in a gain of $45 in box B (i.e., red and green):

Box A:	90% white	6% red	1% green	3% yellow/blue
	$0	win $45	win $30	lose $15
Box B:	90% white	7% red/green	1% blue	2% yellow
	$0	win $45	lose $10	lose $15

In accord with subadditivity, the combination of events yielding the same outcome makes box A more attractive because it packs two losses into one and makes box B less attractive because it packs two gains into one. Indeed, 58% of subjects chose box A in version 2, even though it was dominated by box B. Starmer and Sugden (1993) further investigated the effect of unpacking events with known probabilities (which they called an event-splitting effect) and found that a prospect generally becomes more attractive when an event that yields a positive outcome is unpacked into two components. Such results demonstrate that unpacking affects decisions even when the probabilities are explicitly stated.

The role of unpacking in choice was further illustrated by Redelmeier et al. (1995). Graduating medical students at the University of Toronto ($N = 149$) were presented with a medical scenario concerning a middle-aged man suffering acute shortness of breath. Half of the respondents were given a packed description that noted that "obviously, many diagnoses are possible . . . including pneumonia." The other half was given an unpacked description that mentioned other potential diagnoses (pulmonary embolus, heart failure, asthma, and lung cancer) in addition to pneumonia. The respondents were asked whether or not they would prescribe antibiotics in such a case, a treatment that is effective against pneumonia but not against the other potential diagnoses mentioned in the unpacked version. The unpacking manipulation was expected to reduce the perceived probability of pneumonia and, hence, the respondents' inclination to prescribe antibiotics. Indeed, a significant majority (64%) of respondents given the unpacked description chose not to prescribe antibiotics, whereas respondents given the packed description were almost evenly divided between prescribing (47%) and not prescribing them. Singling out pneumonia increased the tendency to select a treatment that is effective for pneumonia, even though the presenting symptoms were clearly consistent with a number of well-known alternative diagnoses. Evidently, unpacking can affect decisions, not only probability assessments.

Although unpacking plays an important role in probability judgment, the cognitive mechanism underlying this effect is considerably more general. Thus, one would expect unpacking effects even in tasks that do not involve uncertain events. For example, van der Pligt, Eiser, and Spears (1987, experiment 1) asked subjects to assess the current and ideal distribution of five power sources (nuclear, coal, oil, hydro, solar/wind/wave) and found that a given power source was assigned a higher estimate when it was evaluated on its own than when its four alternatives were unpacked (see also Fiedler & Armbruster, 1994; Pelham, Sumarta, & Myaskovsky, 1994). Such results indicate that the effects of unpacking reflect a general characteristic of human judgment.

Extensions

We have presented a nonextensional theory of belief in which judged probability is given by the relative support, or strength of evidence, of the respective focal and alternative hypotheses. In this theory, support is additive for explicit disjunctions of exclusive hypotheses and subadditive for implicit disjunctions. The empirical evidence confirms the major predictions of support theory: (a) probability judgments increase by unpacking the focal hypothesis and decrease by unpacking the alternative hypothesis; (b) subjective probabilities are complementary in the binary case and subadditive in the general case; and (c) subadditivity is more pronounced for probability than for frequency judgments, and it is enhanced by compatible evidence. Support theory also provides a method for predicting judged probability from independent assessments of evidence strength. Thus, it accounts for a wide range of empirical findings in terms of a single explanatory construct.

In this section, we explore some extensions and implications of support theory. First, we consider an ordinal version of the theory and introduce a simple parametric representation. Second, we address the problem of vagueness, or imprecision, by characterizing upper and lower probability judgments in terms of upper and lower support. Finally, we discuss the implications of the present findings for the design of elicitation procedures for decision analysis and knowledge engineering.

Ordinal Analysis

Throughout the chapter, we have treated probability judgment as a quantitative measure of degree of belief. This measure is commonly interpreted in terms of a reference chance process. For example, assigning a probability of two thirds to the hypothesis that a candidate will be elected to office is taken to mean that the judge considers this hypothesis as likely as drawing a red ball from an urn in which two thirds of the balls are red. Probability judgment, therefore, can be viewed as an outcome of a thought experiment in which the judge matches degree of belief to a standard chance process (see Shafer & Tversky, 1985). This interpretation, of course, does not ensure either coherence or calibration.

Although probability judgments appear to convey quantitative information, it might be instructive to analyze these judgments as an ordinal rather than a cardinal scale. This interpretation gives rise to an ordinal generalization of support theory. Suppose there is a nonnegative scale s defined on H and a strictly increasing function F such that, for all A, B in H,

$$P(A, B) = F\left(\frac{s(A)}{s(A) + s(B)}\right),$$ (11)

where $s(C) \leq s(A \vee B) = s(A) + s(B)$ whenever A and B are exclusive, C is implicit, and $C' = (A \vee B)'$.

An axiomatization of the ordinal model lies beyond the scope of the present article. It is noteworthy, however, that to obtain an essentially unique support function in this case, we have to make additional assumptions, such as the following *solvability condition* (Debreu, 1958): If $P(A, B) \geq z \geq P(A, D)$, then there exists $C \in H$ such that $P(A, C) = z$. This idealization may be acceptable in the presence of a random device, such as a chance wheel with sectors that can be adjusted continuously. The following theorem shows that, assuming the ordinal model and the solvability condition, binary complementarity and the product rule yield a particularly simple parametric form that coincides with the model used in the preceding section to relate assessed and derived support. The proof is given in the appendix.

THEOREM 2   Assume the ordinal model (equation 11) and the solvability condition. Binary complementarity (equation 3) and the product rule (equation 5) hold if and only if there exists a constant $k \geq 0$ such that

$$P(A, B) = \frac{s(A)^k}{s(A)^k + s(B)^k}.$$ (12)

This representation, called the power model, reduces to the basic model if $k = 1$. In this model, judged probability may be more or less extreme than the respective relative support depending on whether k is greater or less than one. Recall that the experimental data, reviewed in the preceding section, provide strong evidence for the inequality $\alpha < \delta$. That is, $P(A, B) \leq P(A_1, B) + P(A_2, B)$ whenever A_1, A_2, and B are mutually exclusive; A is implicit; and $A' = (A_1 \vee A_2)'$. We also found evidence (see table 13.2) for the equality $\beta = \gamma$, that is, $P(A_1 \vee A_2, B) = P(A_1, A_2 \vee B) + P(A_2, A_1 \vee B)$, but this property has not been extensively tested. Departures from additivity induced, for example, by regression toward 0.5 could be represented by a power model with $k < 1$, which implies $\alpha < \beta < \gamma < \delta$. Note that, for explicit disjunctions of exclusive hypotheses, the basic model (equations 1 and 2), the ordinal model (equation 11), and the power model (equation 12) all assume additive support, but only the basic model entails additive probability.

Upper and Lower Indicators

Probability judgments are often vague and imprecise. To interpret and make proper use of such judgments, therefore, one needs to know something about their range of uncertainty. Indeed, much of the work on nonstandard probability has been concerned with formal models that provide upper and lower indicators of degree of belief. The elicitation and interpretation of such indicators, however, present both theoretical and practical problems. If people have a hard time assessing a single definite value for the probability of an event, they are likely to have an even harder time assessing two definite values for its upper and lower probabilities or generating a second-order probability distribution. Judges may be able to provide some indication regarding the vagueness of their assessments, but such judgments, we suggest, are better interpreted in qualitative, not quantitative, terms.

To this end, we have devised an elicitation procedure in which upper and lower probability judgments are defined verbally rather than numerically. This procedure, called the *staircase method*, is illustrated in figure 13.6. The judge is presented with an uncertain event (e.g., an eastern team rather than a western team will win the next NBA title) and is asked to check one of the five categories for each probability value. The lowest value that is not "clearly too low" (0.45) and the highest value that is not "clearly too high" (0.80), denoted P_* and P^*, respectively, may be taken as the lower and upper indicators. Naturally, alternative procedures involving a different number of categories, different wording, and different ranges could yield different indicators. (We assume that the labeling of the categories is symmetric around the middle category.) The staircase method can be viewed as a qualitative analog of a second-order probability distribution or of a fuzzy membership function.

Probability (%):	0	5	10	15	20	25	30	35	40	45	50	55	60	65	70	75	80	85	90	95	100
Clearly too high																		×	×	×	×
Slightly too high																×	×				
ABOUT RIGHT															×						
Slightly too low										×	×	×	×	×							
Clearly too low	×	×	×	×	×	×	×	×	×												

Figure 13.6
Example of the staircase method used to elicit upper and lower probabilities.

We model P_* and P^* in terms of lower and upper support functions, denoted s_* and s^*, respectively. We interpret these scales as low and high estimates of s and assume that, for any A, $s_*(A) \leq s(A) \leq s^*(A)$. Furthermore, we assume that P_* and P^* can be expressed as follows:

$$P_*(A, B) = \frac{s_*(A)}{s_*(A) + s^*(B)}$$

and

$$P^*(A, B) = \frac{s^*(A)}{s^*(A) + s_*(B)}.$$

According to this model, the upper and lower indicators are generated by a slanted reading of the evidence; $P^*(A, B)$ can be interpreted as a probability judgment that is biased in favor of A and against B, whereas $P_*(A, B)$ is biased against A and in favor of B. The magnitude of the bias reflects the vagueness associated with the basic judgment, as well as the characteristics of the elicitation procedure. Within a given procedure, however, we can interpret the interval (P_*, P^*) as a comparative index of imprecision. Thus, we may conclude that one judgment is less vague than another if the interval associated with the first assessment is included in the interval associated with the second assessment. Because the high and low estimates are unlikely to be more precise or more reliable than the judge's best estimate, we regard P_* and P^* as supplements, not substitutes, for P.

To test the proposed representation against the standard theory of upper and lower probability (e.g., see Dempster, 1967; Good, 1962), we investigated people's predictions of the outcomes of the NFL playoffs for 1992–1993. The study was run the week before the two championship games in which Buffalo was to play Miami for the title of the American Football Conference (AFC) and Dallas was to play San Francisco for the title of the National Football Conference (NFC). The winners of these games would play each other two weeks later in the Super Bowl. The subjects were 135 Stanford students who volunteered to participate in a study of football prediction in exchange for a single California Lottery ticket. Half of the subjects assessed the probabilities that the winner of the Super Bowl would be Buffalo, Miami, an NFC team. The other half of the subjects assessed the probabilities that the winner of the Super Bowl would be Dallas, San Francisco, an AFC team. All subjects assessed probabilities for the two championship games. The focal and the alternative hypotheses for these games were counterbalanced. Thus, each subject made five probability assessments using the staircase method illustrated in figure 13.6.

Subjects' best estimates exhibited the pattern of subadditivity and binary complementarity observed in previous studies. The average probabilities of each of the four teams winning the Super Bowl added to 1.71; the unpacking factor was 1.92 for the AFC teams and 1.48 for the NFC teams. In contrast, the sum of the average probability of an event and its complement was 1.03. Turning to the analysis of the upper and the lower assessments, note that the present model implies $P_*(A, B) + P^*(B, A) = 1$, in accord with the standard theory of upper and lower probability. The data show that this condition holds to a very close degree of approximation, with an average sum of 1.02.

The present model, however, does not generally agree with the standard theory of upper and lower probability. To illustrate the discrepancy, suppose A and B are mutually exclusive and $C' = (A \vee B)'$. The standard theory requires that $P_*\left(A, \bar{A}\right) + P_*\left(B, \bar{B}\right) \leq P_*\left(C, \bar{C}\right)$, whereas the present account suggests the opposite inequality when C is implicit. The data clearly violate the standard theory: The average lower probabilities of winning the Super Bowl were 0.21 for Miami and 0.21 for Buffalo but only 0.24 for their implicit disjunction (i.e., an AFC team). Similarly, the average lower probabilities of winning the Super Bowl were 0.25 for Dallas and 0.41 for San Francisco but only 0.45 for an NFC team. These data are consistent with the present model, assuming the subadditivity of s_*, but not with the standard theory of lower probability.

Prescriptive Implications

Models of subjective probability or degree of belief serve two functions: descriptive and prescriptive. The literature on nonstandard probability models is primarily prescriptive. These models are offered as formal languages for the evaluation of evidence and the representation of belief. In contrast, support theory attempts to describe the manner in which people make probability judgments, not to prescribe how people should make these judgments. For example, the proposition that judged probability increases by unpacking the focal hypothesis and decreases by unpacking the alternative hypothesis represents a general descriptive principle that is not endorsed by normative theories, additive or nonadditive.

Despite its descriptive nature, support theory has prescriptive implications. It could aid the design of elicitation procedures and the reconciliation of inconsistent assessments (Lindley, Tversky, & Brown, 1979). This role may be illuminated by a perceptual analogy. Suppose a surveyor has to construct a map of a park on the basis of judgments of distance between landmarks made by a fallible observer. Knowledge of the likely biases of the observer could help the surveyor construct a better map. Because observers generally underestimate distances involving hidden areas, for example, the surveyor may discard these assessments and compute the respective distances from other assessments using the laws of plane geometry. Alternatively, the surveyor may wish to reduce the bias by applying a suitable correction factor to the estimates involving hidden areas. The same logic applies to the elicitation of probability. The evidence shows that people tend to underestimate the probability of an implicit disjunction, especially the negation of an elementary hypothesis. This bias may be reduced by asking the judge to contrast hypotheses of a comparable level of specificity instead of assessing the probability of a specific hypothesis against its complement.

The major conclusion of the present research is that subjective probability, or degree of belief, is nonextensional and hence nonmeasurable in the sense that alternative partitions of the space can yield different judgments. Like the measured length of a coastline, which increases as a map becomes more detailed, the perceived likelihood of an event increases as its description becomes more specific. This does not imply that judged probability is of no value, but it indicates that this concept is more fragile than suggested by existing formal theories. The failures of extensionality demonstrated in this article highlight what is perhaps the fundamental problem of probability assessment, namely the need to consider unavailable possibilities. The problem is especially severe in tasks that require the generation of new hypotheses or the construction of novel scenarios. The extensionality principle, we argue, is normatively unassailable but practically unachievable because the judge cannot be expected to fully unpack any implicit disjunction. People can be encouraged to unpack a category into its components, but they cannot be expected to think of all relevant conjunctive unpackings or to generate all relevant future scenarios. In this respect, the assessment of an additive probability distribution may be an impossible task. The judge could, of course, ensure the additivity of any given set of judgments, but this does not ensure that additivity will be preserved by further refinement.

The evidence reported here and elsewhere indicates that both qualitative and quantitative assessments of uncertainty are not carried out in a logically coherent fashion, and one might be tempted to conclude that they should not be carried out at all. However, this is not a viable option because, in general, there are no alternative procedures for assessing uncertainty. Unlike the measurement of distance, in which fallible human judgment can be replaced by proper physical measurement, there are no objective procedures for assessing the probability of events such as the guilt of a defendant, the success of a business venture, or the outbreak of war. Intuitive judgments of uncertainty, therefore, are bound to play an essential role in people's deliberations and decisions. The question of how to improve their quality through the design of effective elicitation methods and corrective procedures poses a major challenge to theorists and practitioners alike.

Acknowledgments

This research has been supported by Grant SES-9109535 from the National Science Foundation to Amos Tversky and by a National Defense Science and Engineering fellowship to Derek J. Koehler. We are grateful to Maya Bar-Hillel, Todd Davies, Craig Fox, Daniel Kahneman, David Krantz, Glenn Shafer, Eldar Shafir, and Peter Wakker for many helpful comments and discussions.

Notes

1. Gigerenzer (1991) has further argued that the biases observed in probability judgments of unique events disappear in judgments of frequency, but the data reviewed here and elsewhere are inconsistent with this claim.

2. Enhancement, like subadditivity, may not hold when a person evaluates these probabilities at the same time because this task introduces additional constraints.

3. We thank the authors for making their data available to us.

References

Aczel, J. (1966). *Lectures on functional equations and their applications*. San Diego, CA: Academic Press.

Bar-Hillel, M., & Neter, E. (1993). How alike is it versus how likely is it: A disjunction fallacy in stereotype judgments. *Journal of Personality and Social Psychology, 65*, 1119–1131.

Briggs, L. K., & Krantz, D. H. (1992). Judging the strength of designated evidence. *Journal of Behavioral Decision Making, 5*, 77–106.

Debreu, G. (1958). Stochastic choice and cardinal utility. *Econometrica, 26*, 440–444.

Dempster, A. P. (1967). Upper and lower probabilities induced by a multivalued mapping. *Annals of Mathematical Statistics, 38*, 325–339.

Dube-Rioux, L., & Russo, J. E. (1988). An availability bias in professional judgment. *Journal of Behavioral Decision Making, 1*, 223–237.

Dubois, D., & Prade, H. (1988). Modelling uncertainty and inductive inference: A survey of recent non-additive probability systems. *Acta Psychologica, 68*, 53–78.

Erev, I., Wallsten, T. S., & Budescu, D. V. (1994). Simultaneous over- and underconfidence: The role of error in judgment processes. *Psychological Review, 101*, 519–527.

Fiedler, K., & Armbruster, T. (1994). Two halfs may be more than one whole. *Journal of Personality and Social Psychology, 66*, 633–645.

Fischhoff, B., Slovic, P., & Lichtenstein, S. (1978). Fault trees: Sensitivity of estimated failure probabilities to problem representation. *Journal of Experimental Psychology: Human Perception and Performance, 4*, 330–344.

Fox, C. R., Rogers, B., & Tversky, A. (1994). Decision weights for options traders. Unpublished manuscript, Stanford University, Stanford, CA.

Gettys, C. F., Mehle, T., & Fisher, S. (1986). Plausibility assessments in hypothesis generation. *Organizational Behavior and Human Decision Processes, 37*, 14–33.

Gigerenzer, G. (1991). How to make cognitive illusions disappear: Beyond "heuristics and biases." In W. Stroche & M. Hewstone (Eds.), *European review of social psychology* (Vol. 2, pp. 83–115). New York, NY: Wiley.

Gilboa, I., & Schmeidler, D. (1994). Additive representations of non-additive measures and the Choquet integral. *Annals of Operations Research, 52*, 43–65.

Good, I. J. (1962). Subjective probability as the measure of a nonmeasurable set. In E. Nagel, P. Suppes, & A. Tarski (Eds.), *Logic, methodology, and philosophy of sciences* (pp. 319–329). Stanford, CA: Stanford University Press.

Johnson, E. J., Hershey, J., Meszaros, J., & Kunreuther, H. (1993). Framing, probability distortions, and insurance decisions. *Journal of Risk and Uncertainty, 7*, 35–51.

Kahneman, D., Slovic, P., & Tversky, A. (Eds.). (1982). *Judgment under uncertainty: Heuristics and biases.* Cambridge, England: Cambridge University Press.

Kahneman, D., & Tversky, A. (1979). Intuitive prediction: Biases and corrective procedures. *TIMS Studies in Management Science, 12*, 313–327.

Kahneman, D., & Tversky, A. (1982). Variants of uncertainty. *Cognition, 11*, 143–157.

Koehler, D. J. (1994). Hypothesis generation and confidence in judgment. *Journal of Experimental Psychology: Learning, Memory, and Cognition, 20*, 461–469.

Koehler, D. J., & Tversky, A. (1993). The enhancement effect in probability judgment. Unpublished manuscript, Stanford University, Stanford, CA.

Krantz, D. H., Ray, B., & Briggs, L. K. (1990). Foundations of the theory of evidence: The role of schemata. Unpublished manuscript, Columbia University, New York, NY.

Lichtenstein, S., Fischhoff, B., & Phillips, L. (1982). Calibration of probabilities: The state of the art to 1980. In D. Kahneman, P. Slovic, & A. Tversky (Eds.), *Judgment under uncertainty: Heuristics and biases* (pp. 306–334). Cambridge, England: Cambridge University Press.

Lindley, D. V., Tversky, A., & Brown, R. V. (1979). On the reconciliation of probability assessments. *Journal of the Royal Statistical Society. Series A (General), 142*, 146–180.

Mehle, T., Gettys, C. F., Manning, C., Baca, S., & Fisher, S. (1981). The availability explanation of excessive plausibility assessment. *Acta Psychologica, 49*, 127–140.

Mongin, P. (1994). Some connections between epistemic logic and the theory of nonadditive probability. In P. W. Humphreys (Ed.), *Patrick Suppes: Scientific philosopher* (pp. 135–172). Dordrecht, the Netherlands: Kluwer.

Murphy, A. H. (1985). Probabilistic weather forecasting. In A. H. Murphy & R. W. Katz (Eds.), *Probability, statistics, and decision making in the atmospheric sciences* (pp. 337–377). Boulder, CO: Westview Press.

Olson, C. L. (1976). Some apparent violations of the representativeness heuristic in human judgment. *Journal of Experimental Psychology: Human Perception and Performance, 2*, 599–608.

Pelham, B. W., Sumarta, T. T., & Myaskovsky, L. (1994). The easy path from many to much: The numerosity heuristic. *Cognitive Psychology, 26*, 103–133.

Peterson, D. K., & Pitz, G. F. (1988). Confidence, uncertainty, and the use of information. *Journal of Experimental Psychology: Learning, Memory, and Cognition, 14*, 85–92.

Redelmeier, D., Koehler, D. J., Liberman, V., & Tversky, A. (1995). Probability judgment in medicine: Discounting unspecified alternatives. *Medical Decision Making*, *15*, 227–230.

Reeves, T., & Lockhart, R. S. (1993). Distributional vs. singular approaches to probability and errors in probabilistic reasoning. *Journal of Experimental Psychology. General*, *122*, 207–226.

Robinson, L. B., & Hastie, R. (1985). Revision of beliefs when a hypothesis is eliminated from consideration. *Journal of Experimental Psychology: Human Perception and Performance*, *4*, 443–456.

Russo, J. E., & Kolzow, K. J. (1992). Where is the fault in fault trees? Unpublished manuscript, Cornell University, Ithaca, NY.

Shafer, G. (1976). *A mathematical theory of evidence*. Princeton, NJ: Princeton University Press.

Shafer, G., & Tversky, A. (1985). Languages and designs for probability judgment. *Cognitive Science*, *9*, 309–339.

Starmer, C., & Sugden, R. (1993). Testing for juxtaposition and event-splitting effects. *Journal of Risk and Uncertainty*, *6*, 235–254.

Statistical abstract of the United States. (1990). Washington, DC: U.S. Department of Commerce, Bureau of the Census.

Suppes, P. (1974). The measurement of belief. *Journal of the Royal Statistical Society. Series B. Methodological*, *36*, 160–191.

Teigen, K. H. (1974a). Overestimation of subjective probabilities. *Scandinavian Journal of Psychology*, *15*, 56–62.

Teigen, K. H. (1974b). Subjective sampling distributions and the additivity of estimates. *Scandinavian Journal of Psychology*, *15*, 50–55.

Teigen, K. H. (1983). Studies in subjective probability III: The unimportance of alternatives. *Scandinavian Journal of Psychology*, *24*, 97–105.

Tversky, A., & Fox, C. (1994). Weighing risk and uncertainty. Unpublished manuscript, Stanford University, Stanford, CA.

Tversky, A., & Kahneman, D. (1983). Extensional vs. intuitive reasoning: The conjunction fallacy in probability judgment. *Psychological Review*, *91*, 293–315.

Tversky, A., & Kahneman, D. (1986). Rational choice and the framing of decisions, Part 2. *Journal of Business*, *59*, 251–278.

Tversky, A., & Sattath, S. (1979). Preference trees. *Psychological Review*, *86*, 542–573.

van der Pligt, J., Eiser, J. R., & Spears, R. (1987). Comparative judgments and preferences: The influence of the number of response alternatives. *British Journal of Social Psychology*, *26*, 269–280.

Van Wallendael, L. R., & Hastie, R. (1990). Tracing the footsteps of Sherlock Holmes: Cognitive representations of hypothesis testing. *Memory & Cognition*, *18*, 240–250.

Walley, P. (1991). *Statistical reasoning with imprecise probabilities*. London, England: Chapman & Hall.

Wallsten, T. S., Budescu, D. V., & Zwick, R. (1992). Comparing the calibration and coherence of numerical and verbal probability judgments. *Management Science, 39*, 176–190.

Zadeh, L. A. (1978). Fuzzy sets as a basis for a theory of possibility. *Fuzzy Sets and Systems, 1*, 3–28.

Zarnowitz, V. (1985). Rational expectations and macroeconomic forecasts. *Journal of Business & Economic Statistics, 3*, 293–311.

Appendix

THEOREM 1:   Suppose $P(A, B)$ is defined for all disjoint $A, B \in$ H, and it vanishes if and only if (iff) $A' = \varnothing$. Equations 3–6 (see text) hold iff there exists a nonnegative ratio scale s on H that satisfies equations 1 and 2.

Proof: Necessity is immediate. To establish sufficiency, we define s as follows. Let E = {$A \in$ H: $A' \in$ T} be the set of elementary hypotheses. Select some $D \in$ E and set $s(D) = 1$. For any other elementary hypothesis $C \in$ E, such that $C' \neq D'$, define $s(C) = P(C, D)/P(D, C)$. Given any hypothesis $A \in$ H such that $A' \neq$ T, $\varnothing$, select some $C \in$ E such that $A' \cap C' = \varnothing$ and define $s(A)$ through

$$\frac{s(A)}{s(C)} = \frac{P(A, C)}{P(C, A)};$$

that is,

$$s(A) = \frac{P(A, C)P(C, D)}{P(C, A)P(D, C)}.$$

To demonstrate that $s(A)$ is uniquely defined, suppose $B \in$ E and $A' \cap B' = \varnothing$. We want to show that

$$\frac{P(A, C)P(C, D)}{P(C, A)P(D, C)} = \frac{P(A, B)P(B, D)}{P(B, A)P(D, B)}.$$

By proportionality (equation 4), the left-hand ratio equals

$$\frac{P(A, C \vee B)P(C, D \vee B)}{P(C, A \vee B)P(D, C \vee B)}$$

and the right-hand ratio equals

$$\frac{P(A, B \vee C)P(B, D \vee C)}{P(B, A \vee C)P(D, B \vee C)}.$$

Canceling common terms, it is easy to see that the two ratios are equal iff

$$\frac{P(C, D \vee B)}{P(B, D \vee C)} = \frac{P(C, A \vee B)}{P(B, A \vee C)},$$

which holds because both ratios equal $P(C, B)/P(B, C)$, again by proportionality.

To complete the definition of s, let $s(A) = 0$ whenever $A' = \varnothing$. For $A' = T$, we distinguish two cases. If A is explicit, that is, $A = B \vee C$ for some exclusive $B, C \in H$, set $s(A) = s(B) + s(C)$. If A is implicit, let $s(A)$ be the minimum value of s over all explicit descriptions of T.

To establish the desired representation, we first show that for any exclusive $A, B \in H$, such that $A', B' \neq T, \varnothing, s(A)/s(B) = P(A, B)/P(B, A)$. Recall that T includes at least two elements. Two cases must be considered.

First, suppose $A' \cup B' \neq T$; hence, there exists an elementary hypothesis C such that $A' \cap C' = B' \cap C' = \varnothing$. In this case,

$$\frac{s(A)}{s(B)} = \frac{P(A, C)/P(C, A)}{P(B, C)/P(C, B)} = \frac{P(A, C \vee B)/P(C, A \vee B)}{P(B, C \vee A)/P(C, B \vee A)} = \frac{P(A, B)}{P(B, A)}$$

by repeated application of proportionality.

Second, suppose $A' \cup B' = T$. In this case, there is no $C' \in T$ that is not included in either A' or B', so the preceding argument cannot be applied. To show that $s(A)/s(B) = P(A, B)/P(B, A)$, suppose $C, D \in E$ and $A' \cap C' = B' \cap D' = \varnothing$. Hence,

$$\frac{s(A)}{s(B)} = \frac{s(A)s(C)s(D)}{s(C)s(D)s(B)}$$
$$= \frac{P(A, C)P(C, D)P(D, B)}{P(C, A)P(D, C)P(B, D)}$$
$$= R(A, C)R(C, D)R(D, B)$$
$$= R(A, B) \quad \text{(by the product rule [equation (5)])}$$
$$= P(A, B)/P(B, A) \quad \text{(as required).}$$

For any pair of exclusive hypotheses, therefore, we obtain $P(A, B)/P(B, A) = s(A)/s(B)$, and $P(A, B) + P(B, A) = 1$, by binary complementarity. Consequently, $P(A, B) = s(A)/[s(A) + s(B)]$ and s is unique up to a choice of unit, which is determined by the value of $s(D)$.

To establish the properties of s, recall that unpacking (equation 6) yields $P(D, C) \leq P(A \vee B, C) = P(A, B \vee C) + P(B, A \vee C)$ whenever $D' = A' \cup B'$, A and B are exclusive, and D is implicit. The inequality on the left-hand side implies that

$$\frac{s(D)}{s(D) + s(C)} \leq \frac{s(A \vee B)}{s(A \vee B) + s(C)};$$

hence, $s(D) \leq s(A \vee B)$. The equality on the right-hand side implies that

$$\frac{s(A \vee B)}{s(A \vee B) + s(C)} = \frac{s(A)}{s(A) + s(B \vee C)} + \frac{s(B)}{s(B) + s(A \vee C)}.$$

To demonstrate that the additivity of P implies the additivity of s, suppose A, B, and C are non-null and mutually exclusive. (If $A' \cup B' = T$, the result is immediate.) Hence, by proportionality,

$$\frac{s(A)}{s(B)} = \frac{P(A, B)}{P(B, A)} = \frac{P(A, B \vee C)}{P(B, A \vee C)} = \frac{s(A)/[s(A) + s(B \vee C)]}{s(B)/[s(B) + s(A \vee C)]}.$$

Consequently, $s(A) + s(B \vee C) = s(B) + s(A \vee C) = s(C) + s(A \vee B)$. Substituting these relations in the equation implied by the additivity of P yields $s(A \vee B) = s(A) + s(B)$, which completes the proof of theorem 1.

THEOREM 2:   Assume the ordinal model (equation 11) and the solvability condition. Binary complementarity (equation 3) and the product rule (equation 5) hold iff there exists a constant $k \geq 0$ such that

$$P(A, B) = \frac{s(A)^k}{s(A)^k + s(B)^k}.$$

Proof: It is easy to verify that equations 3 and 5 are implied by the power model (equation 12). To derive this representation, assume that the ordinal model and the solvability condition are satisfied. Then there exists a nonnegative scale s, defined on H, and a strictly increasing function F from the unit interval into itself such that for all $A, B \in$ H,

$$P(A, B) = F\left[\frac{s(A)}{s(A) + s(B)}\right].$$

By binary complementarity, $P(A, B) = 1 - P(B, A)$; hence, $F(z) = 1 - F(1 - z)$, $0 \leq z \leq 1$. Define the function G by

$$R(A, B) = \frac{P(A, B)}{P(B, A)} = \frac{F\{s(A)/[s(A) + s(B)]\}}{F\{s(B)/[s(B) + s(A)]\}} = G[s(A)/s(B)], \quad B' \neq \emptyset.$$

Applying the product rule, with $s(C) = s(D)$, yields $G[s(A)/s(B)] = G[s(A)/s(C)]G[s(C)/s(B)]$; hence, $G(xy) = G(x)G(y)$, $x, y \geq 0$. This is a form of the Cauchy equation, whose solution is $G(x) = x^k$ (see Aczel, 1966). Consequently, $R(A, B) = s(A)^k/s(B)^k$ and, by binary complementarity,

$$P(A, B) = \frac{s(A)^k}{s(A)^k + s(B)^k}, \quad k \geq 0 \text{ (as required)}.$$

14 Reason-Based Choice

Eldar Shafir, Itamar Simonson, and Amos Tversky

The result is that peculiar feeling of inward unrest known as indecision. *Fortunately it is too familiar to need description, for to describe it would be impossible. As long as it lasts, with the various objects before the attention, we are said to* deliberate; *and when finally the original suggestion either prevails and makes the movement take place, or gets definitively quenched by its antagonists, we are said to* decide . . . *in favor of one or the other course. The reinforcing and inhibiting ideas meanwhile are termed the* reasons *or* motives *by which the decision is brought about.*

—William James (1890/1981)

My way is to divide half a sheet of paper by a line into two columns; writing over the one Pro, *and over the other* Con. *Then, during three or four days' consideration, I put down under the different heads short hints of the different motives, that at different times occur to me for or against the measure. When I have thus got them all together in one view, I endeavor to estimate the respective weights . . . find at length where the balance lies . . . And, though the weight of reasons cannot be taken with the precision of algebraic quantities, yet, when each is thus considered, separately and comparatively, and the whole matter lies before me. I think I can judge better, and am less liable to make a rash step; and in fact I have found great advantage for this kind of equation, ln what may be called* moral *or* prudential algebra.

—Benjamin Franklin, 1772 (cited in Bigelow, 1887)

Introduction

The making of decisions, both big and small, is often difficult because of uncertainty and conflict. We are usually uncertain about the exact consequences of our actions, which may depend on the weather or the state of the economy, and we often experience conflict about how much of one attribute (e.g., savings) to trade off in favor of another (e.g., leisure). In order to explain how people resolve such conflict, students of decision making have traditionally employed either formal models or reason-based analyses. The formal modeling approach, which is commonly used in economics, management science, and decision research, typically associates a numerical value with each alternative and characterizes choice as the maximization of value. Such value-based accounts include normative models, like expected utility theory (von Neumann & Morgenstern, 1947), as well as descriptive models, such as prospect theory (Kahneman & Tversky, 1979). An alternative tradition in the study of decision making, characteristic of scholarship in history and the law, and typical of political and business discourse, employs an informal, reason-based analysis. This approach identifies various reasons and arguments that are purported to enter into and influence decisions and explains choice in terms of the balance of reasons for and against the various alternatives. Examples of reason-based analyses can be found in studies of historic presidential decisions, such as those taken during the Cuban missile crisis (e.g., Allison, 1971), the Camp David accords (Telhami, 1990), or the Vietnam war (e.g., Berman, 1982; Betts & Gelb, 1979). Furthermore, reason-based analyses are commonly used to interpret "case studies" in business and law schools. Although the reasons invoked by researchers may not always correspond to those that motivated the actual decision makers, it is generally agreed that an analysis in terms of reasons may help explain decisions, especially in contexts where value-based models can be difficult to apply.

Little contact has been made between the two traditions, which have typically been applied to different domains. Reason-based analyses have been used primarily to explain nonexperimental data, particularly unique historic, legal, and political decisions. In contrast, value-based approaches have played a central role in experimental studies of preference and in standard economic analyses. The two approaches, of course, are not incompatible: reason-based accounts may often be translated into formal models, and formal analyses can generally be paraphrased as reason-based accounts. In the absence of a comprehensive theory of choice, both formal models and reason-based analyses may contribute to the understanding of decision making.

Both approaches have obvious strengths and limitations. The formal, value-based models have the advantage of rigor, which facilitates the derivation of testable implications. However, value-based models are difficult to apply to complex, real-world decisions, and they often fail to capture significant aspects of people's deliberations. An explanation of choice based on reasons, by contrast, is essentially qualitative in nature and typically vague. Furthermore, almost anything can be counted as a "reason," so that every decision may be rationalized after the fact. To overcome this difficulty, one could ask people to report their reasons for decision. Unfortunately, the actual reasons that guide decision may or may not correspond to those reported by the subjects. As has been amply documented (e.g., Nisbett & Wilson, 1977), subjects are sometimes unaware of the precise factors that determine their choices and generate spurious explanations when asked to account for their decisions. Indeed, doubts about the validity of introspective reports have led many students of decision making to focus exclusively on observed choices. Although verbal reports and introspective accounts can provide valuable information, we use "reasons" in the present article to describe factors or motives that affect decision, whether or not they can be articulated or recognized by the decision maker.

Despite its limitations, a reason-based conception of choice has several attractive features. First, a focus on reasons seems closer to the way we normally think and talk about choices. When facing a difficult choice (e.g., between schools or jobs) we try to come up with reasons for and against each option—we do not normally attempt to estimate their overall values. Second, thinking of choice as guided by reasons provides a natural way to understand the conflict that characterizes the making of decisions. From the perspective of reason-based choice, conflict arises when the decision maker has good reasons for and against each option, or conflicting reasons for competing options. Unlike numerical values, which are easy to compare, conflicting reasons may be hard to reconcile. An analysis based on reasons can also accommodate framing effects (Tversky & Kahneman, 1986) and elicitation effects (Tversky, Sattath, & Slovic, 1988), which show that preferences are sensitive to the ways in which options are described (e.g., in terms of gains or losses), and to the methods through which preferences are elicited (e.g., pricing versus choice). These findings, which are puzzling from the perspective of value maximization, are easier to interpret if we assume that different frames and elicitation procedures highlight different aspects of the options and thus bring forth different reasons to guide decision. Finally, a conception of choice based on reasons may incorporate comparative considerations (such as relative advantages or anticipated regret) that typically remain outside the purview of value maximization.

In this chapter, we explore the logic of reason-based choice and test some specific hypotheses concerning the role of reasons in decision making. The chapter proceeds as follows. Section 1 considers the role of reasons in choice between equally attractive options. Section 2 explores differential reliance on reasons for and against the selection of options. Section 3 investigates the interaction between high and low conflict and people's tendency to seek other alternatives, whereas section 4 considers the relation between conflict and the addition of alternatives to the choice set. Section 5 contrasts the impact of a specific reason for choice with that of a disjunction of reasons. Section 6 explores the role that irrelevant reasons can play in the making of decisions. Concluding remarks are presented in section 7.

1. Choice between Equally Attractive Options

How do decision makers resolve the conflict when faced with a choice between two equally attractive options? To investigate this question, Slovic (1975) first had subjects equate pairs of alternatives, and later asked them to make choices between the equally valued alternatives in each pair. One pair, for example, were gift packages consisting of a combination of cash and coupons. For each pair, one component of one alternative was missing, as shown below, and subjects were asked to determine the value of the missing component that would render the two alternatives equally attractive. (In the following example, the value volunteered by the subject may be, say, $10.)

	Gift package A	Gift package B
Cash		$20
Coupon book worth	$32	$18

A week later, subjects were asked to choose between the two equated alternatives. They were also asked, independently, which dimension—cash or coupons—they considered more important. Value-based theories imply that the two alternatives—explicitly equated for value—are equally likely to be selected. In contrast, in the choice between gift packages above, 88% of the subjects who had equated these alternatives for value then proceeded to choose the alternative that was higher on the dimension that the subject considered more important.

As Slovic (1975, 1990) suggests, people seem to be following a choice mechanism that is easy to explain and justify: choosing according to the more important dimension provides a better reason for choice than, say, random selection, or selection of the right-hand option. Slovic (1975) replicated the above pattern in numerous domains, including choices between college applicants, auto tires, baseball players, and routes to work. (For additional data and a discussion of elicitation procedures, see Tversky et al., 1988.) All the results were consistent with the hypothesis that people do not choose between the equated alternatives at random. Instead, they resolve the conflict by selecting the alternative that is superior on the more important dimension, which seems to provide a compelling reason for choice.

2.   Reasons Pro and Con

Consider having to choose one of two options or, alternatively, having to reject one of two options. Under the standard analysis of choice, the two tasks are interchangeable. In a binary choice situation it should not matter whether people are asked which option they prefer or which they would reject. Because it is the options themselves that are assumed to matter, not the way in which they are described, if people prefer the first they will reject the second, and vice versa.

As suggested by Franklin's opening quote, our decision will depend partially on the weights we assign to the options' pros and cons. We propose that the positive features of options (their pros) will loom larger when choosing, whereas the negative features of options (their cons) will be weighted more heavily when rejecting. It is natural to select an option because of its positive features and to reject an option because of its negative features. To the extent that people base their decisions on reasons for and against the options under consideration, they are likely to focus on reasons for choosing an option when deciding which to choose and to focus on reasons for rejecting an option when deciding which to reject. This hypothesis leads to a straightforward prediction: consider two options, an *enriched* option, with more positive and more negative features, and an *impoverished* option, with fewer positive and fewer negative features. If positive features are weighted more heavily when choosing than when rejecting and negative features are weighted relatively more when rejecting than when choosing, then an enriched option could be both chosen and rejected when compared to an impoverished option. Let P_c and P_r denote, respectively, the percentage of subjects who choose and who reject a particular option. If choosing and rejecting are complementary, then the sum $P_c + P_r$ should equal 100. However, according to the above hypothesis, $P_c + P_r$ should be greater than 100 for the enriched option and less than 100 for the impoverished option. This pattern was observed by Shafir (1993). Consider, for example, the following problem that was presented to subjects in two versions that differed only in the bracketed questions. One half of the subjects received one version, the other half received the other. The enriched option appears last, although the order presented to subjects was counterbalanced.

Problem 1 ($N = 170$):

Imagine that you serve on the jury of an only-child sole-custody case following a relatively messy divorce. The facts of the case are complicated by ambiguous economic, social, and emotional considerations, and you decide to base your decision entirely on the following few observations. [To which parent would you award sole custody of the child?/Which parent would you deny sole custody of the child?]

		Award	Deny
Parent A:	average income	36%	45%
	average health		
	average working hours		
	reasonable rapport with the child		
	relatively stable social life		
Parent B:	above-average income	64%	55%
	very close relationship with the child		
	extremely active social life		
	lots of work-related travel		
	minor health problems		

Parent A, the impoverished option, is quite plain—with no striking positive or negative features. There are no particularly compelling reasons to award or deny this parent custody of the child. Parent B, the enriched option, by contrast, has good reasons to be awarded custody (a very close relationship with the child and a good income), but also good reasons to be denied sole custody (health problems and extensive absences due to travel). To the right of the options are the percentages of subjects who chose to award and to deny custody to each of the parents. Parent B is the majority choice both for being awarded custody of the child and for being denied it. As predicted, $P_c + P_r$ for parent B (64 + 55 = 119) is significantly greater than 100, the value expected if choosing and rejecting were complementary ($z = 2.48$, $p < 0.02$). This pattern is explained by the observation that the enriched parent (parent B) provides more compelling reasons to be awarded as well as denied child custody.

The above pattern has been replicated in hypothetical choices between monetary gambles, college courses, and political candidates (Shafir, 1993). For another example, consider the following problem, presented to half the subjects in the "prefer" and to the other half in the "cancel" version.

Problem 2 (N = 172):

Prefer:

Imagine that you are planning a week vacation in a warm spot over spring break. You currently have two options that are reasonably priced. The travel brochure gives only a limited amount of information about the two options. Given the information available, which vacation spot would you prefer?

Cancel:

Imagine that you are planning a week vacation in a warm spot over spring break. You currently have two options that are reasonably priced, but you can no longer retain your reservation in both. The travel brochure gives only a limited amount of information about the two options. Given the information available, which reservation do you decide to cancel?

		Prefer	Cancel
Spot A:	average weather	33%	52%
	average beaches		
	medium-quality hotel		
	medium-temperature water		
	average nightlife		
Spot B:	lots of sunshine	67%	48%
	gorgeous beaches and coral reefs		
	ultra-modern hotel		
	very cold water		
	very strong winds		
	no nightlife		

The information about the two spots is typical of the kind of information we have available when deciding where to take our next vacation. Because it is difficult to estimate the overall value of each spot, we are likely to seek reasons on which to base our decision. Spot A, the impoverished option, seems unremarkable yet unobjectionable on all counts. By contrast, there are obvious reasons—gorgeous beaches, an abundance of sunshine, and an ultra-modern hotel—for choosing spot B. Of course, there are also compelling reasons—cold water, winds, and a lack of nightlife—why spot B should be rejected. We suggest that the gorgeous beaches are likely to provide a more compelling reason when we choose than when we reject, and the lack of nightlife is likely to play a more central role when we reject than when we choose. Indeed, spot B's share of being preferred and rejected exceeds that of spot A ($P_c + P_r = 67 + 48 = 115$, $p < 0.05$). These results demonstrate that options are not simply ordered according to value, with the more attractive selected and the less attractive rejected. Instead, it appears that the relative importance of options' strengths and weaknesses varies with the nature of the task. As a result, we are significantly more likely to end up in spot B when we ask ourselves which we prefer than when we contemplate which to cancel (67% vs. 52%, $z = 2.83$, $p < 0.001$).

One of the most basic assumptions of the rational theory of choice is the principle of procedure invariance, which requires strategically equivalent methods of elicitation to yield identical preferences (see Tversky et al., 1988, for discussion). The choose–reject discrepancy represents a predictable failure of procedure invariance. This phenomenon is at variance with value maximization, but is easily understood from the point of view of reason-based choice: reasons for choosing are more compelling when we choose than when we reject, and reasons for rejecting matter more when we reject than when we choose.

3. Choice under Conflict: Seeking Options

The need to choose often creates conflict: we are not sure how to trade off one attribute relative to another or, for that matter, which attributes matter to us most. It is commonplace that we often attempt to resolve such conflict by seeking reasons for choosing one option over another. At times, the conflict between available alternatives is hard to resolve, which may lead us to seek additional options or to maintain the status quo. Other times, the context is such that a comparison between alternatives generates compelling reasons to choose one option over another. Using reasons to resolve conflict has some nonobvious implications, which are addressed below. The present section focuses on people's decision to seek other alternatives; the next section explores some effects of adding options to the set under consideration.

In many contexts, we need to decide whether to opt for an available option or search for additional alternatives. Thus, a person who wishes to buy a used car may settle for a car that is currently available or continue searching for additional models. Seeking new alternatives usually requires additional time and effort, and may involve the risk of losing the previously available options. Conflict plays no role in the classical theory of choice. In this theory, each option x has a value $v(x)$ such that, for any offered set, the decision maker selects the option with the highest value. In particular, a person is expected to search for additional alternatives only if the expected value of searching exceeds that of the best option currently available. A reliance on reasons, by contrast, entails that we should be more likely to opt for an available option when we have a convincing reason for its selection, and that we should be more likely to search further when a compelling reason for choice is not readily available.

To investigate this hypothesis, Tversky and Shafir (1992b) presented subjects with pairs of options, such as bets varying in probability and payoff, or student apartments varying in monthly rent and distance from campus, and had subjects choose one of the two options or, instead, request an additional option, at some cost. Subjects first reviewed the entire set of 12 options (gambles or apartments) to familiarize themselves with the available alternatives. In the study of choice between bets some subjects then received the following problem.

Conflict:

Imagine that you are offered a choice between the following two gambles:

(x)   65% chance to win $15

(y)   30% chance to win $35

You can either select one of these gambles or you can pay $1 to add one more gamble to the choice set. The added gamble will be selected at random from the list you reviewed.

Other subjects received a similar problem except that option y was replaced by option x', to yield a choice between the following.

Dominance:

(x)   65% chance to win $15

(x')   65% chance to win $14

Subjects were asked to indicate whether they wanted to add another gamble or select between the available alternatives. They then chose their preferred gamble from the resulting set (with or without the added option). Subjects were instructed that the gambles they chose would be played out and that their payoff would be proportional to the amount of money they earned minus the fee they paid for the added gambles.

A parallel design presented choices between hypothetical student apartments. Some subjects received the following problem.

Conflict:

Imagine that you face a choice between two apartments with the following characteristics:

(x) $290 a month, 25 minutes from campus

(y) $350 a month, 7 minutes from campus

Both have one bedroom and a kitchenette. You can choose now between the two apartments or you can continue to search for apartments (to be selected at random from the list you reviewed). In that case, there is some risk of losing one or both of the apartments you have found.

Other subjects received a similar problem except that option y was replaced by option x', to yield a choice between the following.

Dominance:

(x) $290 a month, 25 minutes from campus

(x') $330 a month, 25 minutes from campus

Note that in both pairs of problems the choice between x and y—the *conflict* condition—is nontrivial because the xs are better on one dimension and the ys are better on the other. In contrast, the choice between x and x'—the *dominance* condition—involves no conflict because the former strictly dominates the latter. Thus, while there is no obvious reason to choose one option over the other in the conflict condition, there is a decisive argument for preferring one of the two alternatives in the dominance condition.

On average, subjects requested an additional alternative 64% of the time in the conflict condition and only 40% of the time in the dominance condition ($p < 0.05$). Subjects' tendency to search for additional options, in other words, was greater when the choice among alternatives was harder to rationalize than when there was a compelling reason and the decision was easy.

These data are inconsistent with the principle of value maximization. According to value maximization, a subject should search for additional alternatives if and only if the expected (subjective) value of searching exceeds that of the best alternative currently available. Because the best alternative offered in the dominance condition is also available in the conflict condition, value maximization implies that the percentage of subjects who seek an additional alternative cannot be greater in the conflict than in the dominance condition, contrary to the observed data.

It appears that the search for additional alternatives depends not only on the value of the best available option, as implied by value maximization, but also on the difficulty of choosing among the options under consideration. In situations of dominance, for example, there are clear and indisputable reasons for choosing one option over another (e.g., "This apartment is equally distant and I save $40!"). Having a compelling argument for choosing one of the options over the rest reduces the temptation to look for additional alternatives. When the choice involves conflict, however, reasons for choosing any one of the options are less immediately available and the decision is more difficult to justify (e.g., "Should I save $60 a month, or reside 18 minutes closer to campus?"). In the absence of compelling reasons for choice, there is a greater tendency to search for other alternatives.

4. Choice under Conflict: Adding Options

An analysis in terms of reasons can help explain observed violations of the principle of independence of irrelevant alternatives, according to which the preference ordering between two options should not be altered by the introduction of additional alternatives. This principle follows from the standard assumption of value maximization and has been routinely assumed in the analysis of consumer choice. Despite its intuitive appeal, there is a growing body of evidence that people's preferences depend on the context of choice, defined by the set of options under consideration. In particular, the addition and removal of options from the offered set can influence people's preferences among options that were available all along. Whereas in the previous section we considered people's tendency to seek alternatives in the context of a given set of options, in this section we illustrate phenomena that arise through the addition of options and interpret them in terms of reasons for choice.

A major testable implication of value maximization is that a nonpreferred option cannot become preferred when new options are added to the offered set. In particular, a decision maker who prefers y over the option to defer the choice should not prefer to defer the choice when both y and x are available. That the "market share" of an option cannot be increased by enlarging the offered set is known as the *regularity condition* (see Tversky & Simonson, 1993). Contrary to regularity, numerous experimental results indicate that the tendency to defer choice can increase with the addition of alternatives. Consider, for instance, the degree of conflict that arises when a person is presented with one attractive option (which he or she prefers to deferring the choice), compared to two competing alternatives. Choosing one out of two competing alternatives can be difficult: the mere fact that an alternative is attractive may not in itself provide a compelling reason for its selection because the other option may be equally attractive. The addition of an alternative may thus make the decision harder to justify and increase the tendency to defer the decision.

A related phenomenon was aptly described by Thomas Schelling, who tells of an occasion in which he had decided to buy an encyclopedia for his children. At the bookstore, he was presented with two attractive encyclopedias and, finding it difficult to choose between the two, ended up buying neither—this, despite the fact that had only one encyclopedia been available he would have happily bought it. More generally, there are situations in which people prefer each of the available alternatives over the status quo but do not have a compelling reason for choosing among the alternatives and, as a result, defer the decision, perhaps indefinitely.

The phenomenon described by Schelling was demonstrated by Tversky and Shafir (1992b) in the following pair of problems, which were presented to two groups of students ($N = 124$ and 121, respectively).

High conflict:

Suppose you are considering buying a compact disc (CD) player and have not yet decided what model to buy. You pass by a store that is having a 1-day clearance sale. They offer a popular SONY player for just $99 and a top-of-the-line AIWA player for just $169, both well below the list price. Do you:

(x) buy the AIWA player? 27%

(y) buy the SONY player? 27%

(z) wait until you learn more about the various models? 46%

Low conflict:

Suppose you are considering buying a CD player and have not yet decided what model to buy. You pass by a store that is having a 1-day clearance sale. They offer a popular SONY player for just $99, well below the list price. Do you:

(y) buy the SONY player? 66%

(z) wait until you learn more about the various models? 34%

The results indicate that people are more likely to buy a CD player in the latter, *low-conflict*, condition than in the former, *high-conflict*, situation ($p < .05$). Both models—the AIWA and the SONY—seem attractive, both are well priced, and both are on sale. The decision maker needs to determine whether she is better off with a cheaper, popular model, or with a more expensive, sophisticated one. This conflict is apparently not easy to resolve, and compels many subjects to put off the purchase until they learn more about the various options. However, when the SONY alone is available, there are compelling arguments for its purchase: it is a popular player, it is very well priced, and it is on sale for 1 day only. In this situation, having good reasons to choose the offered option, a greater majority of subjects decide to opt for the CD player rather than delay the purchase.

The addition of a competing alternative in the preceding example increased the tendency to delay decision. Clearly, the level of conflict and its ease of resolution depend not only on the number of options available, but on how the options compare. Consider, for example, the following problem, in which the original AIWA player was replaced by an inferior model ($N = 62$).

Dominance:

Suppose you are considering buying a CD player and have not yet decided what model to buy. You pass by a store that is having a 1-day clearance sale. They offer a popular SONY player for just $99, well below the list price, and an inferior AIWA player for the regular list price of $105. Do you:

(x′) buy the AIWA player? 3%

(y) buy the SONY player? 73%

(z) wait until you learn more about the various models? 24%

In this version, contrary to the previous *high-conflict* version, the AIWA player is dominated by the SONY: it is inferior in quality and costs more. Thus, the presence of the AIWA does not detract from the reasons for buying the SONY, it actually supplements them: the SONY is well priced, it is on sale for 1 day only, *and* it is clearly better than its competitor. As a result, the SONY is chosen more often than before the inferior AIWA was added. The ability of an asymmetrically dominated or relatively inferior alternative, when added to a set, to increase the attractiveness and choice probability of the dominating option is known as the asymmetric dominance effect (Huber, Payne, & Puto, 1982). Note that in both the *high-conflict* and the *dominance* problems, subjects were presented with two CD players and an option to delay choice. Subjects' tendency to delay, however, is much greater when they lack clear reasons for buying either player than when they have compelling reasons to buy one player and not the other ($p < 0.005$).

The above patterns violate the regularity condition, which is assumed to hold so long as the added alternatives do not provide new and relevant information. In the above scenario, one could argue that the added options (the superior player in one case and the inferior player in the other) conveyed information about the consumer's chances of finding a better deal. Recall that information considerations could not explain the search experiments of the previous section because there subjects reviewed all the potentially available options. Nevertheless, to test this interpretation further, Tversky and Shafir (1992b) devised a similar problem, involving real payoffs, in which the option to defer is not available. Students ($N = 80$) agreed to fill out a brief questionnaire for $1.50. Following the questionnaire, one half of the subjects was offered the opportunity to exchange the $1.50 (the default) for one of two prizes: a metal Zebra pen (henceforth, Zebra) or a pair of plastic Pilot pens (henceforth, Pilot). The other half of the subjects was only offered the opportunity to exchange the $1.50 for the Zebra. The prizes were shown to the subjects, who were also informed that each prize regularly costs a little over $2.00. Upon indicating their preference, subjects received their chosen option. The results were as follows. Seventy-five percent of the subjects chose the Zebra over the payment when the Zebra was the only alternative, but only 47% chose the Zebra *or* the Pilot when both were available ($p < 0.05$). Faced with a tempting alternative, subjects had a compelling reason to forego the payment: the majority took advantage of the opportunity to obtain an attractive prize of greater value. The availability of competing alternatives of comparable value, however, did not present an immediate reason for choosing either alternative over the other, thus increasing the tendency to retain the default option. Similar effects in hypothetical medical decisions made by expert physicians are documented in Redelmeier and Shafir (1993).

In the above study the addition of a competing alternative was shown to increase the popularity of the default option. Recall that the popularity of an option may also be enhanced by the addition of an inferior alternative. Thus, in accord with the asymmetric dominance effect, the tendency to prefer *x* over *y* can be increased by adding a third alternative *z* that is

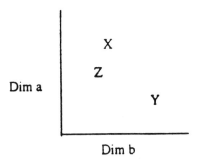

Figure 14.1
A schematic representation of asymmetric dominance. The tendency to prefer *x* over *y* can be increased
by adding an alternative, *z*, that is clearly inferior to *x* but not to *y*.

clearly inferior to *x* but not to *y* (see figure 14.1). The phenomenon of asymmetric dominance
was first demonstrated by Huber, Payne, and Puto (1982) in choices between hypothetical options. Wedell (1991) reports similar findings using monetary gambles. The following
example involving real choices is taken from Simonson and Tversky (1992). One group
(*N* = 106) was offered a choice between $6 and an elegant Cross pen. The pen was selected by
36% of the subjects, and the remaining 64% chose the cash. A second group (*N* = 115) was
given a choice among three options: $6 in cash, the same Cross pen, and a second pen that
was distinctly less attractive. Only 2% of the subjects chose the less attractive pen, but its
presence increased the percentage of subjects who chose the Cross pen from 36% to 46% (*p* <
0.10). This pattern again violates the regularity condition discussed earlier. Similar violations
of regularity were observed in choices among other consumer goods. In one study, subjects
received descriptions and pictures of microwave ovens taken from a "Best" catalog. One
group (*N* = 60) was then asked to choose between an Emerson priced at $110 and a Panasonic
priced at $180. Both items were on sale, one third off the regular price. Here, 57% chose the
Emerson and 43% chose the Panasonic. A second group (*N* = 60) was presented with these
options along with a $200 Panasonic at a 10% discount. Only 13% of the subjects chose the
more expensive Panasonic, but its presence increased the percentage of subjects who chose
the less expensive Panasonic from 43% to 60% (*p* < 0.05).[1]

Simonson and Tversky (1992) have interpreted these observations in terms of "tradeoff
contrast." They proposed that the tendency to prefer an alternative is enhanced or hin-
dered depending on whether the tradeoffs within the set under consideration are favorable
or unfavorable to that alternative. A second cluster of consideration effects, called *extremeness aversion*, refers to the finding that, within an offered set, options with extreme values
are relatively less attractive than options with intermediate values (Simonson, 1989). For
example, consider two-dimensional options *x*, *y*, and *z*, such that *y* lies between *x* and *z*

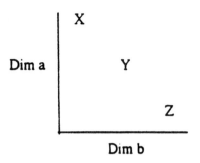

Figure 14.2
A schematic representation of extremeness aversion. Option *y* is relatively more popular in the trinary choice, when both *x* and *z* are available, than in either one of the binary comparisons, when either *x* or *z* are removed.

(see figure 14.2). Considerations of value maximization imply that the middle alternative, *y*, should be relatively less popular in the trinary choice than in either one of the binary comparisons (*y* compared to *x*, or *y* compared to *z*). Extremeness aversion, by contrast, yields the opposite prediction because *y* has small advantages and disadvantages with respect to *x* and to *z*, whereas both *x* and *z* have more extreme advantages and disadvantages with respect to each other. This pattern was observed in several experiments. For example, subjects were shown five 35 mm cameras varying in quality and price. One group (*N* = 106) was then given a choice between two cameras: a Minolta X-370 priced at $170 and a Minolta 3000i priced at $240. A second group (*N* = 115) was given an additional option, the Minolta 7000i priced at $470. Subjects in the first group were split evenly between the two options, yet 57% of the subjects in the second group chose the middle option (Minolta 3000i), with the remaining divided about equally between the two extreme options. Thus, the introduction of an extreme option reduced the "market share" of the other extreme option, but not of the middle option. Note that this effect cannot be attributed to information conveyed by the offered set because respondents had reviewed the relevant options prior to making their choice.

We suggest that both tradeoff contrast and extremeness aversion can be understood in terms of reasons. Suppose a decision maker faces a choice between two alternatives, *x* and *y*, and suppose *x* is of higher quality whereas *y* is better priced. This produces conflict if the decision maker finds it difficult to determine whether the quality difference outweighs the price difference. Suppose now that the choice set also includes a third alternative, *z*, that is clearly inferior to *y* but not to *x*. The presence of *z*, we suggest, provides an argument for choosing *y* over *x*. To the extent that the initial choice between *x* and *y* is difficult, the presence of *z* may help the decision maker break the tie. In the pen study, for example, the addition of the relatively unattractive pen, whose monetary value is unclear but whose inferiority to the elegant Cross pen is apparent, provides a reason for choosing the Cross pen over the cash. Similarly, in the presence of options with extreme values on the relevant dimensions, the middle option can be seen as a compromise choice that is easier to defend than either extreme. Indeed, verbal protocols show that the accounts generated by subjects while making these choices involve considerations of asymmetric advantage and compromise; furthermore, asymmetric dominance is enhanced when subjects anticipate having to justify their decisions to others (Simonson, 1989). It is noteworthy that the arguments leading to tradeoff contrast and extremeness aversion are comparative in nature; they are based on the positions of the options in the choice set, hence they cannot be readily translated into the values associated with single alternatives.

Tversky and Simonson (1993) have proposed a formal model that explains the above findings in terms of a tournament-like process in which each option is compared against other available options in terms of their relative advantages and disadvantages. This model can be viewed as a formal analog of the preceding qualitative account based on reasons for choice. Which analysis—the formal or the qualitative—proves more useful is likely to depend, among other things, on the nature of the problem and on the purpose of the investigation.

5. Definite versus Disjunctive Reasons

People sometimes encounter situations of uncertainty in which they eventually opt for the same course of action, but for very different reasons, depending on how the uncertainty is resolved. Thus, a student who has taken an exam may decide to take a vacation, either to reward herself in case she passes or to console herself in case she fails. However, as illustrated below, the student may be reluctant to commit to a vacation while the outcome of the exam is pending. The following problem was presented by Tversky and Shafir (1992a) to 66 undergraduate students.

Disjunctive version:

Imagine that you have just taken a tough qualifying examination. It is the end of the fall quarter, you feel tired and run-down, and you are not sure that you passed the exam. In case you failed you have to take the exam again in a couple of months—after the Christmas holidays. You now have an opportunity to buy a very attractive 5-day Christmas vacation package in Hawaii at an exceptionally low price. The special offer expires tomorrow, while the exam grade will not be available until the following day. Would you:

(a)	buy the vacation package?	32%
(b)	not buy the vacation package?	7%
(c)	pay a $5 nonrefundable fee in order to retain the rights to buy the vacation package at the same exceptional price the day after tomorrow—after you find out whether or not you passed the exam?	61%

The percentage of subjects who chose each option appears on the right. Two additional versions, called *pass* and *fail*, were presented to two different groups of 67 students each. These two versions differed only in the expression in brackets.

Pass/fail versions:

Imagine that you have just taken a tough qualifying examination. It is the end of the fall quarter, you feel tired and run-down, and you find out that you [passed the exam/failed the exam. You will have to take it again in a couple of months—after the Christmas holidays.] You now have an opportunity to buy a very attractive 5-day Christmas vacation package in Hawaii at an exceptionally low price. The special offer expires tomorrow. Would you:

		Pass	Fail
(a)	buy the vacation package?	54%	57%
(b)	not buy the vacation package?	16%	12%
(c)	pay a $5 nonrefundable fee in order to retain	30%	31%
	the rights to buy the vacation package at the		
	same exceptional price the day after tomorrow?		

The data show that more than half of the students chose the vacation package when they knew that they passed the exam and an even larger percentage chose the vacation when they knew that they failed. However, when they did not know whether they had passed or failed, less than one third of the students chose the vacation and 61% were willing to pay $5 to postpone the decision until the following day, when the results of the exam would be known.[2] Once the outcome of the exam is known, the student has good—albeit different—reasons for taking the trip: having passed the exam, the vacation is presumably seen as a reward following a hard but successful semester; having failed the exam, the vacation becomes a consolation and time to recuperate before a re-examination. Not knowing the outcome of the exam, however, the student lacks a definite reason for going to Hawaii. Notice that the outcome of the exam will be known long before the vacation begins. Thus, the uncertainty characterizes the actual moment of decision, not the eventual vacation.

The indeterminacy of reasons for going to Hawaii discourages many students from buying the vacation, even when both outcomes—passing or failing the exam—ultimately favor this course of action. Tversky and Shafir (1992a) call the above pattern of decisions a *disjunction effect*. Evidently, a disjunction of different reasons (reward in case of success or consolation in case of failure) is often less compelling than either definite reason alone. A significant proportion of the students above were willing to pay, in effect, for information that was ultimately not going to affect their decision—they would choose to go to Hawaii in either case—but that promised to leave them with a more definite reason for making that choice. The willingness to pay for noninstrumental information is at variance with the classical model, in which the worth of information is determined only by its potential to influence decision.

People's preference for definite as opposed to disjunctive reasons has significant implications in cases where the option to defer decision is not available. Consider the following series of problems presented by Tversky and Shafir (1992a) to 98 students.

Win/lose version:

Imagine that you have just played a game of chance that gave you a 50% chance to win $200 and a 50% chance to lose $100. The coin was tossed and you have [won $200/lost $100]. You are now offered a second identical gamble: 50% chance to win $200 and 50% chance to lose $100. Would you:

		Won	Lost
(a)	accept the second gamble?	69%	59%
(b)	reject the second gamble?	31%	41%

The students were presented with the *win* version of the problem above, followed a week later by the *lose* version, and 10 days after that by the following version that is a disjunction of the previous two. The problems were embedded among other, similar problems so that the relation between the various versions was not transparent. Subjects were instructed to treat each decision separately.

Disjunctive version:

Imagine that you have just played a game of chance that gave you a 50% chance to win $200 and a 50% chance to lose $100. Imagine that the coin has already been tossed, but that you will not know whether you have won $200 or lost $100 until you make your decision concerning a second, identical gamble: 50% chance to win $200 and 50% chance to lose $100. Would you:

(a)	accept the second gamble?	36%
(b)	reject the second gamble?	64%

The data show that a majority of subjects accepted the second gamble after having won the first gamble and a majority also accepted the second gamble after having lost the first gamble. However, the majority of subjects rejected the second gamble when the outcome of the first was not known. An examination of individual choices reveals that approximately 40% of the subjects accepted the second gamble both after a gain in the first and after a loss. Among these, however, 65% rejected the second gamble in the disjunctive condition, when the outcome of the first gamble was not known. Indeed, this response pattern (accepting in both conditions but rejecting in the disjunction) was the single most frequent pattern, exhibited by 27% of all subjects. This pattern, which violates Savage's (1954) sure-thing principle, cannot be attributed to unreliability (Tversky & Shafir, 1992a).

The students above were offered a gamble with a positive expected value and an even chance of a nontrivial loss. Different reasons were likely to arise for accepting the second gamble depending on the outcome of the first. In the *win* condition, the decision maker is already up $200, so even a loss on the second gamble leaves him or her ahead overall, which makes this option quite attractive. In the *lose* condition, however, the decision maker is down $100. Playing the second gamble offers a chance to "get out of the red," which for many is more attractive than accepting a sure $100 loss. In the *disjunctive* condition, however, the decision maker does not know whether she is up $200 or down $100; she does not know, in other words, whether her reason for playing the second gamble is that it is a no-loss proposition or, instead, that it provides a chance to escape a sure loss. In the absence of a definite reason, fewer subjects accept the second gamble.

This interpretation is further supported by the following modification of the above problem, in which both outcomes of the first gamble were increased by $400 so that the decision maker could not lose in either case.

Imagine that you have just played a game of chance that gave you a 50% chance to win $600 and a 50% chance to win $300. Imagine that the coin has already been tossed, but that you will not know whether you have won $600 or $300 until you make your decision concerning a second gamble: 50% chance to win $200 and 50% chance to lose $100.

A total of 171 subjects were presented with this problem, equally divided into three groups. One group was told that they had won $300 on the first gamble, a second group was told that they had won $600 on the first gamble, and the third group was told that the outcome of the first gamble—$300 or $600—was not known (the disjunctive version). In all cases, subjects had to decide whether to accept or to reject the second gamble, which, as in the previous problem, consisted of an even chance to win $200 or lose $100. The percentage of subjects who accepted the second gamble in the $300, $600, and disjunctive versions were 69%, 75%, and 73%, respectively. (Recall that the corresponding figures for the original problem were 59%, 69%, and 36%; essentially identical figures were obtained in a between-subjects replication of that problem.) In contrast to the original problem, the second gamble in this modified problem was equally popular in the disjunctive as in the nondisjunctive versions. Whereas in the original scenario the second gamble amounted to either a no-loss proposition or a chance to avoid a sure loss, in the modified scenario the second gamble amounts to a no-loss proposition regardless of the outcome of the first gamble. The increased popularity of the second gamble in the modified problem shows that it is not the disjunctive situation itself that discourages people from playing. Rather, it is the lack of a specific reason that seems to drive the effect: when the same reason applies regardless of outcome, the disjunction no longer reduces the tendency to accept the gamble.

As illustrated above, changes in the context of decision are likely to alter the reasons that subjects bring to mind and, consequently, their choices. Elsewhere (Shafir & Tversky, 1992) we describe a disjunction effect in the context of a one-shot Prisoner's Dilemma game, played on a computer for real payoffs. Subjects ($N = 80$) played a series of Prisoner's Dilemma games, without feedback, each against a different unknown player. In this setup, the rate of cooperation was 3% when subjects knew that the other player had defected and 16% when they knew that the other had cooperated. However, when subjects did not know whether the other player had cooperated or defected (the standard version of the Prisoner's Dilemma game) the rate of cooperation rose to 37%. Thus, many subjects defected when they knew the other's choice—be it cooperation or defection—but cooperated when the other player's choice was not known. Shafir and Tversky (1992) attribute this pattern to the different perspectives that underlie subjects' behavior under uncertainty as opposed to when the uncertainty is resolved. In particular, we suggest that the reasons for competing are more compelling when the other player's decision is known and the payoff depends on the subject alone, than when the other's chosen strategy is uncertain, and the outcome of the game depends on the choices of both players.

The above "disjunctive" manipulation—which has no direct bearing from the point of view of value maximization—appears to influence the reasons for decision that people bring to mind. Another kind of manipulation that seems to alter people's reasons without bearing directly on options' values is described in what follows.

6. Nonvalued Features

Reasons for choice or rejection often refer to specific features of the options under consideration. The positive features of an option typically provide reasons for choosing that option and its negative features typically provide reasons for rejection. What happens when we add features that are neither attractive nor aversive? Can choice be influenced by features that have little or no value?

Simonson and his colleagues have conducted a number of studies on the effects of nonvalued features and tested the hypothesis that people are reluctant to choose alternatives that are supported by reasons that they do not find appealing. In one study, for example, Simonson, Nowlis, and Simonson (1993) predicted that people would be less likely to choose an alternative that was chosen by another person for a reason that does not apply to them. UC Berkeley business students ($N = 113$) were told that, because of budget cuts and in order to save paper and duplicating costs, a questionnaire that they will receive was designed for use by two respondents. Thus, when subjects had to enter a choice, they could see the choice made by the previous "respondent" and the reason given for it. The choices and reasons of the previous respondents were systematically manipulated. One problem, for example, offered a choice between attending the MBA programs at Northwestern and UCLA. In one version of the questionnaire, the previous respondent had selected Northwestern and provided the (handwritten) reason, "I have many relatives in the Chicago area." Because this reason does not apply to most subjects, it was expected to reduce their likelihood of choosing

Northwestern. In a second version, no reason was given for the choice of Northwestern. As expected, those exposed to an irrelevant reason were less likely to choose Northwestern than subjects who saw the other respondent's choice but not his or her reason (23% vs. 43%, $p <$ 0.05). It should be noted that both Northwestern and UCLA are well known to most subjects (Northwestern currently has the highest ranked MBA program; the UCLA program is ranked high and belongs to the same UC system as Berkeley). Thus, it is unlikely that subjects made inferences about the quality of Northwestern based on the fact that another respondent chose it because he or she had relatives in Chicago.

In a related study, Simonson, Carmon, and O'Curry (1994) showed that endowing an option with a feature that was intended to be positive but, in fact, has no value for the decision maker can reduce the tendency to choose that option, even when subjects realize that they are not paying for the added feature. For example, an offer to purchase a collec- tor's plate—that most did not want—if one buys a particular brand of cake mix was shown to lower the tendency to buy that particular brand relative to a second, comparable cake mix brand (from 31% to 14%, $p <$ 0.05). Choosing brands that offer worthless bonuses was judged (in a related study) as more difficult to justify and as more susceptible to criticism. An analysis of verbal protocols showed that a majority of those who failed to select the endowed option explicitly mentioned not needing the added feature. It should be noted that sale pro- motions, such as the one involving the collector's plate offer above, are currently employed by a wide range of companies, and there is no evidence that they lead to any inferences about the quality of the promoted product (e.g., Blattberg & Neslin, 1990).

The above manipulations all added "positive," albeit weak or irrelevant, features, which should not diminish an option's value; yet, they apparently provide a reason against choos- ing the option, especially when other options are otherwise equally attractive. Evidently, the addition of a potentially attractive feature that proves useless can provide a reason to reject the option in favor of a competing alternative that has no "wasted" features.

7. Concluding Remarks

People's choices may occasionally stem from affective judgments that preclude a thorough evaluation of the options (cf. Zajonc, 1980). In such cases, an analysis of the reasons for choice may prove unwarranted and, when attempted by the decision maker, may actually result in a different, and possibly inferior, decision (Wilson & Schooler, 1991). Other choices, furthermore, may follow standard operating procedures that involve minimal reflective effort. Many decisions, nonetheless, result from a careful evaluation of options in which people attempt to arrive at what they believe is the best choice. Having discarded the less attractive options and faced with a choice that is hard to resolve, people often search for a compelling rationale for choosing one alternative over another. In this chapter, we presented an analysis of the role of reasons in decision making, and considered ways in which an analysis based on reasons may contribute to the standard quantitative approach based on the maximization of value. A number of hypotheses that derive from this perspective were investigated in experimental settings.

The reasons that enter into the making of decisions are likely to be intricate and diverse. In the preceding sections we have attempted to identify a few general principles that govern the role of reasons in decision making, and thus some of the fundamental ways in which thinking about reasons is likely to contribute to our understanding of the making of decisions. A reliance on the more important dimensions—those likely to provide more compelling reasons for choice—was shown in section 1 to predict preferences between previously equated options. The notions of compatibility and salience were summoned in section 2 to account for the differential weighting of reasons in a choice versus rejection task. Reasons, it appears, lend themselves to certain framing manipulations that are harder to explain from the perspective of value maximization. In section 3, manipulating the precise relationships between competing alternatives was shown to enhance or reduce conflict, yielding decisions that were easier or more difficult to rationalize and justify. Providing a context that presents compelling reasons for choosing an option apparently increases people's tendency to opt for that option, whereas comparing alternatives that render the aforementioned reasons less compelling tends to increase people's tendency to maintain the status quo or search for other alternatives. The ability of the context of decision to generate reasons that affect choice was further discussed in section 4, where the addition and removal of competing alternatives was interpreted as generating arguments for choice based on comparative considerations of relative advantages and compromise. The relative weakness of disjunctive reasons was discussed in section 5. There, a number of studies contrasted people's willingness to reach a decision based on a definite reason for choice, with their reluctance to arrive at a decision in the presence of uncertainty about which reason is actually relevant to the case at hand. Section 6 briefly reviewed choice situations in which the addition of purported reasons for choosing an option, which subjects did not find compelling, was seen to diminish their tendency to opt for that option, even though its value had not diminished.

The nature of the reasons that guide decision, and the ways in which they interact, await further investigation. There is evidence to suggest that a wide variety of arguments play a role in decision making. We often search for a convincing rationale for the decisions that we make, whether for interpersonal purposes, so that we can explain to others the reasons for our decision, or for intrapersonal motives, so that we may feel confident of having made the "right" choice. Attitudes toward risk and loss can sometimes be rationalized on the basis of common myths or clichés, and choices are sometimes made on the basis of moral or prudential principles that are used to override specific cost–benefit calculations (cf. Prelec & Herrnstein, 1991). Formal decision rules, moreover, may sometimes act as arguments in people's deliberations. Thus, when choosing between options x and z, we may realize that, sometime earlier, we had preferred x over y and y over z and that, therefore, by transitivity, we should now choose x over z. Montgomery (1983) has argued that people look for dominance structures in decision problems because they provide a compelling reason for choice. Similarly, Tversky and Shafir (1992a) have shown that detecting the applicability of the sure-thing principle to a decision situation leads people to act in accord with this principle's compelling rationale. Indeed, it has been repeatedly observed that the axioms of rational choice, which are often violated in nontransparent situations, are generally satisfied when their application is transparent (e.g., Tversky & Kahneman, 1986). These results suggest that the axioms of rational choice act as compelling arguments, or reasons, for making a particular decision when their applicability has been detected, not as universal laws that constrain people's choices.

In contrast to the classical theory that assumes stable values and preferences, it appears that people often do not have well-established values, and that preferences are actually constructed—not merely revealed—during their elicitation (cf. Payne, Bettman, & Johnson, 1992). A reason-based approach lends itself well to such a constructive interpretation. Decisions, according to this analysis, are often reached by focusing on reasons that justify the selection of one option over another. Different frames, contexts, and elicitation procedures highlight different aspects of the options and bring forth different reasons and considerations that influence decision.

The reliance on reasons to explain experimental findings has been the hallmark of social psychological analyses. Accounts of dissonance (Wicklund & Brehm, 1976) and self-perception (Bem, 1972), for example, focus on the reasons that people muster in an attempt to explain their counter-attitudinal behaviors. Similarly, attribution theory (Heider, 1980) centers around the reasons that people attribute to others' behavior. These studies, however, have primarily focused on postdecisional rationalization rather than predecisional conflict. Although the two processes are closely related, there are nevertheless some important differences. Much of the work in social psychology has investigated how people's decisions affect the way they think. The present paper, in contrast, has considered how the reasons that enter into people's thinking about a problem influence their decision. A number of researchers have recently begun to explore related issues. Billig (1987), for example, has adopted a rhetorical approach to understanding social psychological issues, according to which "our inner deliberations are silent arguments conducted within a single self" (p. 5). Related "explanation-based" models of decision making have been applied by Pennington and Hastie (1988, 1992) to account for judicial decisions, and the importance of social accountability in choice has been addressed by Tetlock (1992). From a philosophical perspective, a recent essay by Schick (1991) analyzes various decisions from the point of view of practical reason. An influential earlier work is Toulmin's (1950) study of the role of arguments in ethical reasoning.

In this chapter, we have attempted to explore some of the ways in which reasons and arguments enter into people's decisions. A reason-based analysis may come closer to capturing part of the psychology that underlies decision and thus may help shed light on a number of phenomena that remain counterintuitive from the perspective of the classical theory. It is instructive to note that many of the experimental studies described in this chapter were motivated by intuitions stemming from a qualitative analysis based on reasons, not from a value-based perspective, even if they can later be interpreted in that fashion. We do not propose that accounts based on reasons replace value-based models of choice. Rather, we suggest that an analysis of reasons may illuminate some aspects of reflective choice and generate new hypotheses for further study.

Acknowledgments

This research was supported by US Public Health Service Grant No. 1-R29-MH46885 from the National Institute of Mental Health, by Grant No. 89–0064 from the Air Force Office of Scientific Research, and by Grant No. SES-9109535 from the National Science Foundation. The chapter was partially prepared while the first author participated in a Summer Institute on Negotiation and Dispute Resolution at the Center for Advanced Study in the Behavioral Sciences, and while the second author was at the University of California, Berkeley. Funds for support of the Summer Institute were provided by the Andrew W. Mellon Foundation. We thank Robyn Dawes for helpful comments on an earlier draft.

Notes

1. These effects of context on choice can naturally be used in sales tactics. For example, Williams-Sonoma, a mail-order business located in San Francisco, used to offer a bread-baking appliance priced at $279. They later added a second bread-baking appliance, similar to the first but somewhat larger, and priced at $429—more than 50% higher than the original appliance. Not surprisingly, Williams-Sonoma did not sell many units of the new item. However, the sales of the less expensive appliance almost doubled. (To the best of our knowledge, Williams-Sonoma did not anticipate this effect.)

2. An additional group of subjects ($N = 123$) were presented with both the fail and the pass versions and asked whether or not they would buy the vacation package in each case. Two thirds of the subjects made the same choice in the two conditions, indicating that the data for the disjunctive version cannot be explained by the hypothesis that those who like the vacation in case they pass the exam do not like it in case they fail, and vice versa. Note that while only one third of the subjects made different

decisions depending on the outcome of the exam, more than 60% of the subjects chose to wait when the outcome was not known.

References

Allison, G. T. (1971). *Essence of decision: Explaining the Cuban missile crisis*. Boston, MA: Little, Brown.

Bem, D. J. (1972). Self-perception theory. In L. Berkowitz (Ed.), *Advances in experimental social psychology* (Vol. 6, pp. 1–62). New York, NY: Academic Press.

Berman, L. (1982). *Planning a tragedy*. New York, NY: Norton.

Betts, R., & Gelb, L. (1979). *The irony of Vietnam: The system worked*. Washington, DC: Brookings Institution.

Bigelow, J. (Ed.). (1887). *The complete works of Benjamin Franklin* (Vol. 4). New York, NY: Putnam.

Billig, M. (1987). *Arguing and thinking: A rhetorical approach to social psychology*. New York, NY: Cambridge University Press.

Blattberg, R. C., & Neslin, S. A. (1990). *Sales promotion: Concepts, methods, and strategies*. Englewood Cliffs, NJ: Prentice-Hall.

Heider, F. (1980). *The psychology of interpersonal relations*. New York, NY: Wiley.

Huber, J., Payne, J. W., & Puto, C. (1982). Adding asymmetrically dominated alternatives: Violations of regularity and the similarity hypothesis. *Journal of Consumer Research, 9*, 90–98.

James, W. (1981). *The principles of psychology* (Vol. 2). Cambridge, MA: Harvard University Press.

Kahneman, D., & Tversky, A. (1979). Prospect theory: An analysis of decision under risk. *Econometrica, 47*, 263–291.

Montgomery, H. (1983). Decision rules and the search for a dominance structure: Towards a process model of decision making. In P. Humphreys, O. Svenson, & A. Vari (Eds.), *Analyzing and aiding decision processes* (pp. 343–369). Amsterdam, the Netherlands: North-Holland.

Nisbett, R. E., & Wilson, T. D. (1977). Telling more than we can know: Verbal reports on mental processes. *Psychological Review, 84*, 231–259.

Payne, J. W., Bettman, J. R., & Johnson, E. J. (1992). Behavioral decision research: A constructive process perspective. *Annual Review of Psychology, 43*, 87–131.

Pennington, N., & Hastie, R. (1988). Explanation-based decision making: Effects of memory structure on judgment. *Journal of Experimental Psychology: Learning, Memory, and Cognition, 14*, 521–533.

Pennington, N., & Hastie, R. (1992). Explaining the evidence: Tests of the story model for juror decision making. *Journal of Personality and Social Psychology, 62*, 189–206.

Prelec, D., & Herrnstein, R. J. (1991). Preferences or principles: Alternative guidelines for choice. In R. J. Zeckhauser (Ed.), *Strategy and choice* (pp. 319–340). Cambridge, MA: MIT Press.

Redelmeier, D., & Shafir, E. (1993). Medical decisions over multiple alternatives. Working paper, University of Toronto, Toronto, Ontario, Canada.

Savage, L. J. (1954). *The foundations of statistics.* New York, NY: Wiley.

Schick, F. (1991). *Understanding action: An essay on reasons.* New York, NY: Cambridge University Press.

Shafer, G. (1986). Savage revisited. *Statistical Science, 1,* 463–485.

Shafir, E. (1993). Choosing versus rejecting: Why some options are both better and worse than others. *Memory & Cognition, 21,* 546–556.

Shafir, E., & Tversky, A. (1992). Thinking through uncertainty: Nonconsequential reasoning and choice. *Cognitive Psychology, 24,* 449–474.

Simonson, I. (1989). Choice based on reasons: The case of attraction and compromise effects. *Journal of Consumer Research, 16,* 158–174.

Simonson, I., Carmon, Z., & O'Curry, S. (1994). Experimental evidence on the negative effect of unique product features and sales promotions on brand choice. *Marketing Science, 13,* 23–40.

Simonson, I., Nowlis, S., & Simonson, Y. (1993). The effect of irrelevant preference arguments on consumer choice. *Journal of Consumer Psychology, 2,* 287–306.

Simonson, I., & Tversky, A. (1992). Choice in context: Tradeoff contrast and extremeness aversion. *JMR, Journal of Marketing Research, 29,* 281–295.

Slovic, P. (1975). Choice between equally valued alternatives. *Journal of Experimental Psychology: Human Perception and Performance, 1,* 280–287.

Slovic, P. (1990). Choice. In D. Osherson & E. Smith (Eds.), *An invitation to cognitive science* (Vol. 3, pp. 89–116). Cambridge, MA: MIT Press.

Telhami, S. (1990). *Power and leadership in international bargaining: The path to the Camp David accords.* New York, NY: Columbia University Press.

Tetlock, P. E. (1992). The impact of accountability on judgment and choice: Toward a social contingency model. In M. P. Zanna (Ed.), *Advances in experimental social psychology* (Vol. 25, pp. 331–376). New York, NY: Academic Press.

Toulmin, S. (1950). *The place of reason in ethics.* New York, NY: Cambridge University Press.

Tversky, A., & Kahneman, D. (1986). Rational choice and the framing of decisions. *Journal of Business, 59,* 251–278.

Tversky, A., Sattath, S., & Slovic, P. (1988). Contingent weighting in judgment and choice. *Psychological Review, 95,* 371–384.

Tversky, A., & Shafir, E. (1992a). The disjunction effect in choice under uncertainty. *Psychological Science, 3,* 305–309.

Tversky, A., & Shafir, E. (1992b). Choice under conflict: The dynamics of deferred decision. *Psychological Science, 3*, 358–361.

Tversky, A., & Simonson, I. (1993). Context-dependent preferences. *Management Science, 39*, 1179–1189.

von Neumann, J., & Morgenstern, O. (1947). *Theory of games and economic behavior*. Princeton, NJ: Princeton University Press.

Wedell, D. H. (1991). Distinguishing among models of contextually induced preference reversals. *Journal of Experimental Psychology: Learning, Memory, and Cognition, 17*, 767–778.

Wicklund, R. A., & Brehm, J. W. (1976). *Perspectives on cognitive dissonance*. Hillsdale, NJ: Erlbaum.

Wilson, T. D., & Schooler, J. W. (1991). Thinking too much: Introspection can reduce the quality of preferences and decisions. *Journal of Personality and Social Psychology, 60*, 181–192.

Zajonc, B. (1980). Preferences without inferences. *American Psychologist, 35*, 151–175.

Afterword

Daniel Kahneman

The articles collected in this volume illustrate many of the characteristics that made Amos Tversky a legend in his lifetime. Written decades ago, they still shine. One reason for their longevity is the exemplary clarity and authority of their arguments. Many of Amos's pieces leave the reader with a sense that what he did is definitive and cannot be improved. Amos was not always right, of course, but he never made a claim without a good reason, and the arguments he developed could not be stated better or more persuasively.

Amos Tversky was in graduate school in the early 1960s, when an intellectual movement to bring mathematical thinking to the social sciences was in its heyday. He belonged to the first generation of students who were inspired by that movement, and he collaborated extensively with some of its founders. These early experiences grounded him in the use of formal language, which he used as a tool of thinking for the rest of his life. By itself, formal language guarantees precision but little else. It is entirely possible to be precisely boring, or precisely irrelevant, or precisely wrong. Amos used mathematical precision to avoid being approximately right—he aspired to being precisely right. He was uniquely successful among psychologists in the way he used the language of theory to help both himself and his readers think clearly about things that matter.

Another attribute that protects Amos's work from aging is the quality of his writing. In one famous example, there is a consensus among academic psychologists about the best-written paragraph ever published by *Psychological Review*—the prestige theory journal of the profession—in its 120-year history. The winner by acclamation is the last paragraph of Amos Tversky's "Features of Similarity" (chapter 3 of this collection). Many psychologists have known the last four sentences of this article by heart since they were in graduate school. Here they are:

Consider the simile "An essay is like a fish." At first, the statement is puzzling. An essay is not expected to be fishy, slippery, or wet. The puzzle is resolved when we recall that (like a fish) an essay has a head and a body, and it occasionally ends with a flip of the tail.

The self-referential concluding sentence is quintessentially Tversky: it is witty, it is clear, and it is deep. There are memorable only-Tversky sentences in every chapter of this collection. The adjectives "crisp" and "elegant" were terms of high praise in Amos's own vocabulary, and they perfectly describe his writing.

The readers of this collection can appreciate the unique precision and elegance of what Amos produced, but those who collaborated with him can also report on the unique process. As I had the occasion to observe over many years, Amos's crafting of memorably crisp sentences resembled what many poets have described as the way they write. You start with an idea and a first draft—often written in pencil to make erasing easy. Perfection comes by patient polishing: you start by deleting every superfluous word, and then you consider alternatives for every remaining word. And then you start over and rewrite until you are content. When the initial idea is good—and with Amos it almost always was—you end up with something that cannot be improved further.

Perfection and perfectionism come in several varieties, including anxious, tortured, and dutiful. Amos's perfectionism was the joyous kind. He loved thinking, he loved searching for the best possible word, and he thoroughly enjoyed the slow process of polishing a gem until it shines. The joy he found in his work gave him endless patience, which his collaborators were happy to share. One of his frequent statements during the years we worked together was "let's get it right!"—always said with delight. Coming from Amos, this exhortation promised a long and challenging walk over ever-surprising terrain, but with a clear goal and the complete certainty that the goal would be reached. Sharing these journeys was a thrill for his collaborators, and Amos had many—only one of the articles in this collection is single-authored.

Several of the chapters were written during a period of twelve years in which Amos and I joined in an exceptionally close partnership. The work that we did together on judgment and on decision making turned out to be much more influential than we had expected. Its impact was due in part to a successful synthesis of approaches, but an almost fortuitous choice of research method and expository format was probably even more important.

Amos was a theorist by temperament and a decision theorist by training. It was natural for him to see people's judgments and choices as imperfect attempts to approximate the logic of probability and decision making. My background was in studies of visual perception, and it was natural for me to understand thinking and choice in terms of how people represent the world. The blending of these different approaches proved fruitful.

Style was perhaps more important than substance in explaining the impact of our joint work. Amos and I rarely reported complex experiments. Instead, we constructed examples in which responses to a single question (or a matched pair of questions) illustrated a specific theoretical point. We included these questions word for word in our published papers, using format to separate them from the rest of the text. The readers were therefore compelled to share the experience of participants in our research. They usually found themselves tempted to make all the responses (including predictable errors) that our reports described and explained. The personal experience of cognitive illusions and incoherent choices had a strong impact on readers. It is now apparent that the unusual influence of our research on other fields was largely due to a fortunate accident: no other area of cognitive or social psychology lends itself so naturally to a personal conversation with the reader.

Demonstrations were crucial to the spread of our work across the boundaries of disciplines. Lawyers, philosophers, political scientists, physicians, and some economists were surprised and impressed by their experiences and keen to apply what they had learned to their field of interest. Illusions of judgment and incoherent choices were soon documented in many fields of application, including—among others—nuclear reactor safety, the conduct of complex negotiations, the selection of football players, and the promotion of retirement saving.

Amos was delighted with the influence of our work on other fields, but he was most involved in what came to be called "the great rationality debate," the conversation with scholars in decision theory and economics who hoped to retain rational models as descriptive theories of how humans think and choose. Although we did not explicitly discuss rationality in our early work, the observations we reported were quickly identified as a significant challenge to the rational agent model and soon elicited a variety of defensive reactions. Amos was especially provoked by attempts to modify the axioms of rationality so that apparent violations of rationality could be reclassified as rational. He viewed these defenses of human rationality as "lawyerly" and inelegant and was eager to show their flaws. Amos did almost all the new work on the choice and framing article (chapter 5 in this collection), which reused earlier empirical findings to make a new set of theoretical points.

From the start of his career, Amos strove to develop a precise account of the ways that human minds violate rules of rationality. A recurrent theme was the contrast between extensional logic and intensional intuitions, which is the motivating idea of several articles in this collection. The related distinction between reality and description was another focus of Amos's thinking. Much of his subsequent work with other collaborators was concerned with these contrasts between normative and descriptive rules.

There are few scholars whose work can be republished twenty years after their death, not as historical documents but as enduring intellectual contributions. Amos Tversky is one of these few.

Index

Page numbers in italics indicate references to figures.